BUSINESS PROGRAMMING LOGIC

A Structured Approach

JAY SINGELMANN
William Rainey Harper College

JEAN LONGHURST
William Rainey Harper College

Prentice-Hall, Inc., Englewood Cliffs, New Jersey 07632

Printed in the United States of America

10 9 8 7 6 5 4 3 2 1

Prentice-Hall International, Inc., London

Prentice-Hall of Australia Pty. Limited, Sydney

Prentice-Hall of Canada, Ltd., Toronto

Prentice-Hall of India Private Limited, New Delhi

Prentice-Hall of Japan, Inc., Tokyo

Prentice-Hall of Southeast Asia Pte. Ltd., Singapore

Whitehall Books Limited, Wellington, New Zealand

Contents

Preface

This volume covers the flowcharting of typical types of business applications programs. The topics include symbols and their usage, documentation practices, typical applications logic, decision tables and necessary terminology. A structured approach has been used in flowcharting examples. The material presented is language independent, although some examples draw on COBOL for explanation.

There are several important highlights to this volume, the first of which is the informal presentation. It is meant for the beginning student in a data processing program at either a junior college or a four-year institution. It can be used as the primary book in a business applications flowcharting course or as a supplement if flowcharting is taught as a part of a programming course.

The depth of the material is sufficient to facilitate the learning of the material. It has been our experience in class testing this text that there is sufficient material for a full semester of study. We have also found that students who have studied this material have more success in future programming language courses. This is true because they are then free to concentrate on the syntax of the particular language.

Another point is the scope of material covered. Standard business applications such as listing programs, input edits, updates, extracts and file matching are covered. Also present is material on documentation, decision tables and file maintenance.

The whys are emphasized along with the hows so that the student will see the reason for doing something in a particular manner. There is an abundance of examples throughout the volume. The examples are explained in detail to aid the student in grasping the topic.

Each chapter starts with a list of behavioral objectives. These emphasize what material the student should master in the chapter. Each chapter also has a variety of questions at the end of the chapter. The questions are suitable for assignments, class discussions or quiz questions.

We would like to express our appreciation to those who have aided us in the preparation of this volume. Credit goes to our students whose constructive criticism has been invaluable in preparing this material. Credit also goes to our colleagues at William Rainey Harper College for their support of this project and to Dr. Charles Falk, the Chairman of the Business Division at Harper College for his enthusiasm and support at various stages in the project.

We are grateful to the reviewers; Darrell DeGeeter, Waubonsee Community College; John J. Dineen, Middlesex County College; Mario Farina, Author/Consultant; Kenneth Lebeiko, Oakton Community College; Harice L. Seeds, Los Angeles City College and John Westley, Illinois Central Community College for their ideas, comments and criticisms which were helpful in preparing the final draft.

We are indebted to Judith Rothman of Prentice-Hall for her interest in and support of this text. We thank Julie Read Hildebrand for her early interest and enthusiasm. Preparation of the manuscript was made easier by the efforts of Dorothy Miller and Audrey Longhurst.

Our greatest thanks goes to our spouses, Merlyn Longhurst and Barbara Singelmann, without whose patience and understanding this would not have been possible.

Jay Singelmann
Jean Longhurst

CHAPTER 1

Data Processing

OBJECTIVES

As a result of studying this chapter the student should be able to perform the following activities.

1. Describe the data processing cycle.

2. Define the units of data.

3. Differentiate between device and media, core storage and auxiliary storage, data and instructions.

4. List the major types of programs in a system.

5. List the steps required to convert a flowchart to an operational program.

INTRODUCTION

One of the most important competencies needed in computer programming is problem analysis. It is only through a clear understanding of what is desired that a reasonable solution to a problem may be developed. This process is greatly enhanced by the use of flowcharts and decision tables to quantify and structure the procedures to be accomplished. However, before we can pursue the main topic of the book, some background information about data processing is needed.

In general a data processing project is started because there is an objective to meet. We want to produce something which will be useful. The various departments in a company have ideas for reports and procedures that will make their job easier and their area more productive.

DATA PROCESSING CYCLE

When communication begins between the data processing department and a department requiring its services, the discussion is usually in terms of the end results desired. This is termed the output of the data processing operation. If the output is to be in printed form it is called a report.

The next step is to determine if the necessary data is available to produce the desired output. If it isn't currently available, can it be collected? The data needed to produce the output is called the input. Knowing what we must produce and what we have to work with brings us to the last step -- how are we going to do it? This is the process step. These three items; input, process and output constitute what is known as the data processing cycle.

UNITS OF DATA

When we start to discuss the output we'd like, or the input we need to produce it; new vocabulary is required to describe the units of data we work with. Data is classified as shown in Figure 1-1.

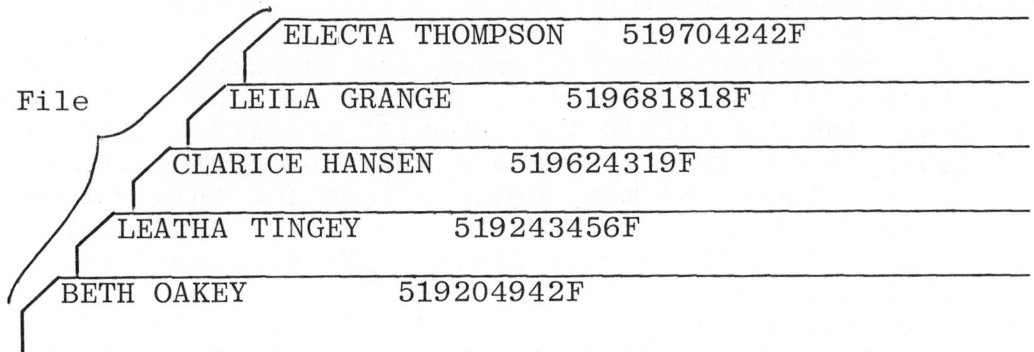

File - A collection of one or more related records organized for a particular purpose.

Example - The records for every student in a school.

Record - A group of one or more related fields that refer to one person, place or thing.

Example - the data the school maintains concerning one student.

Field - One or more consecutive characters of related data.

Example - Individual items of data such as name, social security number, etc.

Character - A single symbol.

Example - A letter of the alphabet used to spell a name or a digit in a date.

Figure 1-1

INPUT/OUTPUT DEVICES AND STORAGE

In order to manipulate data using the computer, we need a means of transferring the data into primary storage of the computer (storage located within the computer itself). After it has been manipulated, we need a means of transferring it back out of storage. There are many devices used for this purpose. A general name for these pieces of equipment is input/output (I/O) devices. Among the common devices are card readers, tape drives, disk drives, terminals and optical scanners. Each of these devices uses a medium on which the data is recorded. Examples of the recording media are punched cards, magnetic tape, disks and optically readable marks and characters. The term auxiliary storage refers to the storage of data on these and other types of media outside the computer.

DATA VERSUS INSTRUCTIONS

In respect to a program, two types of items are placed in primary storage, the instructions (processing steps) and the data as it is required by the program. It is important to make a distinction between the two items.

ADD A, B GIVING C is an example of an instruction. This instruction has two parts, an operation code (op code) and operands. The operation code tells the computer what we want done, (ADD). The operands give the names of the items to be used in the addition. These item names represent the storage areas where the actual values of the data can be found.

This instruction infers that values of the data items A and B have already been established and stored. The computer will calculate a value for C as this instruction is executed and store it in the storage area referred to as C. To use this instruction areas must be provided for A, B, and C in primary storage, The method for providing these storage areas in primary storage depends on the programming language being used.

PLANNING A PROJECT

Let's consider a request that might come to us from the accounting department. They want the payroll converted from a manual operation to a computerized operation. After determining that this is feasible, we agree to proceed.

What output will they require? The most obvious answer is paychecks. However, this is only one of many forms of output needed by the accounting department's payroll operation. They will need Federal Tax Reports, State Tax Reports, Payroll Registers, Voluntary Deduction Reports and W2's to name some of the more common reports. The output required and all of the steps necessary to produce the output comprise a payroll system.

The planning for this system should be a joint effort of the accounting and data processing departments. The better informed each department is about the needs of the other, the more smoothly the project will progress.

SYSTEMS FLOWCHART

A graphic representation of a system is made by drawing a system flowchart. A systems flowchart shows the flow of data from the original source (employment records and time cards) through the creation of all the necessary output (printed reports, etc.). The individual programs shown in a systems flowchart are merely shown as rectangles containing a program name with nothing said about the actual logic of the program itself. Systems flowcharts are covered in Chapter 13.

This systems flowchart needs approval from both departments before programming is begun. Our object in this text is not to plan the system or draw the system flowchart. It is to take an individual program shown within a system and break it down into processing steps.

There are at least five basic types of programs found in most systems:

1. Report programs
2. Extract programs
3. Input edit programs
4. Update programs
5. Utility programs

Report programs - (discussed in Chapters 5, 6 and 9) - are programs that utilize the data from one or more input files to produce a report containing the necessary information from the files. This information that is produced is usually in the same sequence as the files. The bulk of the records in the files are usually referenced.

Extract programs - (discussed in Chapter 7) - are programs that utilize only a portion of the data on a given file to produce a report. The report is often in a sequence different from that of the original file

Input edit programs - (discussed in Chapter 8) - are programs used to validate the data in a file. This file will ultimately be used as part of the input to some other program. Input edit programs are used to make sure that the data is as correct as possible in order to avoid errors of greater magnitude in future programs.

Update programs - (discussed in Chapter 10) - are programs used to bring a master file up to date. This is done by altering it to reflect transactions that have taken place during the period between the last update and the present time.

Utility programs - (not discussed in any greater detail) - are programs that may be either provided by the manufacturer or written by the user. They perform such standardized functions as sorting, merging, copying and listing the data on files.

CONVERSION FROM FLOWCHART TO PROGRAM

As we proceed through the book examples of the output we are planning to produce will be provided along with the format of the input record or records needed to produce the output. With these items provided we are then free to concentrate on the processing required to produce the output.

As stated earlier, flowcharts are used to help us quantify and structure the processing step. Once the flowchart is complete, we test it with all of the possible types of input we can reasonably expect (and some unreasonable types also). This process is called desk checking. After we have proved to our satisfaction that the logic we used will produce the output we require, we are ready to code the actual computer program. Coding is converting the flowchart into a particular programming language. The computer programming language used will depend on what is available to us at our facility.

After the program is coded, it should be checked for correctness in respect to both the logic and the rules of the programming language. The coding is then converted to a form which can be accepted by the computer. Two possible methods would be entering the code directly into the computer through a terminal keyboard or punching it into cards to be read by a card reader connected to a computer.

At this stage, the instructions are inspected by a program called a compiler, interpreter or assembler, depending on the programming language being used. Such a program exists for every programming language. It checks each instruction to see if it complies with all of the rules of the programming language. It also converts the source program we have written into an object program. An object program is a machine executable equivalent of the source program. If any of the program statements contain errors, they are identified so they can be corrected. This conversion process concerns itself with the rules of the programming language only, it does not check the logic of the program or the spacing of the output.

Once the programming language errors are removed, the program is executed (run) in an attempt to produce output. If input data is required for the program it is provided at this time. If the logic was developed correctly, the output will be as it was planned. On the other hand, if the output is incorrect it may be simple spacing errors or more serious logic errors. Corrections are made until the output is acceptable.

To go from a flowchart to a properly executing program requires care at each step. Time spent in careful planning during the developmental stages pays dividends in terms of the time required to complete the project.

When the output is acceptable we should prepare a documentation package. This documentation is a means of communication between the programmer and the user. It is also useful, if the need arises for a revision of the program.

The majority of the chapters in this book are devoted to planning and flowcharting the processing steps necessary to convert the input we have, to the output we require. One exception is Chapter 4 which discusses the documenting of a program. The concept of documentation and the components of a documentation package will be presented at that time.

For the purposes of this text we have tried to remain as language independent as possible. We have, though, concentrated on business applications in which there are large volumes of input and output. Because of this the handling of files is an important part of the processing to be done. The second chapter introduces the flowcharting symbols and the concepts involved in moving data through a computer.

REVIEW QUESTIONS

Matching

A. Report Program

B. Extract Program

C. Input Edit Program

D. Update Program

E. Report

F. Systems Flowchart

G. File

H. Data Processing Cycle

__________ 1. Utilizes only a portion of the data in a file to produce a report that is often in a different sequence than the original file.

__________ 2. Used to bring a file (usually a master file) up to a point where it reflects the current status for the data in the file.

__________ 3. Used to summarize data from one or more input files into a written form.

__________ 4. Used to validate the data in a file prior to further processing.

__________ 5. Shows the flow of data from the original source through the creation of all the necessary output.

__________ 6. Output which is in a printed form.

__________ 7. Consists of input, process and output.

__________ 8. A collection of records organized for some particular purpose.

True/False

T F 1. A systems flowchart show much of the logic of the individual programs.

T F 2. Utility programs may be either provided by the manufacturer or written by the user.

T F 3. Flowcharts are used to quantify and structure the process step.

T F 4. In computer programming the words data and instruction have the same meaning.

T F 5. Once a program is coded, it need be checked for correctness only in respect to the logic.

T F 6. A file is a collection of records.

T F 7. Data is stored on a device.

T F 8. Storage inside the computer is called auxiliary storage.

Exercises

1. Draw a tree showing the relationship of the units of data.

2. List any devices or media that you are aware of. Specify whether they are suitable for input or output or both.

3. List the steps required to convert a flowchart to an operational program.

Discussion Questions

1. Why are we likely to use output as our starting point when developing a system?

2. Identify what would consititute a file, record, item and character in various data processing systems. Examples: student registration, inventory, accounts receivable.

3. Give examples of logic errors versus breaking the rule of a programming language.

4. What business courses would you want a programmer you hire to have taken?

CHAPTER 2

Introduction to Flowcharting

OBJECTIVES

As a result of studying this chapter the student should be able to perform the following activities.

1. Describe the purpose of program flowcharting.
2. Define desk checking.
3. Identify the various program flowcharting symbols.
4. Describe the difference between START/STOP and NAME/EXIT in the terminal symbol.
5. Describe destructive readin and its effects on the contents of an input area.
6. Describe the difference between internal and external predefined processes.

PROGRAM FLOWCHARTS

We are now going to concentrate on program flowcharts. A program flowchart is planned and drawn by a programmer. When it is complete, the programmer tests it by pretending to be a computer. He moves the data through each step of the flowchart, doing with the data exactly what each step specifies. If the flowchart was correctly drawn then the results (what happened to the data) will be exactly as planned. This process, called desk checking, is important as it helps to discover surprises in the flowchart or details that have been forgotten.

When the programmer is satisfied that the flowchart has been drawn correctly, he will code it in the programming language used at his facility. Coding the program entails translating the process in each symbol to the appropriate form for the programming language chosen. If the flowchart has been drawn in detail the result would be one programming statement per flowcharting symbol. While there are many views on how detailed a program flowchart should be let's simply say that it only needs to be detailed enough to show the logical decisions being made and general processing to be done. An experienced programmer will recognize situations where one symbol in a flowchart must be expanded into more than one programming statement. As a beginner it is better to have too much rather than too little detail.

The next step is to transcribe the coded program into a machine readable form and compile it. Error diagnostics will be provided by the compiler for any rules of the programming language that have been broken. The programmer must correct any errors pointed out by the compiler. With all of the language errors removed the program will now execute the instructions in the order specified. It is here that any lack of planning in the flowchart will show up. With incorrect planning, the output will be what you asked for -- but, not what you wanted. Any corrections that have to be made to the logic after it is in the form of a program take an excessive amount of time. An "I'll fix it as it falls apart" attitude leads to sloppy programming and continued headaches.

FLOWCHARTING SYMBOLS

Program flowcharts are the graphic representation of the actual logic in a program needed to produce the desired output. There are several standard symbols used in program flowcharting which have specific meanings. The remainder of the chapter will be devoted to presenting these symbols and their meanings.

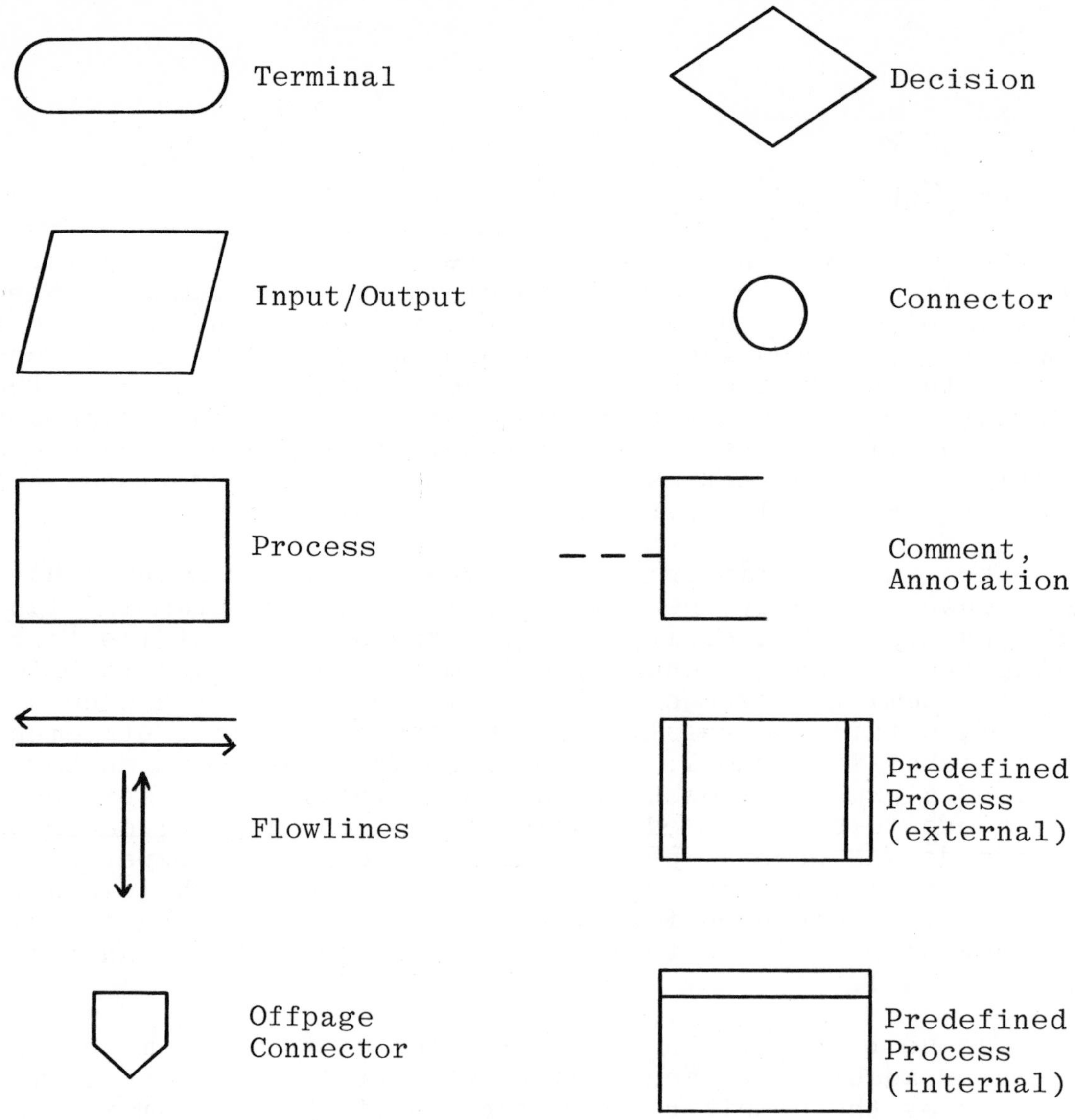

Figure 2-1

STANDARDS

This material* is reproduced with permission from American National Standards X3.5-1970 by the American National Standards Institute, copies of which may be purchased from the American National Standards Institute at 1430 Broadway, New York, New York 10018.

*All flowcharting symbols (except the offpage connector which is an IBM symbol) and the definitions for the following symbols in Chapter 13: Punched Card Symbols, Online Storage, Magnetic Tape, Punched Tape, Magnetic Drum, Magnetic Disk, Core, Document, Manual Input, Display, Communications Link, Offline Storage, Preparation, Manual Operation, Auxiliary Operation, Merge, Extract, Sort and Collate.

TERMINAL SYMBOL

The terminal symbol indicates a starting or stopping point in the logic. It is depicted in Figure 2-2.

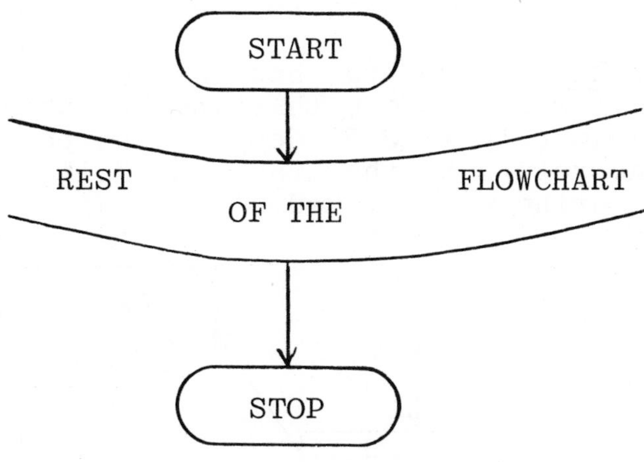

Figure 2-2

The terminal symbol is also used at the beginning of a subroutine. It is used to indicate not only the beginning of the subroutine but the name of the subroutine. A subroutine is a small task such as printing headings or computing gross pay. Subroutines are drawn or written as separate entities with their own beginning and ending points. In subroutines however, we do not use START and STOP within the terminal symbols. Instead we use the name of the subroutine in place of START and EXIT in place of STOP. Figure 2-3 shows the beginning of a routine (subroutine) with the name of the routine in the terminal symbol.

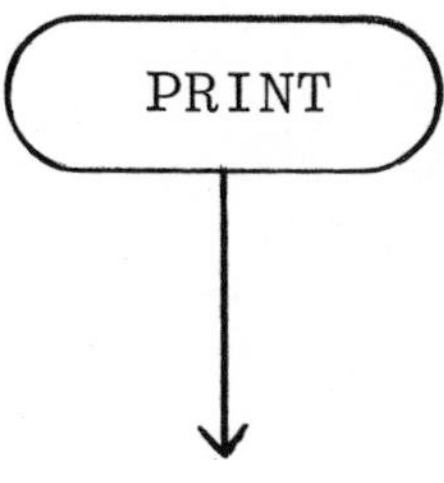

Figure 2-3

The terminal symbol should also be used at the end of the subroutine to show the end of the specific task and an exit to a point in the logic of the program (see Figure 2-4).

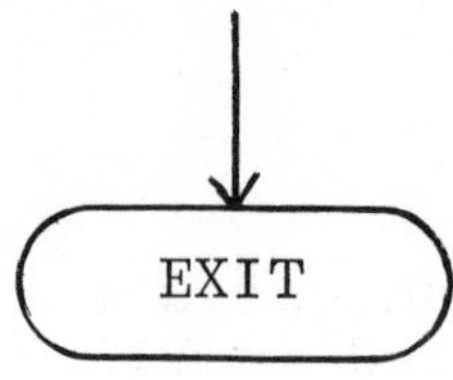

Figure 2-4

The word EXIT is used to show the return to the statement immediately following the one that invoked the subroutine. The following diagram (Figure 2-5) depicts the performance of a subroutine and the return to the statement following the one in which the subroutine was invoked.

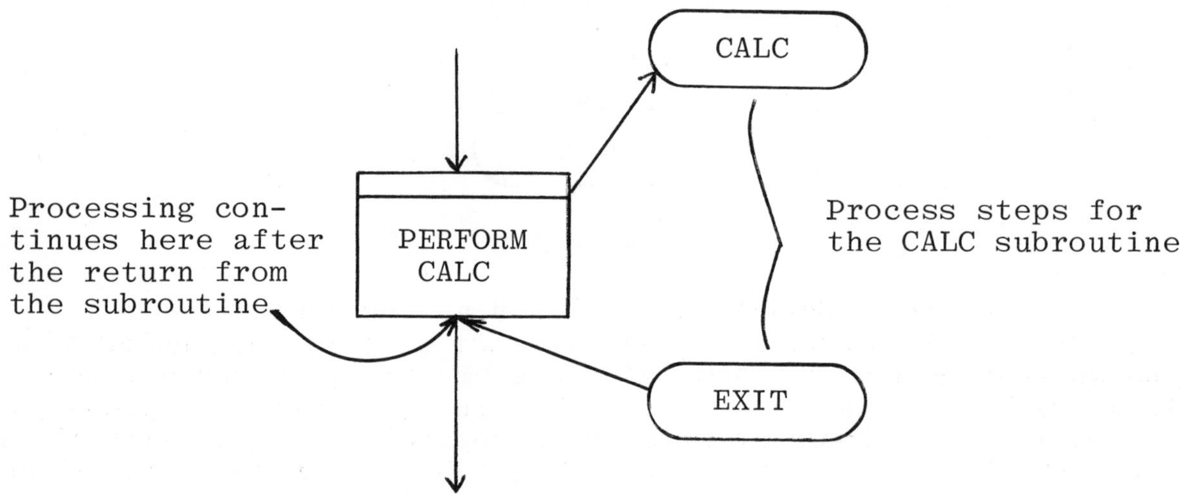

Figure 2-5

INPUT/OUTPUT SYMBOL

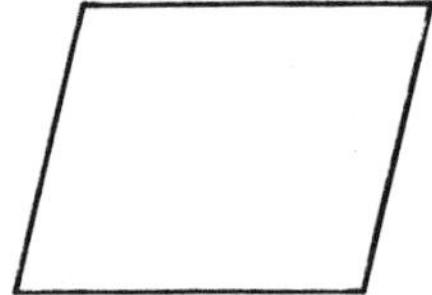

The input/output symbol is used to show the reading or writing of one logical (individual) record. This is a general purpose input/output symbol. More specific symbols which indicate a particular type of input/output device are used in a system flowchart. These symbols as well as the concept of system flowcharting will be covered in Chapter 13.

There are normally separate areas in primary storage for

accepting data that is read into storage and for holding data as it is prepared for output to some device. Figure 2-6 is a diagram of these areas in primary storage.

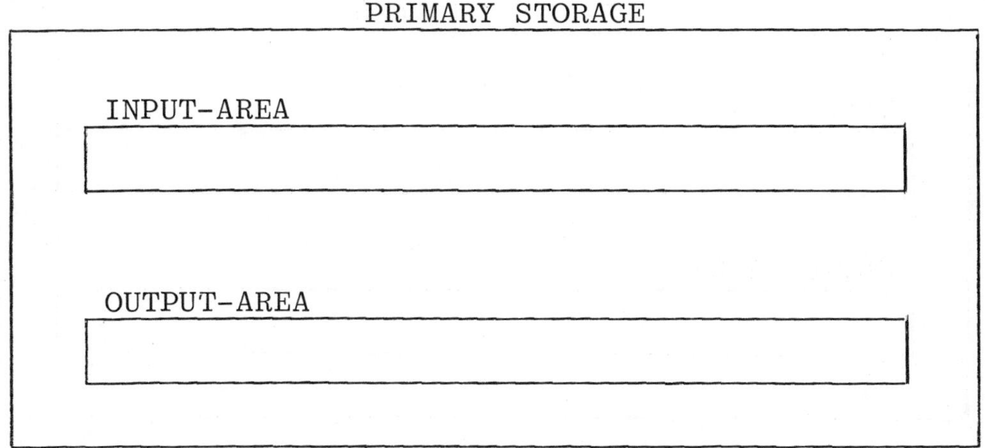

Figure 2-6

The area in primary storage shown as INPUT-AREA will be used to hold data that is read into storage from some file. The file we will use is represented by Figure 2-7

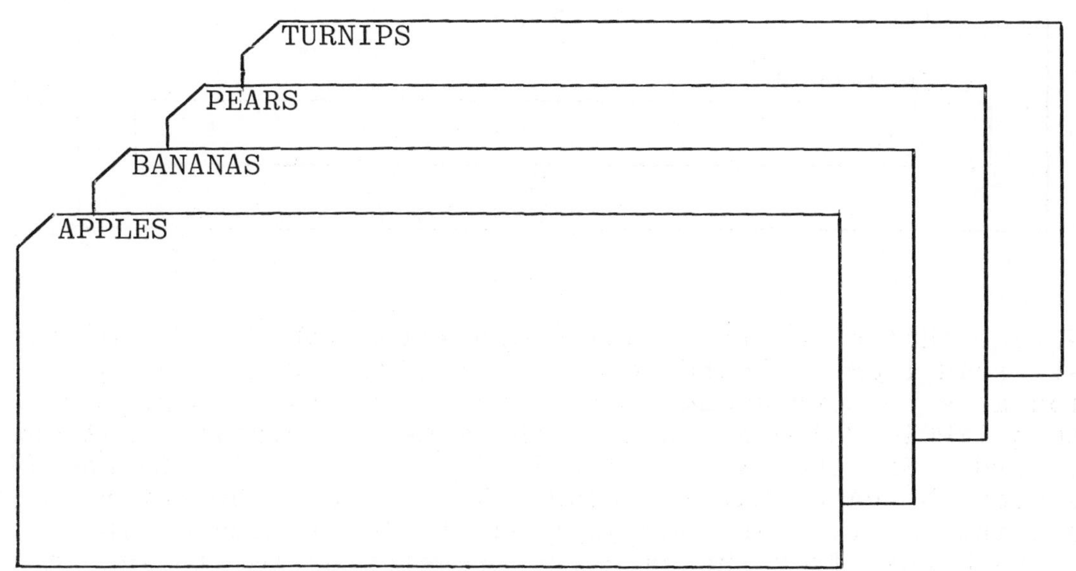

Figure 2-7

We will assume that INPUT-AREA contains blanks at the beginning of the process. If we read one card record into storage that contains the word APPLES in the first 6 columns of the card the result is shown in Figure 2-8.

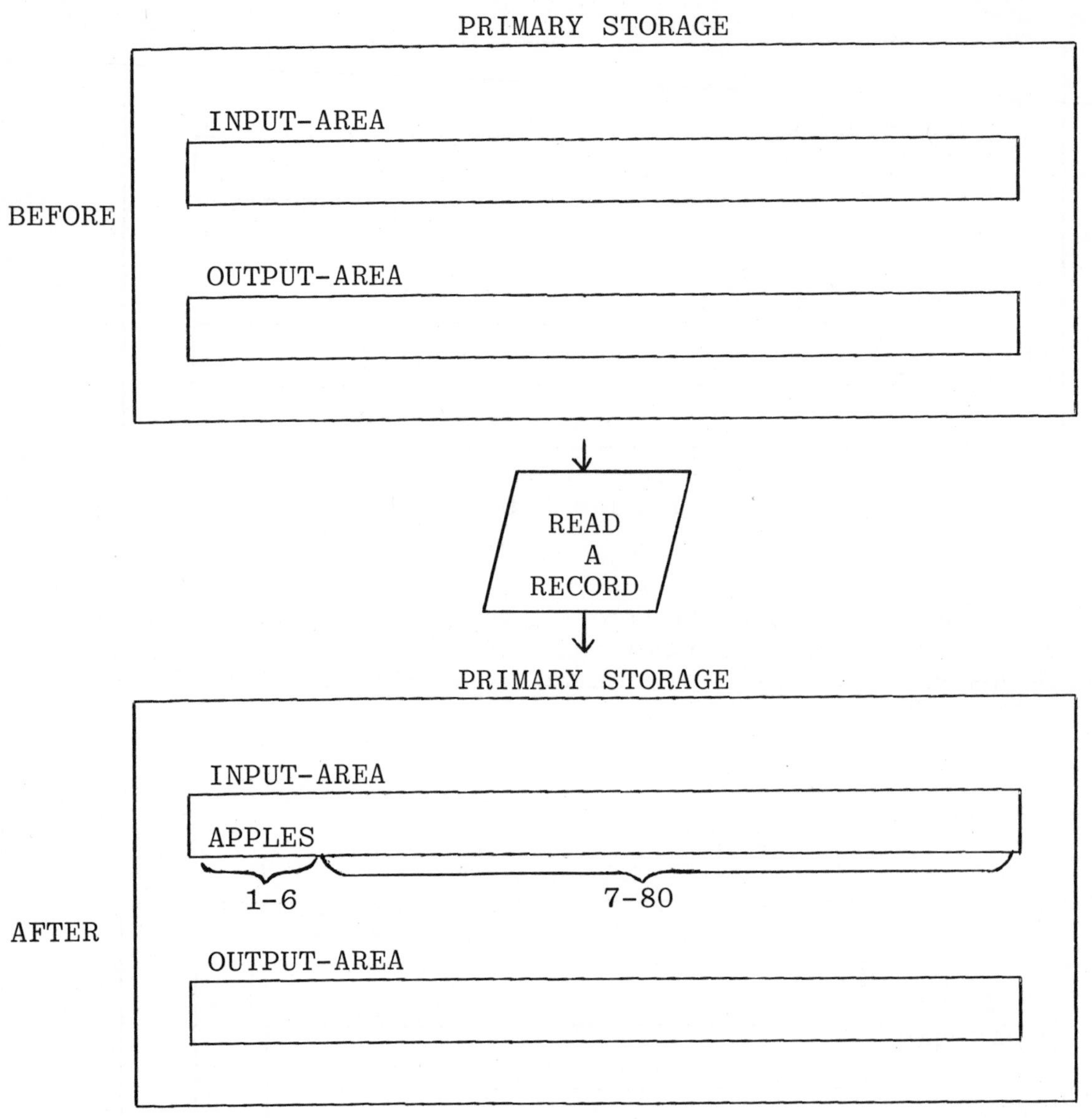

Figure 2-8

Notice that after the reading operation INPUT-AREA contains the data read from the card record. If INPUT-AREA is an 80 position area to correspond to the size of a standard punched card then INPUT-AREA now contains the same information that was on the card. In other words, INPUT-AREA contains APPLES and 74 blanks from the card that was read. Notice that the entire card was read into storage and not just one field or area on the card. The blanks from the card are transferred to storage in the same manner that the alphabetic characters are. The reading operation had no effect on the contents of OUTPUT-AREA. To modify the contents of OUTPUT-AREA further processing would be necessary.

Now let us presume that we are going to read the four cards one after another with no other processing being done. While the odds are not good that any program would just read four cards and stop, this example will serve to point out the effect of a repetitive reading process.

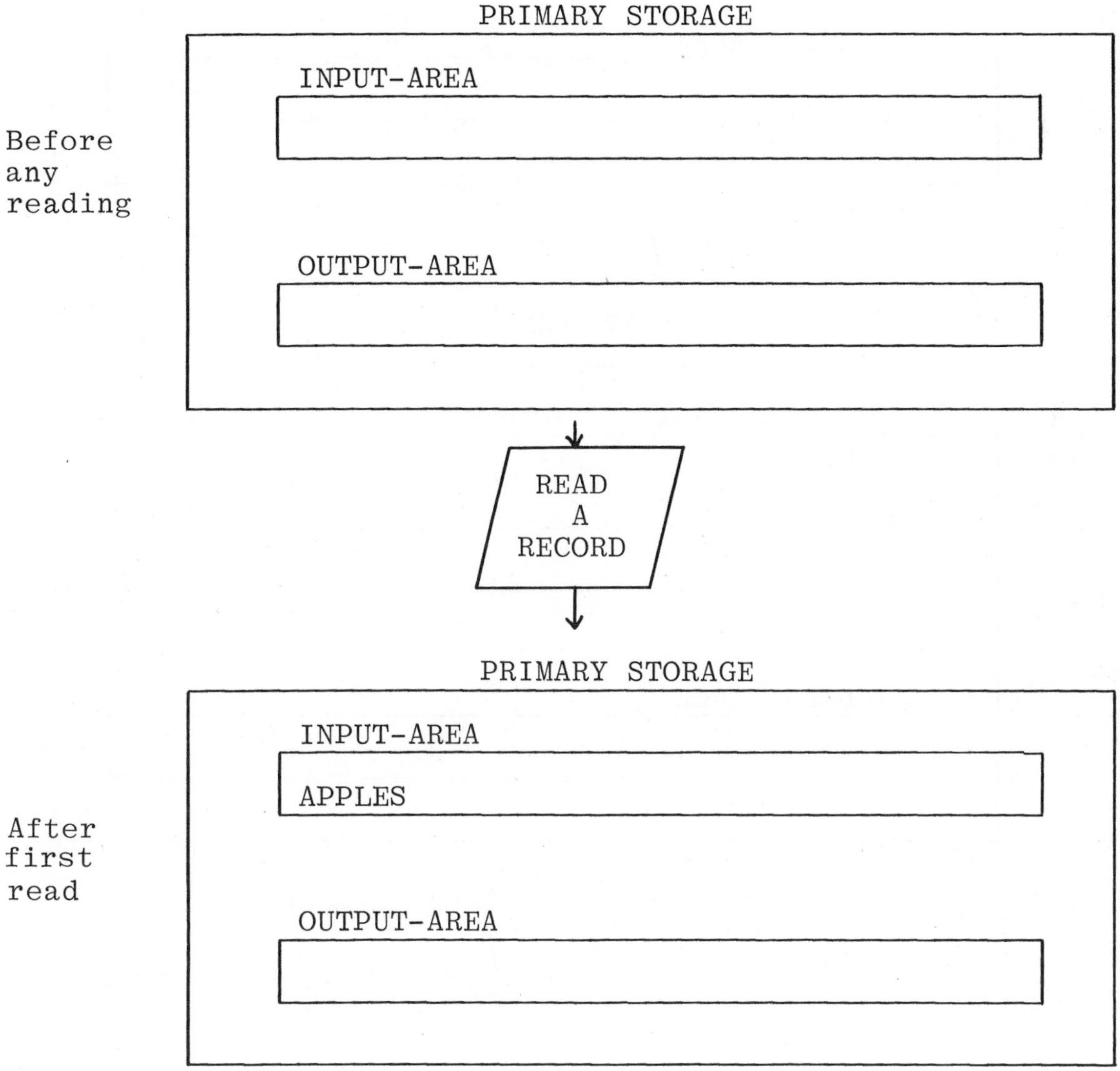

Figure 2-9

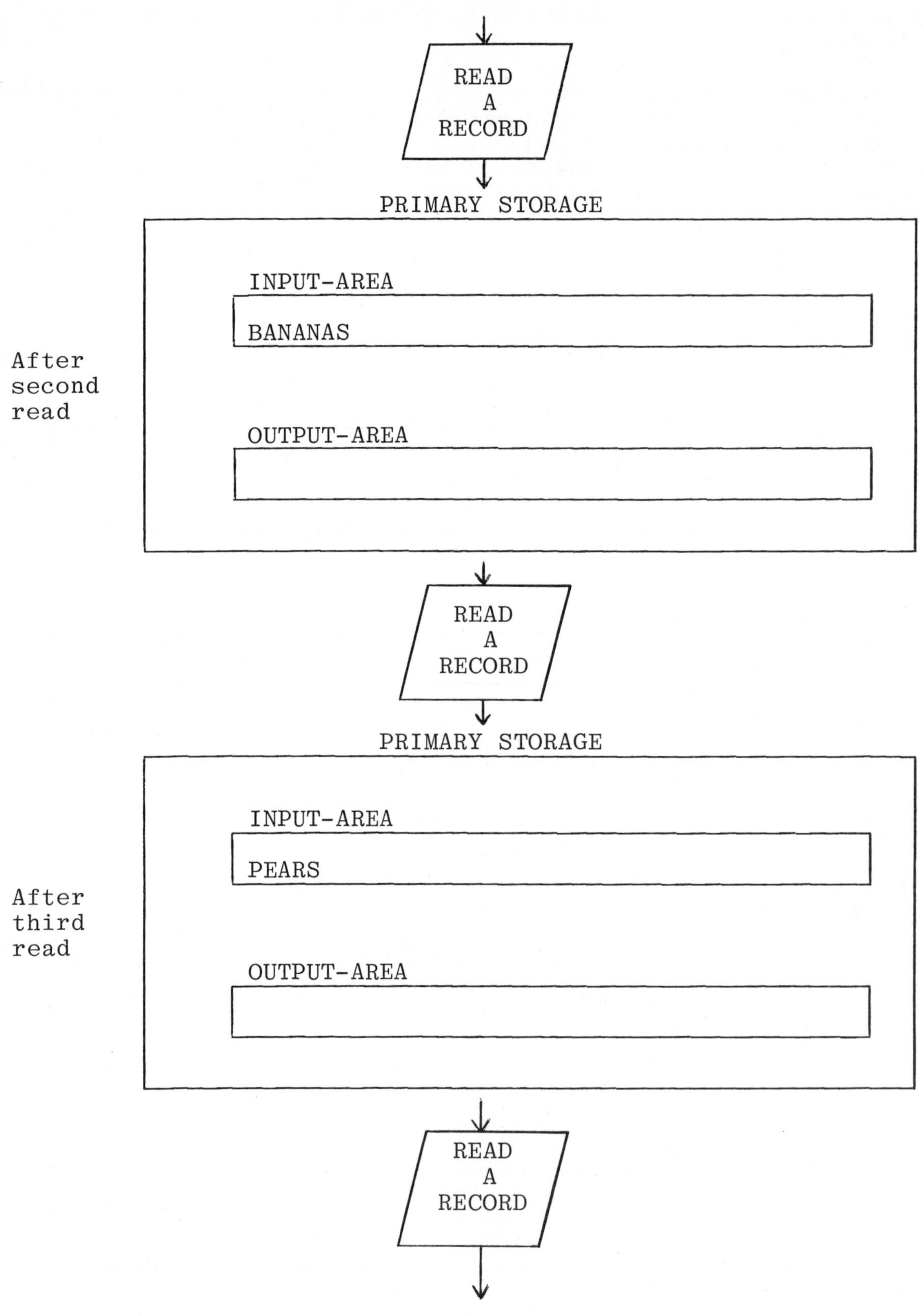

Figure 2-9 (cont.)

PRIMARY STORAGE

After fourth read

INPUT-AREA
TURNIPS

OUTPUT-AREA

Figure 2-9 (cont.)

The first read is very similar to the previous example. Notice that after the first read is accomplished the contents of INPUT-AREA now reflect the contents of the first card. The contents of INPUT-AREA are APPLES and the remaining blanks or spaces from the card (74 of them to be exact).

After the second read the contents of INPUT-AREA have been altered completely so that they now reflect the contents of the second card. The word APPLES has been completely overlayed with the word BANANAS (and 73 spaces) from the second card.

After the third read the data from the third card (that is PEARS and 75 spaces) has replaced BANANAS (and 73 spaces) in INPUT-AREA. In a similar manner when the fourth card is read, the data from it (TURNIPS and 73 spaces) will completely overlay PEARS.

There are two very important concepts in this example. First, when you read you read only one logical (individual) record at a time and not the whole file. Second, since you read each successive record into the same area (INPUT-AREA in this case), the contents of the previous record are lost as each new card is read. The contents can be saved with other types of processing which we will cover under the process symbol. The concept of overlaying data as each successive record is read is called destructive readin.

The other half of the Input/Output process is that of writing data out of storage to some media such as tape, disk or a printed report. In other words we are now going to write one logical (individual) record. Using our original example where we read only one card that had APPLES and 74 spaces in it let us presume that the card has already been read and that storage now looks like Figure 2-10.

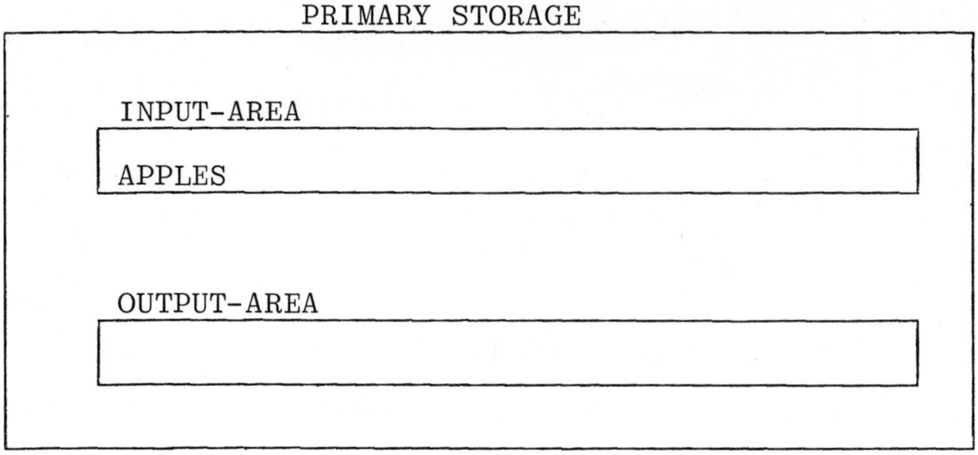

PRIMARY STORAGE

INPUT-AREA
APPLES

OUTPUT-AREA

Figure 2-10

Transfer of the data from INPUT-AREA to OUTPUT-AREA is necessary before we can produce any output. The steps necessary to accomplish this are explained in the section for the PROCESS symbol. For the moment, assume the transfer has been made as shown in Figure 2-11.

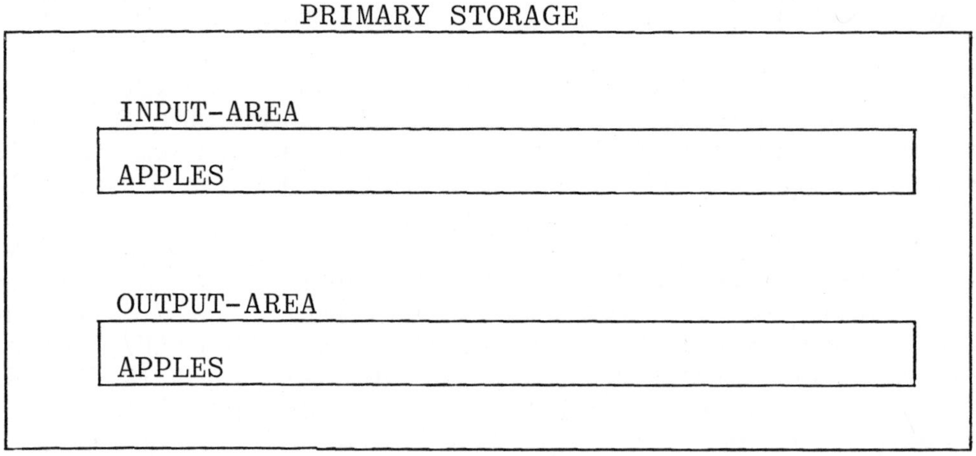

PRIMARY STORAGE

INPUT-AREA
APPLES

OUTPUT-AREA
APPLES

Figure 2-11

If we now want the contents of OUTPUT-AREA to be written on the printer, we instruct the system to write a line and the data will be transferred to the output device we indicate (a printer in our example). In flowcharting form this instruction is shown in Figure 2-12.

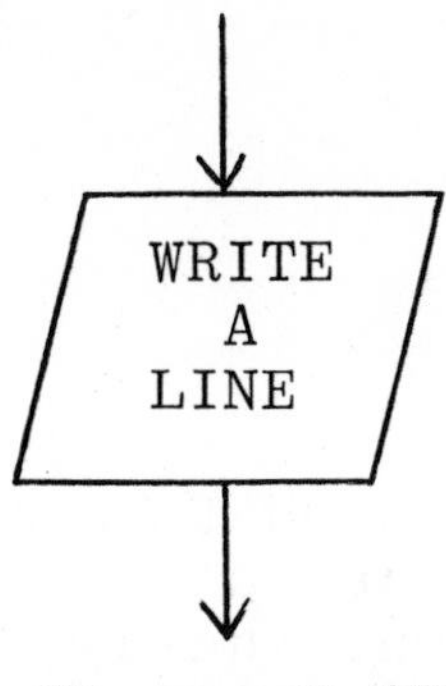

Figure 2-12

The instruction in Figure 2-12 causes the following printer output to be produced (Figure 2-13):

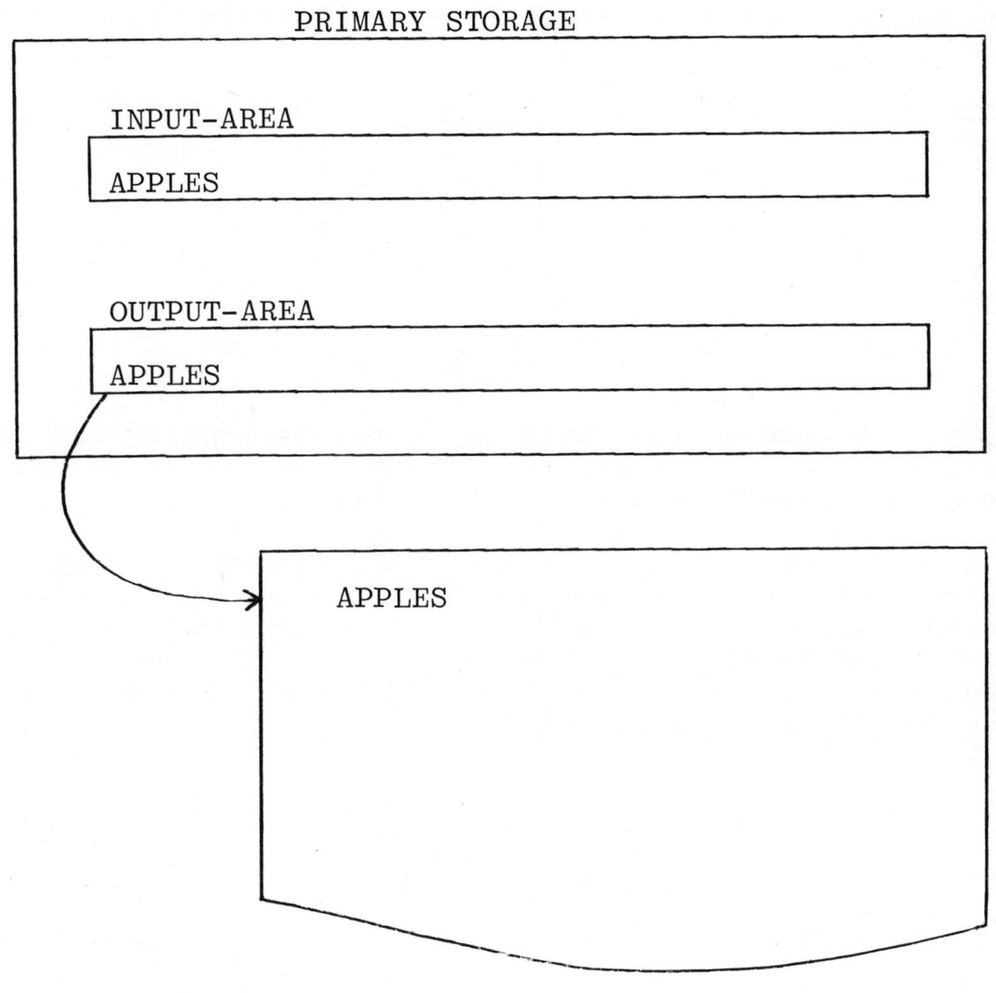

Figure 2-13

PROCESS SYMBOL

The process symbol is used to show individual steps in the processing of data which takes place between input and output operations. Such steps might include transferring data from one part of storage to another (called moving) or mathematical operations such as addition, subtraction, multiplication or division.

In the COBOL or assembler programming languages one of the most common processing steps is moving data from one storage location to another such as from INPUT-AREA to OUTPUT-AREA. This process would be flowcharted as shown in Figure 2-14.

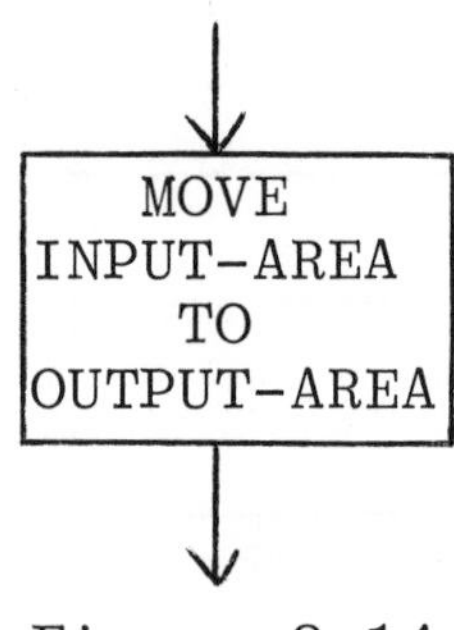

Figure 2-14

If we combine this with our previous reading and writing operations, we can produce a routine that will read and write one card record. This is shown in Figure 2-15.

Notice the contents of INPUT-AREA after the MOVE operation. The contents of INPUT-AREA are not affected by the move. Moving does not affect the contents of a sending area, which in this case is INPUT-AREA. It merely duplicates the contents of the sending area in some other area of storage called the receiving area (OUTPUT-AREA in our example).

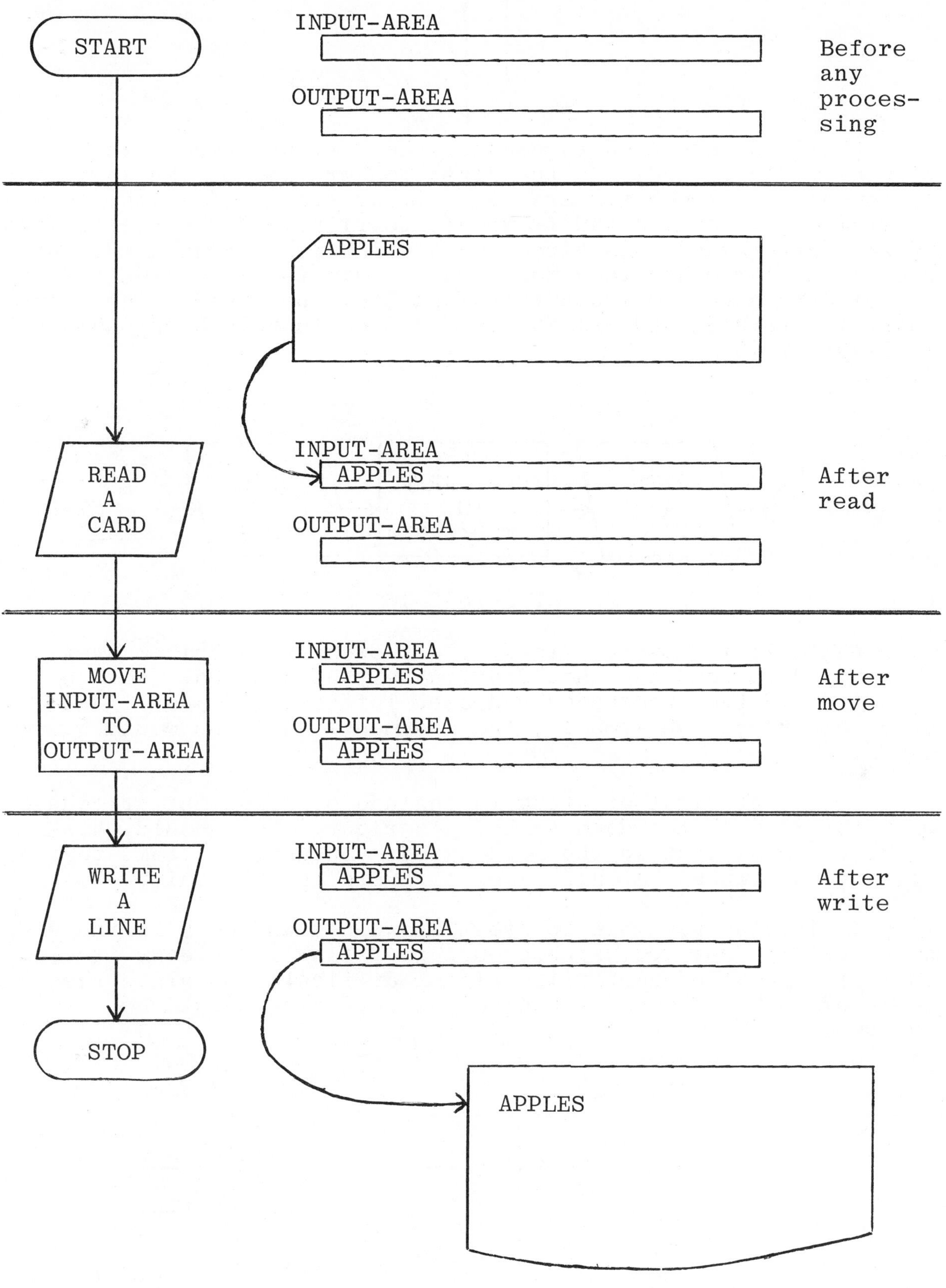
START
INPUT-AREA
OUTPUT-AREA
Before any processing
APPLES
READ A CARD
INPUT-AREA
APPLES
OUTPUT-AREA
After read
MOVE INPUT-AREA TO OUTPUT-AREA
INPUT-AREA
APPLES
OUTPUT-AREA
APPLES
After move
WRITE A LINE
INPUT-AREA
APPLES
OUTPUT-AREA
APPLES
After write
STOP
APPLES

Figure 2-15

FLOWLINES

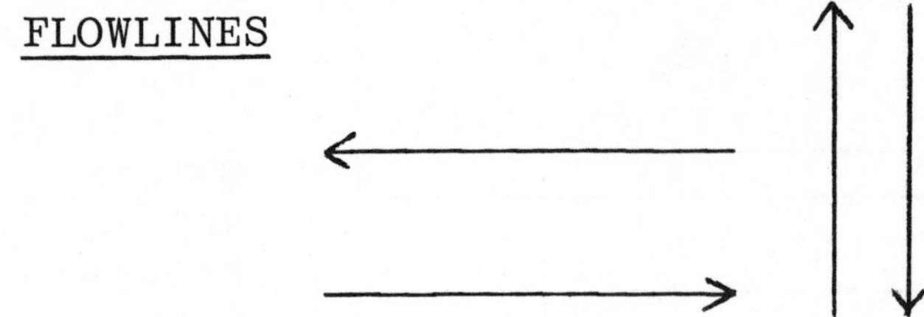

Flowlines are used to connect the various symbols in a flowchart and to indicate the direction or flow of the logic in a flowchart. Flowcharts are normally written so that the flow is from top to bottom and from left to right. If your flowlines have no arrowheads this direction of flow will be assumed. Directional flow other than top down or left to right requires the use of arrowheads to indicate the path of the logic. The flowchart for reading and writing one card could have been shown as in Figure 2-16.

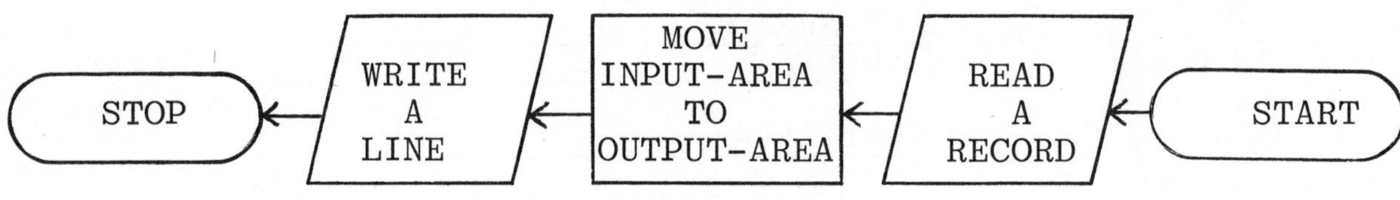

Figure 2-16

While it is possible to draw a flowchart in this manner, it is awkward to read and should definitely be avoided. Notice also that if the arrowheads had been left off and just lines used to connect the symbols, the assumed first step would be to STOP.

It is not right or wrong to include or leave out arrowheads when the flow is top down or left to right. You should, however, be consistent in the method that you use. In this text we will use arrowheads at all times to avoid any ambiguity.

It is also possible to cross flowlines as shown in the example below. However, such crossing of flowlines lends itself to a great deal of ambiguity. It is difficult to follow the logic of such a flowchart and so this practice should be avoided.

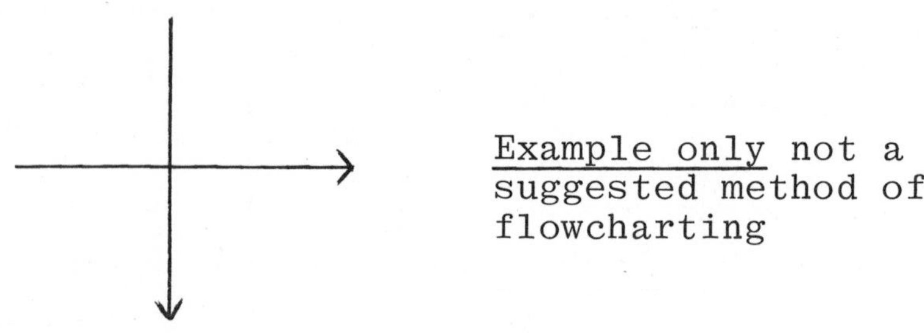

Figure 2-17

OFFPAGE CONNECTOR

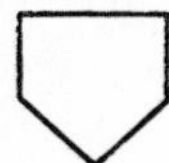

The offpage connector symbol is used to show a continuation of a logic path from one page of a flowchart to another page of the flowchart. To illustrate this point let us take another look at the flowchart we created to read only one card and write a line on the printer. See Figures 2-18, and 2-19. The small size of the pages in this example is unrealistic but they give us the opportunity to illustrate how a page change is made.

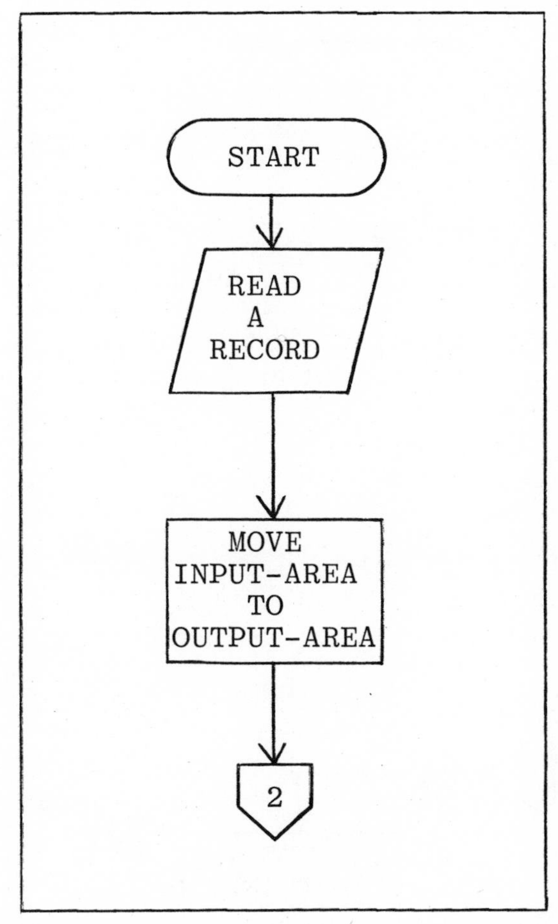

Figure 2-18

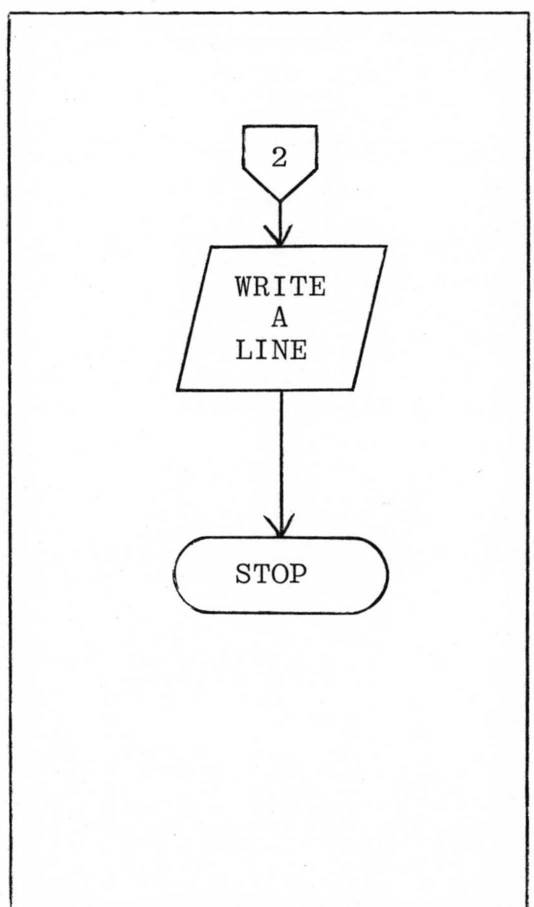

Figure 2-19

Notice that the number in both offpage connector symbols is the same. On the bottom of Page 1 it indicates the page you are continuing to and on the top of Page 2 it indicates where the continuation actually takes place. At times the symbolism within the offpage connector symbol becomes more extensive to facilitate following a logic path. This is especially true in rather large programs with a great number of subroutines.

DECISION SYMBOL

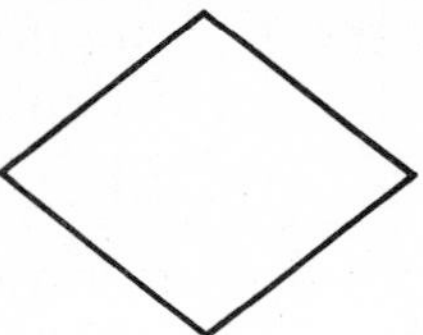

The decision symbol is used to depict a decision being made and the alternate paths to be followed as a result of that decision. There is one entrance into a decision symbol and at least two exit paths away from the symbol. See Figure 2-20.

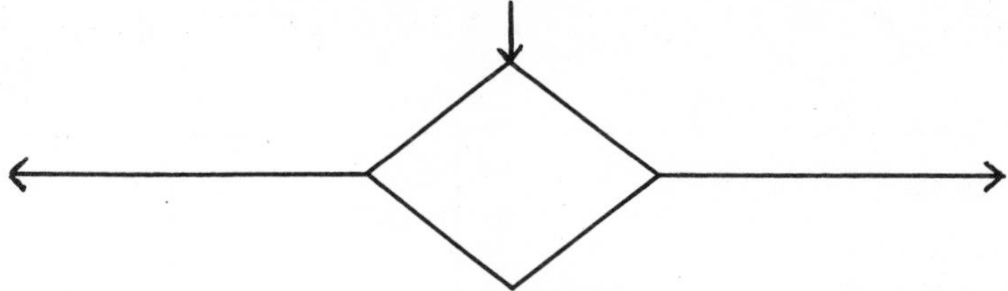

Figure 2-20

The simplest form of decision is a two way exit. In our example flowchart that reads one card and writes one line, let's add the requirement that we will print or write the contents of the card only if the first letter of that card is a B. This will produce the somewhat more sophisticated flowchart shown in Figure 2-21.

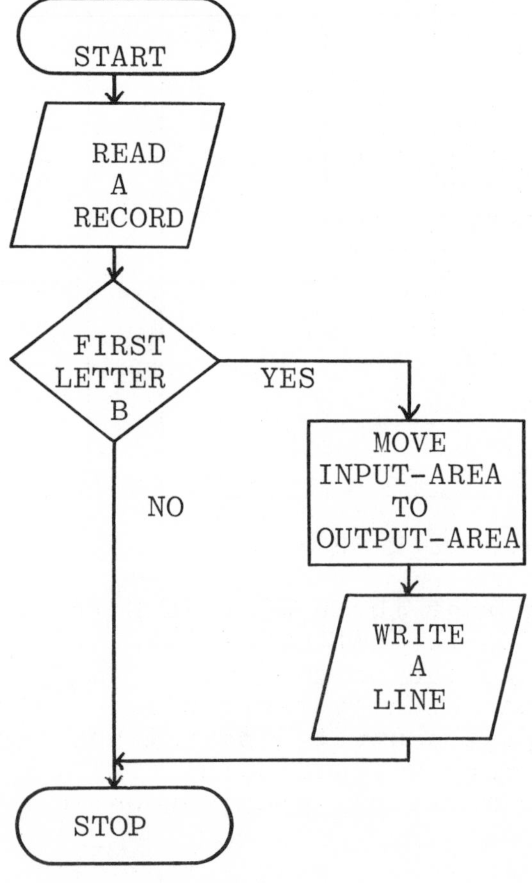

Figure 2-21

This example reads only one card and decides whether or not to print it. Suppose we expand this flowchart to read a whole file of cards and print only those cards whose first column contains a B. The flowchart would be as shown in Figure 2-22.

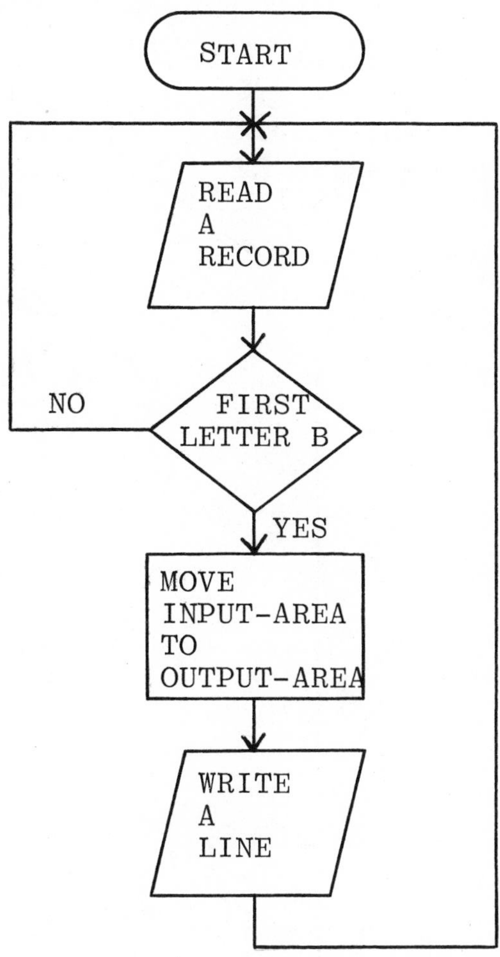

Figure 2-22

We will now check each card that is read and either print it if the first letter on the card is a B or bypass the printing of the card and go back to read the next card. The concept of reexecuting the same series of instructions over and over is called looping. In this particular example the loop sends us back to the beginning of the flowchart so we are able to read additional cards. The finer points of looping and how it can be used will be covered in Chapter 3.

There is, however, one thing wrong with our flowchart as it now exists for the reading of a file of cards and printing those cards whose first letter is a B. What happens when we have finished reading our file? We have made no provision for running out of cards. Let's modify the logic to take care of this situation.

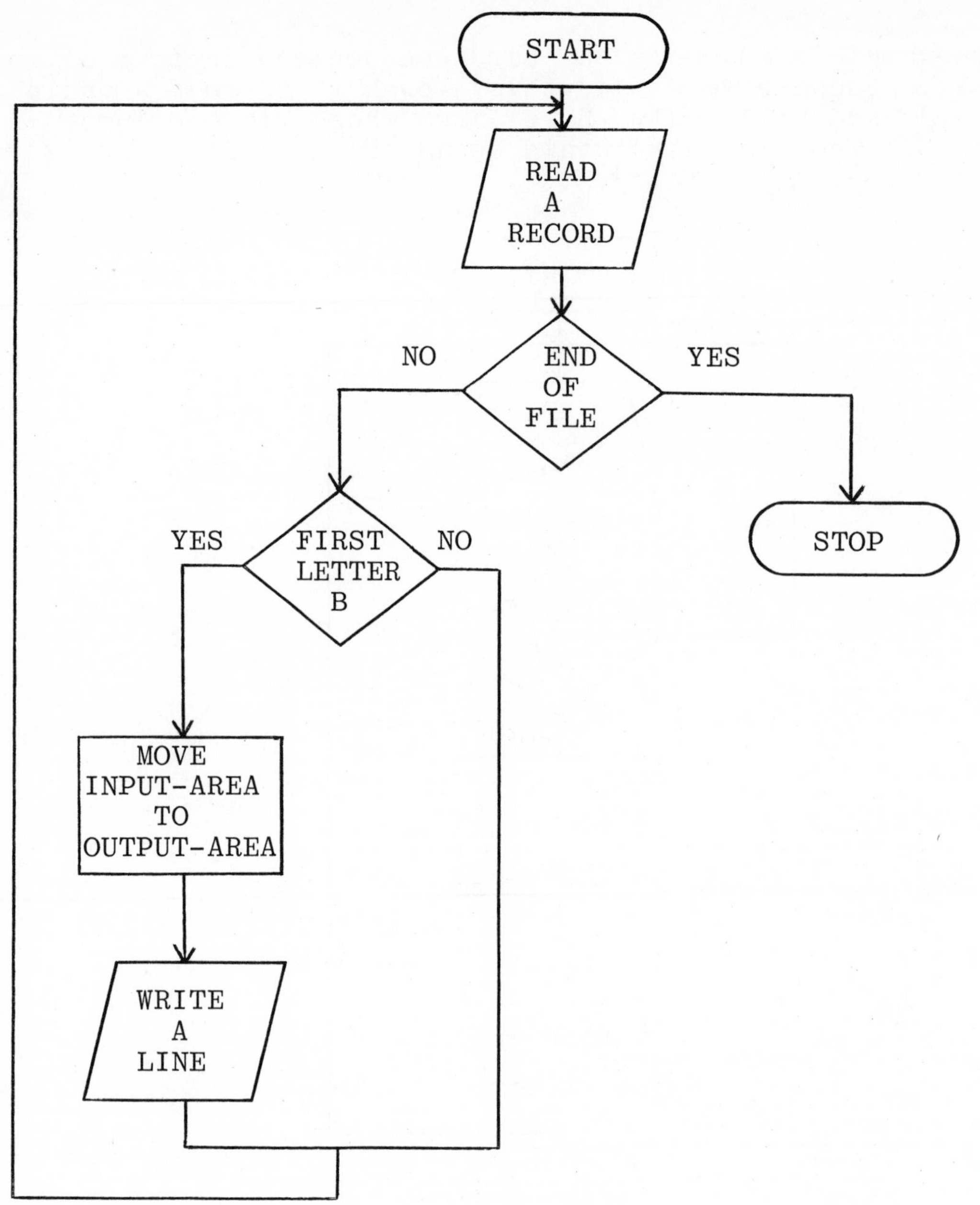

Figure 2-23

Now we will read and process cards only until we run out of data cards at which point we will stop processing. However, we need to say something about the symbol that asks if it is a data card that has been read.

Most computers today provide the ability to test for an out of data or more accurately an end of file condition on a sequential reading operation (reading the file from beginning to end including all records in the file). Sequential files which are files that have been sorted into some predetermined order such as Social Security Number or Part Number have a record at the end which is not actually data but indicates to the system that all data records have been read and processed. When this record is found at the end of a file you do not process it since it is not data but merely an indicator that all data has already been processed. On System/360 and 370 computers a card end of file situation is indicated with /* in Columns 1 and 2 respectively. While this code may vary with the manufacturer or specific computer, the principle remains the same. For our purposes we will show this situation in future flowcharts as testing for an end of file condition (see Figure 2-24).

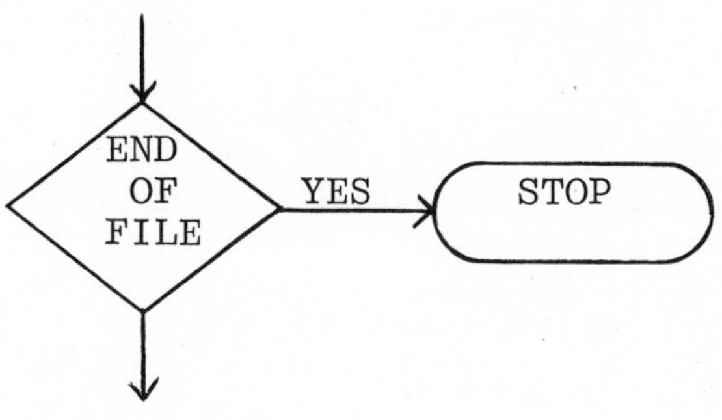

Figure 2-24

There are other possible decision symbol uses other than a simple two way test. One of the most common is the situation where you are testing to see if one number is greater than, less than or equal to another number. This is typically shown as follows (Figure 2-25).

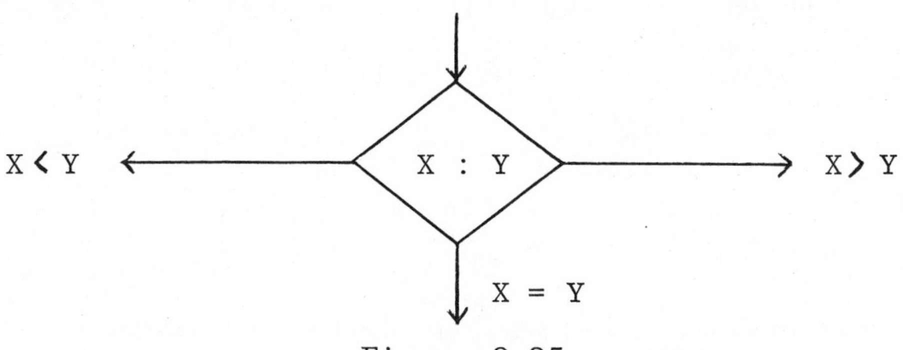

Figure 2-25

Another possibility is that one of several exit paths may be taken depending on the value of some variable. Two very common ways of depicting this are shown in Figure 2-26.

Based on the value of the variable (X in this case) various paths in the logic may be followed.

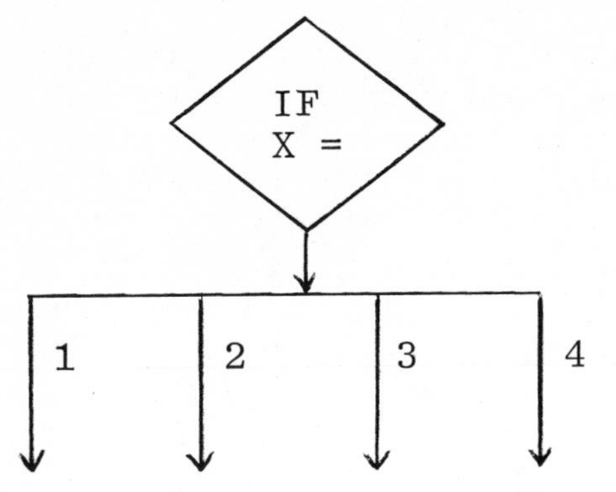

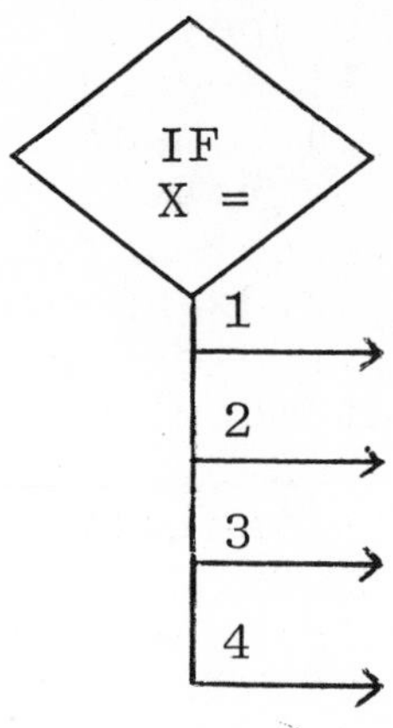

Figure 2-26

CONNECTOR SYMBOL

The connector symbol is used to show an exit from or an entrance into the logic of a flowchart. When it is used to show that you are leaving one part of the flowchart and going to some other part of the same flowchart it is called an exit. Exits are typically shown in one of the ways indicated in Figure 2-27.

An exit symbol (often called a branch) is usually identified with a letter that indicates where in the logic you are branching to for further processing. The point you are branching to is also indicated by a connector with the same letter in it and this point is called an entry.

Exits and entries may also have page references in them indicating where you are branching to (for exits) and where you are branching from (for entries). Entry symbols are typically shown in one of the ways indicated in Figure 2-28.

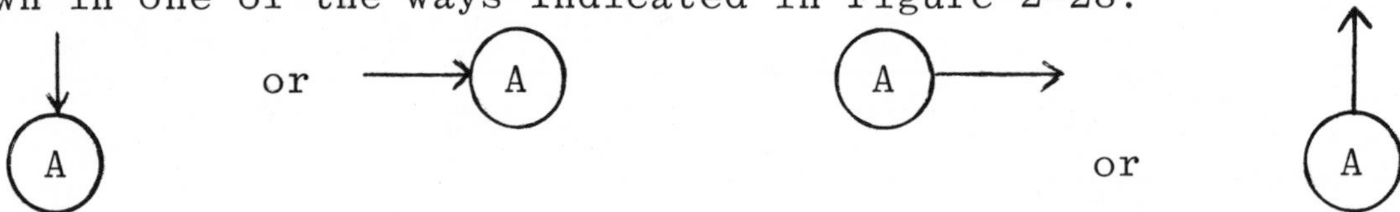

Figure 2-27

Figure 2-28

In most cases connectors are used as replacements for flowlines to avoid having lines running all over the place and to present a neater, easier to follow flowchart. There is at least one case where connectors are definitely used in place of flowlines. This is when the branch is to another place in the flowchart that is on a different page. After all, you can't (or shouldn't) have lines going from one page to another.

Let's take another look at our flowchart for reading a file of cards and printing those cards whose first letter is B. Figure 2-29 utilized flowlines while Figure 2-30 utilizes connectors. The individual symbols are numbered to facilitate cross-referencing.

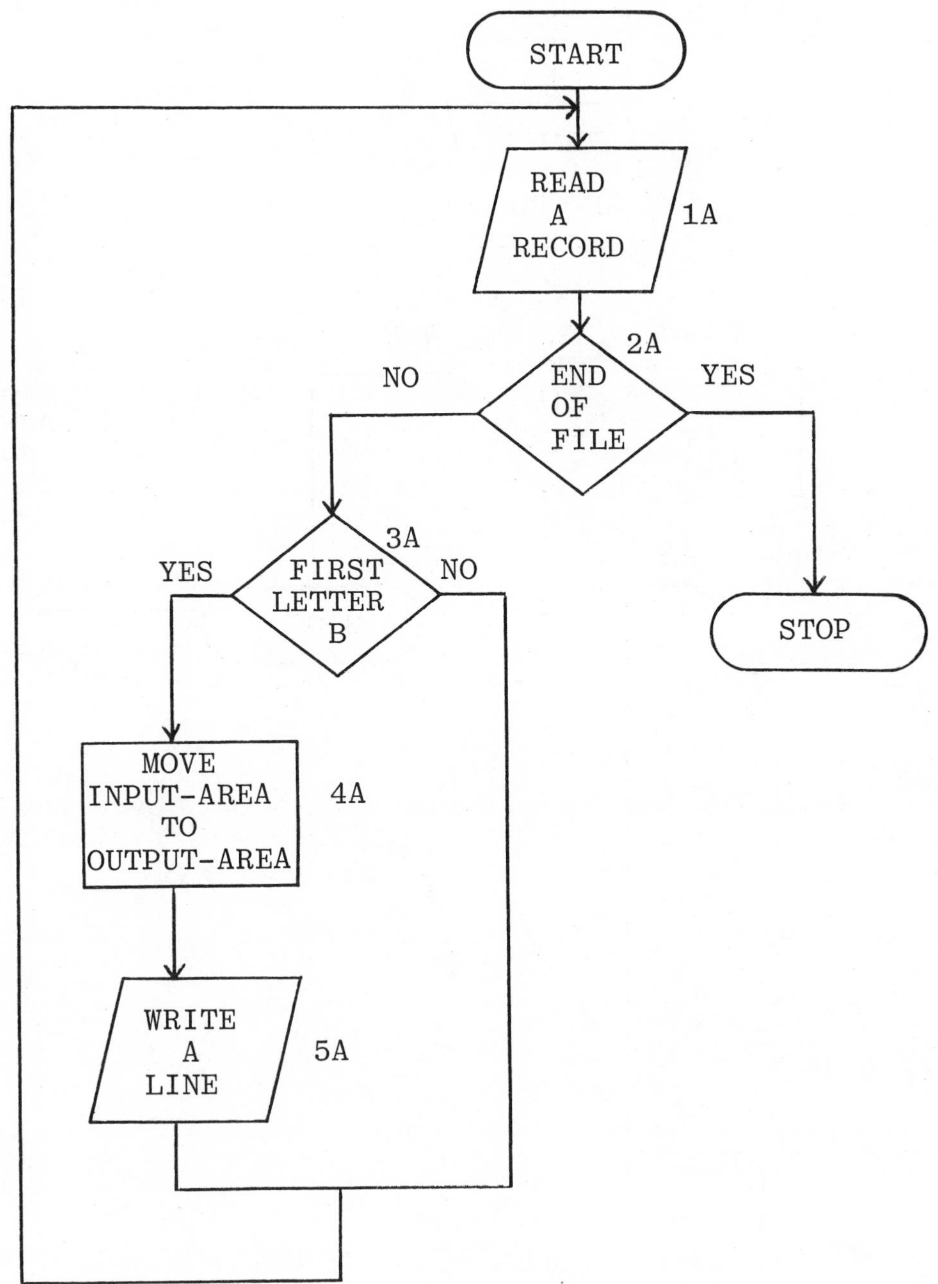
START
READ
A
RECORD
1A
2A
NO
END
OF
FILE
YES
3A
YES
FIRST
LETTER
B
NO
STOP
MOVE
INPUT-AREA
TO
OUTPUT-AREA
4A
WRITE
A
LINE
5A

Figure 2-29

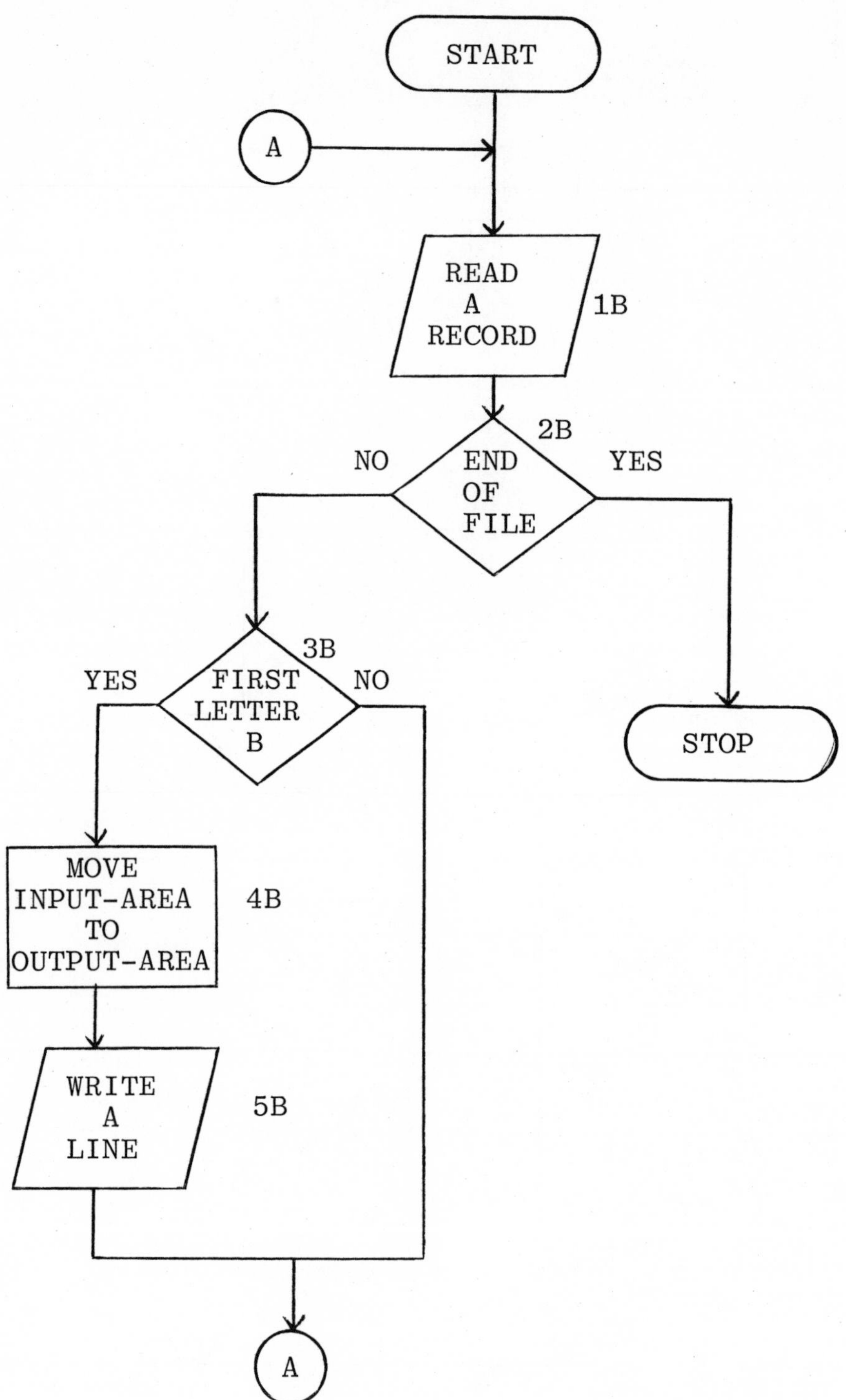
START
A
READ
A
RECORD
1B
2B
NO
END
OF
FILE
YES
3B
YES
FIRST
LETTER
B
NO
STOP
MOVE
INPUT-AREA
TO
OUTPUT-AREA
4B
WRITE
A
LINE
5B
A

Figure 2-30

The path back to read the next card in Figure 2-29 is done via flowlines from blocks 3A and 5A, whereas in Figure 2-30 it is done via connectors from blocks 3B and 5B. The connector leaving blocks 3B and 5B is an exit. The connector going in to read the next card just above block 1B is an entry.

Now that we have enough of the basics to read and write multiple records and test for end of file, we need one more concept covered before we go too far. Most likely any file would have more than one field on each record. To illustrate the fact that each field must be moved individually, we will read and print each record from the card file shown in Figure 2-31.

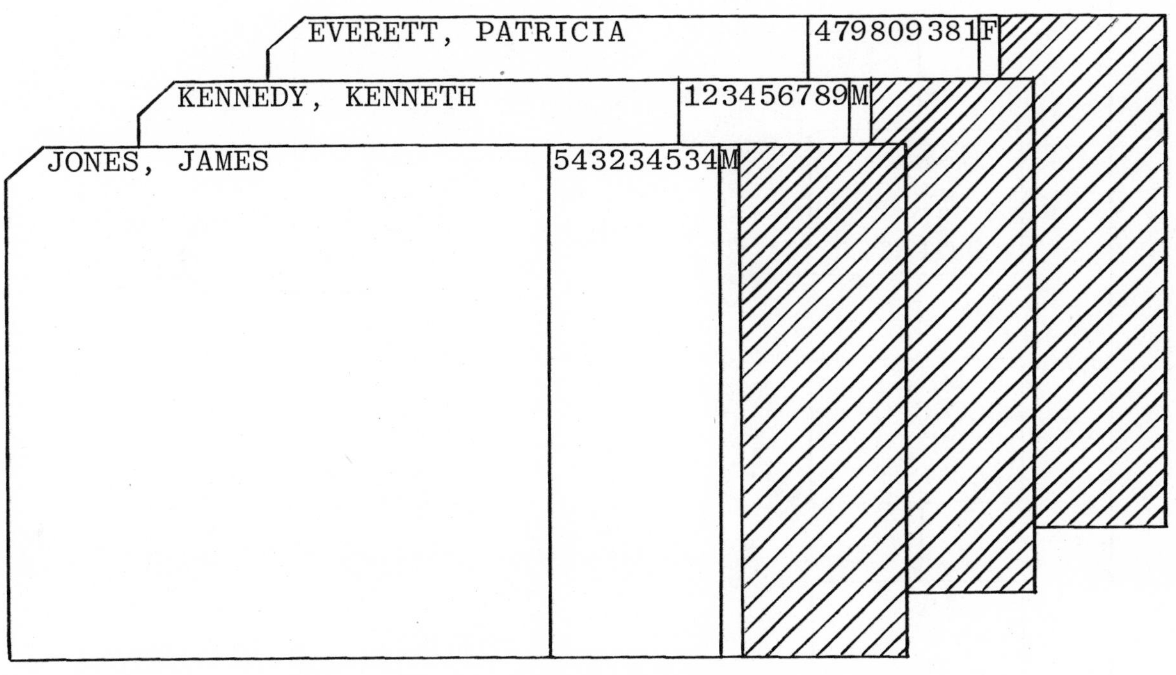

Figure 2-31

On the printer report we want blank space of some size to appear between the fields for readability. (See Figure 2-32).

```
JONES, JAMES        543234534      M
KENNEDY, KENNETH    123456789      M
EVERETT, PATRICIA   479809381      F
```

Figure 2-32

Each card contains 3 fields (name, social security number and sex). The shaded areas on the cards are not used in the output. Figure 2-33 shows the flowchart to accomplish the listing of this file.

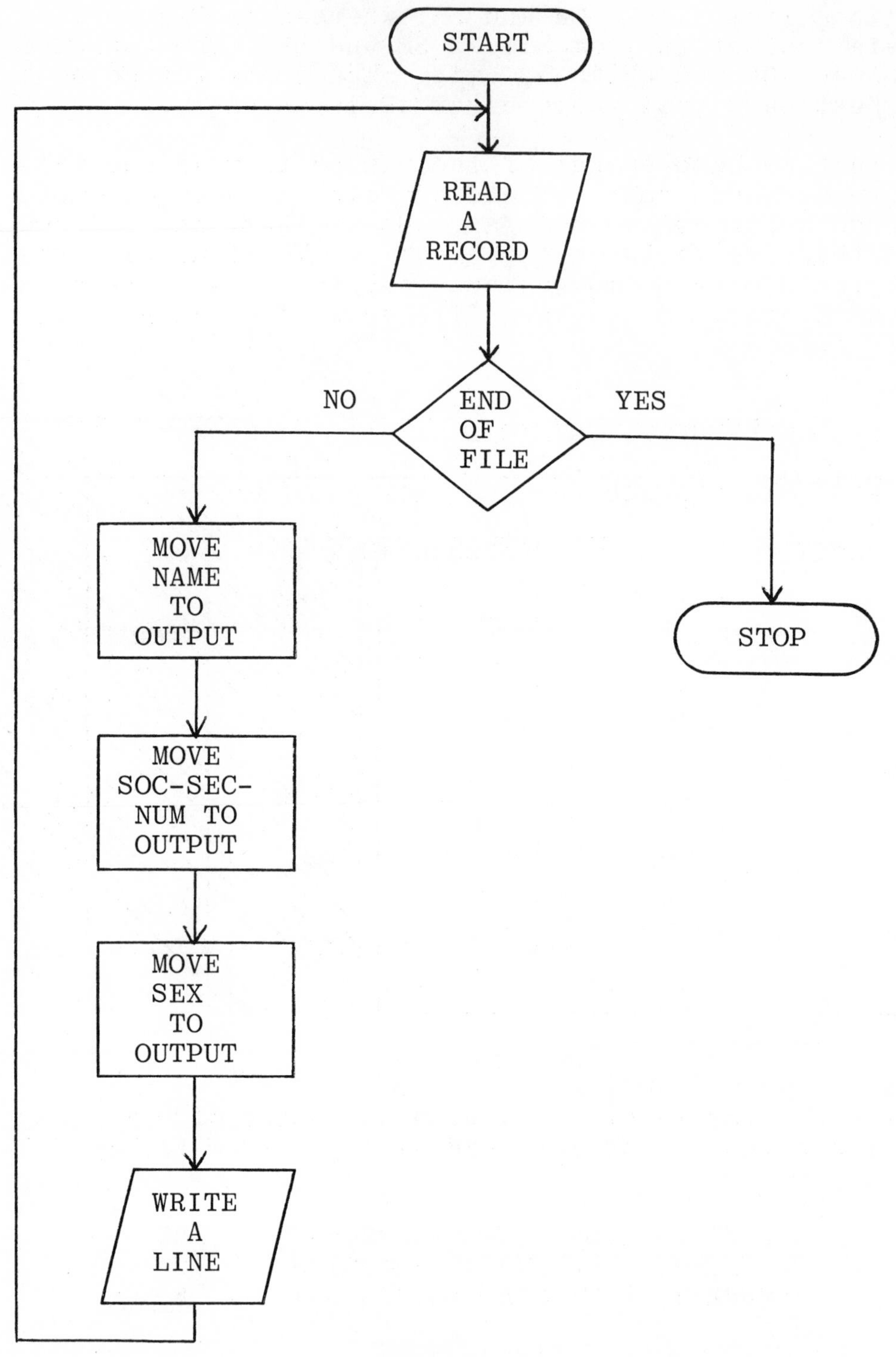

Figure 2-33

The most important idea in Figure 2-33 is that if we are concerned with the individual fields on a record rather than the entire record, then each of the input fields from the card must be moved separately to the output line. If we follow one card through the process the actual steps that are followed should become clearer (see Figure 2-34).

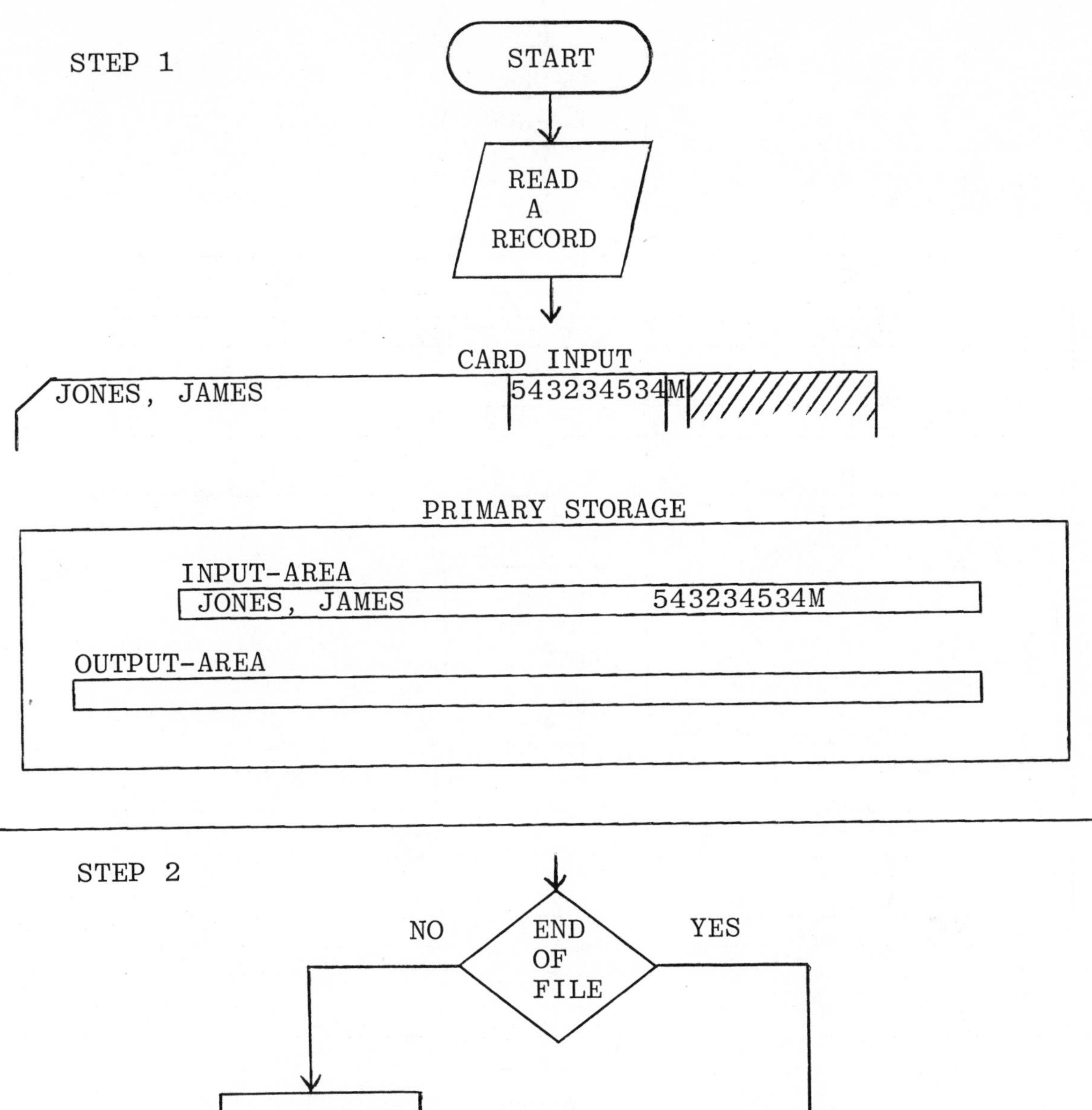

PRIMARY STORAGE

INPUT-AREA

JONES, JAMES 543234534M

OUTPUT-AREA

JONES, JAMES

Figure 2-34

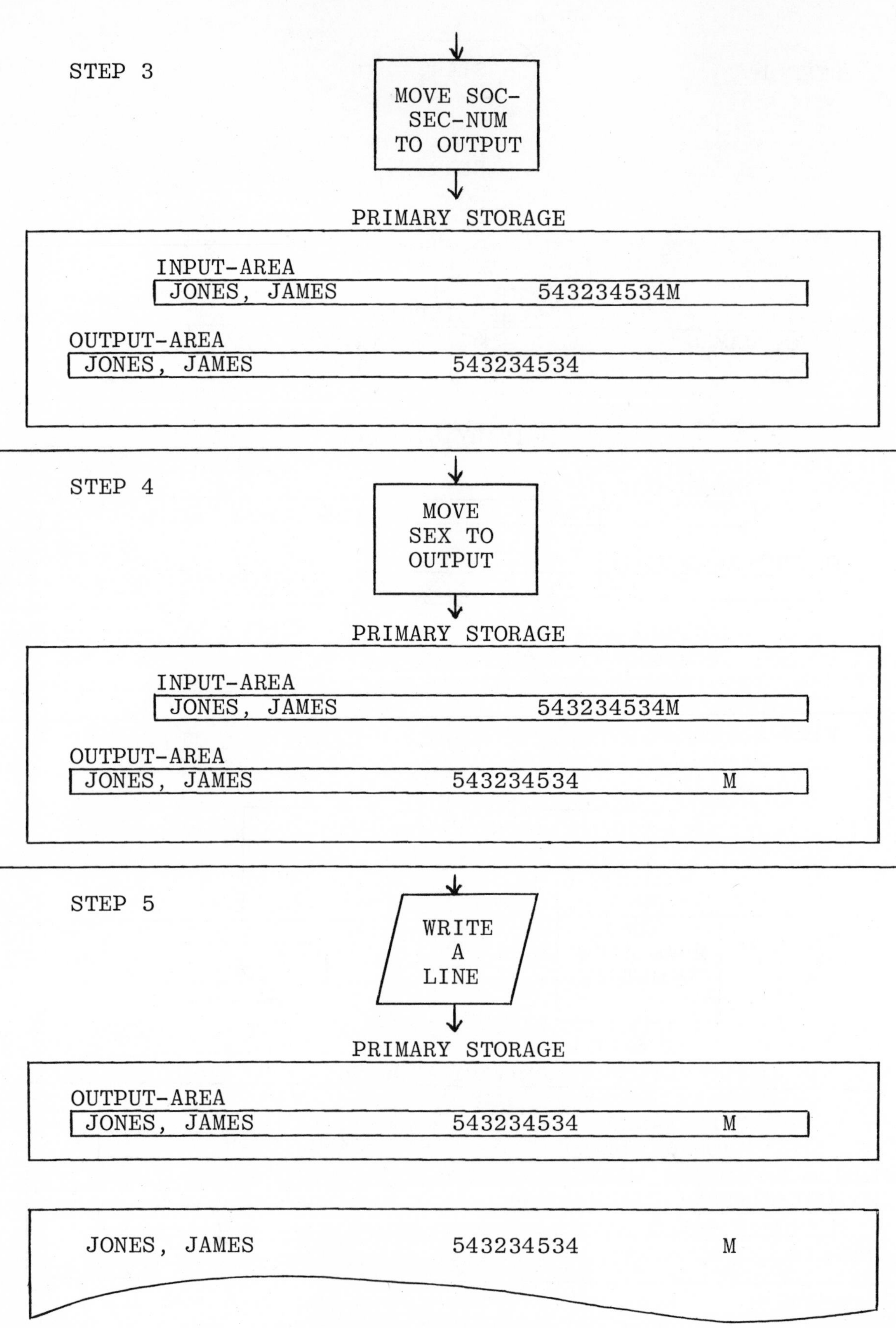

Figure 2-34 (cont.)

Step 1 - This step reads the next record on the input file.

Step 2 - This step checks to see if we have reached the end of the input file. If the end of file is found we terminate processing. If the end of file is not reached, and in our case it was not, we move the contents of the first field (name) to the OUTPUT-AREA.

Step 3 - This step moves the contents of the second field (soc-sec-num) to the OUTPUT-AREA.

Step 4 - This step moves the contents of the third field (sex) to the OUTPUT-AREA.

Step 5 - This step prints the contents of the OUTPUT-AREA on the report. Note that all items were moved prior to writing the line and that only one line was written.

ANNOTATION SYMBOL

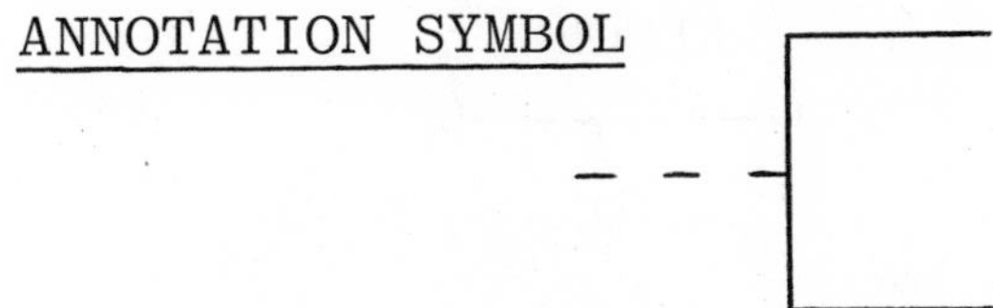

The annotation symbol is used to add additional comments to a flowcharting symbol. While you normally indicate what action is being taken in any given block, there are times when additional wording is needed to indicate more detail about the action being taken. For instance in using the reading process above we merely said to read a record but we did not say from what file. It is possible we may wish to clarify which file is being used. To accomplish this we could use the annotation symbol as shown in Figure 2-35.

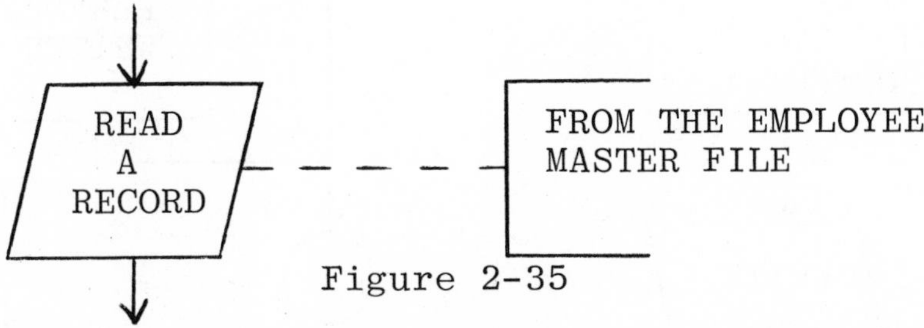

Figure 2-35

By adding this note it is now obvious that we are reading a record from the employee master file. This same type of notation may be used in many ways on various symbols to provide more detail for clarification. However, its use should not become so extensive that it serves only to clutter up the flowchart and hinder readability.

PREDEFINED PROCESS SYMBOL

EXTERNAL INTERNAL

The predefined process symbol is used to show a routine that has been described elsewhere. It normally says to perform the set of instructions described elsewhere (usually a subroutine) and return to the next symbol in the flowchart. The next symbol being the one that immediately follows the predefined process symbol. Let's reuse our flowchart for reading a file of cards and printing the ones whose first letter is a B. The original flowchart for doing this is provided for comparison with a flowchart in which a subroutine is used (see Figure 2-36).

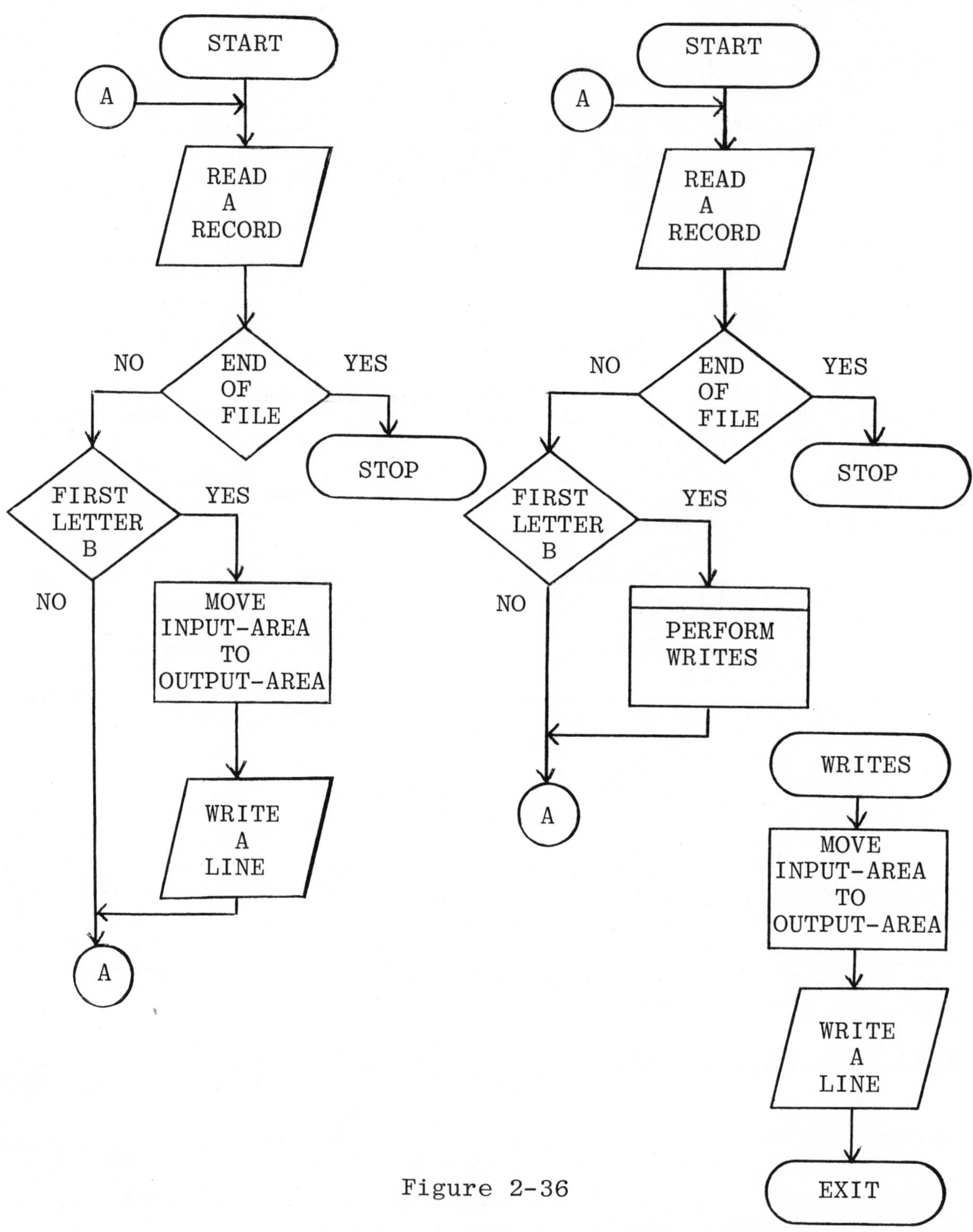

Figure 2-36

We have substituted the symbols for moving and writing the data with a predefined process symbol that performs a routine called WRITES which is shown to the right of the main flowchart. As you can see, the WRITES routine is totally described as a separate piece of logic that is invoked or called when needed by the main logic in the program. After the WRITES routine has been executed, control is transferred to the next instruction following that instruction which executed the subroutine. In this case it is a branch to read the next card. Some of the reasons for utilizing subroutines will be covered in Chapter 5.

The concepts that have been presented so far regarding the flowcharting symbols will be reemphasized in succeeding chapters. Chapter 3 will introduce you to processing sequences and how they may be altered.

REVIEW QUESTIONS

Matching

A.

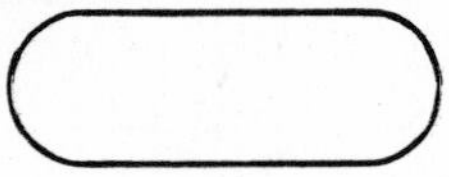

B.

C.

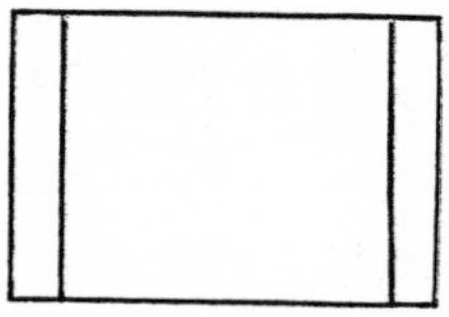

D.

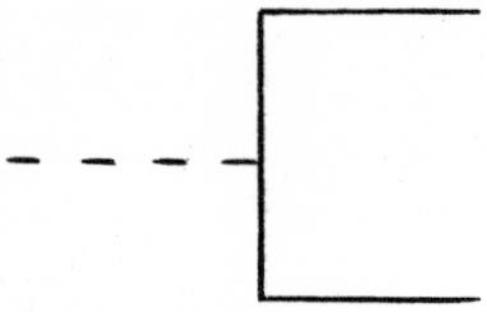

E.

F.

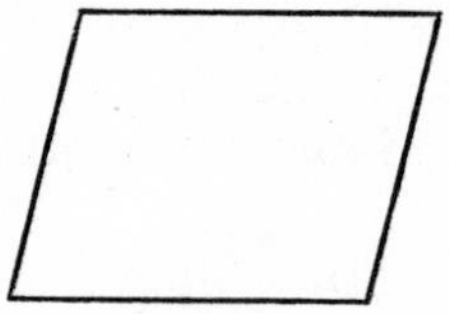

G.

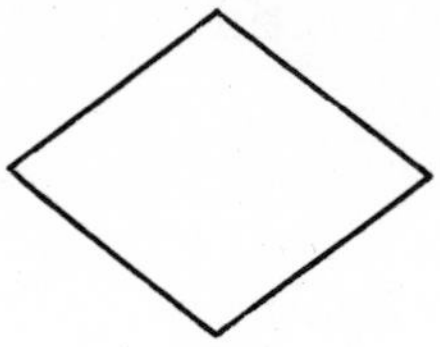

H.

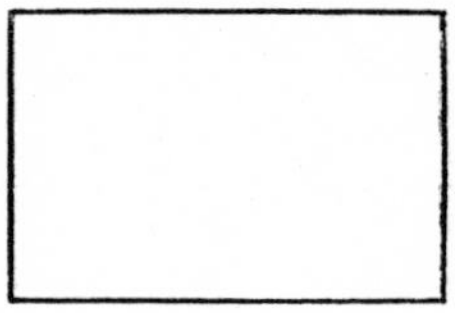

__________ 1. Used to insert additional comments on a flowchart.

__________ 2. Indicates the reading or writing of data.

__________ 3. Indicates a predefined process.

__________ 4. Indicates a decision being made in a flowchart.

__________ 5. Indicates a continuation of the logic to a succeeding page.

__________ 6. May be either an exit or an entry point.

__________ 7. Used to represent the statement 'MOVE INPUT TO OUTPUT'.

__________ 8. Indicates the beginning or ending point in a flowchart.

True/False

T F 1. Terminal symbols are never used in conjunction with subroutines.

T F 2. Two symbols that are interchangeable in program flowcharts are: ◯ ⬠

T F 3. Flowcharts are normally read from top to bottom and right to left unless otherwise noted.

T F 4. An (EXIT) symbol on a subroutine indicates that control is to return to that point in the logic immediately following the statement that invoked the subroutine.

T F 5. Moving data from one storage area to another causes destruction of the contents of the sending area.

T F 6. Repeating a series of steps in a flowchart over and over again is called looping.

T F 7. In the following flowchart segment the (A) represents an entry point.

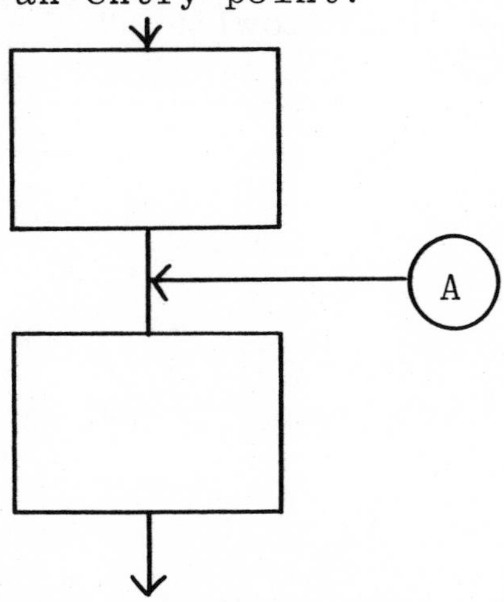

T F 8. Arrowheads are always required in the construction of a program flowchart.

T F 9. Decision symbols always have at least two exit paths.

T F 10. Reading two consecutive cards into an input area causes the data from the second card read to overlay the data from the first card.

Exercises

1. Draw a flowchart to read one card, print its contents and stop.

2. Draw a flowchart to read multiple cards and print their contents. When the card input has been exhausted, print a message that indicates the end of processing and stop. Utilize flowlines for branching back in the logic.

3. Same as number two but use connectors for branching back in the logic.

4. Same as number two except that only those cards with a code of 1, 2 or 7 are to be printed. All other cards are merely to be bypassed.

Discussion Questions

1. What is the purpose of preparing a program flowchart?

2. Why use top down and left to right structure in preparing a flowchart?

3. What is destructive readin and what are its implications?

4. Why would or would not connector symbols be more advantageous at times than flowlines?

CHAPTER 3

Branching and Structuring

OBJECTIVES

As a result of studying this chapter the student should be able to perform the following activities.

1. Describe the process of branching and explain why it is an important aspect of flowcharting or programming.
2. Differentiate between conditional and unconditional branching.
3. Identify typical places where both conditional and unconditional branching might be found in a flowchart.
4. Describe the process of looping and indicate its importance to flowcharting.
5. Identify and describe the four major steps of the looping process.
6. Describe what is meant by a nested loop.
7. Identify the four basic structures and explain their individual usage.
8. Draw and explain the generalized logic common to most programs as the main part of the program.

INTRODUCTION

A computer normally executes the instructions in a program one after the other in the order that they are written. Without some way of altering this sequential instructional flow, programs would be severely handicapped. They would have to have the same instructions written over and over and over again for each processing cycle to be done. Realizing this potential limitation the designers of computers and programming languages developed a way of altering this sequential processing of instructions. This process is called branching.

Additionally some of the basic concepts of structured flowcharting will be presented following the section on branching.

UNCONDITIONAL BRANCHING

Branching is merely causing the execution sequence of the instructions to be altered. Two types of branching are possible to accomplish this alteration in sequence. The first of these is referred to as unconditional branching. An unconditional branch is an instruction that alters the flow regardless of what particular situation is present.

Let's take a look at a flowchart (see Figure 3-1) for a program that would do nothing but read the records in a payroll master file and list them on a report. Once the end of the file has been reached we will terminate processing.

Notice in Figure 3-1 that after each employee record is printed on the report (WRITE A LINE) a 'branch' is taken to read the next record. This branch to A will take place each time we reach that point in the flowchart. The branch is not dependent on any condition being present at the point which it is executed.

CONDITIONAL BRANCHING

The second type of branching that is utilized in programs is called conditional branching. Conditional branching is when one of two or more paths in the logic will be followed based on some condition either being true or not being true. One of the simplest forms of conditional branching is found in Figure 3-1 when we tested to see if the record that was just read was a data record or if it is the end of the file. If the record just read was not a data record a branch was taken to terminate processing. If the record was a data record a branch was taken to move its contents to the output area and print them on a report.

The particular path in the logic that was followed at this point was dependent on whether or not the record just read was a data record.

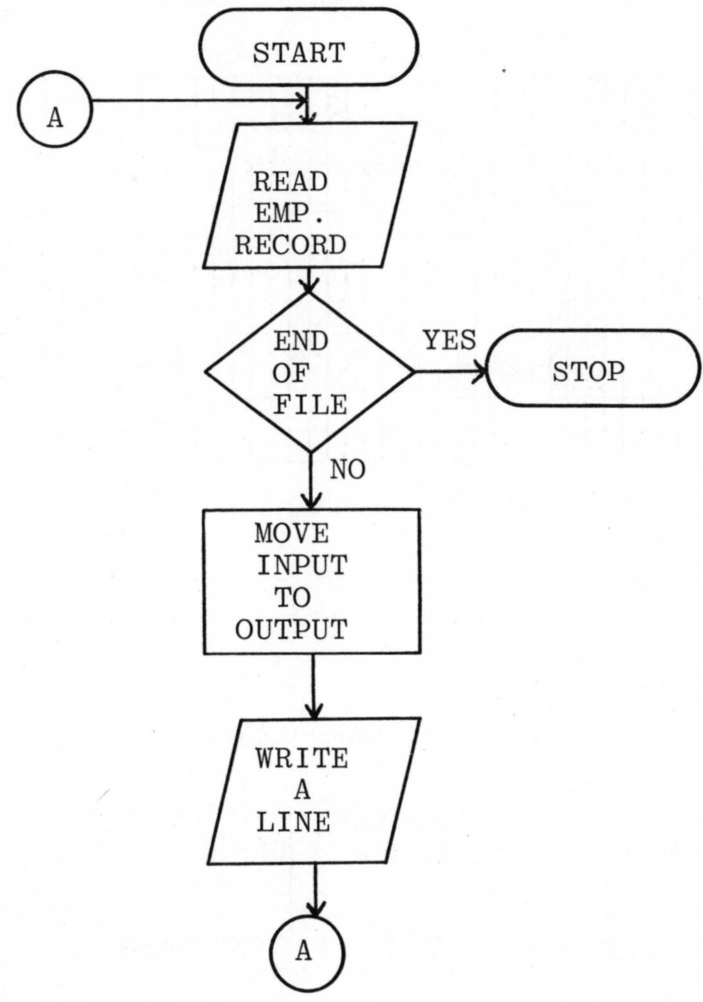

Figure 3-1

Conditional branching was also used in Chapter 2 (Figure 2-22) When we either printed the contents of the card if it had a B in Column 1 or bypassed it if any character other than a B appeared in Column 1. For our purpose let's expand the problem at the start of this chapter to cover the computation of an employee's net pay in two different ways, that is for either hourly or monthly payroll types. Without getting bogged down in how either of these would be computed. In addition to computing the net pay we will also still be listing the other data about the employees that is found in each input record on the report. The logic needed to add this requirement is shown in Figure 3-3. The card format and printer layout are shown in Figure 3-2.

The logic for producing the headings on the report is not shown in the flowchart. They were included on the printer layout at this time only to allow you to identify the fields. The logic for producing headings will be presented in Chapter 5.

PRINTER LAYOUT

```
         1111111111222222222233333333334444444444555555555566666
1234567890123456789012345678901234567890123456789012345678901234
                                        TYPE
                EMPLOYEE     REG   OT   OF    PAY
EMPLOYEE NAME    NUMBER      HRS   HRS  PAY   RATE  DEDUCTIONS

X-----------X  XXX-XX-XXXX  XX.X  XX.X   X  XXXX.XX  XXXX.XX
X-----------X  XXX-XX-XXXX  XX.X  XX.X   X  XXXX.XX  XXXX.XX
X-----------X  XXX-XX-XXXX  XX.X  XX.X   X  XXXX.XX  XXXX.XX
```

CARD LAYOUT

EMPLOYEE NAME	EMPLOYEE NUMBER	REG HRS	OT HRS	TYPE OF PAY	RATE OF PAY	DEDUC- tions	
9 9 9 9 9 9 9 9 9 9 9 9 9	9 9 9 9 9 9 9 9 9	9 9 | 9	9 9 | 9	9	9 9 9 9 | 9 9	9 9 9 9 | 9 9	9 9 9
1 2 3 4 5 6 7 8 9 10 11 12 13	14 15 16 17 18 19 20 21 22	23 24 | 25	26 27 | 28	29	30 31 32 33 | 34 35	36 37 38 39 | 40 41	42 43 44

Figure 3-2

Just after we move the majority of data to the output area to print it we make a decision as to whether the employee is an hourly or monthly person. Based on their type of pay we compute either a monthly or an hourly salary and move it to the output area for printing. It should be pointed out that all input fields and items originating from processing in the program such as gross pay must be moved to the output area prior to writing the output record. Which type of pay is computed is based on a conditional branch to the appropriate logic. This same type of process (conditional branching) could be carried to decisions with three or more possible paths in the logic being followed based on the result of some comparison or series of comparisons being made.

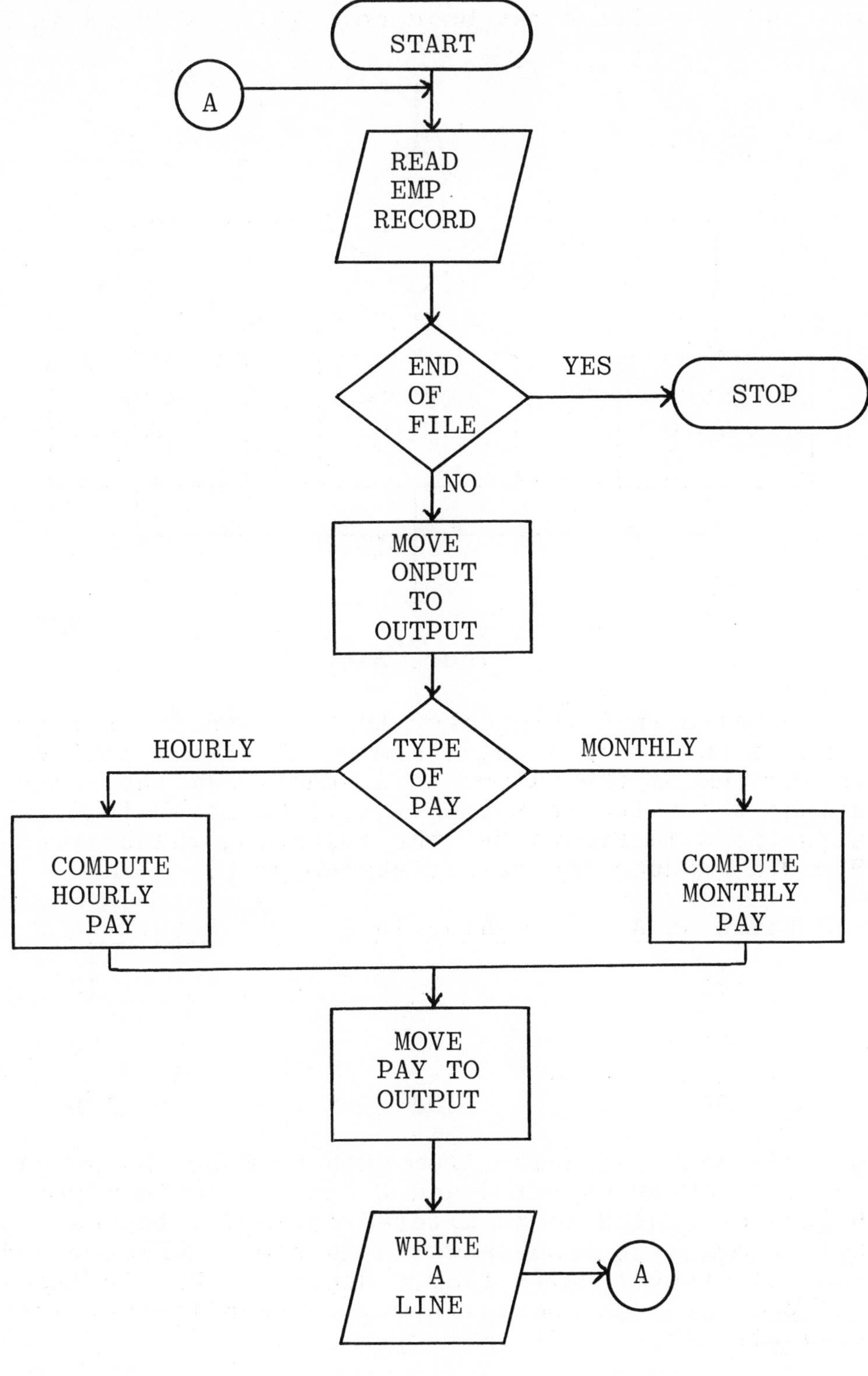

Figure 3-3

THREE WAY BRANCHING

One of the most common types of three-way decisions is to check the contents of two items against each other. Depending on which item is high in value or whether they are equal in value various activities may be done. This is shown in Figure 3-4.

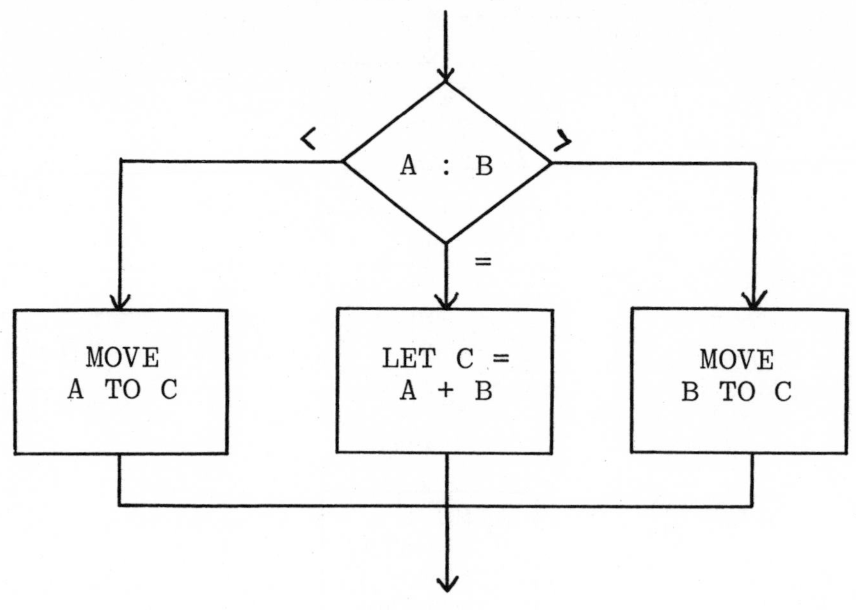

Figure 3-4

If the value in A is greater than the value in B then B will be moved to C. If A and B are equal then C will be set equal to the sum of the values in A and B. If the value in A is less than the value in B then A will be moved to C. Given the instructions in Figure 3-4 the following values present in A and B would produce the values shown for C.

	Value in A	Value in B	Resulting C Value
1.	24	19	19
2.	36	82	36
3.	54	54	108

Not only can a separate item such as C be changed as a result of the comparison of A and B but the logic might require the contents of A or B to be altered following the comparison. It is not so much the process which is used in Figure 3-4 as it is the use of several exits from a decision that is important. Each exit path from the decision will have different activities associated with it.

This same process could be extended to something such as checking a particular code for its value and performing various activities depending on the value of the code as shown in Figure 3-5.

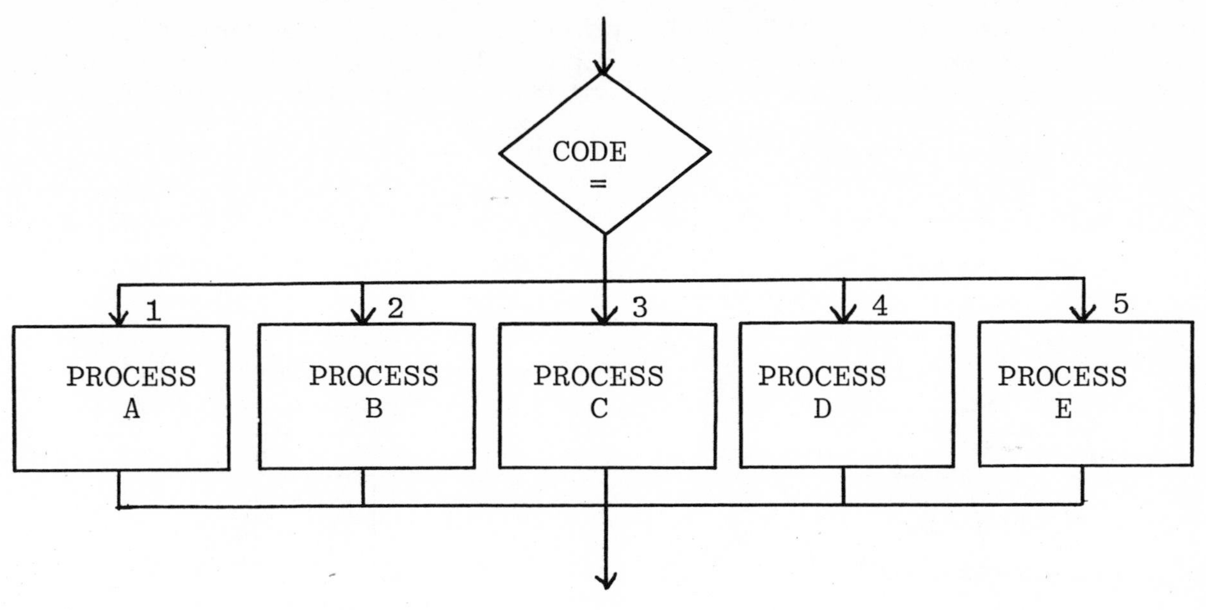

Figure 3-5

LOOPING

In all of the flowcharts involving multiple cards or records being read so far we have always branched back to the beginning of the program to read the next card or record after printing the data. This process of reusing the same set of logic for each record to be processed is an example of looping. Looping is executing any series of instructions repeatedly. Loops however do not have to include the whole flowchart, they may cover only a small part of the overall flowchart. It is also possible for a flowchart to have multiple loops in it and for one loop to be inside of a larger loop. When a loop is inside of a larger loop the one on the inside is said to be nested. Let's start with a relatively simple looping operation. Presume that we have a card file where each card has ten fields in it that contain numeric data. What we are going to do is read each card, add the amounts in each of the ten fields together and print the total.

Since we are going to be producing a total of the fields we are going to need some place to accumulate the total. For lack of a better name let's accumulate our total in an area of storage that we will call TOTAL. In order to control how many times we add the next field to TOTAL we will also need a counter. Let's name our counter COUNT. The logic needed to accomplish the totaling of the ten fields is shown in Figure 3-6.

Let's follow one card through this process to see how it operates. After the card is read and determined to be a data card the CALCS routine is then performed. It is the CALCS routine that will actually produce the total and contains the loop for adding the 10 fields. The first step in CALCS is to zero out the area called COUNT. We need to initialize the value of COUNT since we are going to use the value in COUNT to tell us when we have added the contents of all ten fields to TOTAL.

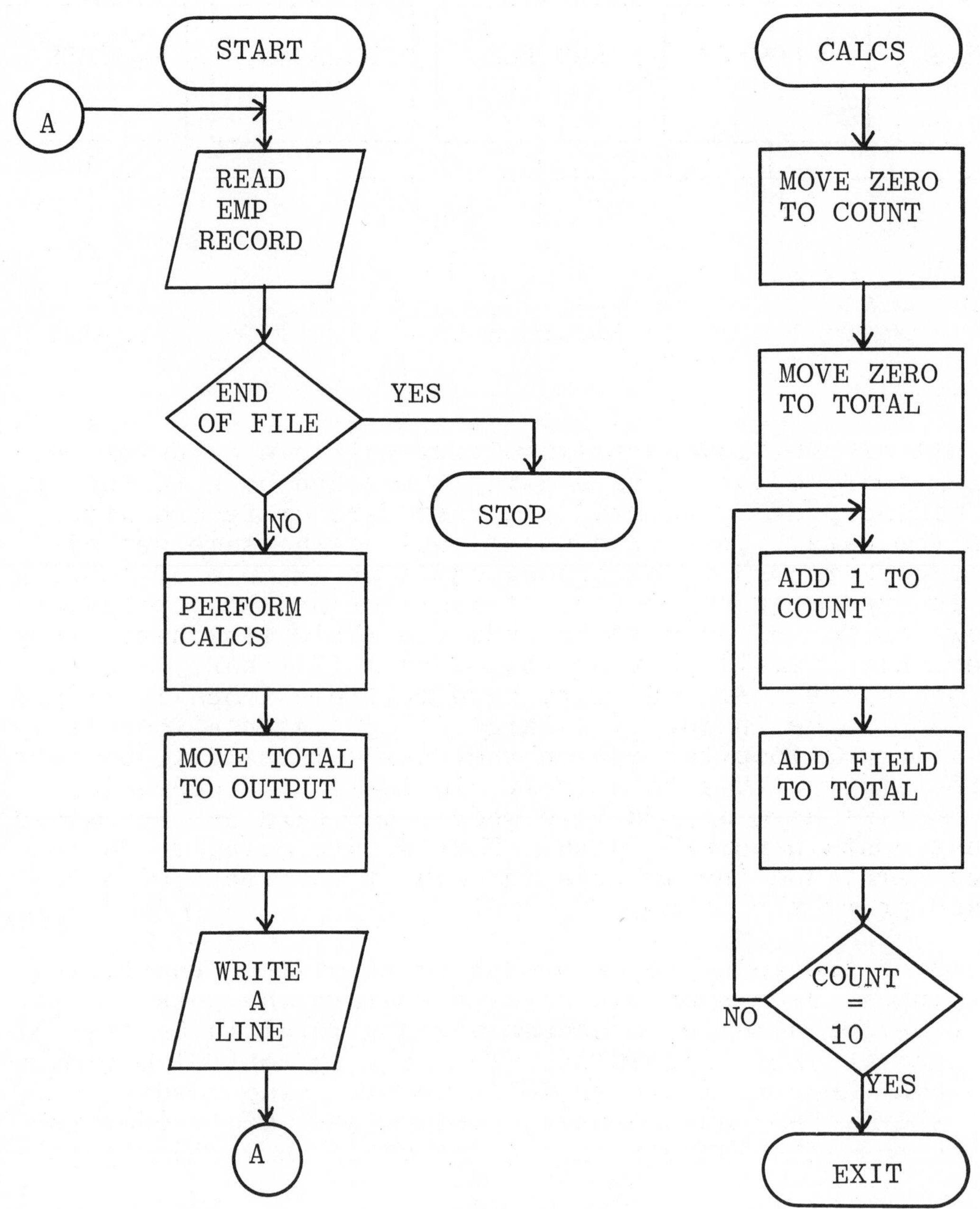

Figure 3-6

The next step is to zero out the TOTAL area. This is necessary if our total is to be only for the fields in the card we just read. If TOTAL were not initially set to zero our total would be erroneous. We would be adding to whatever was left over in that area of storage. Notice that both of these operations (zeroing out COUNT and TOTAL) are done at the time that the subroutine is performed so that each card that is processed will start at the same point.

The next step in CALCS is to increment COUNT by 1. We are adding 1 to indicate that 1 more field is being processed. This process will take place as each of the 10 fields are processed (added to TOTAL). The value in COUNT can be used to point to the field to be added to TOTAL. After incrementing COUNT the next field's value is added to TOTAL. This topic is further explained in Chapter 11.

At this point we check to see if the value in COUNT is equal to 10. If it is then the contents of all 10 fields have been added and we exit the subroutine. If the value in COUNT is not yet equal to 10 then we return to the step that increments COUNT.

Once the exit path in CALCS is taken we return to the next step in the logic of the program. This is immediately after the perform that invoked the CALCS routine. At this point we move and print the total and return to read the next card.

The symbols containing ADD 1 TO COUNT, ADD FIELD TO TOTAL and COUNT = 10 comprise the loop. These are executed over and over again while the value in COUNT progresses from 1 to 10.

LOOPING STEPS

There are some inherent steps that are present in any loop. The steps, except for the first step, may be in just about any order necessary to produce the desired effect. The major difference is where the modification and testing are done. Depending on where these two steps appear in the loop the loops are referred to as top driven or bottom driven loops. Depending on the language being used to implement the flowchart the processes of initialization, modification and testing may require two or more actual programming instructions to accomplish the necessary actions.

1. Initialization - the step in which items are given a beginning value. These items will be used to determine when the loop should be terminated. This may involve moving a value such as 1 to an area. In the case of the loop used to add the contents of 10 fields on a card, this step is when zero was moved to COUNT and TOTAL.

2. Processing - the step or steps in which the actual processing present within the loop is performed.

3. Modification - the step in which some sort of alteration is done to an item which was initialized in Step 1. This might be adding 1 to a counter or reading the next available record.

4. Testing - the step in which the value of an item is tested (such as whether the record is a data card or whether the value in a counter has exceeded a given value) to determine whether the loop should be continued or terminated.

Our sample loop added the values in the fields on a card and printed the result. The initialization step in this sample is moving zero to COUNT and TOTAL. The processing step is the addition of the contents of the field to TOTAL. Modification takes place when 1 is added to COUNT. Testing is when we check the value in COUNT to see if it is greater than 10.

NESTED LOOPS

In order to discuss nested loops let's use the flowchart in Figure 3-7.

Both ROUTINE A and ROUTINE B contain loops. In this case ROUTINE B is a nested loop in that it is executed within ROUTINE A. Let's follow this process through the processing of a single record.

After a card has been read and verified that it is a data card ROUTINE A is performed. ROUTINE A will continue to be performed until the value in COUNT1 is greater than 3 or a total of 4 times. The extra execution of the routine comes from the fact that PROCESS A is executed for the values 0, 1, 2 and 3 in COUNT1. Each time ROUTINE A is performed ROUTINE B is invoked as a part of executing ROUTINE A. Each time that ROUTINE B is invoked it will be executed a total of 6 times. Since ROUTINE B is executed 6 times for each execution of ROUTINE A then ROUTINE B will be executed a total of 24 times during the processing of each card. PROCESS A and PROCESS B could contain any type of processing and have no effect on how the loops are handled as long as neither routine (PROCESS A or PROCESS B) does anything to the contents of COUNT1 and COUNT2.

In a similar manner, ROUTINE A is a nested loop. It is performed or invoked for each card that is read until an end of file condition occurs.

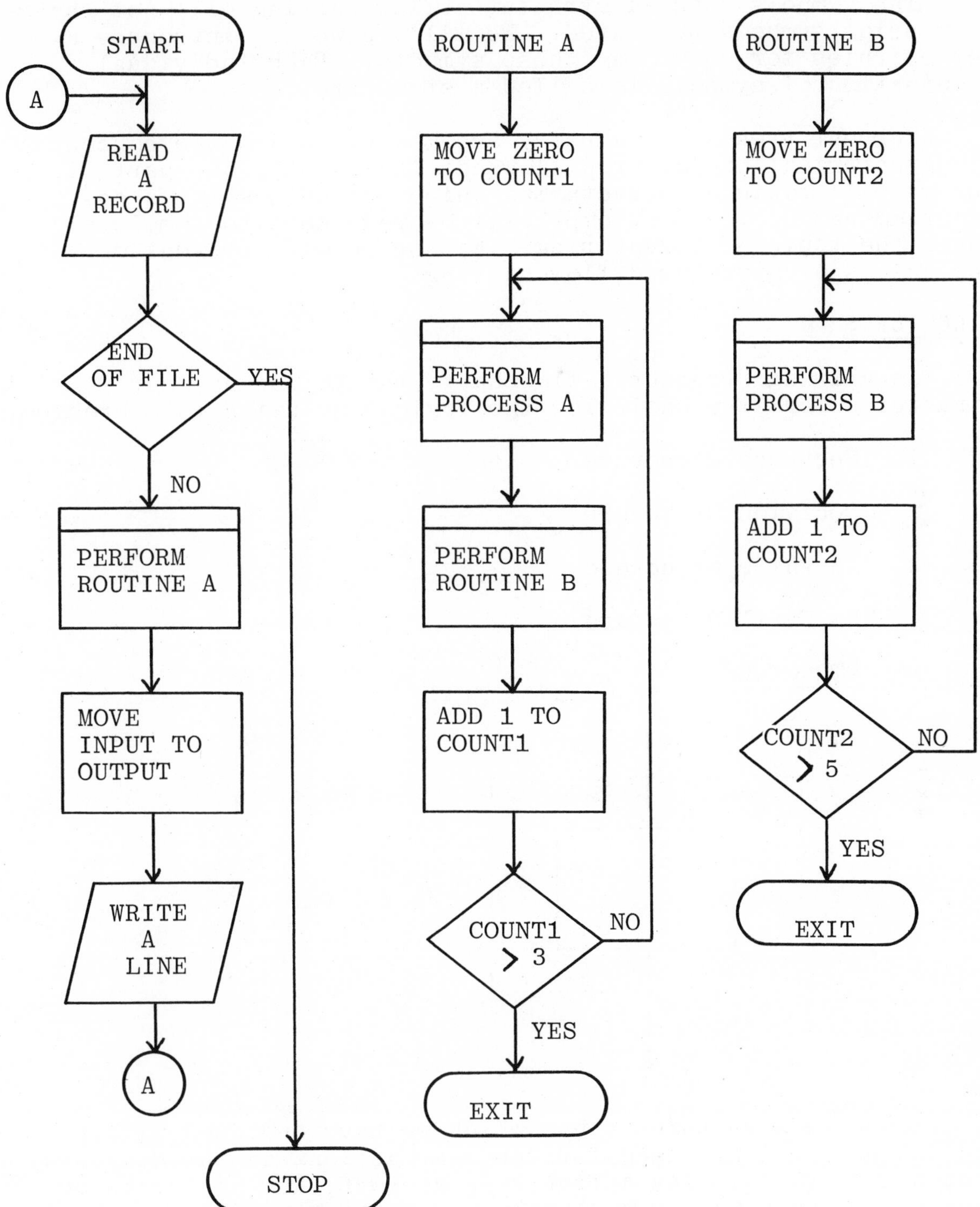
START
A
READ
A
RECORD
END
OF FILE
YES
NO
PERFORM
ROUTINE A
MOVE
INPUT TO
OUTPUT
WRITE
A
LINE
A
STOP
ROUTINE A
MOVE ZERO
TO COUNT1
PERFORM
PROCESS A
PERFORM
ROUTINE B
ADD 1 TO
COUNT1
COUNT1
> 3
NO
YES
EXIT
ROUTINE B
MOVE ZERO
TO COUNT2
PERFORM
PROCESS B
ADD 1 TO
COUNT2
COUNT2
> 5
NO
YES
EXIT

Figure 3-7

STRUCTURED FLOWCHARTING

The symbols used in structured flowcharting will not change from prior symbols presented. We will, however, introduce a set of rules for combining these symbols. Each individual combination of symbols is called a structure.

Current trends in industry are moving toward the concept of structuring. Structured flowcharting is only one part of the overall topic of structuring which includes systems design, programming, etc. No attempt will be made here to completely cover the topic of structuring. Rather we will present only the basics of structured flowcharting.

STRUCTURES

In drawing structured flowcharts the following four structures form the basis for the logical solution to a problem.

1. Sequence Structure

2. Decision Structure

3. Do While Structure

4. Do Until Structure

SEQUENCE STRUCTURE

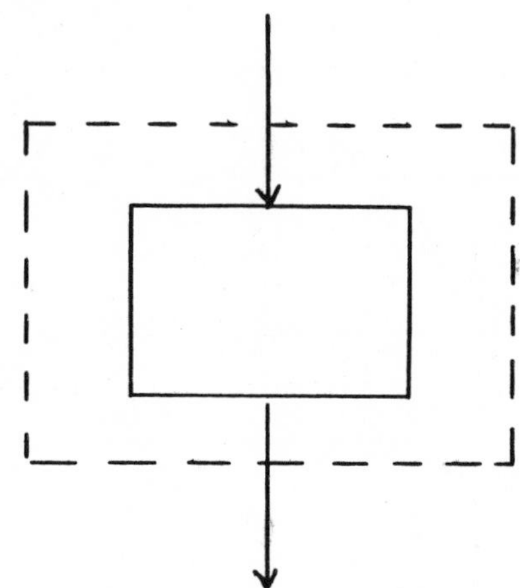

Sequence structures (that which we have enclosed within the dotted line) are used for the same actions as the standard processing symbol. Any action such as MOVE, ADD, etc. can be represented by a sequence structure. It is also possible to have multiple activities within a sequence structure. The dotted line in Figure 3-8 shows the structure which contains multiple processing activities. Note that there is only one entrance into and one exit from the structure. This concept will be true for all of the structures.

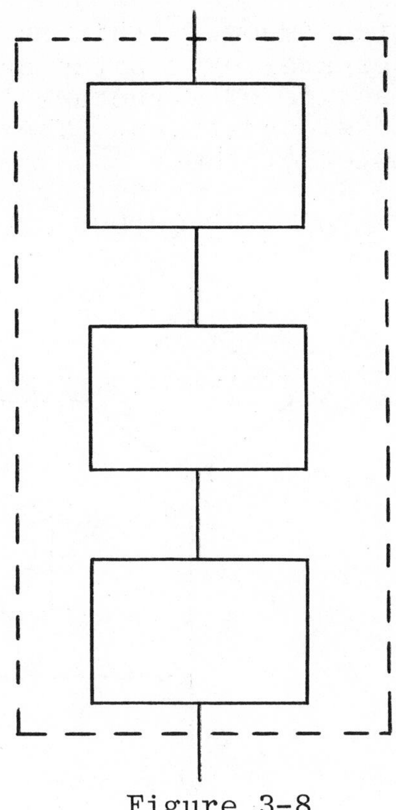

Figure 3-8

DECISION STRUCTURE

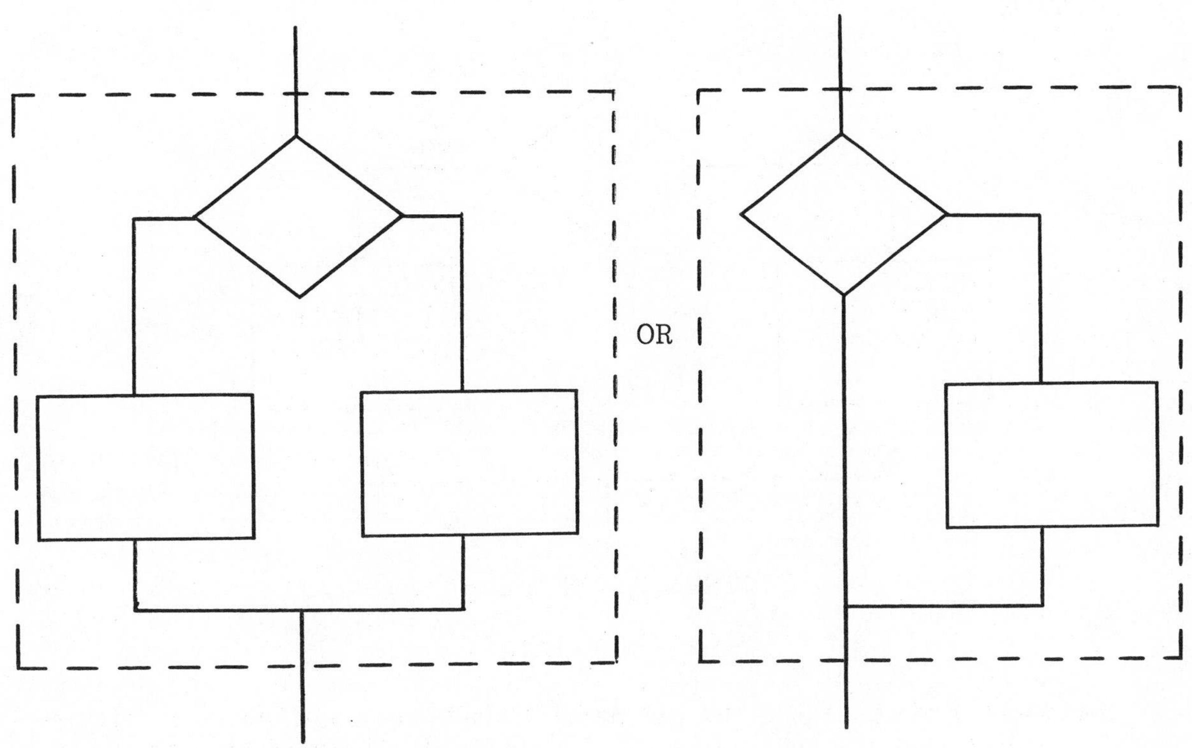

Decision structures (shown within the dotted lines) are used to represent alternate logic paths based on the result of some comparison. This type of structure is used to depict If/Then or If/Then, Else conditions. The following programming instructions are examples of these two forms of statements.

IF A = B MOVE STARTDATE TO OUTPUT AREA.

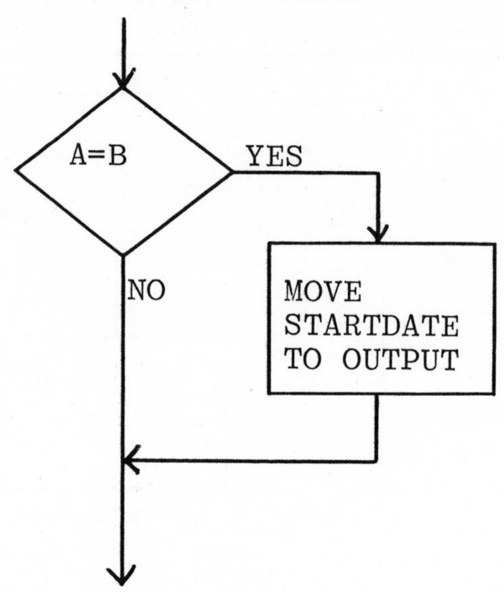

IF/THEN example

Figure 3-9

IF A = B MOVE STARTDATE TO OUTPUT ELSE MOVE ENDDATE TO OUTPUT.

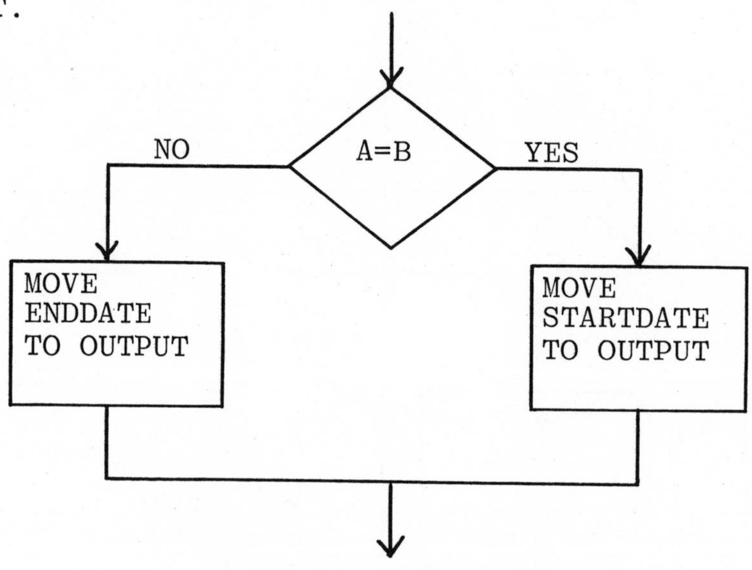

IF/THEN, ELSE example

Figure 3-10

Several points need to be made relative to decision structures. First, it is possible to have 2, 3, 4 or many paths in a structure. This can be seen in Figure 3-11.

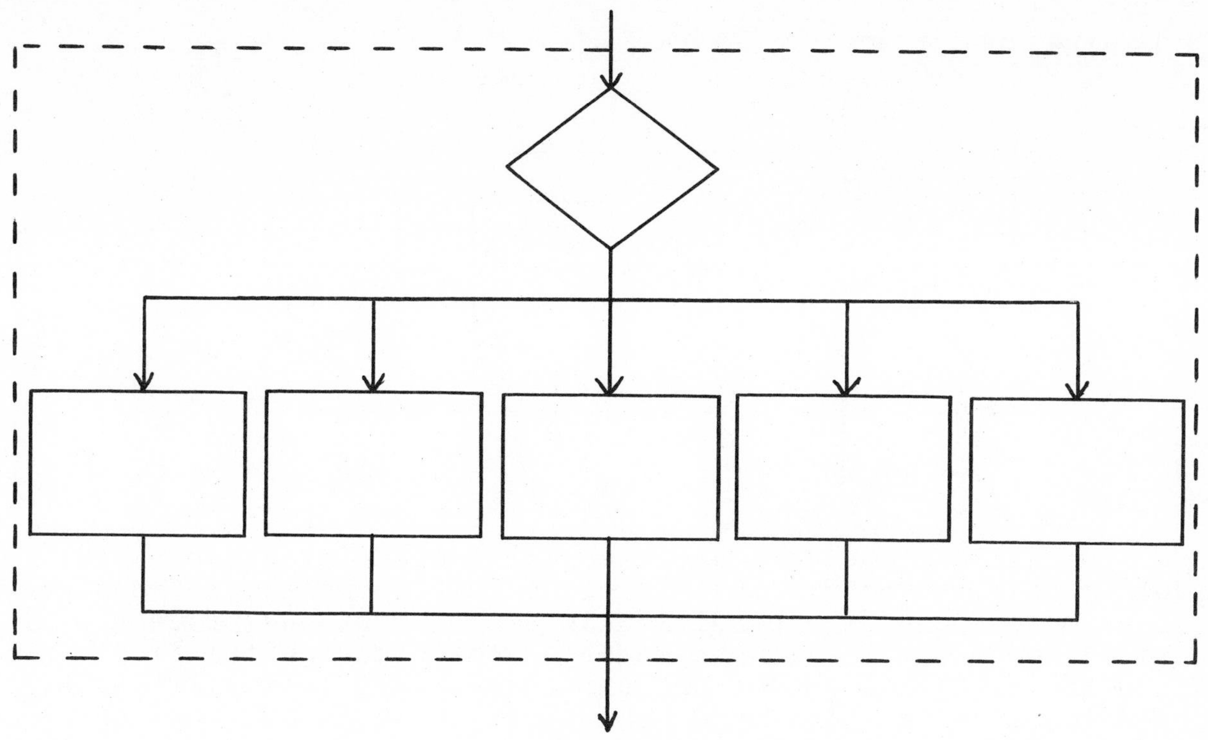

Figure 3-11

Second, regardless of the number of alternate paths possible, there is only one entrance into and one exit from the structure. Third, the process boxes within the decision may themselves contain a decision structure. This last point is illustrated in Figure 3-12.

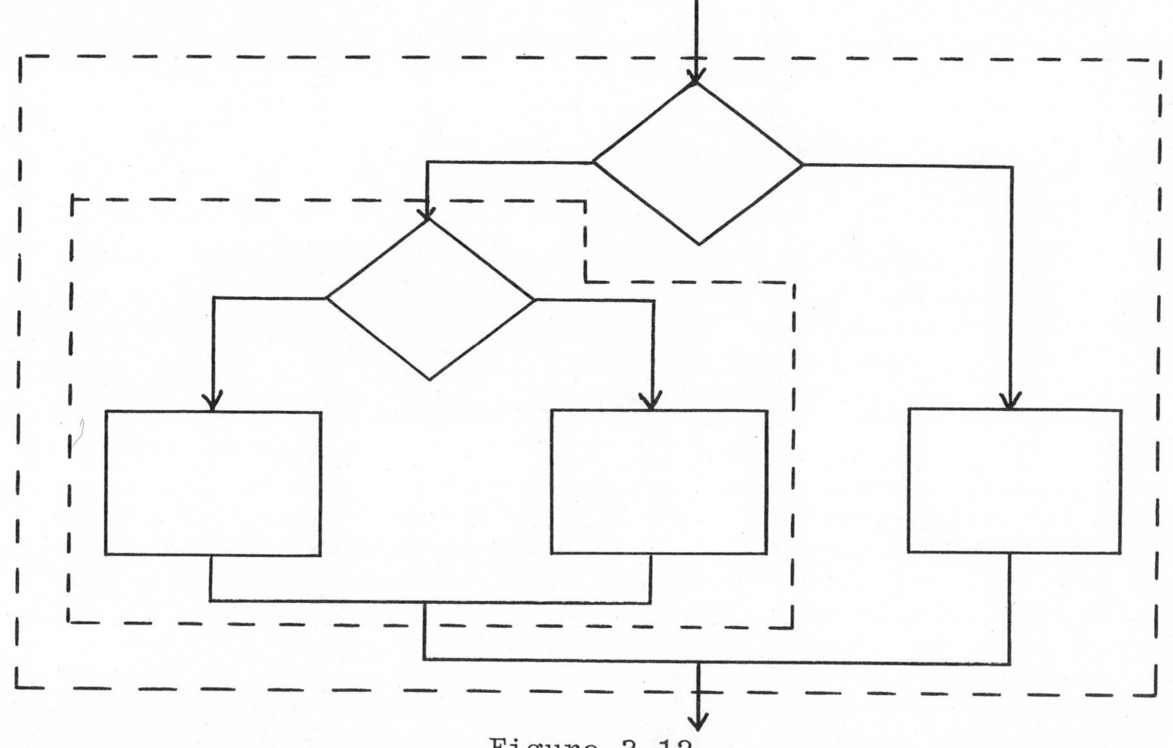

Figure 3-12

DO WHILE STRUCTURE

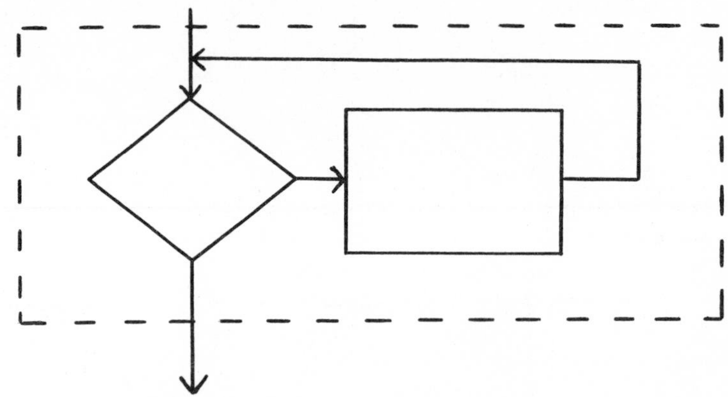

Do While structures are used for looping processes. As long as a given condition is present some process will continue to be done. Once the condition is not present the process will no longer be done. If upon entering the decision the first time the condition is not present then the process will not be executed at all. Note once again that there is only one entrance into and one exit from the structure.

DO UNTIL STRUCTURE

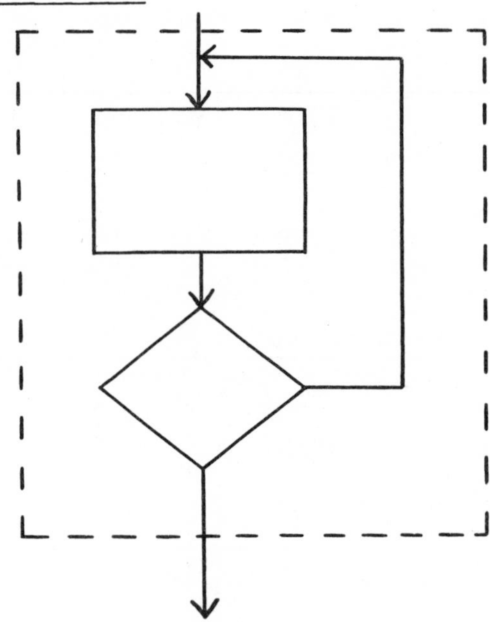

Do Until structures are also used for looping processes. They differ from Do While structures in that the process will be performed at least once regardless of whether or not the condition is present. After the first time through the process the presence or absence of the condition being tested determines whether the process will be done again or whether we will exit the structure. As with previous structures the Do Until structure has only one entrance into and one exit from the structure.

When using structures it is permissible to use the terminal symbol. Also, the process structure can be shown as a subroutine symbol (PERFORM CALCS in Figure 3-6). Subroutines and their symbols will be presented in detail in Chapter 5. Additionally, the read/write symbol is permissible as a process structure.

In structured flowcharting the use of connector symbols of any type is diminished if not completely eliminated. In this regard it becomes more efficient to have two reads in a program. The first read is done at the beginning of the program. The second read is done at the end of the processing steps for a data record. Let's take another look at Figure 3-6, this time in a structured form (Figure 3-13).

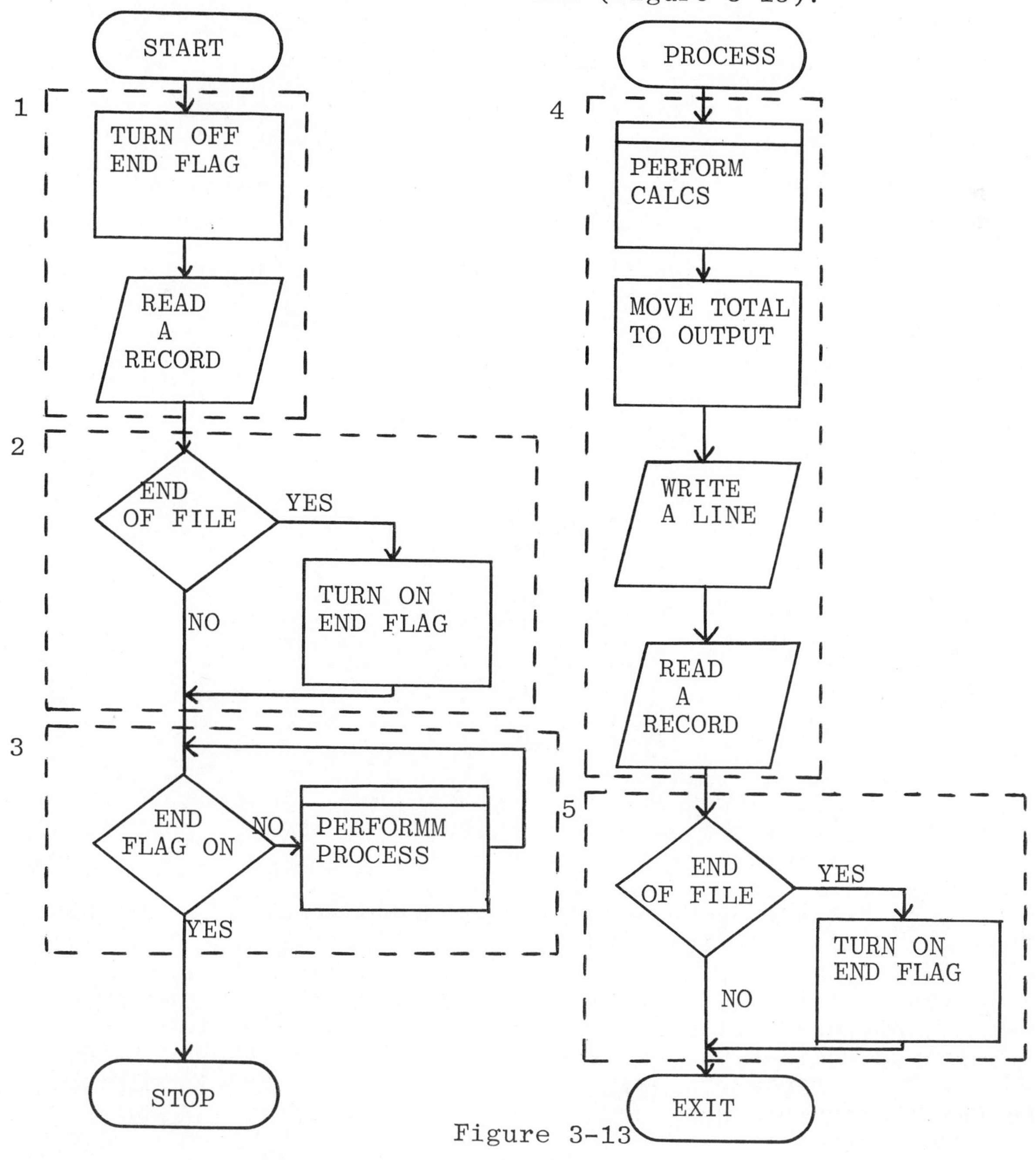

Figure 3-13

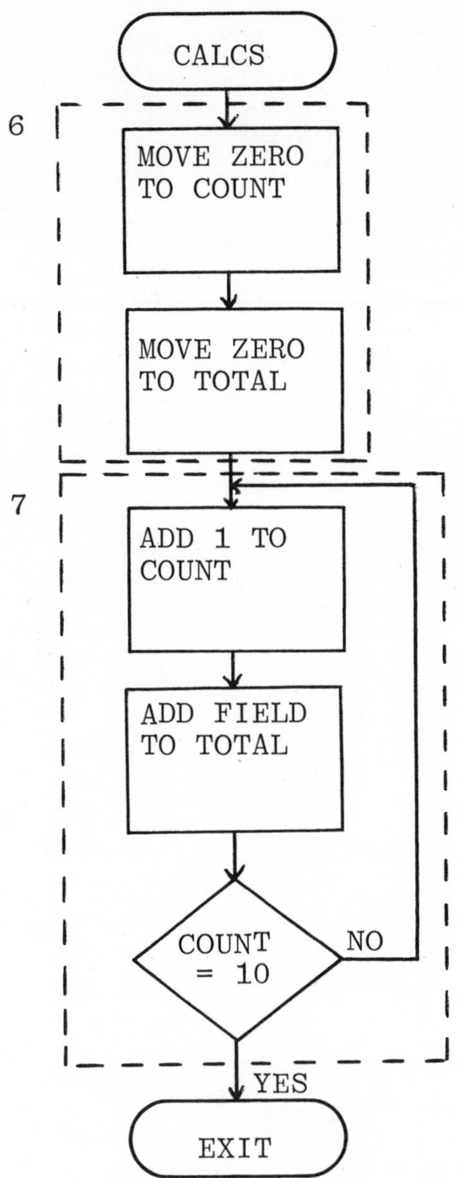

Figure 3-13 (cont.)

The following is a discussion of Figure 3-13 structure by structure. The dotted lines are present only to aid you in identifying the structures. The structures have been numbered for reference in the discussion.

Structure 1 - This is a sequence structure which turns of END FLAG and reads the first record on the file.

Structure 2 - This is a decision structure which checks to see if the initial reading process actually found a data record. If for some reason no data records were present in the file END FLAG is turned on to indicate that the end of file has been reached.

Structure 3 - This is a Do While structure which will continue to do the PROCESS routine until END FLAG has been turned on. Presuming we actually read a data record on our initial read then we should at least perform the PROCESS routine one time.

Structure 4 - This is a sequence structure that does four processing steps within the structure. That is it performs CALCS, moves a total to the output, prints the total and reads the next record.

Structure 5 - This is a decision structure which tests to see if an end of file condition occurred in trying to read a data record. If an end of file condition occurs, END FLAG is turned on. When we exit structure 5 and the PROCESS routine we return to the test for END FLAG. If an end of file was found in the last time through PROCESS, END FLAG is on and we end the program. If no end of file was found on the last time through PROCESS, END FLAG is still off so we once again perform PROCESS.

Structure 6 - This is a sequence structure that moves zeros to two counters called COUNT and TOTAL.

Structure 7 - This is a Do Until structure that does the processes of adding 1 to COUNT and adding the contents of a field to TOTAL until COUNT = 10. Once COUNT = 10, we exit both structure 7 and the CALCS routine.

Our approach throughout this book will make use of structures. There are three major routines which are common to all of our programs. We can arrange these routines into a generalized flowchart which will act as the framework for all of our flowcharts (see Figure 3-14). The individual steps for these three routines will vary with the problem we are flowcharting. The following paragraphs outline some of the common actions taken that might be in the three routines.

HSK contains items that are done only once at the beginning of the program. One of these items is the initial read to read the first record on the file. Once completed the HSK routine is not executed again during the duration of the program. In Figure 3-13 this would include structures 1 and 2.

The PROCESS routine contains actions being done by the program. This includes such items as calculations, writing output, moving data from input areas to output areas, etc. The last item in PROCESS is to read the next data record. If an end of file condition is encountered END FLAG is turned on. The name of this routine may be changed to fit the situation.

EOJ is a routine whose steps we have not yet presented. It contains processing steps that are to be done after an end of file condition has occurred. These steps will be identified in succeeding chapters.

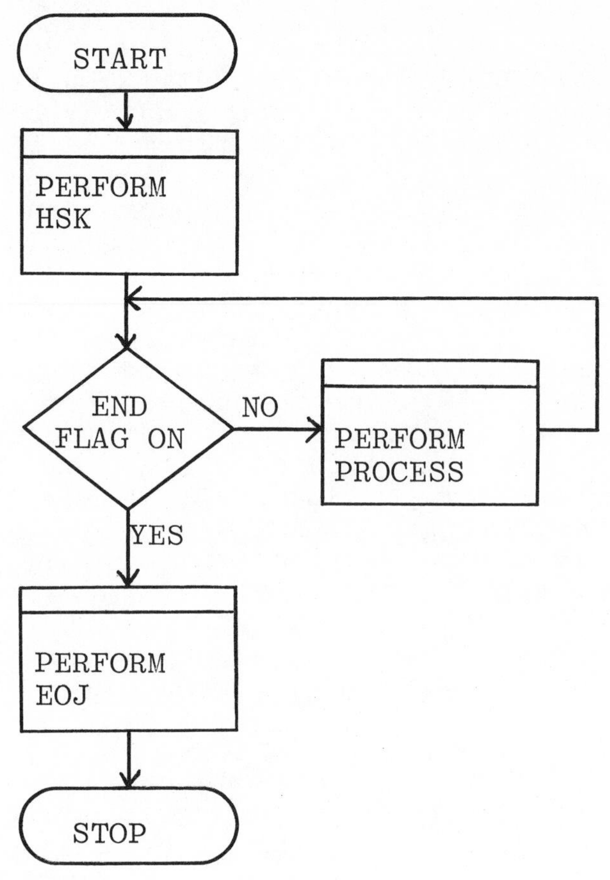

Figure 3-14

As with any topic, structured programming or structured flowcharting has its good and bad points. One of its attributes is consistency in flowcharting methods among people in a department. It also provides for easily converting flowcharts into an actual programming language. Flowcharts and programs which are structured are also a great deal easier to maintain or change in the future. The one drawback of structured programs is their tendency to take longer to execute. Depending on the environment in which they are being run (both computer and support programs) structured programs can take up to three or more times as long to run. As with many items it becomes a tradeoff of good vs. bad when deciding whether or not to use structuring or how deeply to become involved. In general it seems better to structure than not to structure a program. Structuring is the direction in which the business community is moving today.

In Chapter 4 you will be introduced to various types of documentation and why they are important to the overall process of designing the solution to a problem.

REVIEW QUESTIONS

Matching

A. Unconditional branch

B. Loop

C. Connectors or flowlines

D. Modification

E. Initialization

F. Conditional branch

G. Nested loop

H. Normal instruction sequence

I. Testing

__________ 1. An alteration in the flow of the logic that takes place regardless of anything being or not being true.

__________ 2. The repetition of a series of instruction or symbols in a flowchart over and over again.

__________ 3. The step in the looping process that must always be first.

__________ 4. A loop which is performed inside of another loop.

__________ 5. An alteration in the flow of the logic based on some situation being true or not true.

__________ 6. In the order that they are written.

__________ 7. The step in the looping process responsible for the alteration of some component which will be used to determine whether or not the loop should be continued.

__________ 8. Can be used to show where either type of branch will proceed to next.

__________ 9. The step in the looping process which determines whether the loop should be terminated or continued.

True/False

T F 1. Loops may not be performed more than 500 times in a program or a flowchart.

T F 2. Altering the sequence in which the instructions will be executed is called sequencing.

T F 3. The step(s) in which the processing in a loop takes place is referred to as modification.

T F 4. Conditional branching requires that at least three exit paths exist coming out of any decision symbol on a flowchart.

T F 5. A loop could be avoided by merely rewriting the desired instructions as many times as you wanted them performed.

T F 6. Do While structures perform the process before testing the condition.

T F 7. Connectors are used commonly and plentifully in structuring.

T F 8. Decisions are limited to 2-way choices in structuring.

Exercises

1. Draw a flowchart segment to depict both unconditional and conditional branching to a routine called PROCESS. The conditional version should go to the routine only if the end of file has been reached and there were over 100 records read. If the conditions are not true the program should go to a routine called ERRS.

2. Draw a flowchart segment that shows the logic in a program performing RTN-A, RTN-B, RTN-C, RTN-D or RTN-E depending on whether the contents of a field called CODE is 1, 2, 3, 4, or 5 respectively. If the value in code is none of these, the program should perform ERR-RTN.

3. Draw a flowchart to show the reading of twenty cards and stop. The contents of the cards should be printed as they are read. Use a loop to control the reading process.

4. The same as number 3 with the following additions. Each card now contains 5 fields with numeric data in them. As each card is read these fields are to be summed and the sum is to be printed along with the contents of the card. Nested loops should be used to solve the problem.

Discussion Questions

1. Differentiate between conditional and unconditional branching and give examples of where each of them might be used.

2. Describe what branching is and why it is necessary in the construction of flowcharts.

3. Describe looping and indicate why it is an important part of the flowcharting process.

4. Identify the steps in the looping process and what their function is within this process.

5. Describe the effects of having the initialization step as something other than the first step in a loop.

6. Describe nested looping and how it works.

7. Describe each of the various structures.

8. Depict and describe the general mainline logic of a program using structured concepts.

CHAPTER 4

Documentation

OBJECTIVES

As a result of studying this chapter the student should be able to perform the following activities.

1. Describe the need for documentation.
2. Describe the need for and create a card layout.
3. Describe the need for and create a tape/disk layout.
4. Describe the need for and create a record description.
5. Describe the need for and design a print chart.
6. Describe the need for and be able to prepare a program narrative.
7. Describe the need for and be able to prepare a run sheet.
8. Assemble a documentation package upon completion of a programming project.

INTRODUCTION

Flowcharting, while essential to the planning of a program, is only one part of the documentation usually required by a company. Each company has its own standards for documentation and the forms used vary somewhat from company to company. No matter what the format of the documentation, the underlying concept is the desire to communicate information about a program or an entire system as completely and efficiently as possible.

Documentation for every program and system is usually kept in a centralized location within the data processing department. This makes it easily accessible to all members of the department. A set of standards for documentation is usually supplied to each programmer so that he can prepare his documentation package in accordance with the company's standards.

Programmers and systems analysts come and go within an organization but the projects they work on remain as a part of the data processing system of the company. These systems and programs require revision as changes are made within the company. If the program or system has not been documented, then changes will require an excessive amount of time. This extra time is required to track down all of the details of the project.

DOCUMENTATION COMPONENTS

This chapter will provide examples of commonly used types of documentation. We will also point out the basics of when each piece of documentation is created and by whom. We will identify the users of the documentation and the reasons for their need of each item. Six of the more common documentation items are listed below.

1. Card layout
2. Tape/disk layout
3. Record description
4. Print chart
5. Program narrative
6. Run sheet

When a program has been completed (written and tested), a documentation package is prepared. Final versions of the items above are prepared, and the following items would be added to complete the documentation package.

1. A table of contents for the documentation package.

2. A flowchart.

3. A listing of the source program (a machine produced listing of the program as coded by the programmer). This is the final version of the source program after all errors have been corrected and the program has produced correct output.

4. Samples of any printed reports produced by the program and in particular, any special preprinted forms that may be used when producing output.

5. A systems flowchart may be included to show where this program fits into the system.

SYSTEMS FLOWCHART

The examples of documentation in this chapter will draw from a payroll system. We can use a systems flowchart to show the section of a payroll system we are going to document.

A systems flowchart depicts the flow of data through a system. Symbols are used which represent the media on which the data files are recorded (see Figure 4-1). For a description of the systems flowcharting symbols see Chapter 13.

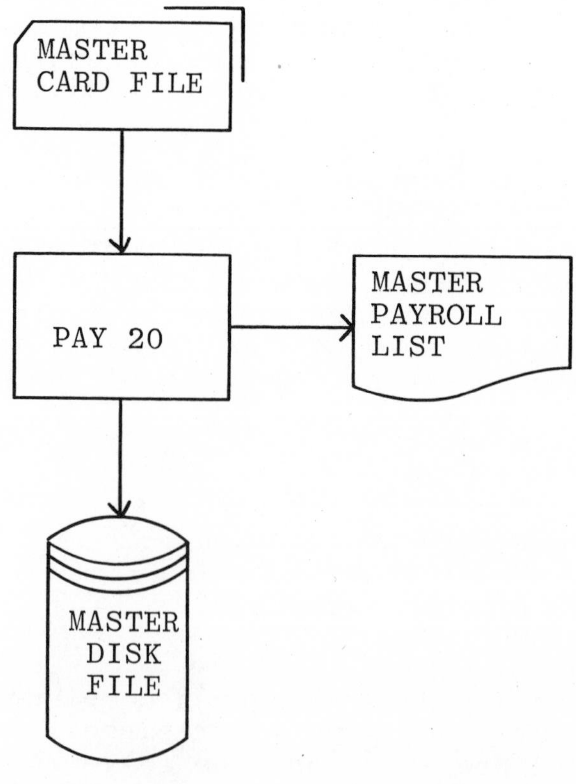

Figure 4-1

This portion of a systems flowchart indicates that a card file containing permanent information about each employee will be input to a program named PAY 20. The PAY 20 program creates as output a master disk file and a listing of the master file. Each of the output files is simply a copy of the data on the card file, but in a form more suitable for its future use within the system.

The transfer of the data from a card file to a disk file offers many advantages.

1. The data on the file can be accessed or retrieved either sequentially or randomly. Sequential retrieval means reading the records one after another in the order in which they exist. Every record must be passed over whether you wish to process it or not. Random retrieval is the ability to access any one record as easily as any other. This eliminates the need to read any records you do not wish to process.

2. Less physical space is required for the storage of the data.

3. Access to the data is faster.

4. The need for constant rehandling of the card file is eliminated.

The purpose of printing the master listing is to provide a visual check of the contents of the records loaded on the master disk file. Such a listing would become a reference document for the payroll department.

The planning and design for a systems flowchart are done by a systems analyst. It is his graphic way of showing the general plan of action for a particular project.

PROGRAM FLOWCHART

A program flowchart is first drawn by the programmer when he is assigned the portion of the system that includes the program. Many of the six items listed on the previous page are used in preparation of the program flowchart. The first program flowchart is generally a rough planning tool. Then, depending upon the size of the company and its procedures, he will either code from this rough flowchart or produce a more finished copy and have it reviewed by the project leader. The programmer will then code the program. When the coding is complete and the program has been tested, a finished flowchart should be drawn reflecting any changes that may have occurred between the planning stage and the operational program.

The program flowchart we will use as an example of documentation gives more detail of how the print and disk files are created. It is shown in Figure 4-2.

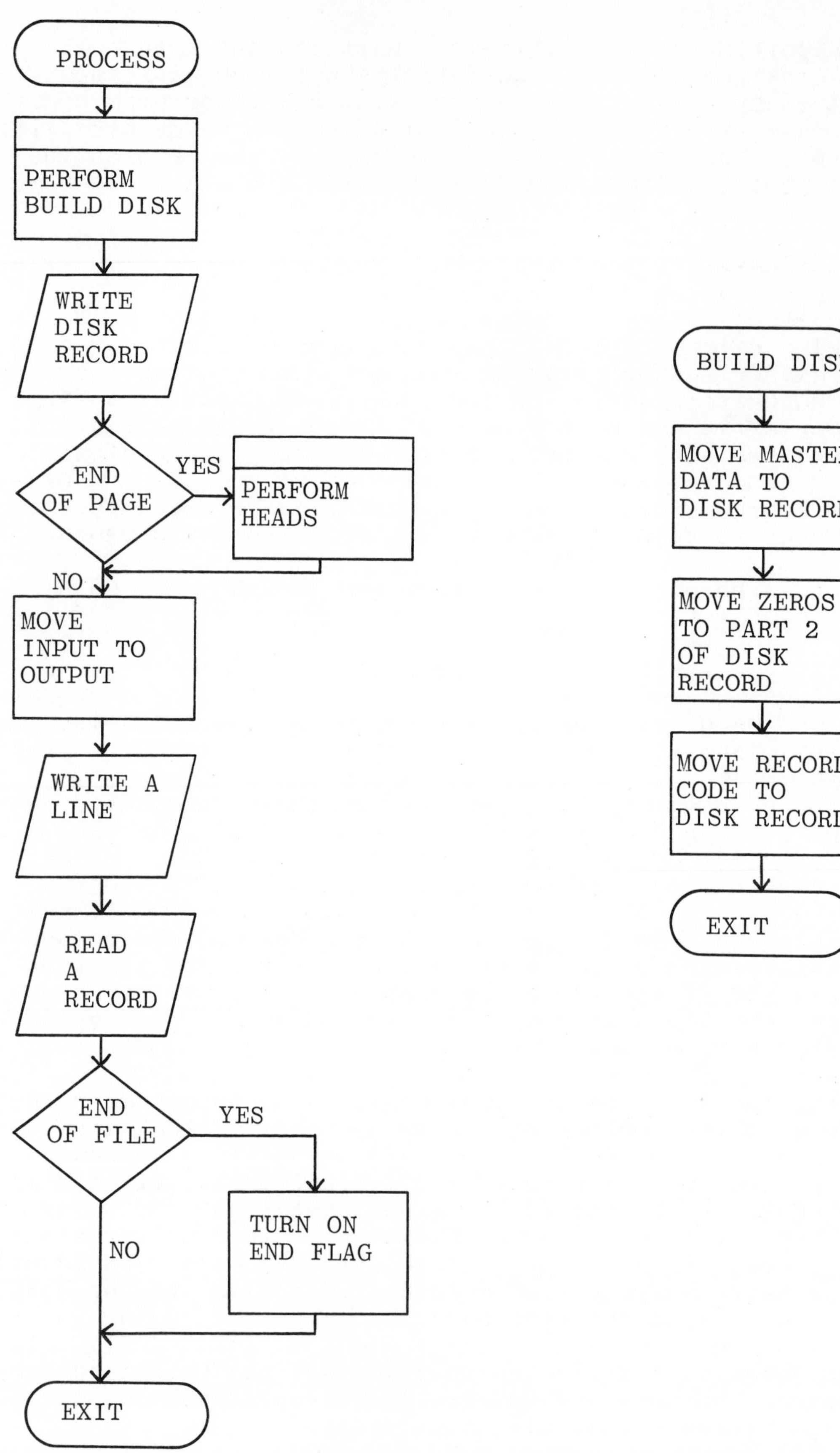
PROCESS
PERFORM
BUILD DISK
WRITE
DISK
RECORD
END
OF PAGE
YES
PERFORM
HEADS
NO
MOVE
INPUT TO
OUTPUT
WRITE A
LINE
READ
A
RECORD
END
OF FILE
YES
TURN ON
END FLAG
NO
EXIT
BUILD DISK
MOVE MASTER
DATA TO
DISK RECORD
MOVE ZEROS
TO PART 2
OF DISK
RECORD
MOVE RECORD
CODE TO
DISK RECORD
EXIT

Figure 4-2

In Figure 4-2 the disk record that is being created is made up of two parts. The first portion of each disk record will contain the data read in from the master record. The second portion of the disk record will contain areas necessary for future processing. These areas will eventually contain year-to-date figures for the payroll. Since no value for the year-to-date figures exists when the file is created, these fields are set to zero so that they will not contain any extraneous data.

After each card record is written to disk, a print record is written. Prior to printing each record, a test for end of page is made. If there is additional room on the page for more items to be printed, the logic proceeds directly to the building and printing of a line. If the page is full a routine is performed which ejects to the top of a new page and prints headings, then the line is built and printed. After the printing is accomplished, we read the next master record. The subroutine which writes the page headings will be further explained in Chapter 5.

THE CARD LAYOUT

Card layouts are developed as a part of the design for a system. Any time cards are to be used as the input or output medium for a program a layout is drawn of the card records. Programmers using the records can then have a visual reference of the record's contents. Consistency between programmers working on a system is essential and a card layout provides a portion of the information and standards for this purpose.

The design of the card entails keypunching and programming, considerations not covered in this book. Such information is found in many systems analysis and design books. The conventions for drawing a card layout, given the size and relative positions of the fields, will be sufficient for our purposes. The process usually begins with a list similar to the one in Figure 4-3.

Under FIELD we find the name we will use when referring to this item of data. COLUMNS gives us the size of each field and its relative position in the record. The notation in parenthesis indicates the placement of a decimal in the field. In the case of PAY-RATE, the field is six positions wide. Two of the six positions are to the right of the decimal point. No decimal point is actually punched into the card. We identify its position to the computer so that it can align the numbers properly when making calculations.

Each field on the list is then transferred to a card layout as shown in Figure 4-4. This figure represents one strip from a form called a multiple card layout.

FIELD	COLUMNS
CARD-CODE	1 - 2
SOC-SEC-NUM	3 - 11
DIVISION-NUM	12 - 12
DEPARTMENT	13 - 13
EMP-NAME	14 - 38
PAY-RATE	39 - 44 (6.2)
MARITAL	45 - 45
FED-DEPS	46 - 47
STATE-DEP	48 - 49
CREDIT-UNION	50 - 54 (5.2)
HOSP-INS	55 - 59 (5.2)
UNUSED	60 - 80

Figure 4-3

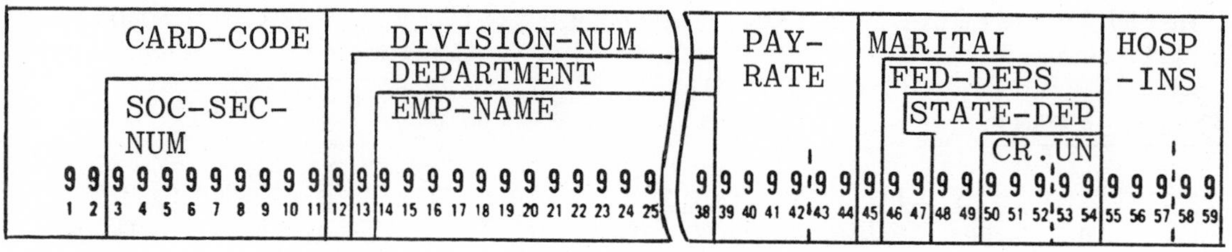

CARD-CODE
SOC-SEC-NUM
DIVISION-NUM
DEPARTMENT
EMP-NAME
PAY-RATE
MARITAL
FED-DEPS
STATE-DEP
CR. UN
HOSP -INS

Figure 4-4

Accuracy in transferring the information from the list to the card layout is important. This card layout will be used by the programmer to describe to the computer where the data can be found in the card record. The programmer will also use it to specify under what name the areas of the card will be stored in the computer. An example of how this information might be conveyed to the computer in the COBOL programming language would be as shown in Figure 4-5. Each 9 represents a card column to be occupied by numeric data. Each X represents a card column to be occupied by alphanumeric (either alphabetic or numeric) data. A V represents the position for an <u>assumed</u> decimal. The V does not occupy a card column and no decimal point is punched into the card. FILLER is a word used in COBOL to describe an unused area.

```
01  PAYROLL-CARD.

    02  CARD-CODE             PICTURE 99.
    02  SOC-SEC-NUM           PICUTRE 9(9).
    02  DIVISION-NUM          PICTURE 9.
    02  DEPARTMENT            PICTURE 9.
    02  EMP-NAME              PICTURE X(25).
    02  PAY-RATE              PICTURE 9(4)V99.
    02  MARITAL               PICTURE 9.
    02  FED-DEPS              PICTURE 99.
```

```
02  STATE-DEP             PICTURE 99.
02  CREDIT-UNION          PICTURE 9(3)V99.
02  HOSP-INS              PICTURE 9(3)V99.
02  FILLER                PICTURE X(21).
```

Figure 4-5

If the card layout is made incorrectly or the storage description made from it is inaccurate, the consequences are incorrect information on the output or a program interrupt. A program interrupt is when the computer stops processing the program and prints a message indicating a problem of some type. One reason this could happen is the computer does not find the appropriate numeric values in storage areas where it attempts arithmetic operations.

For example, if EMP-NAME had been mistakenly set at PICTURE X(24) then PAY-RATE would be assumed by the computer to be stored in card columns 38 through 43 instead of columns 39 through 44. The first position of PAY-RATE would now be a blank or contain the last letter from someone's name. When any attempt was made to use PAY-RATE in a calculation it could cause a program interrupt. Every field from EMP-NAME to the end of the card would also be referenced incorrectly.

For the same reason, if there are any unused areas on the card they should be identified and space allocated so that they may be described to the computer as physically occupying space on the card. Otherwise, the alignment of each succeeding field will be off just as if we had described the length of the field incorrectly. In terms of the card layout itself, if the area is unused it should be marked as blanks or spaces to make it clear that this area has not been overlooked.

Notice that money fields such as PAY-RATE (Figure 4-3) have a figure in parenthesis to the right of the column designation. The (6.2) on PAY-RATE indicates that the entire field is 6 positions wide and the portion to the right of the decimal place is two positions wide. In order to do arithmetic properly in high level languages such as FORTRAN and COBOL, it is necessary for the computer to be able to align numeric fields on their decimal position. The position of the decimal point may be expressed as in (6.2) or if no notation is present the decimal is implied to be to the right of the field.

Actual decimal points are seldom punched into cards, a savings of punching time and storage space. Their assumed position is shown on the card layout and conveyed to the computer when storage of the card is described to the computer as in the COBOL example. In the COBOL example (Figure 4-5) the V indicates the assumed position of the decimal point. In the card layout (Figure 4-4) the broken lines extending part of the way up the field indicates the assumed decimal position.

The card layout is a preliminary piece of documentation. This means that it is created prior to the programming, while the system is in the planning stages. The size of the company has a great deal to do with who creates the card layout. Large companies often have documentation analysts whose primary job is to create documentation for systems. If such a position does not exist, the card layout may be done by the systems analyst. In an even smaller shop the programmer may double as systems analyst and create the documentation.

In addition to the programmer using the card layout to describe the needed storage area to the computer, a data entry operator usually deeps a card (or record) layout of every record format they have occasion to enter. They use this layout to program their machine to aid themselves in entering the data more efficiently.

TAPE/DISK LAYOUT

The rules for creating a tape or disk layout are essentially the same as for a card layout. There are two differences we will consider here.

Record length Card records are fixed at 51, 80, 90 or 96 columns in length depending on the equipment being used. Tape or disk records may vary greatly in size. Many tape and disk records exceed the more ordinary 80 column length. For this reason a card layout form is not adequate to describe a tape or disk record. Tape or disk layouts are created to accomodate the longer record lengths.

Format When a field contains numeric data it is often in a format called packed decimal. This is essentially recording two digits per position. Tape and disk layouts provide the extra space necessary for indicating this. The concept of packed data is not essential to flowcharting and will not be developed further in this book. An example of a disk layout for the master file is shown in Figure 4-6.

RECORD DESCRIPTION

Often a listing of the fields in a record is created with more extensive explanation of each field than the space on a card or record layout form will allow. Such a record description, created from the card layout in this chapter would be as shown in Figure 4-7.

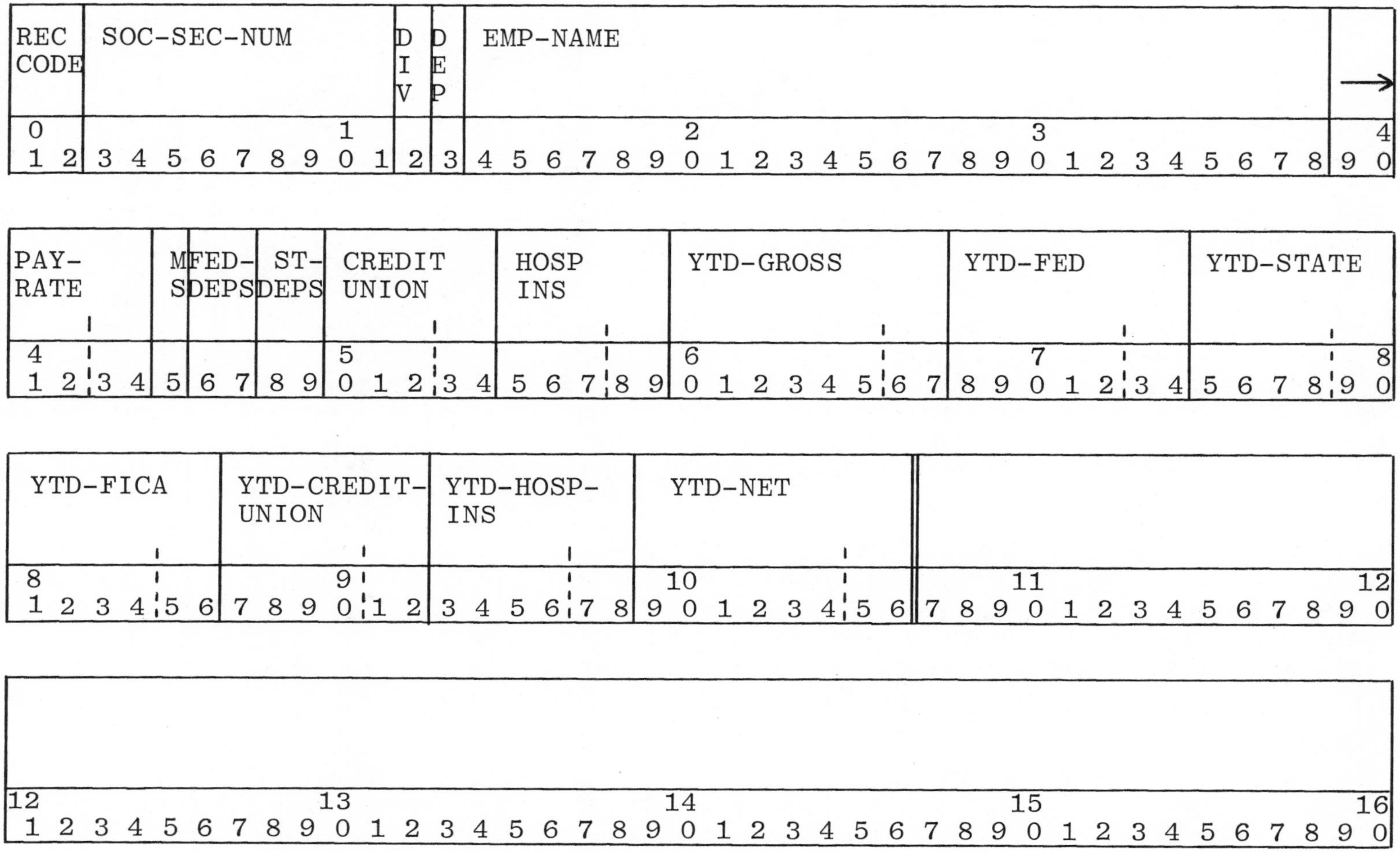

REC CODE	SOC-SEC-NUM	DIV	DEP	EMP-NAME	→
0	1			2 3	4
1 2	3 4 5 6 7 8 9 0 1	2	3	4 5 6 7 8 9 0 1 2 3 4 5 6 7 8 9 0 1 2 3 4 5 6 7 8	9 0

PAY-RATE	MS	FED-DEPS	ST-DEPS	CREDIT UNION	HOSP INS	YTD-GROSS	YTD-FED	YTD-STATE
4				5		6	7	8
1 2 ¦ 3 4	5	6 7	8 9	0 1 2 ¦ 3 4	5 6 7 ¦ 8 9	0 1 2 3 4 5 ¦ 6 7	8 9 0 1 2 ¦ 3 4	5 6 7 8 ¦ 9 0

YTD-FICA	YTD-CREDIT-UNION	YTD-HOSP-INS	YTD-NET	
8	9		10	11 12
1 2 3 4 ¦ 5 6	7 8 9 0 ¦ 1 2	3 4 5 6 ¦ 7 8	9 0 1 2 3 4 ¦ 5 6	7 8 9 0 1 2 3 4 5 6 7 8 9 0

12 13 14 15 16
1 2 3 4 5 6 7 8 9 0 1 2 3 4 5 6 7 8 9 0 1 2 3 4 5 6 7 8 9 0 1 2 3 4 5 6 7 8 9 0

Figure 4-6

RECORD DESCRIPTION

POSITION	DATA NAME	TYPE	FORMAT	SIZE	EXPLANATION
1 - 2	CARD-CODE	N	D	2	The number 10, a code unique to this card.
3 - 11	SOC-SEC-NUM	N	D	9	Social Security Number unique to each person.
12 - 12	DIVISION-NUM	N	D	1	A number from 1 to 5 representing the divisions of the company as follows: 1 - West Coast 2 - Rocky Mountain 3 - Midwest 4 - South Atlantic 5 - Eastern
13 - 13	DEPARTMENT	N	D	1	A number from 1 to 5 representing the departments within the divisions of the company as follows: 1 - Administrative 2 - Marketing 3 - Production 4 - Accounting 5 - Data Processing
14 - 38	EMP-NAME	X	D	25	The employee's name, entered as follows: last name, space, first name, space, middle initial.
39 - 44	PAY-RATE	N	D	6.2	The rate in dollars for either hourly or monthly pay.
45 - 45	MARITAL	X	D	1	The marital status for the employee for federal income tax purposes. S - Single M - Married
46 - 47	FED-DEPS	N	D	2	The number of dependents claimed for federal income tax purposes.
48 - 49	STATE-DEP	N	D	2	The number of dependents claimed for state income tax purposes.

POSITION	DATA NAME	TYPE	FORMAT	SIZE	EXPLANATION
50 - 54	CREDIT-UNION	N	D	5.2	Amount to be deducted from the employee's pay for the credit union.
55 - 59	HOSP-INS	N	D	5.2	Amount to be deducted from the employee's pay for hospital insurance.
60 - 80	UNUSED	X	D	21	Blanks

Figure 4-7

An explanation of some of the columns in Figure 4-7 is needed. For a card record, position corresponds to the card columns a field is located in. In the case of a tape or disk record, the numbers refer to the position of the field within the record relative to the beginning.

The data name portion should be the same name that will be used when the program is actually written in a programming language. The computer is not concerned with the way a data name is spelled or its meaning in the English language. It only requires that when you use a data name to refer to a particular field on a record that it be spelled exactly the same way every time. The rules for constructing data names vary with each programming language. The names we have chosen to use as an example here are suitable for the COBOL programming language. Our reason for using COBOL type names is that COBOL is written in near English terms allowing us to make the data names understandable to a non-programmer.

The type portion of the record description has three possibilities.

N	meaning numeric	includes 0 - 9
X	meaning alphanumeric	includes 0 - 9, A - Z and special characters
A	meaning alphabetic	includes A - Z and blanks

When writing a computer program it is usually necessary to declare a type for each field. How you can use the field within the program depends partially on its type. For example, arithmetic can be done only with fields that have been declared numeric.

The format indicates the manner in which the field is stored in the computer. The D in our example indicated zoned decimal. Other possibilities for the format would be binary (B) and packed (P).

The size of a numeric field is of the form w.d, where w is equal to the total size of the field and d equals the positions to the right of the decimal.

The explanation column is used to explain the codes used and provide other useful information.

A record description with all of its detail is useful to departments of a company that prepare source (original) documents or forms for eventual input to the computer. It provides guidance for these people in assigning codes to various items. In our example, S represents single and M represents married. The use of such codes saves considerable storage space on a record and at the same time reduces the cost of preparing the input record. Other items which have been coded in our record description are the division and department numbers. Refer to Figure 4-7 (the record description) for an interpretation of these codes.

Upon receiving the source document, the data input operators use the record description as a reference to insure that the data they are entering is coded properly and appropriate for each field.

Programmers will use the record description as reference when they describe the record for storage in the computer. Some of their programming techniques will be dependent upon the type and format of the data, as well as its possible values. The record description is a part of the preliminary documentation and is created in conjunction with the record layouts.

PRINT CHART

When a printed copy of information from a file is needed, it is necessary for someone to design the format of the printed copy. This must be done before the program can be written as the design will be used as an aid in coding the program. A special form called a print chart or printer layout is used for this purpose. This form is marked off in boxes corresponding to the size of the type on the printer being used. There are generally 10 vertical columns to an inch and 6 horizontal rows to an inch. Output is normally printed 6 lines per inch, however, many printers can be adjusted to 8 lines per inch. Forms can be designed for either 6 or 8 lines per inch and care should be taken when ordering preprinted forms that the proper vertical spacing is specified. It is also important that adequate space is provided for all field lengths when designing forms.

Preprinted forms and blank stock for a computer printer come in a variety of sizes. The standard print chart has 150 vertical columns and 50 horizontal rows to accomodate almost any needed design. If smaller paper or forms are used the print chart can be lined off to indicate the form size and shape.

If the 80 columns of input were transferred directly to output with no space inserted between fields, it would look like Figure 4-8.

```
1012345678912KENNEDY KENNETH J          215090S00000000001220
1016323453413GABLE ANDREW L             176250S02220900001665
1020346972915SIMPSON JANET A            190000M03030600001400
1023965938721CARUSO LUCY D              162361M04031500002090
1031624953222GONZALES JANET             229020S00001000001600
1032649876524EDISON KEITH U             100250M05050000001775
1036162901632HILL ANNA W                150010S01002000001550
1038311211773SMITH ALICE K              098000S00000800001322
1039694321935JOHNSON EDWARD M           185615M02200000001000
1041962349141ALEXANDER WILLIAM D        120050M30302500001075
1047980938143EVERETT EDSIL R            098975M02010500001700
1091236125145SWANSON SHARON S           137510S01011050001592
1054323445341JONES JAMES N              107900M04040900002000
1059153270153LONG MARILYN G             146300S02020670000000
1061921161353STANDFORM ALLEN B          117120S01000750001900
1063291236555METTLESON GREGORY C        210900S01010000003000
```

Figure 4-8

Figure 4-8 contains all of the necessary data but its readability leaves something to be desired. In order to create a readable report, spaces need to be inserted between each field forming the information into columns.

Normally when a printed output is described to the computer, space is alloted to each variable to be printed on a line and space is also allocated between each variable for readability. When the actual instructions to the computer are coded, each variable is transferred from input to output individually. When <u>all</u> of the variables on a line have been transferred, a write command is issued to print the entire line at one time. For the sake of brevity, our flowchart will say MOVE INPUT TO OUTPUT followed by WRITE A LINE. An experienced programmer will understand this to mean that every variable on the line must have a current value in the output record before a write command is issued for that line.

For our report we will use paper which has 90 horizontal print positions and 66 vertical print lines (14-7/8 x 11). Our job is to make the form look as attractive and readable as possible within our space constraints.

Although there are a number of places where judgment and not simple mathematics is useful in forms layout, let's approach this first layout on a mathematical basis.

It is usually easier to create the detail line first and then work upward, filling the headings in later. In order to create the detail line first it is necessary to know the number of heading lines there will be and the vertical spacing you wish between them. For this form there will be three lines of report headings and two lines of column headings with five blank lines used for vertical spacing. Since we are devoting 10 lines to headings we will start the detail line on line 11 of the print chart.

There are 59 columns of information on the card (shown in Figure 4-3) which must be printed out. Three of the fields represent money and would become more understandable if a decimal point were inserted in the proper space. The addition of these decimal points would increase the needed print positions to 62. Hyphens would improve the readability of the social security number, so two more print positions are needed. This brings the totals to 64.

```
    90 positions possible
  - 64 positions used
    26 positions available for spacing
```

with 11 columns to be printed there are

```
    10 gaps between columns
  +  2 margins needed
    12 areas which require spacing
```

The object is to divide the 26 spaces available among the 12 blank areas. Since 12 will go into 26 only twice and a fraction, two is the approximate number of spaces that can be allocated to each area. The 2 remaining spaces can be placed as desired. Often they are needed around the narrow columns to accommodate the width of the column headings. One solution for printing out the contents of our master card file would be as shown in Figure 4-9.

Notice the characters that are used to express the fields on the detail line. In general, X's are used to indicate both variable numeric and alphanumeric data fields. If other editing characters are to be a part of the output ($, -, *, etc.), they can be shown on the print chart.

After placing the detail line on the print chart, the column headings can be centered above each column. Working from the detail line up makes the centering of the column headings easier. Most of the placement can be done by sight at this point. It is possible that some shifting of detail line items may be necessary to accomodate long column headings. The company name, report name, date and page numbering can be added at this time (see Figure 4-10).

NARRATIVE

The program narrative is an overview of the purpose of a particular program. It can either be preliminary or finished documentation or both. As preliminary documentation it may be something the systems analyst gives to the programmer. The programmer uses this description to draw his flowchart. In a smaller shop it may be preliminary documentation with only a few notes a programmer writes concerning what he needs to accomplish with a particular program. In either case when the documentation is finished, the narrative should identify the structure and impact on the system of the working program.

PRINTER LAYOUT

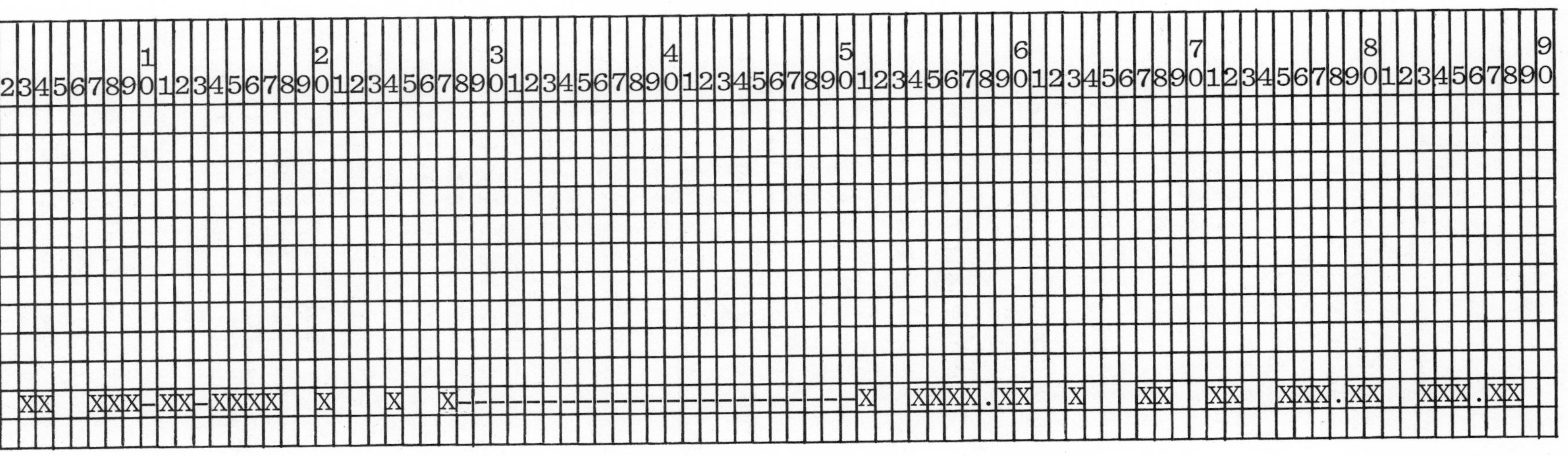

Figure 4-9

```
         1         2         3         4         5         6         7         8         9
123456789012345678901234567890123456789012345678901234567890123456789012345678901234567890

                                      ZYX COMPANY

                                   EMPLOYEE LISTING

                                       11/09/77

 CARD    SOCIAL                                              MAR  FED ST  CREDIT   HOSP
 CODE SECURITY NO DIV DEPT         NAME               RATE   STAT DEP DEP UNION    INS

  XX  XXX-XX-XXXX  X   X  X-----------------------X  XXXX.XX  X   XX  XX  XXX.XX  XXX.XX
```

Figure 4-10

See Figure 4-11 for an example of a simple narrative for the program we have used in this chapter. A good narrative should contain at least the following items.

It should identify all input files and their source.

It should specify if there is to be any editing (verification of the data) of these files. If so, there should be a list of the fields within the records that are to be edited. The process of editing is further explained in Chapter 8.

It should specify any fields which are to be updated or changed.

It should specify the disposition of the input files.

It should describe the general processing necessary to accomplish the goals of the program.

It should emphasize any special processing unique to the program.

It should describe the output files (printed or otherwise) and their disposition.

It should specify if any files are used as both input and output and outline the changes made to such a file.

PROGRAM NARRATIVE

PAY 20

INPUT

Edited master card file which has been sequenced by employee (social security number). This file is prepared by the payroll department and returned to them for permanent storage after the completion of this program.

PROCESSING

The master card file is loaded to disk creating the master disk file. All year-to-date fields are initialized at zero. A listing is made of the master file to allow visual confirmation of its contents at the time of the loading.

OUTPUT

Master disk file sequenced by employee (social security number) to be used as input to PAY 30, PAY 50 and PAY 60. It will be updated in PAY 70 with new year-to-date figures and used as input to PAY 80.

Figure 4-11

RUN SHEET

Once a programmer has completed the programming and testing of a system, the system is turned over the operations department. An important part of the documentation to the operations department is the run sheets for the program. A copy of these sheets is incorporated into a run book. Depending on the complexity of the installation, there may be a run book for each system or just one run book for the entire shop.

A run sheet (Figures 4-12 and 4-13) provides operations with a detailed list of all inputs and outputs for each program as well as the source and disposition of these items. The amount of information on the run sheet varies with the size of the organization. In a large organization the source and disposition of files may only be the input/output room where a more detailed set of instructions has been developed for the handling of these items. Assuming an input/output room exists shifts much of the detail away from operations with respect to the handling, storage and distribution of files. Existence of a mailroom may further isolate some of the functions that could be found on a run sheet in a small company.

The printer portion of the form enables the operator to identify the appropriate size paper or special form to be loaded into the printer and instructions for aligning the form in the printer so that the output will be placed properly on the form. At the end of the form, (bottom of Figure 4-13) information is found about the treatment of the report after it has been produced. Burst, as found on the run sheet, means to separate continuous forms into single units or pages as one would do with paychecks. Decollate is the separation of multiple-ply forms and the removal of any carbon paper they may contain.

The card portion of the form identifies any card input or output for the program. It also shows where the card input is coming from or the card output is to be sent.

The mass storage portion of the form identifies any disk, tape, drum, etc. files used by the program. It shows their name, ID number, where they are coming from, type of file (tape, disk, etc.) and where they should go after processing.

Recovery procedures represent special situations which the programmer anticipates may occur and the actions he expects operations to take if these situations do occur. The operations department usually runs two or three shifts a day. It is to the advantage of the programmer who normally works a day shift to make his instructions not only as clear as possible but to cover all potential trouble spots with error handling instructions The alternative is loss of sleep when a call comes from the operations department in the middle of the night.

The operator should be provided with the section of the systems flowchart which applies to the program run (Figure 4-14).

RUN SHEET

JOB NUMBER PAY 20 JOB NAME MASTER LOAD

PARTITION/CLASS F1/A EST. RUN TIME 15 DATE 11/09/77

(X) SEE SPECIAL INSTRUCTIONS ON REVERSE

PRINTER	LOGICAL UNIT	FORM NUMBER	CARRIAGE TAPE #	ALIGNMENT
	SYS 020	STD 1	STD	CHANNEL 1 = LINE 3 CENTERED

CARD	LOGICAL UNIT	I/O	POCKET	CARD IDENTIFICATION/ VOLUME	SOURCE/ DISPOSITION
	SYS018	I	4	PAYROLL MASTER/1000	PAYROLL

MAGNETIC STORAGE DEVICES	LOGICAL UNIT	I/O	T/D	FILE IDENTIFICATION	VOLUME ID	SOURCE/ DISPOSITION
	SYS005	O	D	PAYROLL MASTER	072540	PAY 30,50

Figure 4-12

R E C O V E R Y   P R O C E D U R E S

PHASE NAME	STEP DESCRIPTION	EST. TIME	STEP NUMBER

PROCEDURE

SPECIAL INSTRUCTIONS

PAY 20 is run only after PAY 10 is error free

BURST NO

DECOLLATE NO

Figure 4-13

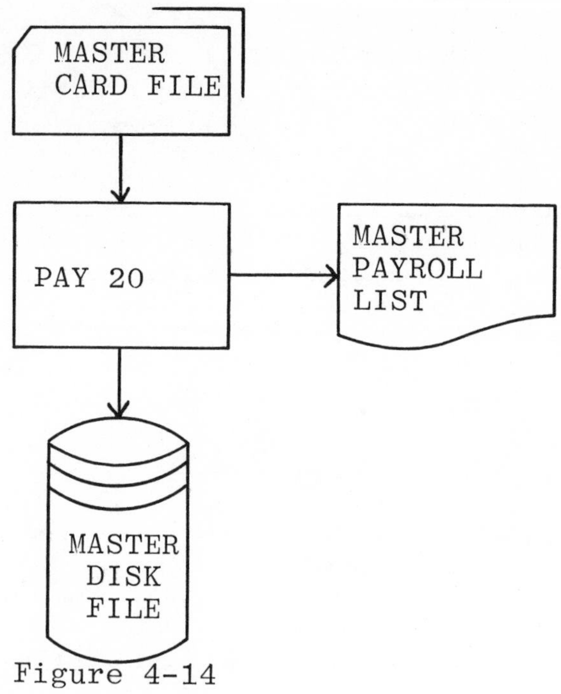

Figure 4-14

A listing of the job control language is also provided (see Figure 4-15). Job control language is a set of instructions to the computer concerning the actions to be performed by the computer.

JOB CONTROL FOR PAY 20

```
// JOB PAY20J
// OPTION DUMP
// ASSGN SYS018,X'00C'
// ASSGN SYS020,X'00E'
// ASSGN SYS005,X'193'
// DLBL MASTER,'PAYROLL MASTER',,SD
// EXTENT SYS005,072540,1,1,100,40
// EXEC PAY20
      (data)
/*
/&
```

Figure 4-15

A brief explanation of the job control is all we require for our purposes. The // JOB card identifies a new job to the computer. The // OPTION card allows us to request special options, otherwise, we take the standard options available. The // ASSGN cards specify the I/O devices we will use. The // DLBL and // EXTENT cards identify our disk pack and the storage area on it we will use. The // EXEC card begins the execution of the program. The data is read as required by the instructions in the program. The /* card identifies the end of the data and the /& identifies the end of the job. A more complete explanation of job control is covered in programming courses as the need arises.

REVIEW QUESTIONS

Matching

A. Card layout

B. Tape/disk layout

C. Record description

D. Print chart

E. Narrative

F. Run sheet

G. Documentation

H. Vertical spacing

I. Decimal alignment

J. Job control

K. Type

L. Format

_________ 1. Instructions which control the execution of a computer run.

_________ 2. Spacing between lines on a printed report.

_________ 3. Graphic description of card fields.

_________ 4. Extensive written description about a group of fields.

_________ 5. Written instructions to the operations staff concerning all details of running a program.

_________ 6. The sum total of information conveyed in written form concerning an entire system or an individual program.

_________ 7. The form in which a field is stored, such as decimal or binary.

_________ 8. Positioning of a numeric field in storage.

_________ 9. Graphic description of a tape or disk file.

_________ 10. Whether a field is alphabetic, numeric or alphanumeric.

_________ 11. An overview of the purpose and mechanics of a program.

_________ 12. A design for printed output.

True/False

T F 1. Vertical spacing on a print chart means the space left between columns.

T F 2. Since no actual decimal point is punched in a card, its location is ignored on a card layout.

T F 3. Type, on a record description, describes the contents of a field such as alphabetic, numeric or alphanumeric.

T F 4. The print chart is usually drawn after the program is written.

T F 5. Blank fields or areas on a card layout should be identified.

T F 6. Record descriptions are superfluous if a layout of the record has been made.

T F 7. A documentation package consists of a flowchart and a copy of the program only.

T F 8. A run sheet is used by the keypunch operator for punching data.

T F 9. If the operator maintains job control in some other form, a listing of it is unnecessary.

T F 10. Tape/disk layout forms usually allow for a longer record than a card layout.

Exercises

1. Create a card layout, record description and print chart for the following case. Add any editing characters you think appropriate to the output.

   Problem Description

   A listing will be produced from the card input showing the personal information for each employee. The input is already in sequence. Output formats will be designed by the student and will include the items indicated below. Headings and column heads should appear at the top of each page. The current date should be included in the heading.

   Input

Data Name	Columns
EMPLOYEE NAME	1 - 15
EMPLOYEE NUMBER	16 - 20
SOCIAL SECURITY NUMBER	21 - 29
SEX CODE	30 - 30
MARITAL STATUS CODE	31 - 31
START DATE (MMDDYY)	32 - 37
SALARY CODE	38 - 39
POSITION	40 - 54
RATE	55 - 61 (7.2)

DATE OF BIRTH (MMDDYY)	69 - 74
NUMBER OF DEPENDENTS	75 - 76
DATE OF LAST RAISE (MMYY)	77 - 80

Output

All fields on the input should be included on the output.

2. Prepare a card layout and printer layout for the following case.

Input

Data Name	Columns
NAME	1 - 15
ADDRESS	16 - 35
CITY/STATE	36 - 50
ZIP	51 - 55
DATE	56 - 61
DESCRIPTION	62 - 74
AMOUNT	75 - 80

Processing

You have been presented with a large supply of a poorly designed mailer. Print a politely worded threat on the left and a list of the items that will be repossesed by a collection agency on the right. The shaded areas can be used only for addresses because of the placement of the carbon. There may be as many as 12 cards per customer (items to be repossesed). Put all items for each customer on a single sheet.

Output (actual size)

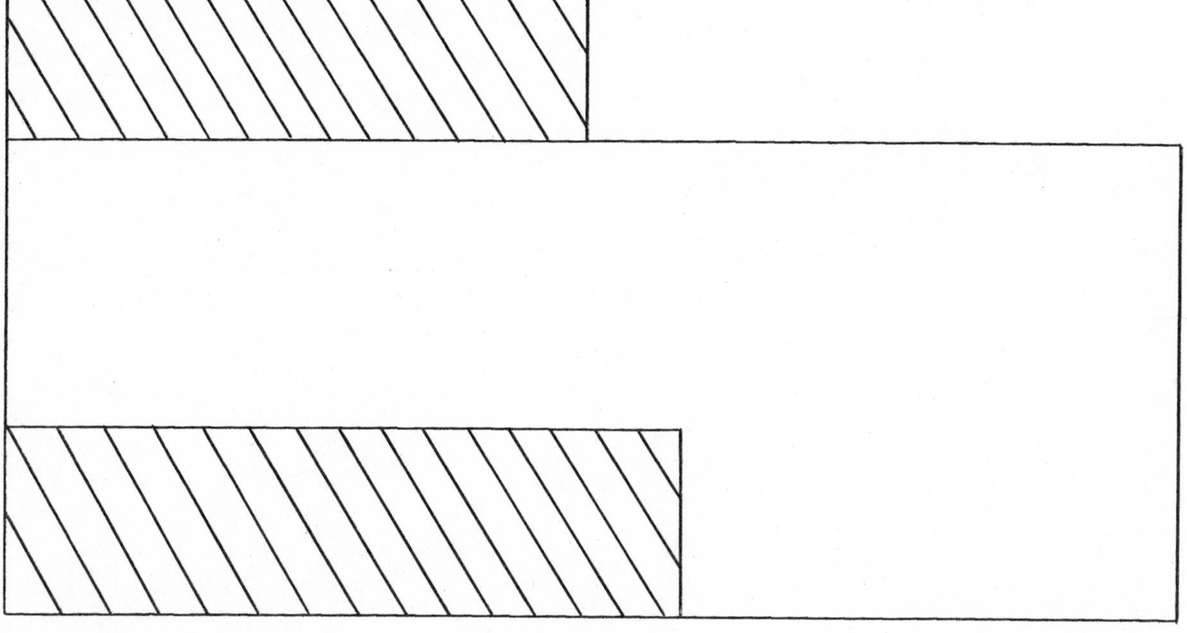

Discussion Questions

1. Which pieces of documentation must be prepared before the program can be written? Why?

2. Which pieces of documentation are likely to be prepared after the program is written? Why?

3. List the pieces of documentation in the order they would be created (include the flowchart). Give your reasons for the order you selected.

4. Is a documentation package really worth all the time it takes to prepare it?

5. How large should a company be before they document formally?

6. Once a program or system is put into operation, will the documentation ever require modification?

CHAPTER 5

Single Input Programs 1

OBJECTIVES

As a result of this chapter the student should be able to perform the following activities.

1. Describe what a housekeeping routine is and what function it has in a program or flowchart.

2. Describe a simple listing process including checking for an end of forms condition.

3. Describe what control breaks are and what types of activities normally take place on a control break.

4. Describe what a subroutine is and indicate the difference between open and closed subroutines.

5. Describe what headings are and how they are put on the top of new pages for both forms overflow and control break situations.

6. Describe the difference between internal and external subroutines.

7. Describe when heading and control break control fields should be updated and why this is necessary.

INTRODUCTION

One of the more common types of programs in industry is one which reads a single file and produces a report relative to the data contained in the file. This chapter will cover such a procedure using employee data from a payroll system that will eventually be used to create the payroll master file. The report that will be created will be a listing of the contents of the employee file for verification by the personnel department at each of the company's various locations. The portion of a systems flowchart representing this listing process is shown in Figure 5-1.

Figure 5-1

This process will be presented in five separate steps the first of which deals with housekeeping routines.

HOUSEKEEPING ROUTINES

A housekeeping routine is one which appears at the beginning of the program and is executed only once during the actual execution of the program. It is used to set up or condition the program for future processing needs. There are several types of activities typically done in a housekeeping routine. Some of these activities are opening the files to be processed, accessing the current date, reading a header card or cards, setting switches, reading the first record on a file, printing headings etc.

At this point we will show examples of opening the files to be used and accessing the current date. Other types of uses will be pointed out in future chapters as the need for such routines arises.

Flowcharting the opening of files is a rather simple process as can be seen by Figure 5-2.

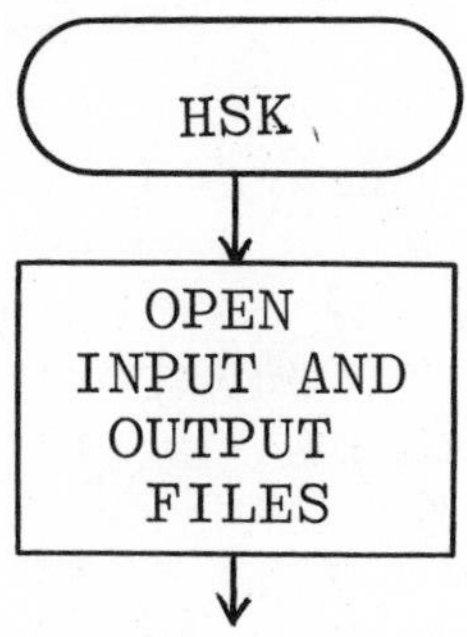

Figure 5-2

Unless a large number of files are being used at various times in the program which may require multiple opening processes it is more typical to show the opening process as shown in Figure 5-3.

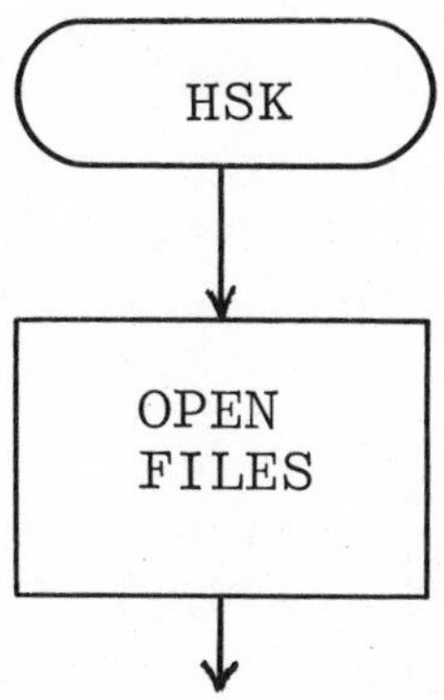

Figure 5-3

The opening of files that are to be used is a very important process. It is here that the files are made ready for processing. Trying to use a file that has not been opened is somewhat similar to trying to get the beans out of a can of beans before removing the lid. This is the point at which header labels found on most files are checked to be sure that the right file is being used if it is an input file. If it is an output file this is the point where the header labels are created. Sometimes files are created without any labels present. In this case the open process merely makes the file available for processing.

In the case of magnetic tape the labels (header and trailer) are found (recorded) on the file itself. They are for machine usage and not for human readability. The general format of how they exist on magnetic tape is shown in Figure 5-4.

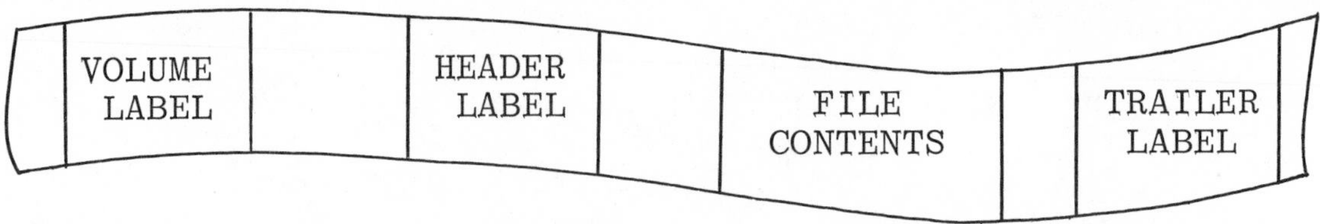

Figure 5-4

The volume label identifies the particular reel of tape or other physical medium on which the file is recorded. The header label identifies the name of the file, when it was created, how long it is to be kept, and which reel it is if the file is contained on multiple reels, etc. The trailer label contains such things as record counts.

While the technical data about what is on header and trailer labels is not usually needed for flowcharting you should at least be aware of their existence. There are times when additional labels are used (called user labels) which may require flowcharting consideration. When this is true they are shown on the flowchart in much the same way as opening the files (see Figure 5-5).

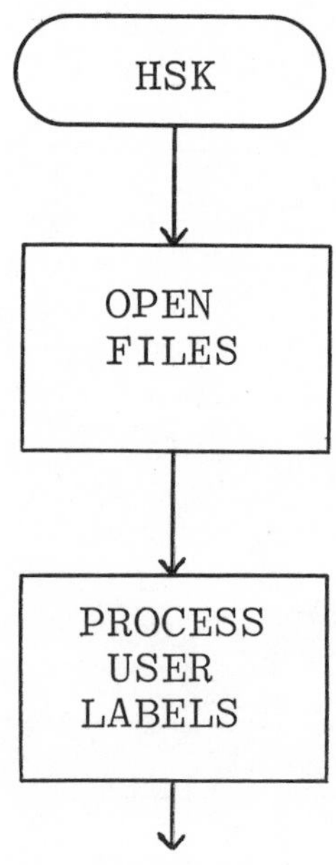

Figure 5-5

The actual processing of user labels would vary depending on what they contained and why they were being used.

The current date may be obtained in various ways. Many computer systems have the current date stored in them which is available to the programmer. This date is usually stored by the operator at the beginning of each day. The actual programming to retrieve this date varies with the programming language and the computer being used. In terms of flowcharting the process of retrieving this date is shown in Figure 5-6.

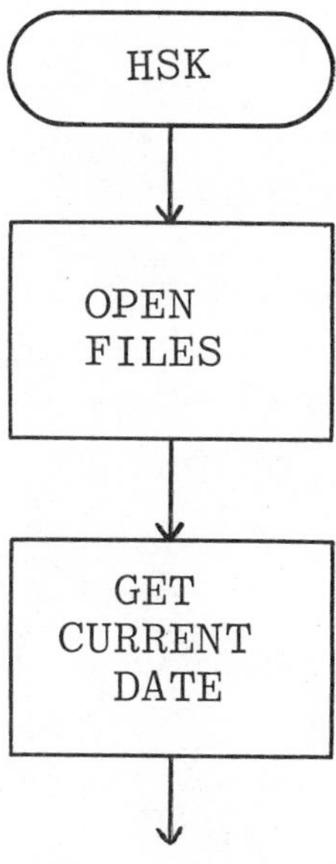

Figure 5-6

THE LISTING PROCESS

Our problem now is to read the cards in the file and list them on a report. The only condition to be checked at this point is forms overflow. This is checking to see if there is any more room left on the page to print additional data lines without going over the perforations that exist between the pages on continuous form paper. If there is no more room left we will eject to a new page. How this ejecting process actually happens varies with the language used to write the program and with the type of printer.

How the end of a page is sensed on different printers varies but one is via a carriage control tape. A carriage control tape as seen in Figure 5-7 is a paper loop which has holes punched in it at specific points (note the arrows). These holes, as they are sensed by wire brushes, indicate such things as end of page and first print line to the computer. When we test for an end of page condition we are testing to see if one of these punches has been sensed.

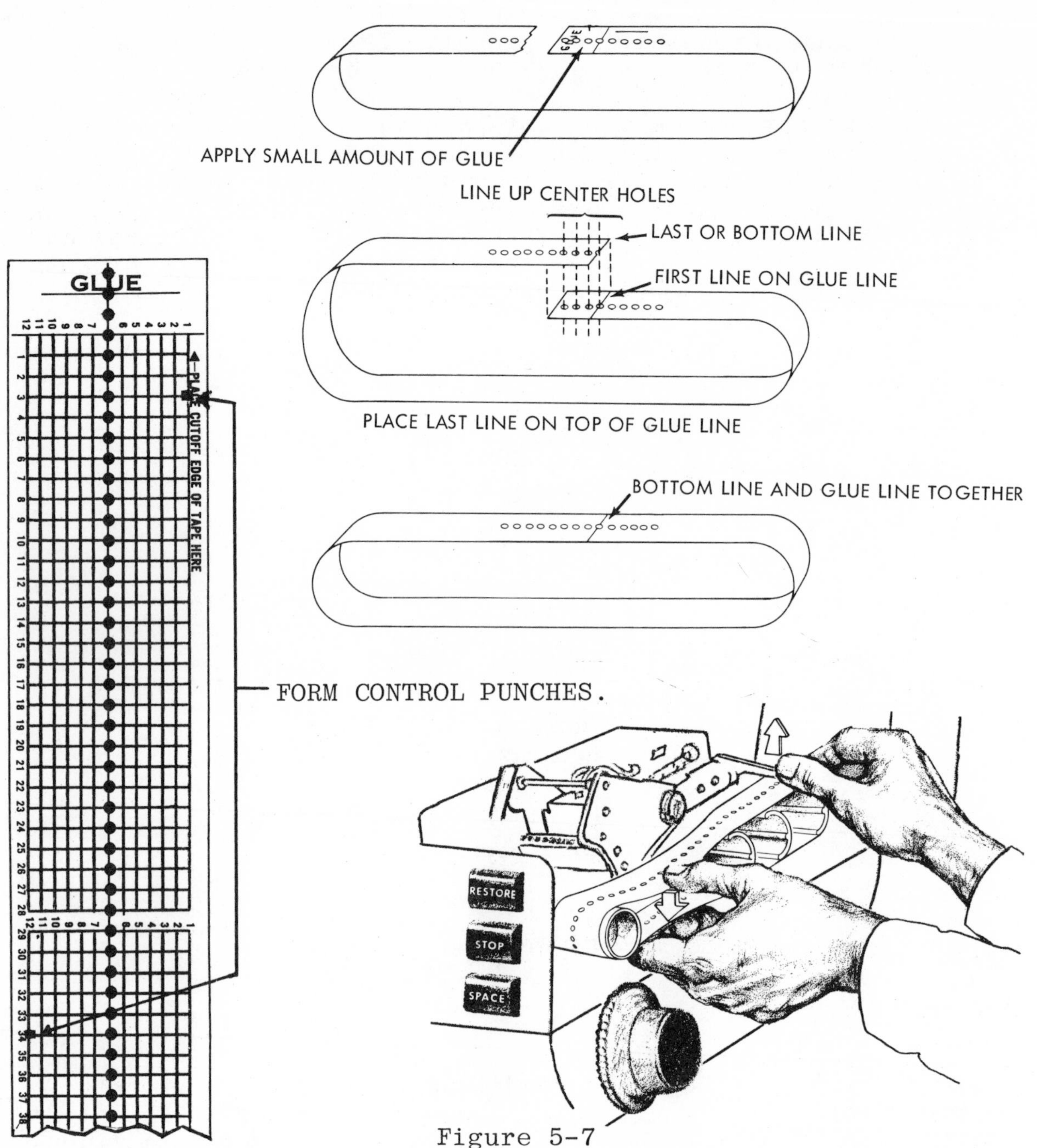

Figure 5-7

On the carriage control tape a channel 1 punch represents the first printing line and a channel 12 punch represents the end of page. These are represented in Figure 5-8.

At this point it only needs to be said that if a channel 12 punch is sensed we are going to go to the top of a new page. The flowchart for this process is Figure 5-9.

This process will continue to read and print data from the card file until the end of the file is reached at which point processing will be terminated. Notice that the files were opened prior to any processing. The open does not do any processing of the data itself. Also, notice that the files were closed

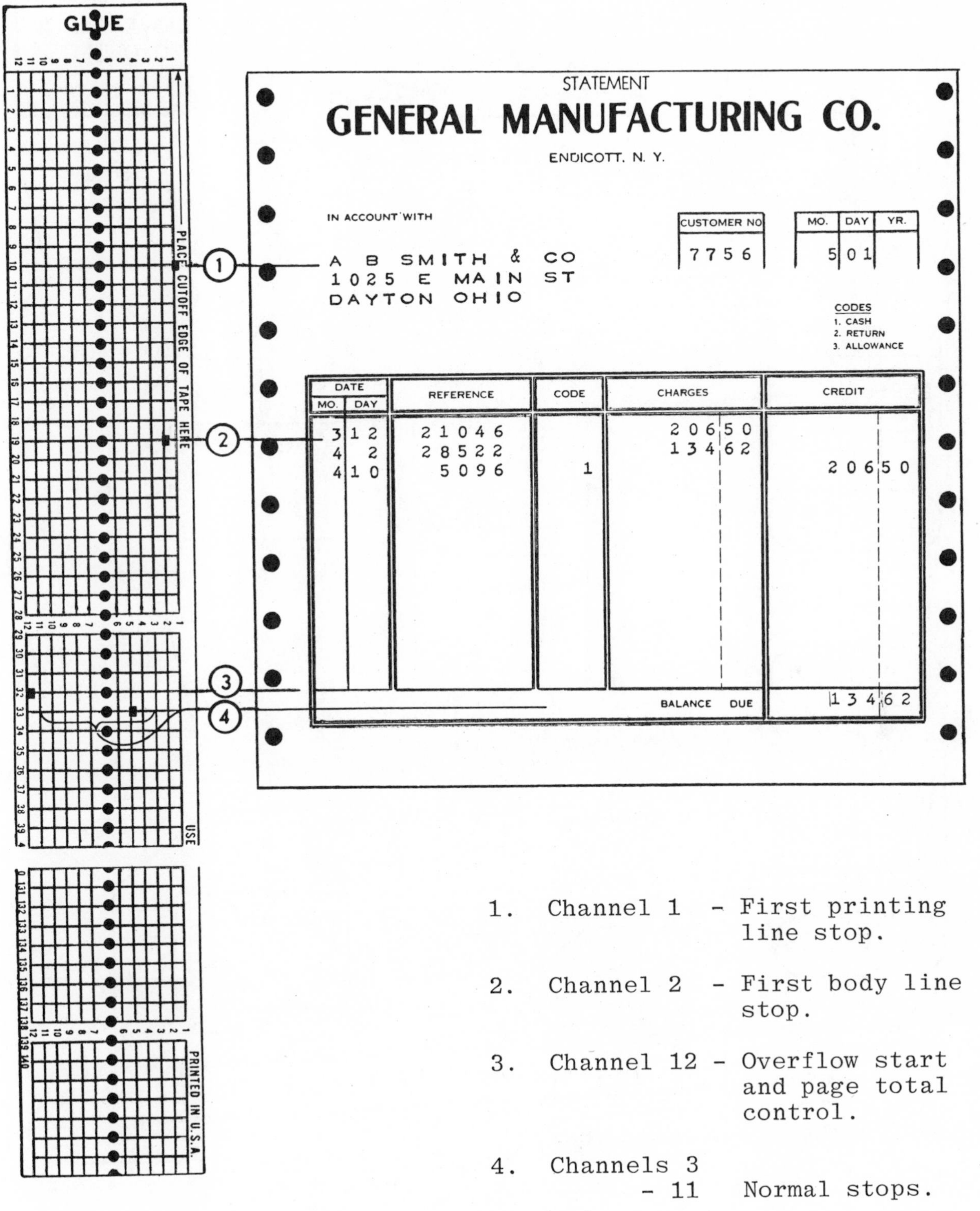

1. Channel 1 - First printing line stop.

2. Channel 2 - First body line stop.

3. Channel 12 - Overflow start and page total control.

4. Channels 3 - 11 Normal stops.

Figure 5-8

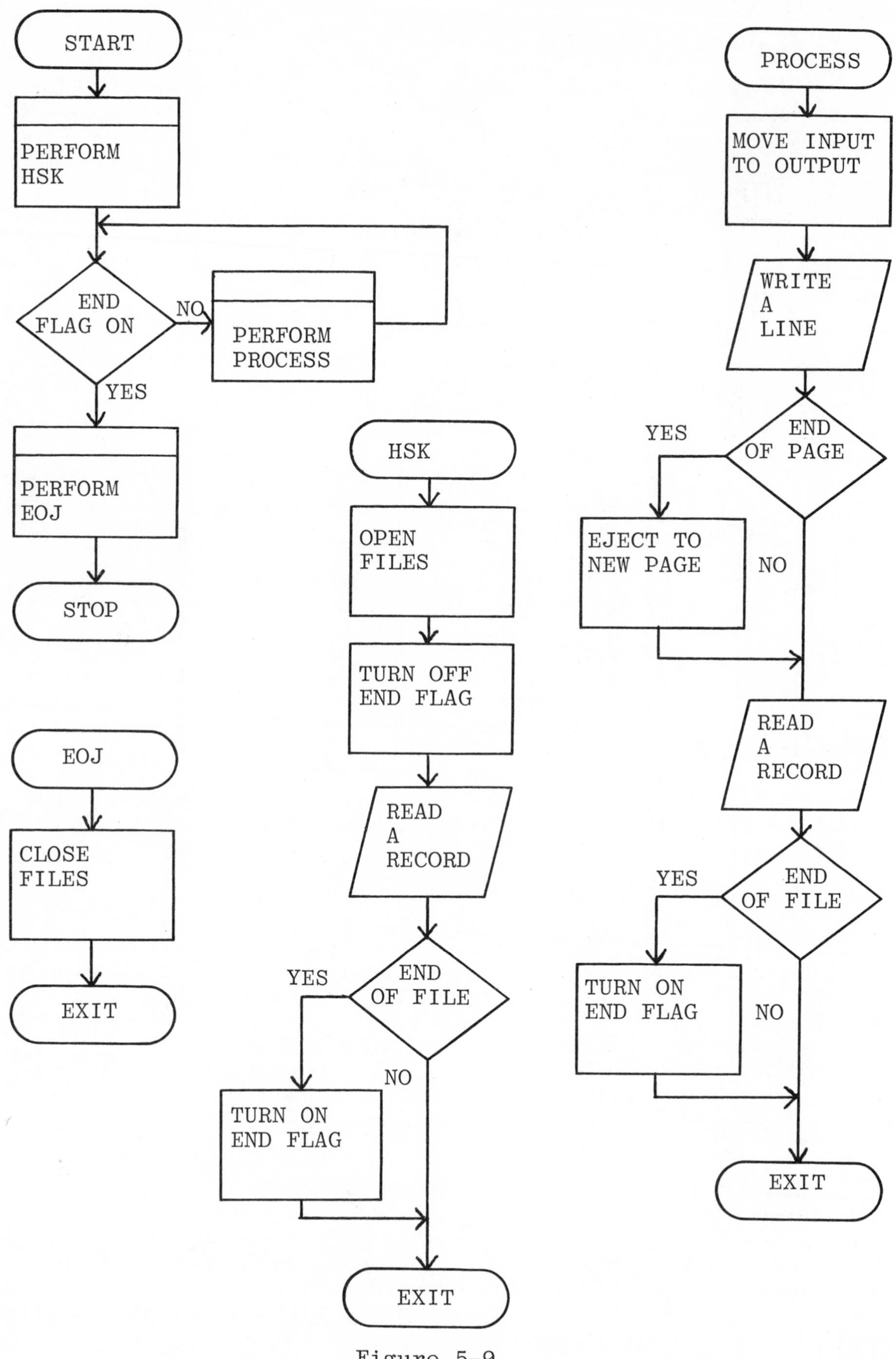
START
PERFORM HSK
END FLAG ON
NO
YES
PERFORM PROCESS
PERFORM EOJ
STOP
EOJ
CLOSE FILES
EXIT
HSK
OPEN FILES
TURN OFF END FLAG
READ A RECORD
END OF FILE
YES
NO
TURN ON END FLAG
EXIT
PROCESS
MOVE INPUT TO OUTPUT
WRITE A LINE
END OF PAGE
YES
NO
EJECT TO NEW PAGE
READ A RECORD
END OF FILE
YES
NO
TURN ON END FLAG
EXIT

Figure 5-9

before ending the program.

The closing process is much like the open process in reverse. For input files that were being processed it checks record counts etc. and for output files it creates the trailer or end of file labels. For files without labels it merely makes the file no longer available for processing. An example of a report using overflow processing is shown in Figure 5-10.

CONTROL BREAKS

The next item to add to our problem is control breaks. Control breaks are a method of breaking a report down into smaller units so that the data becomes more meaningful. A control break exists when the contents in a given field or fields changes. This field is the one on which the file has been sequenced. Presume a file is in sequence by divisions in a company. When we go from division 1 to division 2 we have a control break. It is also rather common to produce totals at the time that a control break occurs. The totaling process will be covered in Chapter 6.

In our example of listing employee file data for verification by personnel at the various divisions it would be better if we broke the listing down so that each division's information started on a new page. This way the report could be easily broken up and sent to the various divisions. In looking at this as a manual process it sounds rather easy - we simply want to start at the top of a new page as each new division is encountered.

In essence this process is what happens in a computerized version of the problem. To know if we have encountered a new division in computer processing we have to have some way of comparing the current record being processed with the previous record processed. This comparison process requires that the number from the previous card be maintained or stored somewhere. To accomplish this we will establish a hold area in which we can save the number from a card. We can then compare the number we saved with the number on the next card after the next card has been read. If a difference occurs during the comparing process then we have encountered a new division. When a new division is encountered we store the new division number in the hold area. Figure 5-11 shows this process including the hold area in storage. This hold area is designed via programing to be the same size as the item being compared.

Notice that at the beginning of the flowchart this hold area was set to zero. This is done to force a new division condition on the first card read. This presumes there is no division numbered zero. Without initializing this area to zero (or less than the lowest division number) there is no way of knowing what its contents would be and we would be playing control break roulette on the first card.

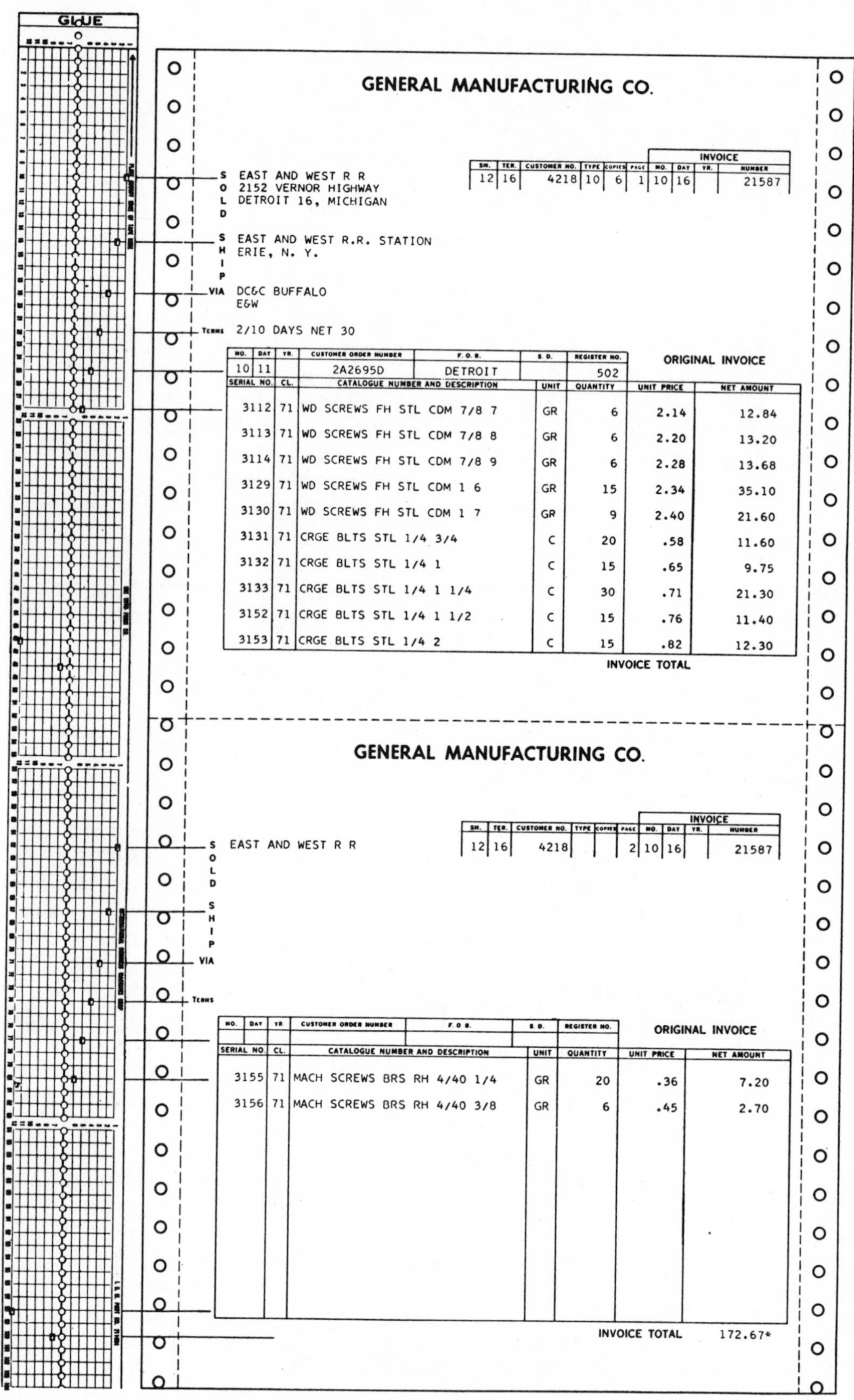

GLUE

GENERAL MANUFACTURING CO.

INVOICE									
SH.	TER.	CUSTOMER NO.	TYPE	COPIES	PAGE	NO.	DAY	YR.	NUMBER
12	16	4218	10	6	1	10	16		21587

SOLD: EAST AND WEST R R
2152 VERNOR HIGHWAY
DETROIT 16, MICHIGAN

SHIP: EAST AND WEST R.R. STATION
ERIE, N. Y.

VIA: DC&C BUFFALO
E&W

TERMS: 2/10 DAYS NET 30

NO.	DAY	YR.	CUSTOMER ORDER NUMBER	F.O.B.	S.O.	REGISTER NO.
10	11		2A2695D	DETROIT		502

ORIGINAL INVOICE

SERIAL NO.	CL.	CATALOGUE NUMBER AND DESCRIPTION	UNIT	QUANTITY	UNIT PRICE	NET AMOUNT
3112	71	WD SCREWS FH STL CDM 7/8 7	GR	6	2.14	12.84
3113	71	WD SCREWS FH STL CDM 7/8 8	GR	6	2.20	13.20
3114	71	WD SCREWS FH STL CDM 7/8 9	GR	6	2.28	13.68
3129	71	WD SCREWS FH STL CDM 1 6	GR	15	2.34	35.10
3130	71	WD SCREWS FH STL CDM 1 7	GR	9	2.40	21.60
3131	71	CRGE BLTS STL 1/4 3/4	C	20	.58	11.60
3132	71	CRGE BLTS STL 1/4 1	C	15	.65	9.75
3133	71	CRGE BLTS STL 1/4 1 1/4	C	30	.71	21.30
3152	71	CRGE BLTS STL 1/4 1 1/2	C	15	.76	11.40
3153	71	CRGE BLTS STL 1/4 2	C	15	.82	12.30

INVOICE TOTAL

GENERAL MANUFACTURING CO.

INVOICE									
SH.	TER.	CUSTOMER NO.	TYPE	COPIES	PAGE	NO.	DAY	YR.	NUMBER
12	16	4218			2	10	16		21587

SOLD: EAST AND WEST R R

SHIP:

VIA:

TERMS:

NO.	DAY	YR.	CUSTOMER ORDER NUMBER	F.O.B.	S.O.	REGISTER NO.

ORIGINAL INVOICE

SERIAL NO.	CL.	CATALOGUE NUMBER AND DESCRIPTION	UNIT	QUANTITY	UNIT PRICE	NET AMOUNT
3155	71	MACH SCREWS BRS RH 4/40 1/4	GR	20	.36	7.20
3156	71	MACH SCREWS BRS RH 4/40 3/8	GR	6	.45	2.70

INVOICE TOTAL 172.67*

Figure 5-10

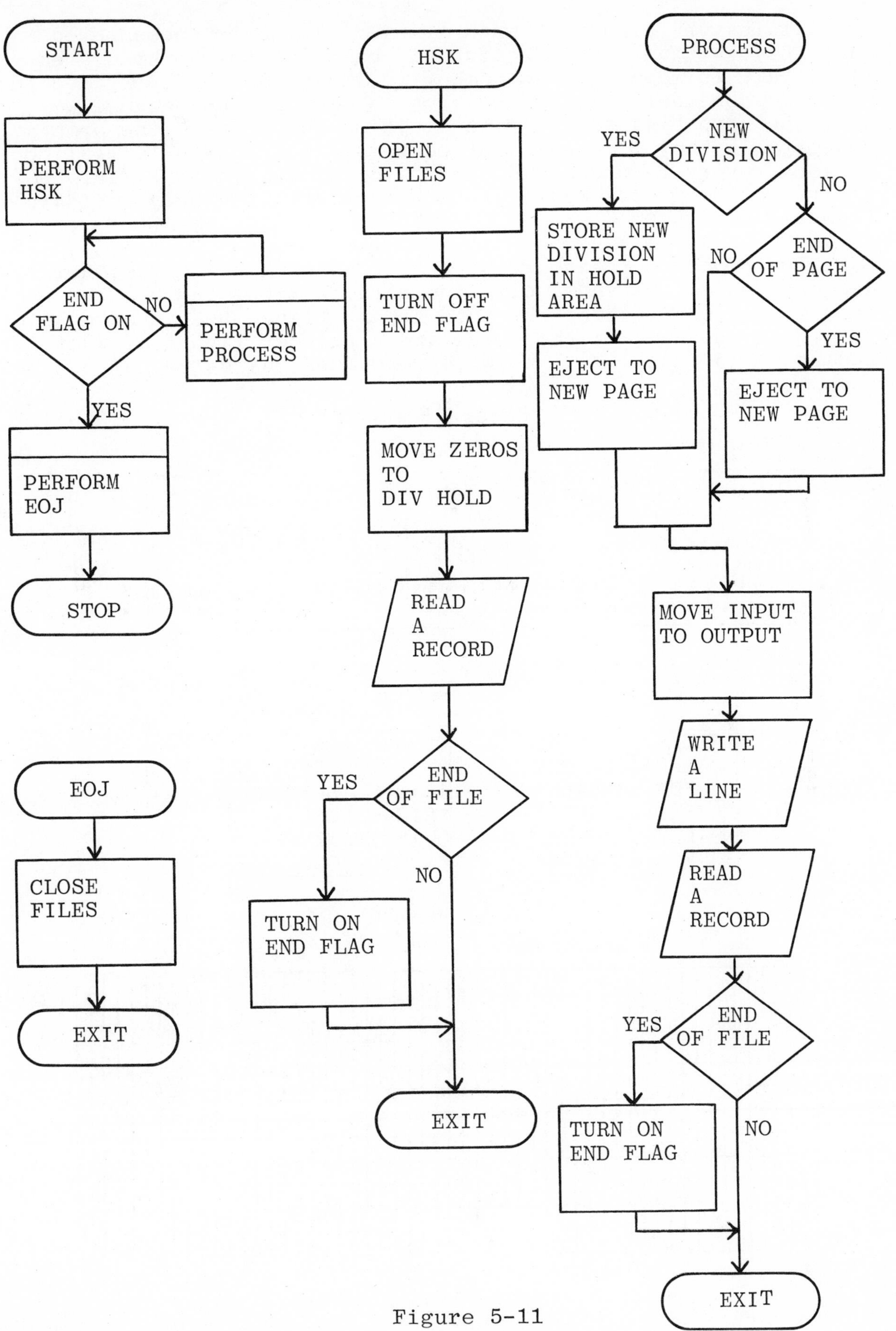
START
PERFORM HSK
END FLAG ON
NO
PERFORM PROCESS
YES
PERFORM EOJ
STOP
HSK
OPEN FILES
TURN OFF END FLAG
MOVE ZEROS TO DIV HOLD
READ A RECORD
END OF FILE
YES
TURN ON END FLAG
NO
EXIT
PROCESS
NEW DIVISION
YES
STORE NEW DIVISION IN HOLD AREA
EJECT TO NEW PAGE
NO
END OF PAGE
NO
YES
EJECT TO NEW PAGE
MOVE INPUT TO OUTPUT
WRITE A LINE
READ A RECORD
END OF FILE
YES
TURN ON END FLAG
NO
EXIT
EOJ
CLOSE FILES
EXIT

Figure 5-11

It is very important when a new division is encountered that the new division number should be moved to the hold area. If we fail to move the new number to the hold area every record would be considered a new division. This is true because we would be comparing each card's division number with the original contents in the hold area. Since the hold area was initialized to zero, every record would cause a control break. Failure to update the hold area would produce a report with only one data line per page.

The process of saving the number as each new division is encountered can be shown with the data in Figure 5-12. The process is called updating the hold area. Figure 5-12 shows the format of the data on the cards and a printer layout of what the report is to look like. We will read these cards one at a time.

Record Format

DIVISION NUMBER	EMPLOYEE NAME	START DATE MM	START DATE DD	START DATE YY	POSITION	BLANK
1	2–21	22–23	24–25	26–27	28–43	44–80

Sample Data

1	2 – 21	22 – 27	28 – 43
1	PETER JOHNSON	032842	CLERK
1	RALPH TOLSTORY	061860	BOOKKEEPER
2	CLYDE SAMUALS	101258	LIBRARIAN
2	BETTY BARKER	121649	SECRETARY
2	SALLY TINKERBY	091271	LAWYER
3	GREGORY GARTNER	072565	PROGRAMMER

Printer Layout

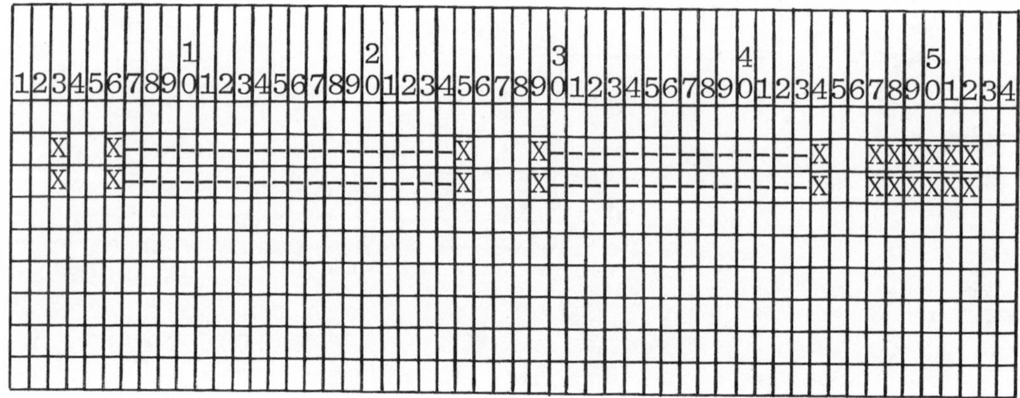

Figure 5-12

If we follow the first few of these cards through the flowchart in Figure 5-11 the comparing/updating process should become clear. The division hold area is initially set to zero.

After the first card is read and we determine that the END FLAG is off, the division field in the card (division 1) is compared to the hold area. Since 1 is not equal to zero, a new division is indicated. Thus we store (move) the new division number to the hold area and eject to a new page. The hold area now contains a 1. Next the data from the card is moved to the print area and a line is written. Figure 5-13 shows the current contents of the hold area and the line on the report. Following this we go back to read the next card.

1 Hold area

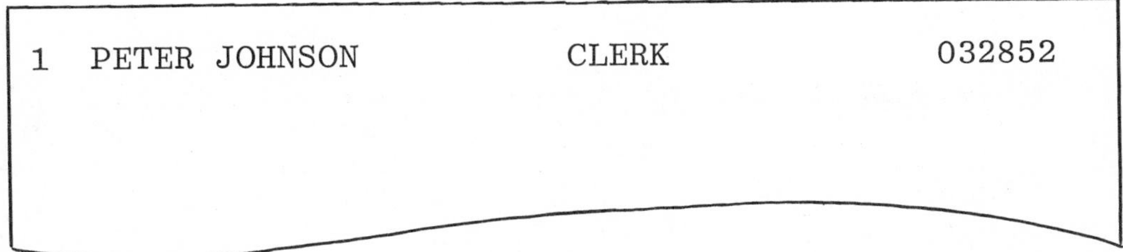

Figure 5-13

After reading the second card and finding END FLAG still off, we compare the division field in the card (also division 1) to the hold area. Since 1 is equal to 1 we fall through to checking for the end of the page. As no end of page exists, we build and write the line and read the next card. Figure 5-14 shows the current status of the hold area and the report.

1 Hold area

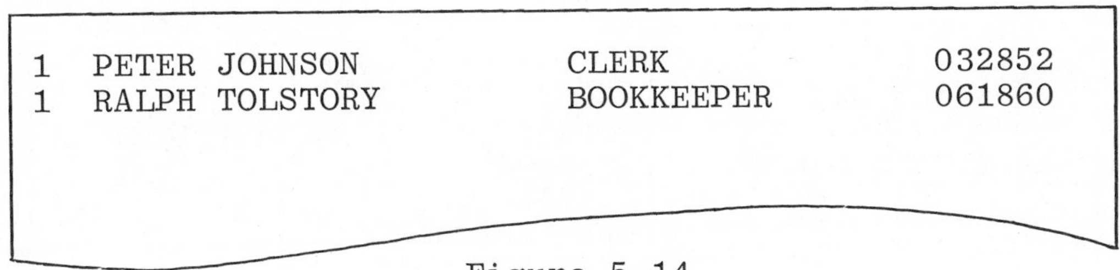

Figure 5-14

When the third card is read and found to be a data card we compare the division field in the card (division 2) with the hold area. Since 2 is not equal to 1 (from the hold area) we have encountered a new division. This forces the paper to be ejected to a new page and the new division number (2) to be stored in the hold area. The data is then moved and printed and we read the next card. The result of this is shown in Figure 5-15. The dotted line is used to indicate the top of a new page.

[2] Hold area

1	PETER JOHNSON	CLERK	032852
1	RALPH TOLSTORY	BOOKKEEPER	061860
	top of page 2		
2	CLYDE SAMUALS	LIBRARIAN	101258

Figure 5-15

The process of comparing the current card value with the hold area and moving the new division number to the hold area when one is encountered is a standard method of handling control breaks. It continues until the end of file is reached. At the end of the input file we turn on the END FLAG. When we return again to test the END FLAG we find it on and therefore close the files and stop. In Chapter 6 we will be adding more to this process (both totals and multiple level breaks) but the basics will not change. The completed output of our example is depicted in Figure 5-16.

[3] Hold area

1	PETER JOHNSON	CLERK	032852
1	RALPH TOLSTORY	BOOKKEEPER	061860
	top of page 2		
2	CLYDE SAMUALS	LIBRARIAN	101258
2	BETTY BARKER	SECRETARY	121649
2	SALLY TINKERBY	LAWYER	091271
	top of page 3		
3	GREGORY GARTNER	PROGRAMMER	072565

Figure 5-16

SUBROUTINES

There comes a time in even the easiest of programs when it

is desirable to utilize subroutines. A subroutine is a group of instructions that performs some identifiable part of the overall problem. Typical examples of items that might be found in subroutines are:

1. Housekeeping routines
2. Heading routines
3. Calculation routines
4. Table processing routines
5. Editing routines
6. Setting counters to zero

Subroutines may be either internal or external. Internal subroutines are those that are physically in your program and are used by it in processing. External subroutines are routines used by your program that are not physically a part of it and must somehow be accessed in order to be used. In this text we will stick to internal subroutines. The basic flowcharting concepts however apply to either type and it is beyond the scope of this text to describe how external routines are accessed.

In a flowchart the symbols used to represent the two different types of subroutines are shown in Figure 5-17. Either of these symbols may be used as a process structure.

External Subroutine Internal Subroutine

Figure 5-17

<u>OPEN vs. CLOSED SUBROUTINES</u>

Both of these indicate a set of instructions or logic path that has been described in detail elsewhere (either internally or externally). Internal subroutines may also be catagorized as open or closed. Open subroutines are written within the mainline logic of the program whereas closed subroutines are outside of the mainline logic of the program and must be branched to in order to be executed. Closed subroutines are normally used when the routine is to be executed at several points in the program to avoid redundancy. Without closed subroutines the process done by the subroutine would need to be redone or recoded every place in the program where we want to do the subroutine. The way in which the two different types are flowcharted is shown in Figure 5-18.

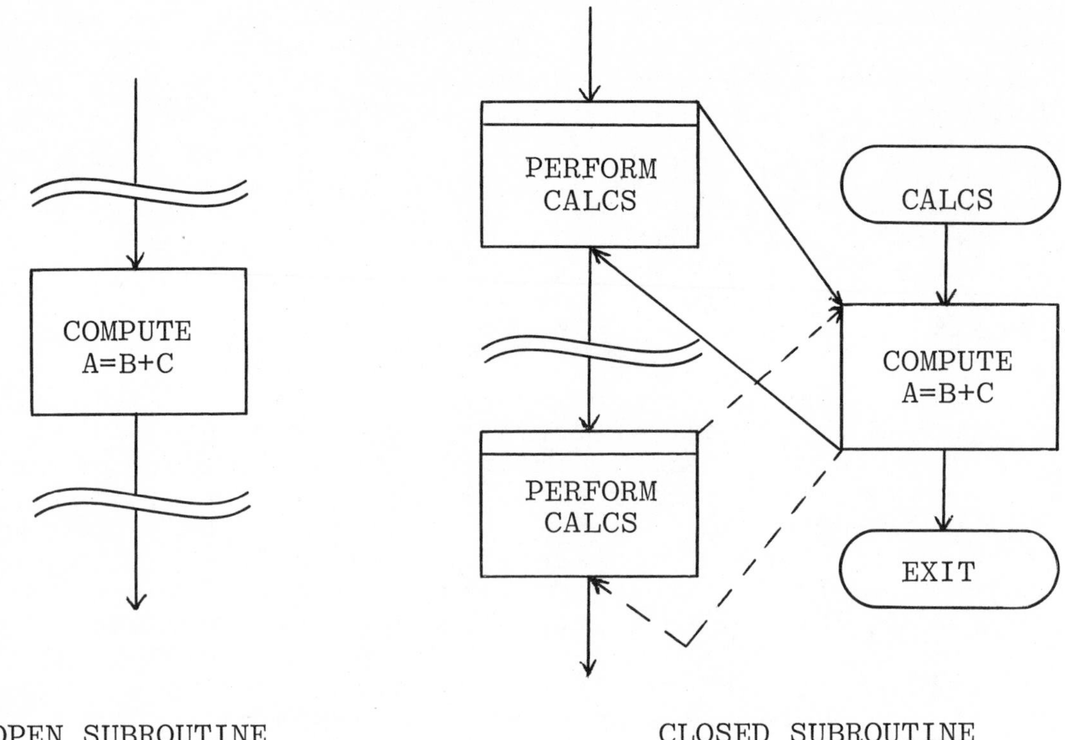

Figure 5-18

In the open version the code is written into the main portion or mainline of the program as it is needed. If it were needed at three different places in the program then the code would be duplicated at each point where it is needed. In the closed version PERFORM indicates that at this point in the logic the subroutine is to be executed. Control goes to whatever routine is being performed and does everything that is in that routine. After the routine has been completed, control is returned to the next symbol or instruction following the PERFORM that invoked the routine. This is shown in Figure 5-18 by the solid and dotted lines. The solid lines show one execution of the CALC routine. The dotted lines show another execution of the same routine at another point in the program.

It is also worth noting how the subroutine itself is depicted when it is a closed subroutine. The first symbol is always a terminal symbol with the name of the subroutine. The last symbol is always a terminal symbol with EXIT (or RETURN) in it. EXIT (or RETURN) indicates a return to the mainline logic immediately following where the subroutine was invoked. Although it is common in some shops to find the word RETURN the word EXIT is by far more prevalent. In the next section you will see how closed routines can readily be applied to headings.

HEADINGS

Headings are descriptive information at the top of a page that indicate what the report is and what information is contained on the page. Headings may be quite simple or very complex. For our purposes we will start with only the simplest of headings. We will only read one card and print it under an appropriate heading and then stop. This flowchart is shown in Figure 5-19.

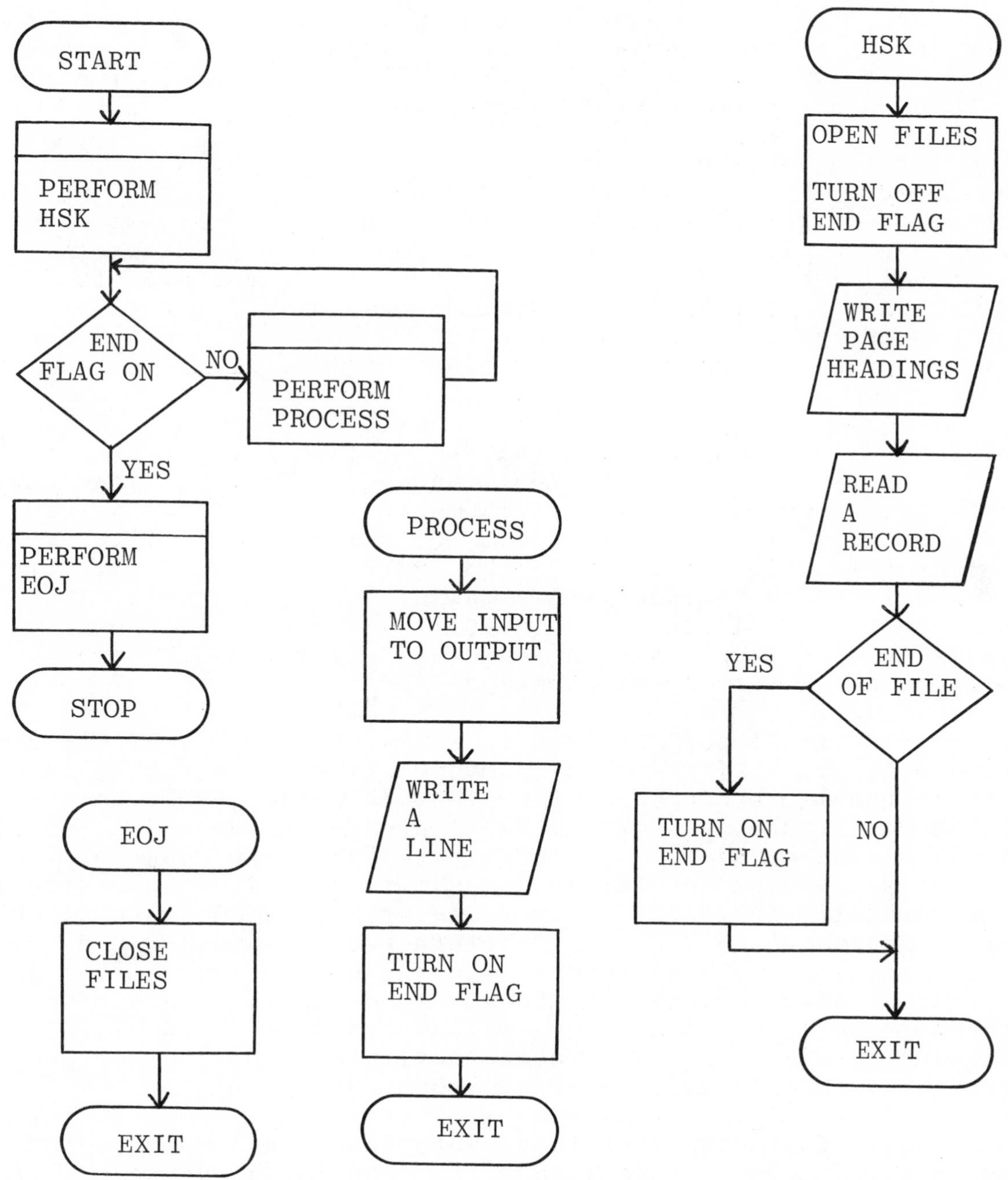

Figure 5-19

It is much more realistic, however, to assume that there will be many cards coming in and that the possibility of forms overflow may exist (that is, we may need more than one page for the output). Forms overflow means that the end of page has been reached and that before any more detail lines are printed the paper should be ejected to a new page and the headings should be printed on the new page. For our purposes we will print up to 12 lines on any page before going to the next page. The logic for this can be seen in Figure 5-20.

It varies with the actual language being used to implement the flowchart how you skip to the top of a new page. We will only infer that any heading routine will first skip to the top of a new page before printing any headings. Therefore, when the routine or symbol says WRITE PAGE HEADINGS, it infers that this is to be done at the top of a new page.

Notice that the line counter in Figure 5-20 was initially set to 12. This is to make sure that heads will appear at the top of the first page since we are producing headings if the line count > 11. There are many approaches to printing the first set of headings but this is one of the easiest methods. It will not produce a set of useless headings if the file is not present and does not require the use of switches (presented in Chapter 6) to control their being printed.

In following through the flowchart, after each card is read and found to be a data card (that is we find the END FLAG to be off) we test to see if the line count > 11. If the line count is not > 11, we move the input items to the output areas and write the detail line. After each detail line is written we increment the line count by 1, thus reflecting the total detail lines printed on the page. If, on any pass through the logic, the line count > 11, the page is full. According to the specifications we set up, when the page is full (12 lines printed) we need to eject to a new page and print another set of headings.

It is also important to note that the test for line count being > 11 came before building or printing the output line. This is usually preferable to prevent an extra set of headings from being produced. For instance, presume we have just printed the 12th line on a page and incremented the line counter. If we now check the line counter we would find it > 11. According to plan we would eject to a new page and print another set of headings. Following this we would return to read another record. If we find that we have reached the end of the input file, our flowchart indicates that we should close the files and stop. Thus we have a set of headings which we did not need. This will be pointed out again in the next section which discusses headings for both overflow and control breaks.

The next complication to be introduced into our problem is that of control break headings. If a control break occurs (that is we encounter a new division), we want to print a new set of headings to identify the new division. This may well require

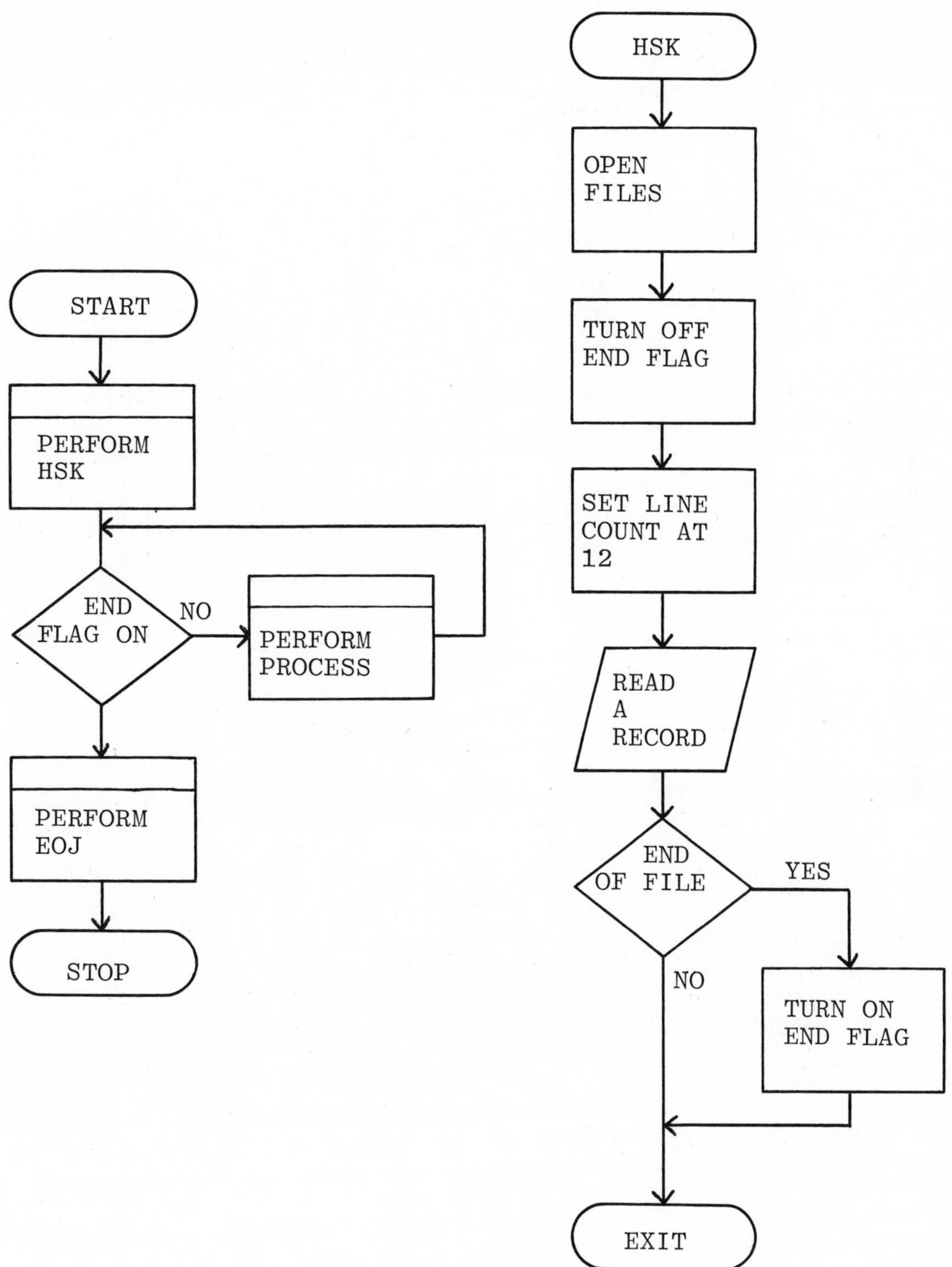
START
PERFORM
HSK
END
FLAG ON
NO
PERFORM
PROCESS
PERFORM
EOJ
STOP
HSK
OPEN
FILES
TURN OFF
END FLAG
SET LINE
COUNT AT
12
READ
A
RECORD
END
OF FILE
YES
NO
TURN ON
END FLAG
EXIT

Figure 5-20

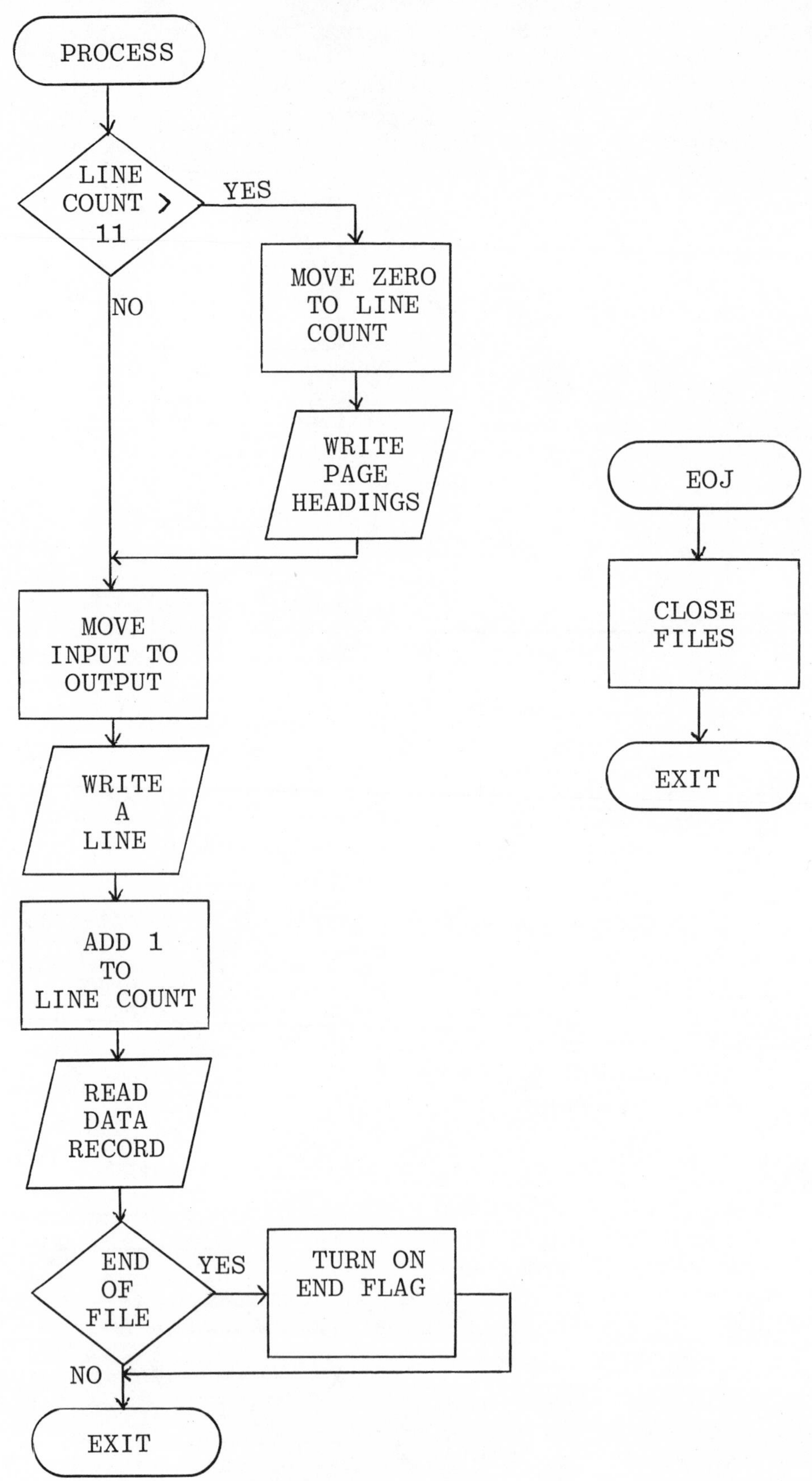

Figure 5-20 (cont.)

that certain data in the headings be updated or changed prior to printing the headings in order for them to properly reflect the new division. This is in addition to the forms overflow headings already taken into account (except that we forced a new page after 50 lines rather than waiting for the physical end of the page). This is a more efficient approach than waiting for the end of the page.

For the purposes of discussion we will develop a flowchart to produce a divisional listing of some of the data in an employee master card file. The format for this report along with the card layout for the input records are shown in Figure 5-21.

The actual flowchart for this expanded problem is shown in Figure 5-22. It incorporates new headings as each new division is encountered as well as for forms overflow. A segment of the output is shown in Figure 5-23.

As with previous flowcharts the flowchart in Figure 5-22 has the logic in separate subroutines, one of which is called PROCESS. PROCESS is in fact a closed subroutine which is performed as long as END FLAG remains off. END FLAG will continue to be off until we reach an end of file condition. The HEADS routine also is a closed subroutine which is performed when needed as a part of PROCESS. When a subroutine is performed within a subroutine that is itself being performed it is said to be nested.

The hold area for division was set to zero at the beginning of the logic. This was done to set it up for control break testing. As each new division is encountered, this hold area is updated to reflect the new division number (UPDATE DIVISION HOLD). When a new division is encountered the heading information is also updated (UPDATE HEADING AREA) to reflect the new divisional information. When control breaks are being checked there is no need to initialize the line counter. This is true because the first group will force a control break and thus give us our first set of headings. Notice in Figure 5-23 that as either control breaks (page 1 to page 2) or overflow (page 2 to page 3) occurred, headings were printed at the top of the new page. On control breaks the headings were also altered to reflect the new division.

To reiterate a point, suppose the test for line count came after building and writing a line and incrementing the line counter (as shown in Figure 5-24). What would happen if we had forms overflow occurring just before a control break? Presume that the following two cards (Figure 5-25) are the 50th and 51st cards to be processed.

As card number 50 (last card in division 1) is read, we check to see whether it is a new division and it is not. Therefore we move and print the information from card 50 and add 1 to the line counter. Next we check to see if line count is 49. It is so we eject to a new page, print the headings, reset the line count to zero and go back to read the next card.

PRINTER LAYOUT

```
         1         2         3         4         5         6
1234567890123456789012345678901234567890123456789012345678901234

                        EMPLOYEE LISTING

                           DIVISION X

                 EMPL     PAY     START                   BIRTH
EMPLOYEE NAME    NUMB    RATE     DATE      POSITION      DATE

X-------------X  XXXXX  XXX.XX  XX/XX/XX X------------X XX/XX/XX
X-------------X  XXXXX  XXX.XX  XX/XX/XX X------------X XX/XX/XX
```

CARD LAYOUT

DIVISION	EMPLOYEE NAME	EMPL NUMB	PAY RATE	START DATE			POSITION	BIRTH DATE		
				MM	DD	YY		MM	DD	YY
1	2–16	17–21	22–26	27–28	29–30	31–32	33–46	47–48	49–50	51–52

Figure 5-21

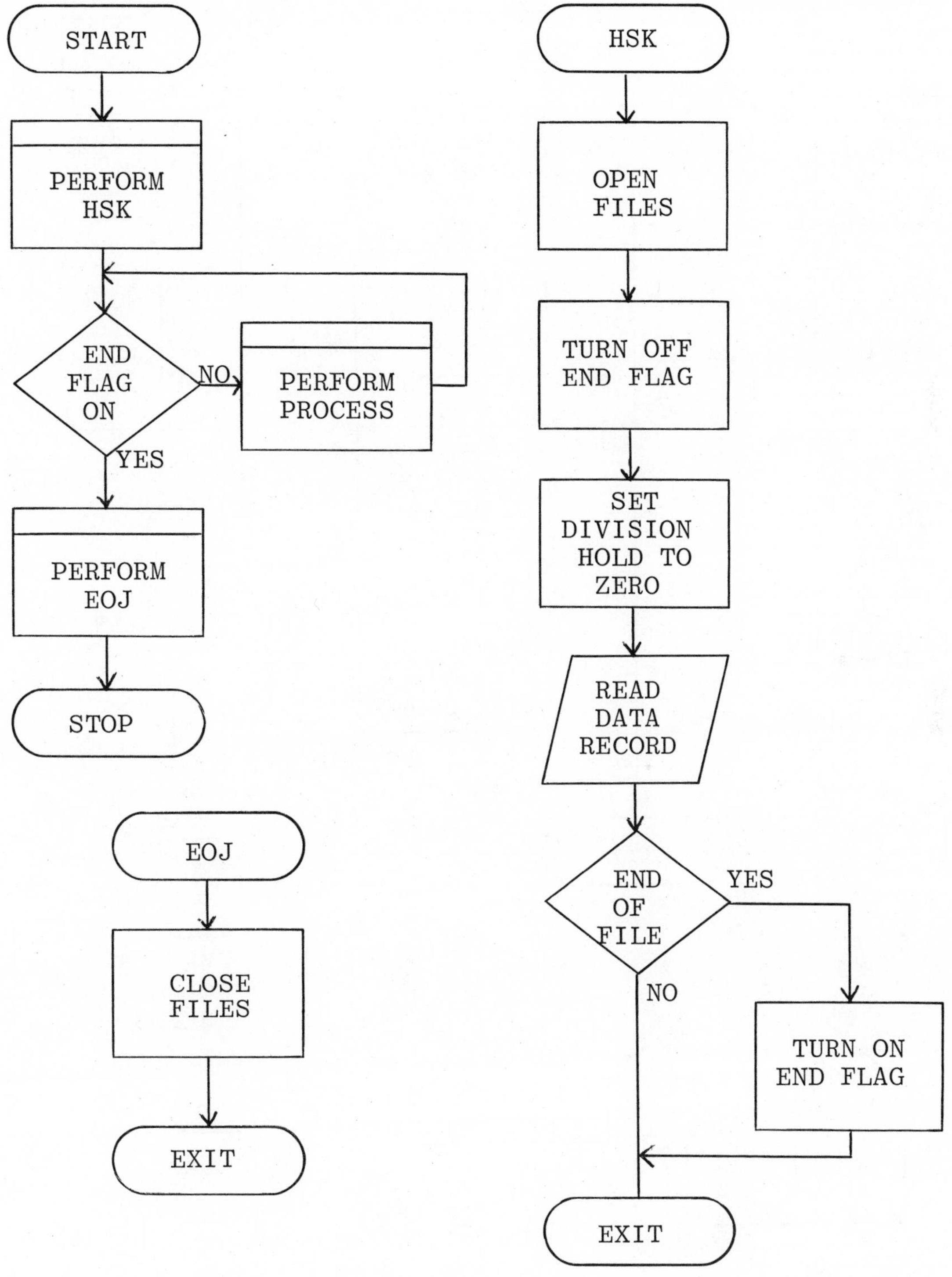

START
PERFORM HSK
END FLAG ON
NO
PERFORM PROCESS
YES
PERFORM EOJ
STOP
EOJ
CLOSE FILES
EXIT
HSK
OPEN FILES
TURN OFF END FLAG
SET DIVISION HOLD TO ZERO
READ DATA RECORD
END OF FILE
YES
NO
TURN ON END FLAG
EXIT

Figure 5-22

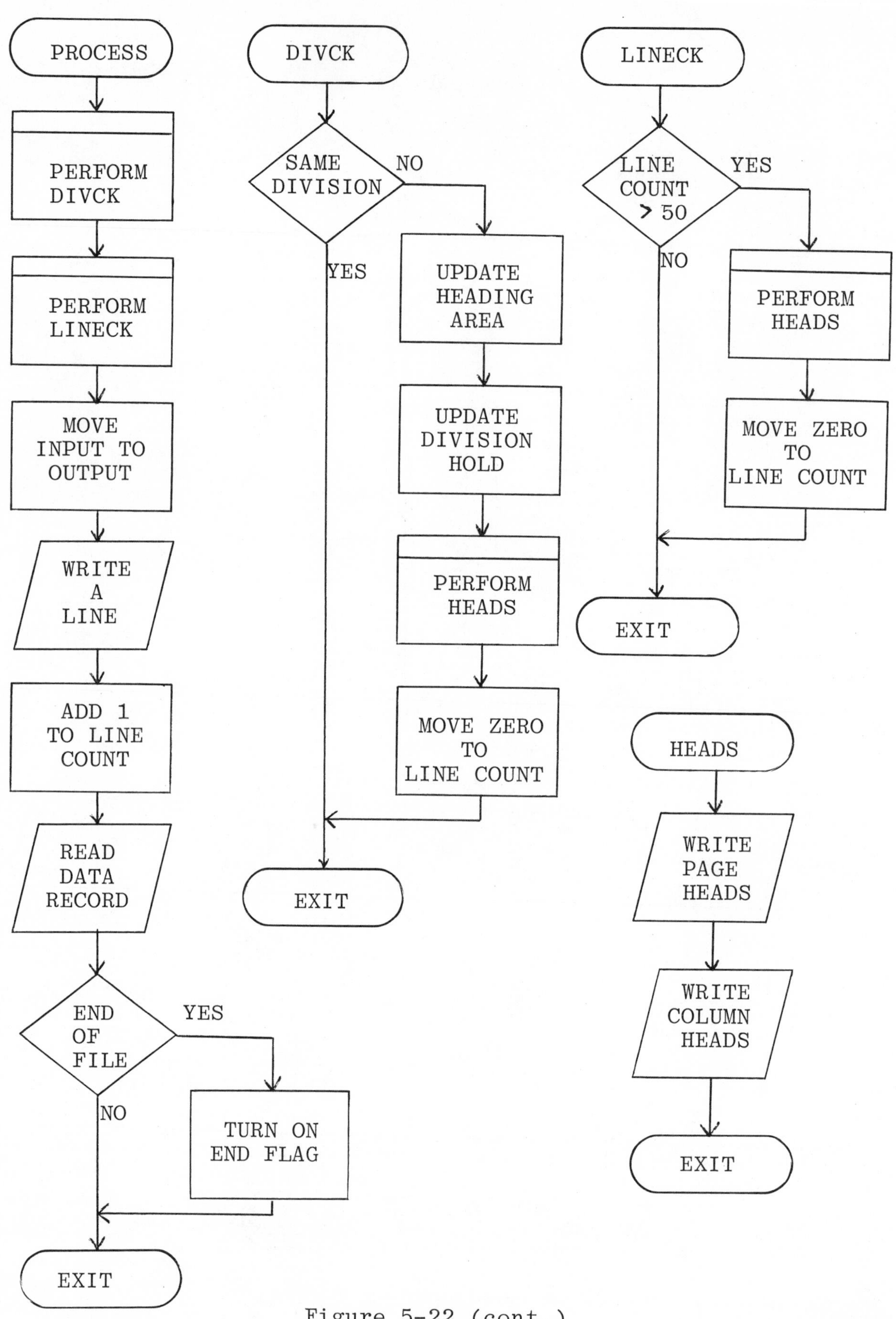

Figure 5-22 (cont.)

EMPLOYEE LISTING

DIVISION 1

EMPLOYEE NAME	EMPL NUMB	PAY RATE	START DATE	POSITION	BIRTH DATE
SANDRA ABBOTT	21374	600.00	08/13/69	SECRETARY	07/21/35
CINDY BABCOCK	42071	525.00	10/14/70	SECRETARY	11/18/40
THOMAS CONWICKE	39462	725.00	04/27/73	SALESMAN	02/15/50
JAMES DAVIDS	78525	825.00	09/11/71	SALESMAN	06/25/42
GRACE EVERETT	10274	750.00	11/22/75	SALESMAN	09/04/51
ED FRANKLIN	82443	800.00	03/19/72	SALESMAN	12/17/48
BARB GAREIS	57224	490.00	06/10/76	CLERK	02/13/57
WILSON HINGLS	68392	980.00	12/28/64	MANAGER	10/22/34
SALLY SMITH	90874	570.00	06/01/71	CLERK	10/23/56

- -

EMPLOYEE LISTING

DIVISION 2

EMPLOYEE NAME	EMPL NUMB	PAY RATE	START DATE	POSITION	BIRTH DATE
MARGE ISAACSON	42375	650.00	11/12/62	SECRETARY	05/13/39
BEVERLY JONES	84962	600.00	02/22/70	SECRETARY	10/18/44
CLAUDIA KENT	73214	580.00	05/17/74	SECRETARY	09/07/49
BILL LAWSON	27536	740.00	09/07/73	SALESMAN	11/12/52
SAMEUL MILLER	58947	810.00	03/19/77	SALESMAN	12/02/55
ROBERTA NELSON	93271	750.00	10/02/69	SALESMAN	01/30/48
SUE OBRYCKI	60725	900.00	04/15/74	SALESMAN	08/07/51
ROBERT PETERS	30341	830.00	06/25/66	SALESMAN	02/06/42
TERRENCE RUTH	21896	770.00	12/30/62	SALESMAN	10/25/38
CHARLES SMITH	62184	680.00	10/13/71	SALESMAN	08/30/45
SALLY THOMAS	15423	480.00	07/10/75	CLERK	11/14/55
JOE ULRICH	35792	495.00	04/05/74	CLERK	04/07/54

- -

EMPLOYEE LISTING

DIVISION 2

EMPLOYEE NAME	EMPL NUMB	PAY RATE	START DATE	POSITION	BIRTH DATE
SANDOR VASQUEZ	57562	890.00	07/13/70	SALESMAN	05/12/42
AL WILSON	73836	880.00	09/29/71	SALESMAN	07/22/44
THOMAS YOUNG	36243	995.00	11/17/68	MANAGER	12/15/39

Figure 5-23

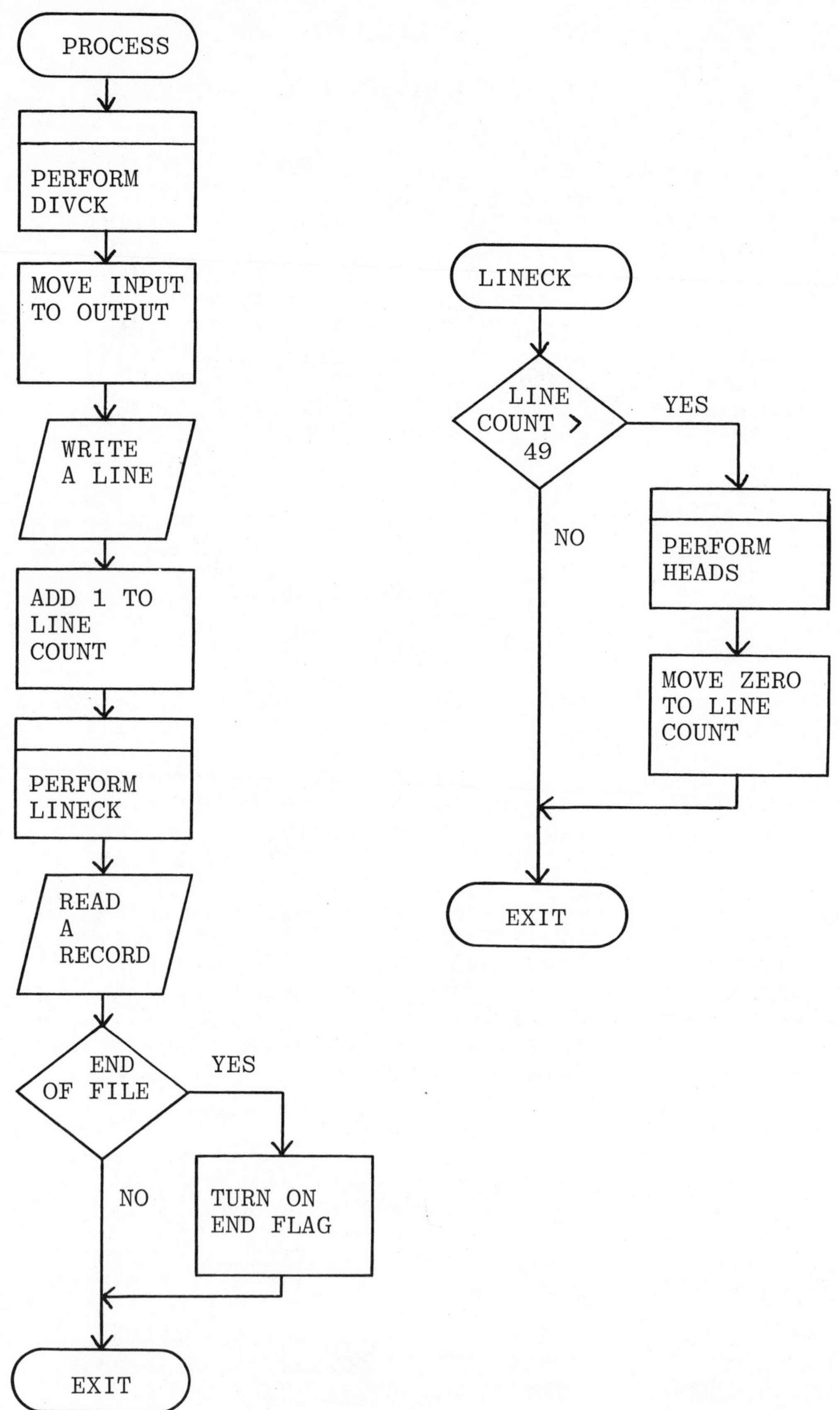

PROCESS
PERFORM DIVCK
MOVE INPUT TO OUTPUT
WRITE A LINE
ADD 1 TO LINE COUNT
PERFORM LINECK
READ A RECORD
END OF FILE
YES
NO
TURN ON END FLAG
EXIT
LINECK
LINE COUNT > 49
YES
NO
PERFORM HEADS
MOVE ZERO TO LINE COUNT
EXIT

Figure 5-24

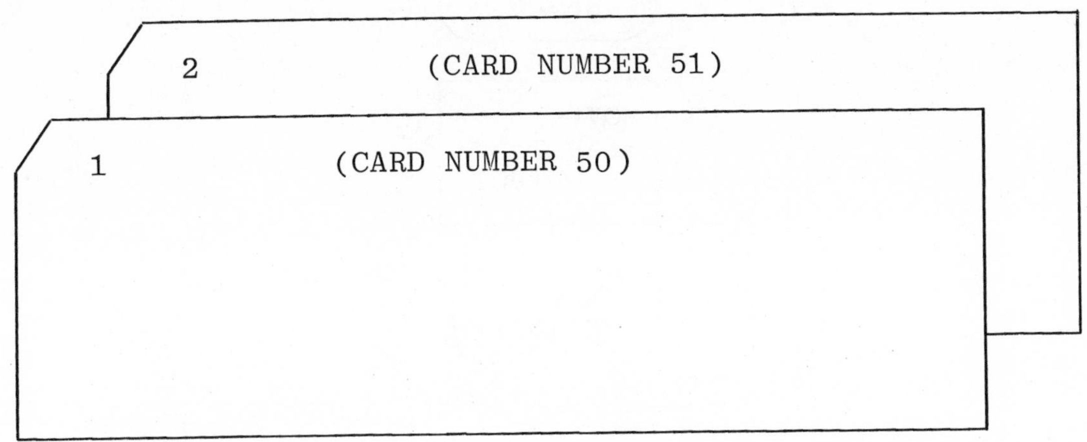

Figure 5-25

When we read card no. 51 (first card in division 2) we check to see if it is a new division. We find that it is and therefore update the headings, update the hold area, eject to a new page, print the new heads and continue on with moving and printing the data from card 51. We now have an extra, and useless, set of headings for division 1. This again is why it is usually better to check for overflow prior to building and printing a detail line.

The same heading routine is used as an internal closed subroutine (both page and column headings) for forms overflow and control break situations. In the HEADS routine we showed two write symbols to produce all the page and column headings as well as zeroing the line counter. If desired this could be expanded to show each of the actions that are needed to do this process (which is not a bad idea for the beginning student). If you wanted to show the expanded version it would appear as shown in Figure 5-26.

The same type of expansion could be done for moving the input fields to the output fields and for beginning students this is a good idea. It points out that in the actual programming of the problem each of these input fields needs to be individually moved to the output fields one at a time. Once they have all been moved then the completely built output record can be written.

The next chapter will introduce the ideas of producing various types of totals and the use of switches.

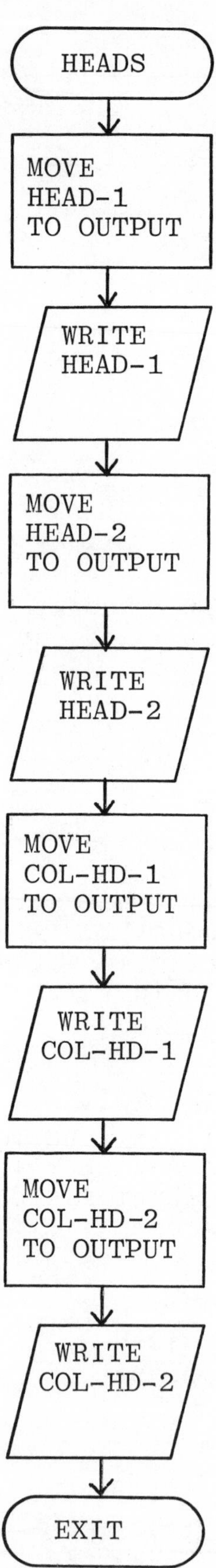

HEADS
MOVE HEAD-1 TO OUTPUT
WRITE HEAD-1
MOVE HEAD-2 TO OUTPUT
WRITE HEAD-2
MOVE COL-HD-1 TO OUTPUT
WRITE COL-HD-1
MOVE COL-HD-2 TO OUTPUT
WRITE COL-HD-2
EXIT

Figure 5-26

REVIEW QUESTIONS

Matching

A. Housekeeping routine

B. Closed subroutines

C. Closing files

D. Subroutine

E. Forms overflow

F. Open subroutines

G. Opening files

H. Exit

I. External subroutine

J. Control break

_______ 1. Indicated by a change in the value of a control field.

_______ 2. A subroutine written outside the mainline logic of the program but within the program.

_______ 3. The last symbol in the flowcharting of a closed subroutine.

_______ 4. A group of instructions that perform some identifiable part of the overall problem.

_______ 5. Reaching the end of the page on a printed report

_______ 6. Performed once at the beginning of a program.

_______ 7. A subroutine written within the mainline logic of the program.

_______ 8. Produces trailer labels as one of its functions if they are needed.

_______ 9. A subroutine that is not a part of the program itself.

_______ 10. Responsible for processing header labels if they exist.

True/False

T F 1. Accessing the current date and reading header records is typically part of housekeeping.

T F 2. Control breaks provide a method of breaking a report down into more meaningful units.

T F 3. Hold areas for determining control breaks are initialized at the beginning of the program and do not have to be modified during processing.

T F 4. Internal subroutines may be open or closed.

T F 5. Open subroutines are typically used when the routine will be executed at many different points in the program.

T F 6. External subroutines are typically shown by the following symbol:

T F 7. After a closed subroutine is finished control is automatically passed back to the statement following the one that invoked it.

T F 8. Headings usually appear only at the top of the first page in a report.

T F 9. It is necessary to update the heading information when headings are being produced because of either a control break or forms overflow.

Exercises

1. Draw a flowchart (including opening and closing files) to read a deck of cards and print their contents. Provision should be made for forms overflow but no headings.

2. Same as Number 1 except provide for headings. There is one page heading and two column headings.

3. Draw a flowchart to produce a departmentalized listing of an employee file. The file is in sequence on department number. Headings should be provided at the top of each new page and each new department should start at the top of a new page. The name of the department is in the headings and can be found by reading the employee file.

Discussion questions

1. Describe what a housekeeping routine is, where it is found, when it is used and what it is used for in a program.

2. Describe what control breaks are and what types of activities usually take place on a control break.

3. Differentiate between open and closed subroutines.

4. Differentiate between internal and external subroutines.

5. Describe what headings are and how and when they are put on a report.

CHAPTER 6

Single Input Programs 2

OBJECTIVES

As a result of studying this chapter the student should be able to perform the following activities.

1. Describe the difference between single and multiple level totals.
2. Indicate typical types of items that might be used as single level totals.
3. Indicate when and why single level totals need to be reset to zero.
4. Describe what is meant to roll totals and show how this is accomplished.
5. Describe how a first card switch or indicator can be used in conjunction with control break totals.
6. Describe the difference between minor, intermediate and major level breaks.
7. Describe what is meant by higher level breaks always forcing all lower level breaks.

INTRODUCTION

One of the most common needs in programming is to keep track of various totals. Totals can be broken down into two basic groups - single level and multiple level totals.

SINGLE LEVEL TOTALS

One of the easiest single level totals used is an item count. It is used to determine the number of records processed. This total can be produced as a file is created. It may be recorded at the end of the file in a special record. This is one place where a user label (as presented in Chapter 5) might be used. Each time the file is processed in the future the records can be counted during processing and compared with the count in the special record to see whether records were gained or lost. As an example let's read an employee master file and write it on magnetic tape with a record-count record as the last record created on the tape. This process is shown in Figure 6-1.

As each record is read and written on tape the counter is incremented by 1. Note that this counter was set to zero at the beginning of the flowchart (in HSK). When we reach the end of the input file this counter will have a value equal to the number of records processed. This value is then written as a separate record on the tape prior to closing the files and stopping. Figure 6-2 shows how a record-count record might look on tape.

Another very common single level total is that of a page counter. Most reports have their pages sequentially numbered from 1 to n with n being the number of the last page. The page counter is typically set to zero in the housekeeping routine and incremented in the heading routine. From the previous chapter you will remember an operation that updated the headings. One of the actions to update headings is to increment the page counter. This is shown in Figure 6-3.

Totals are not limited to page numbers or record counts. Let's take a look at a program which processes a payroll summary file. A separate page will be produced at the end of the report showing the totals for the entire company. Figure 6-4 shows the format of the records in the payroll summary file and a printer layout of the report to be produced. The *'s indicate those fields for which totals are to be accumulated. Figure 6-5 shows the logic needed to produce the report.

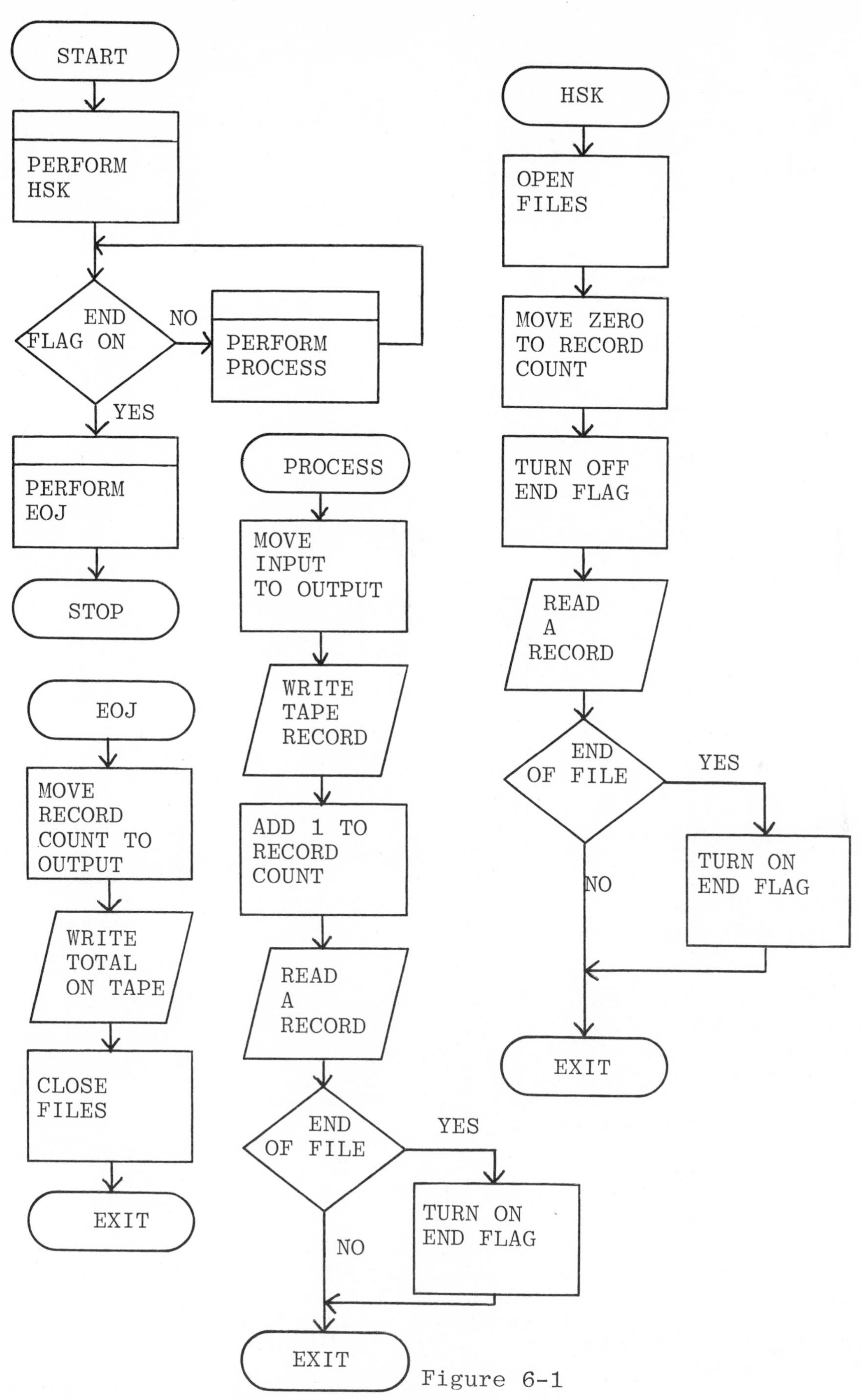
START
PERFORM HSK
END FLAG ON
NO
PERFORM PROCESS
YES
PERFORM EOJ
STOP
EOJ
MOVE RECORD COUNT TO OUTPUT
WRITE TOTAL ON TAPE
CLOSE FILES
EXIT
PROCESS
MOVE INPUT TO OUTPUT
WRITE TAPE RECORD
ADD 1 TO RECORD COUNT
READ A RECORD
END OF FILE
YES
TURN ON END FLAG
NO
EXIT
HSK
OPEN FILES
MOVE ZERO TO RECORD COUNT
TURN OFF END FLAG
READ A RECORD
END OF FILE
YES
TURN ON END FLAG
NO
EXIT
Figure 6-1

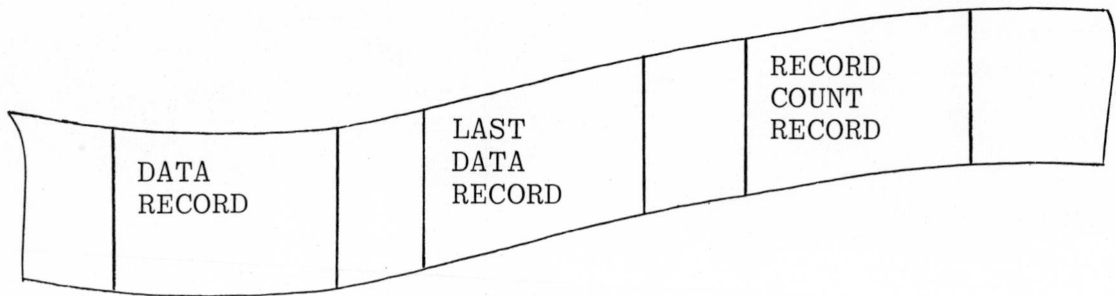

Figure 6-2

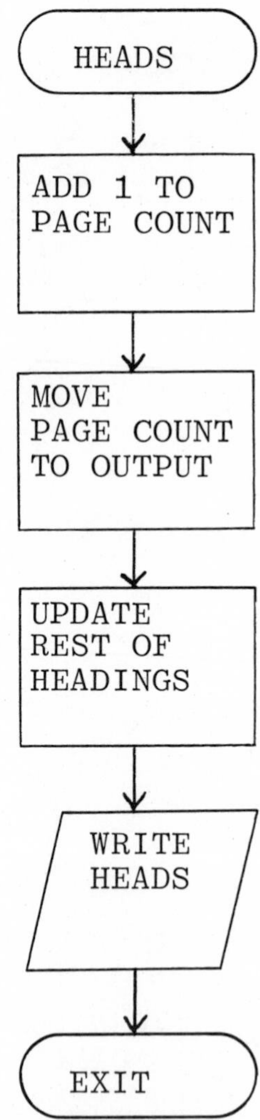

Figure 6-3

CARD LAYOUT

RECORD CODE	EMPLOYEE NUMBER	GROSS PAY *	FED TAX *	STATE TAX *	FICA *	CREDIT UNION *	HOSP INS *	NET PAY *	DIVISION	DEPARTMENT	UNUSED		
9 9	9 9 9 9 9 9 9 9 9	9 9 9 9 9 9	9 9 9 9 9 9	9 9 9 9 9	9 9 9 9 9	9 9 9 9 9	9 9 9 9 9	9 9 9 9 9 9	9	9	9 9 9 9 9 9 9 9	9 9 9 9 9 9 9 9	9 9 9 9
1 2	3 4 5 6 7 8 9 10 11	12 13 14 15 16 17	18 19 20 21 22 23	24 25 26 27 28	29 30 31 32 33	34 35 36 37 38	39 40 41 42 43	44 45 46 47 48 49	50	51	52 53 54 55 56 57 58 59	60 61 62 63 64 65 66 67	77 78 79 80

PRINTER LAYOUT

```
         1         2         3         4         5         6         7         8
12345678901234567890123456789012345678901234567890123456789012345678901234567890

                          PAYROLL SUMMARY REPORT

                                DIVISION X                         PAGE XXX

             EMPLOYEE      GROSS         FED       STATE           CREDIT     HOSP       NET
 DEPT         NUMBER        PAY          TAX         TAX     FICA   UNION      INS       PAY

   X    XXX-XX-XXXX   XXXX.XX    XXXX.XX   XXX.XX   XXX.XX   XXX.XX   XXX.XX   XXXX.XX
   X    XXX-XX-XXXX   XXXX.XX    XXXX.XX   XXX.XX   XXX.XX   XXX.XX   XXX.XX   XXXX.XX


                          PAYROLL SUMMARY TOTALS

                    GROSS PAY                     XXX,XXX.XX
                    FEDERAL TAX                   XXX,XXX.XX
                    STATE TAX                      XX,XXX.XX
                    FICA                           XX,XXX.XX
                    CREDIT UNION                   XX,XXX.XX
                    HOSPITAL INSURANCE             XX,XXX.XX
                    NET PAY                       XXX,XXX.XX
```

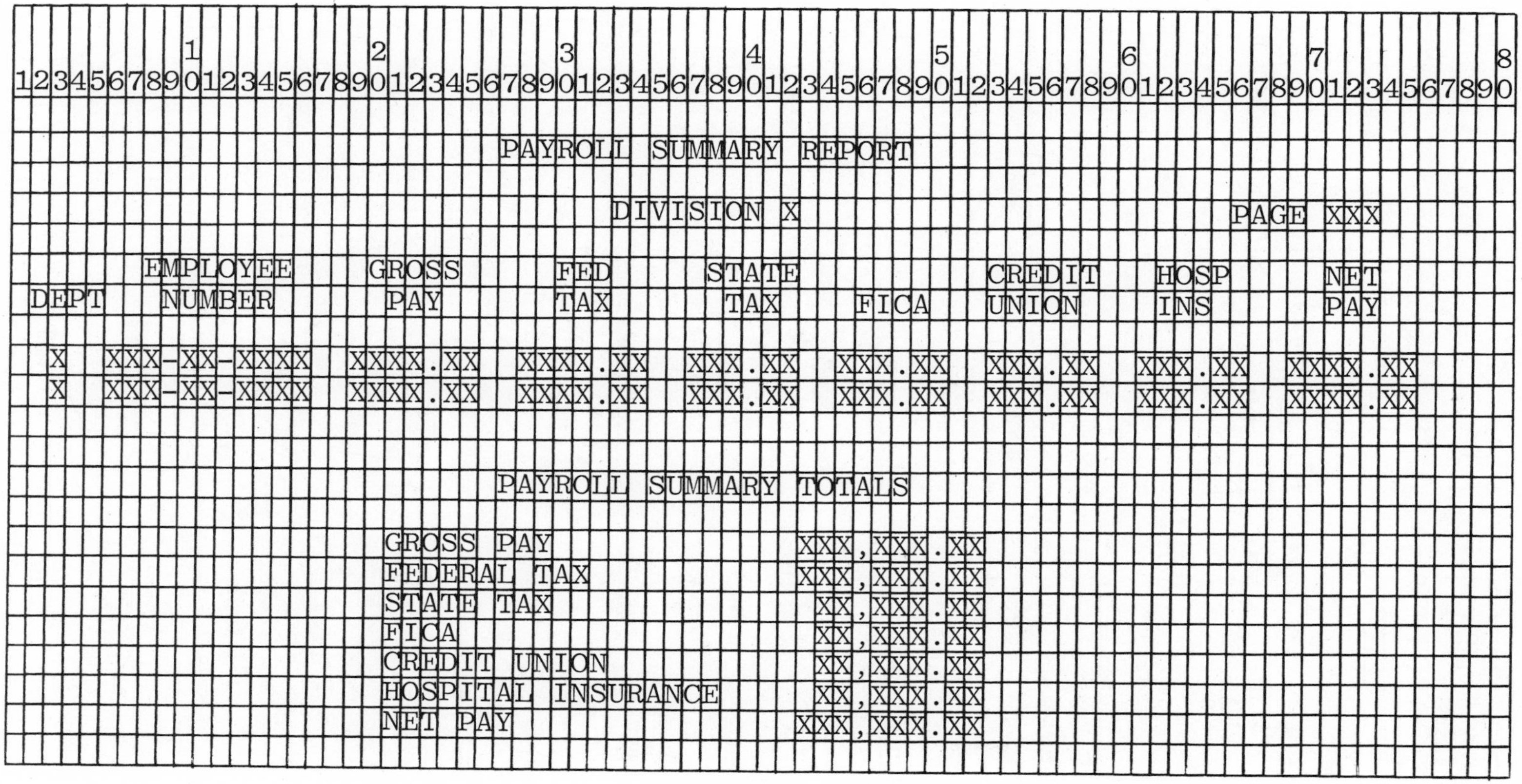

Figure 6-4

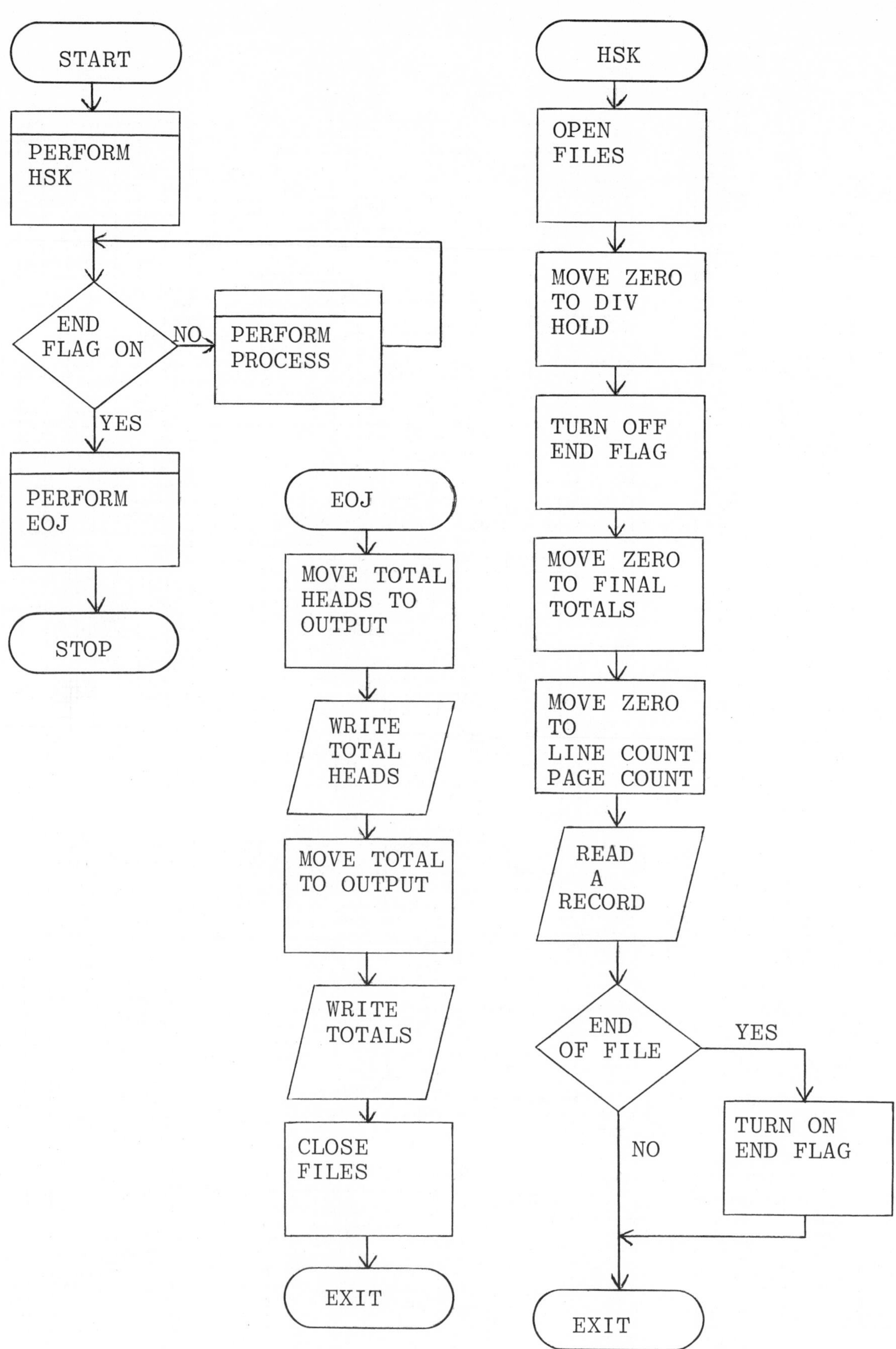
START
PERFORM HSK
END FLAG ON
NO
PERFORM PROCESS
YES
PERFORM EOJ
STOP
EOJ
MOVE TOTAL HEADS TO OUTPUT
WRITE TOTAL HEADS
MOVE TOTAL TO OUTPUT
WRITE TOTALS
CLOSE FILES
EXIT
HSK
OPEN FILES
MOVE ZERO TO DIV HOLD
TURN OFF END FLAG
MOVE ZERO TO FINAL TOTALS
MOVE ZERO TO LINE COUNT PAGE COUNT
READ A RECORD
END OF FILE
YES
TURN ON END FLAG
NO
EXIT

Figure 6-5

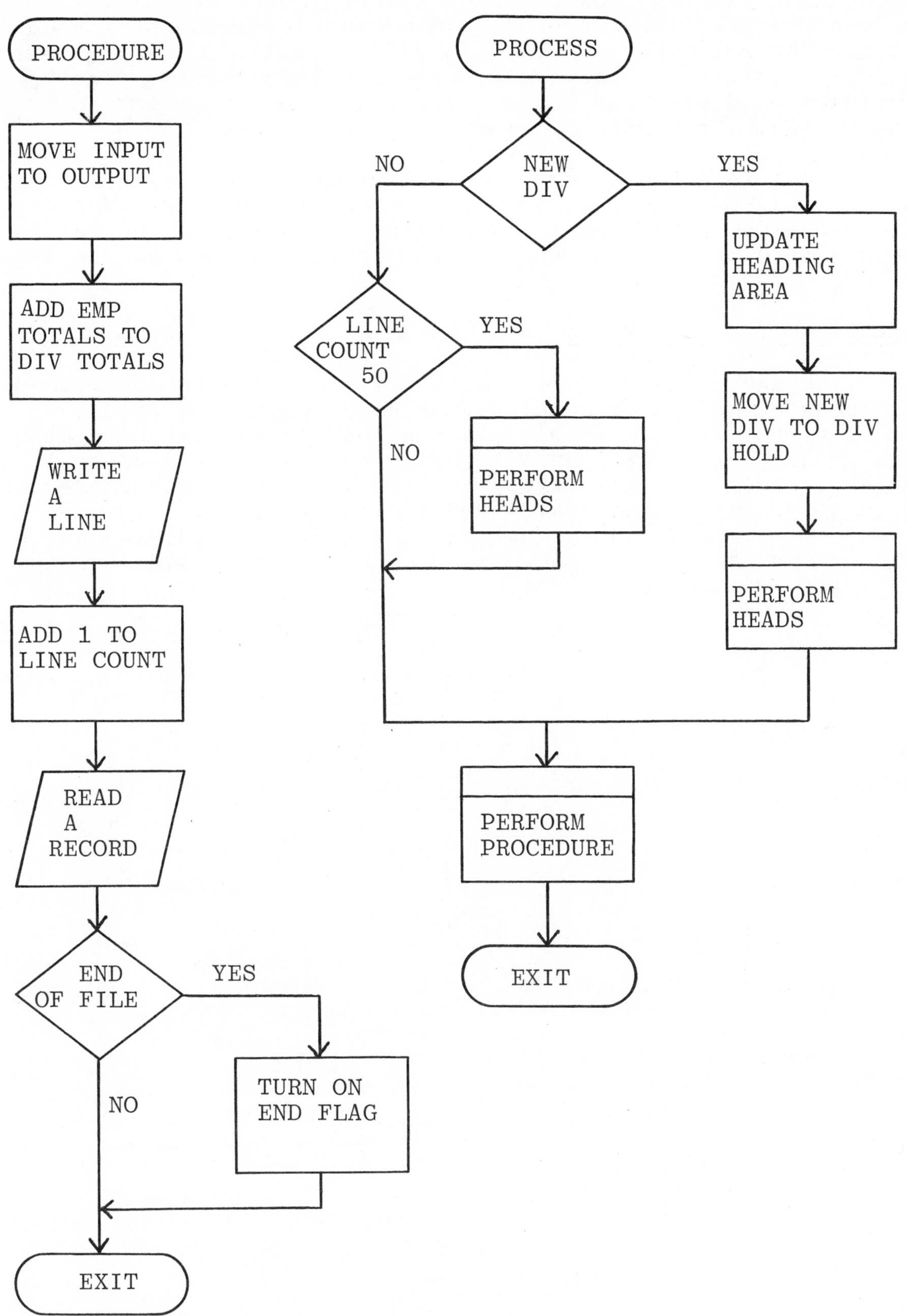

Figure 6-5 (cont.)

It is important to note that the division (DIV) hold area is updated with the new division number when a new division is encountered (see Figure 6-5). This step is always performed when a control break occurs. If it were not done, every record past the first division would cause a control break. The division hold area was also initialized to zero in HSK to insure that the first division will cause a break to occur.

The totals are accumulated at the same time (either before or after is OK) the data is moved from the input record area to the output record area. The actual printing of the totals occurs as a part of the EOJ routine after the data has been read.

RESETTING SINGLE LEVEL TOTALS

The above examples of single level totals are continuously incremented and never reset to any given value. There is another type of single level total called control break totals that require the total area to be reset each time a control break occurs. For this type of total let's switch our previous problem around a little and produce the listing by division with the totals of the deductions developed and printed at the end of each division. There will be no final totals developed this time (see Figure 6-6).

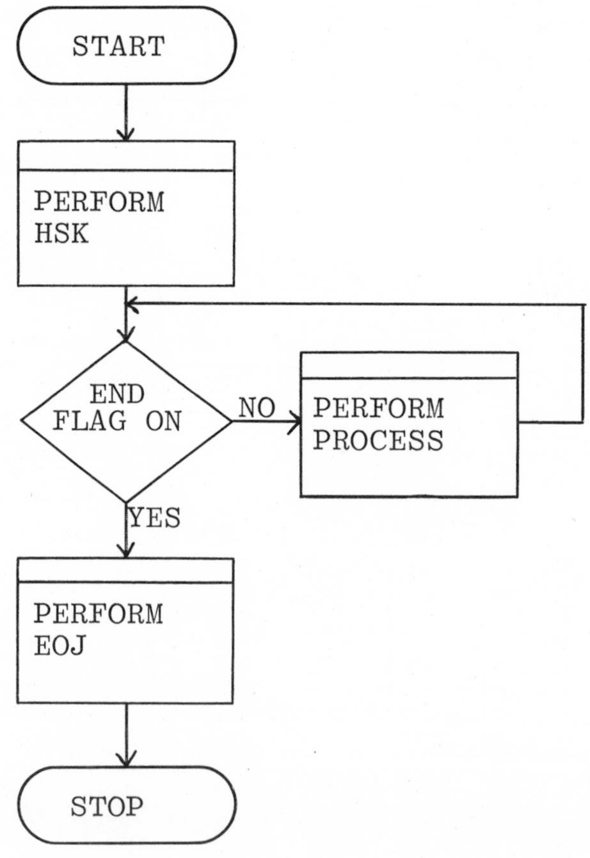

Figure 6-6

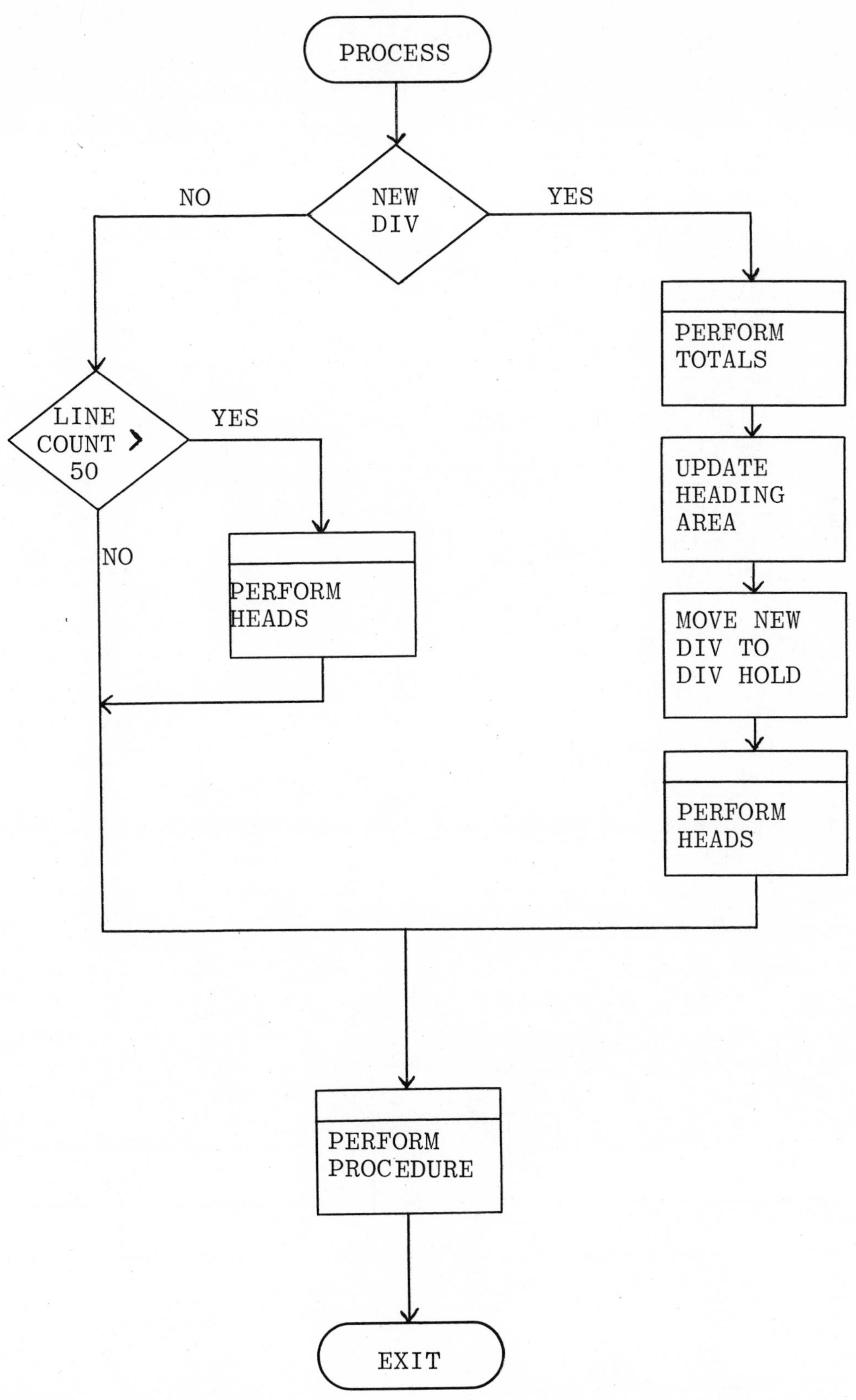

Figure 6-6 (cont.)

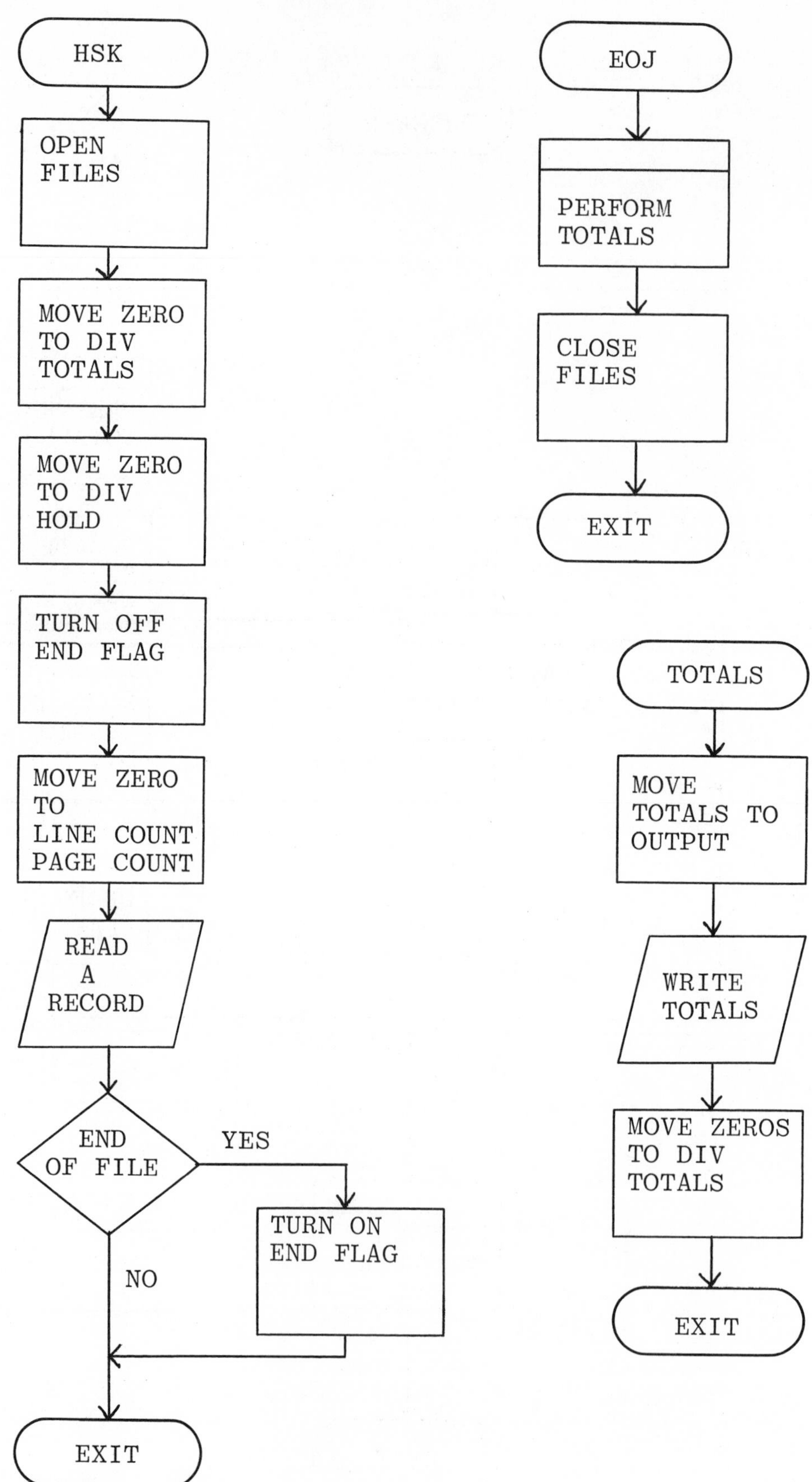

Figure 6-6 (cont.)

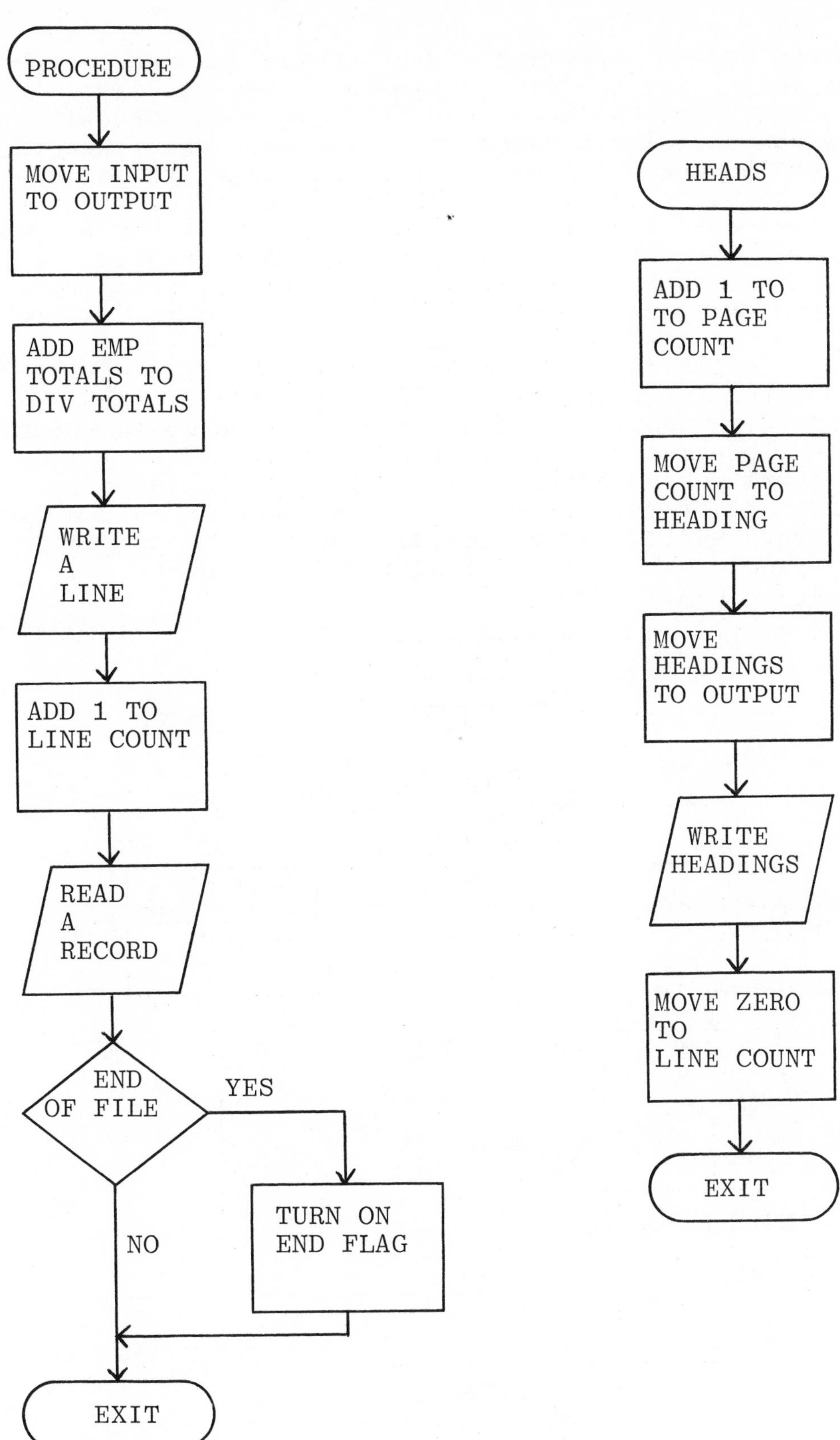

Figure 6-6 (cont.)

Notice in Figure 6-6 that the TOTALS routine is done as each new division (DIV) is encountered and also at the end of job. The end of job execution of the routine is necessary to obtain the totals for the last division. When the last card of the last division has been read there is no opportunity to test for a new division because the YES branch was taken to terminate processing. It is therefore necessary to include the TOTALS routine prior to closing the files and terminating the program. Also note that the division totals were set to zero within the TOTALS routine (after they had been printed) to get them ready for the next division. If the division totals were not reset to zero the division totals would be cumulative.

There is still one problem present in the flowchart. What happens when the first card is read? Following it through the flowchart we find that it is a new division and we therefore are supposed to print the totals for the previous division. Whoops -- there was no previous division. While there are several ways out of this dilemma, the most common is the use of a first card switch to prevent totals on the first card read. This would change our TOTALS routine flowchart as shown in Figure 6-7.

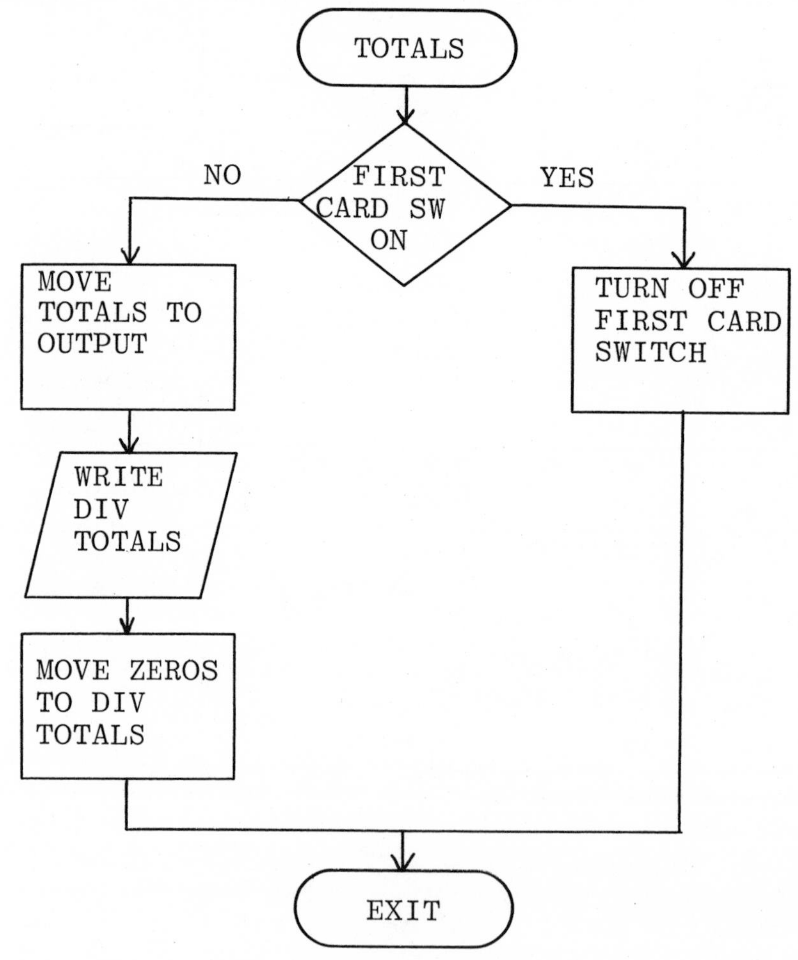

Figure 6-7

Now when the TOTALS routine is executed on the first card it will find that it is the first card and instead of printing totals it will turn off the first card switch and exit the routine. Now you ask, just where did this switch get turned on? It was turned on in a portion of the housekeeping routine at the same point we opened the files. The following segment of the housekeeping routine (HSK) shows this being done (see Figure 6-8).

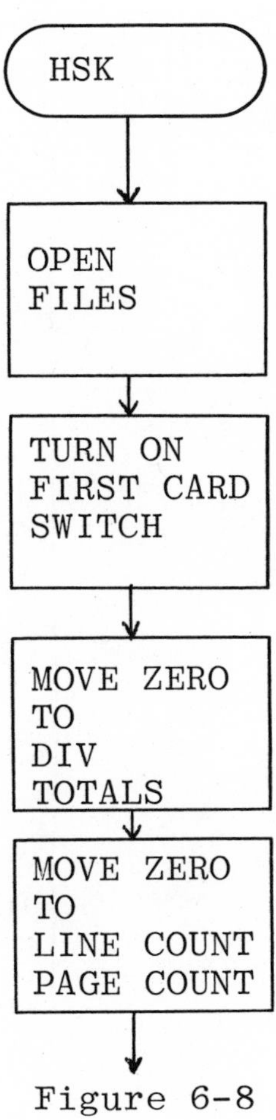

Figure 6-8

MULTIPLE LEVEL TOTALS

The next obvious extension of this is to produce both control break totals and final totals on the same report. This involves a concept of rolling totals at the time of the control break (see Figure 6-9).

Notice in the BREAK routine that after the division totals have been moved and printed they are added to the final totals, thus rolling the division totals into the final total. After being added to the final totals the division totals are set to zero to accommodate the totals for the next division. When the end of file is reached the BREAK routine is invoked to print the totals for the last group and add them to the final totals. It would, however, have been possible to do this differently by placing BREAK routine in the FINAL routine (see Figure 6-10).

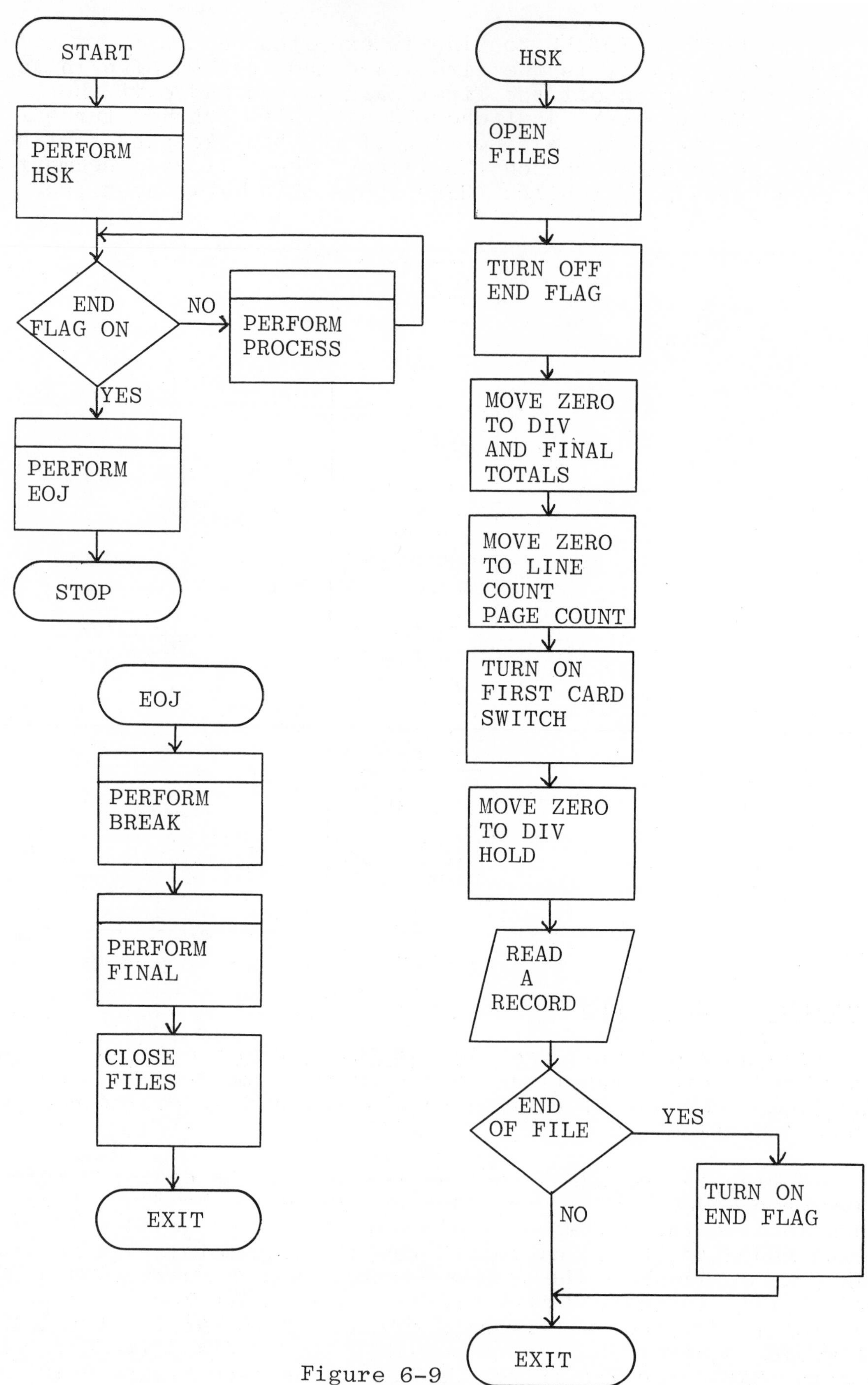
START
PERFORM HSK
END FLAG ON
NO
PERFORM PROCESS
YES
PERFORM EOJ
STOP
EOJ
PERFORM BREAK
PERFORM FINAL
CLOSE FILES
EXIT
HSK
OPEN FILES
TURN OFF END FLAG
MOVE ZERO TO DIV AND FINAL TOTALS
MOVE ZERO TO LINE COUNT PAGE COUNT
TURN ON FIRST CARD SWITCH
MOVE ZERO TO DIV HOLD
READ A RECORD
END OF FILE
YES
TURN ON END FLAG
NO
EXIT
Figure 6-9

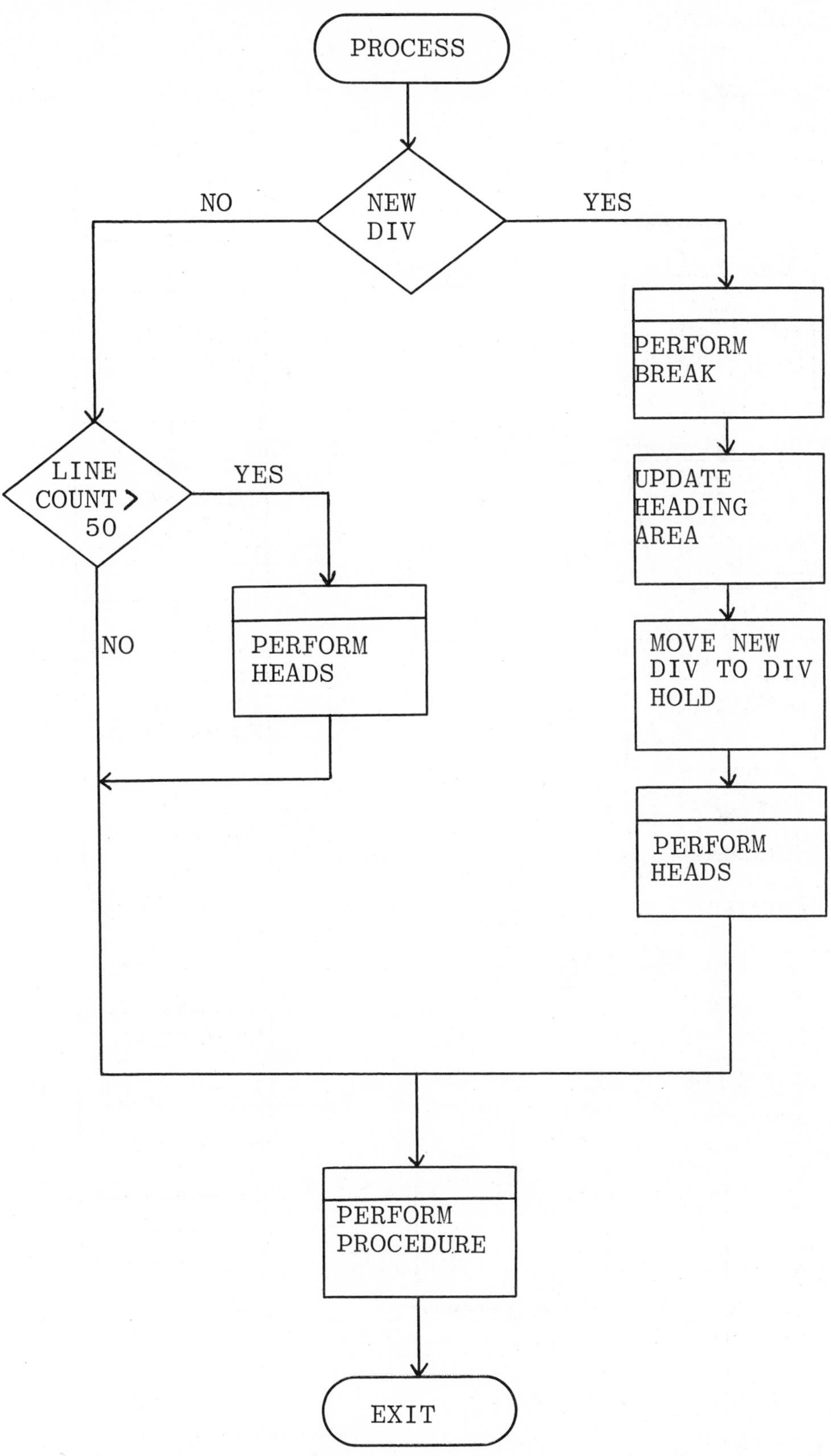

Figure 6-9 (cont.)

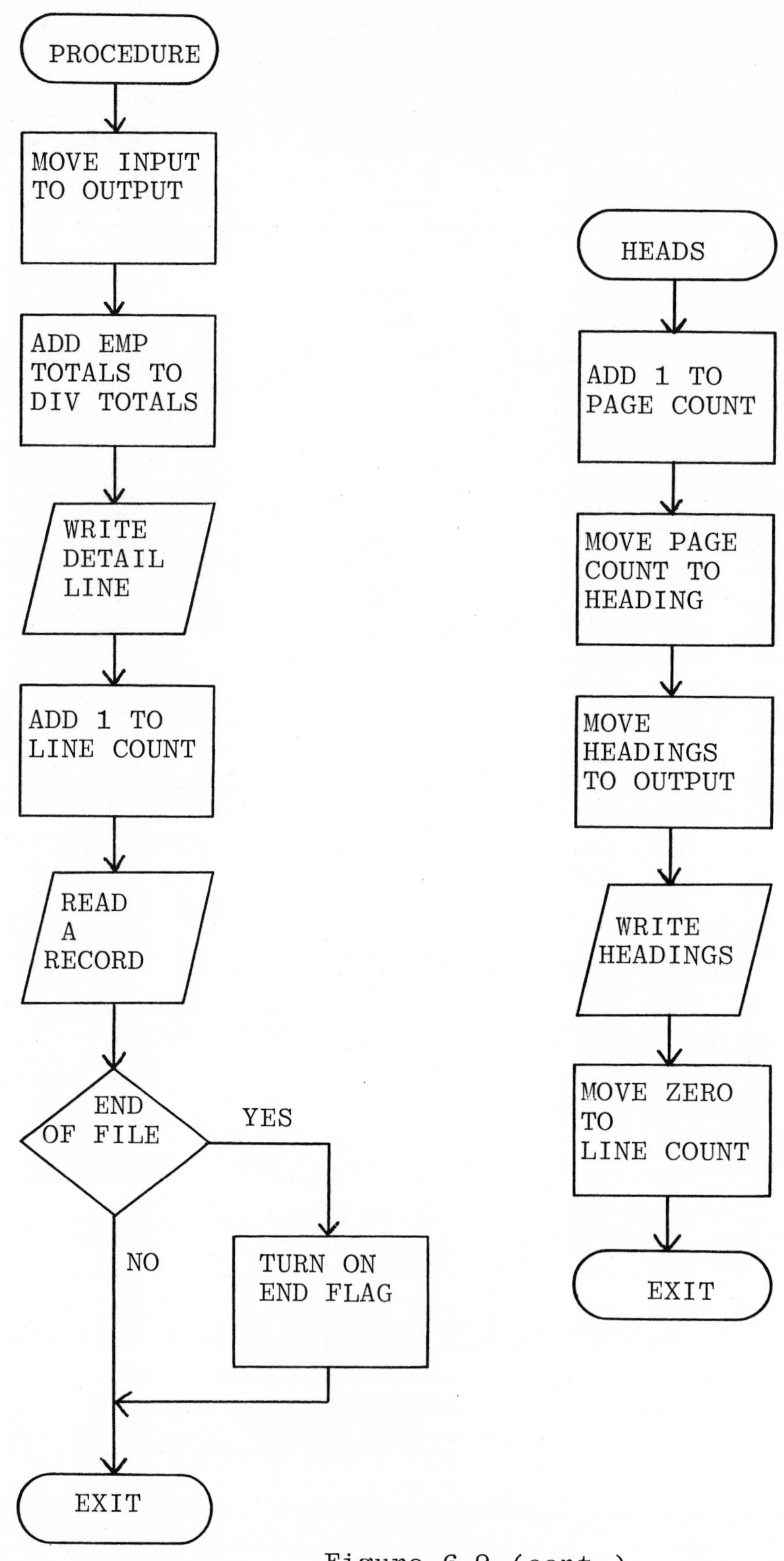

Figure 6-9 (cont.)

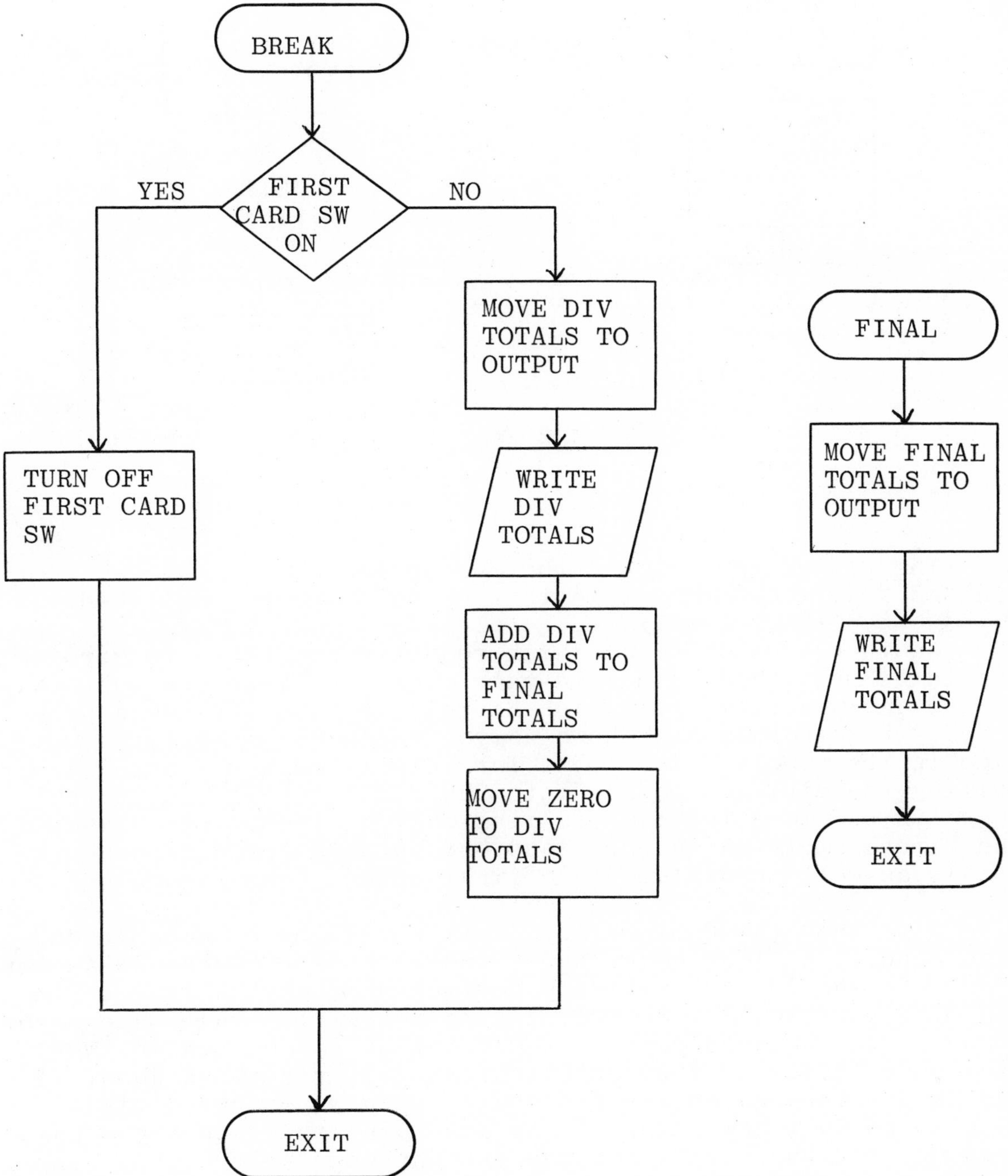

Figure 6-9 (cont.)

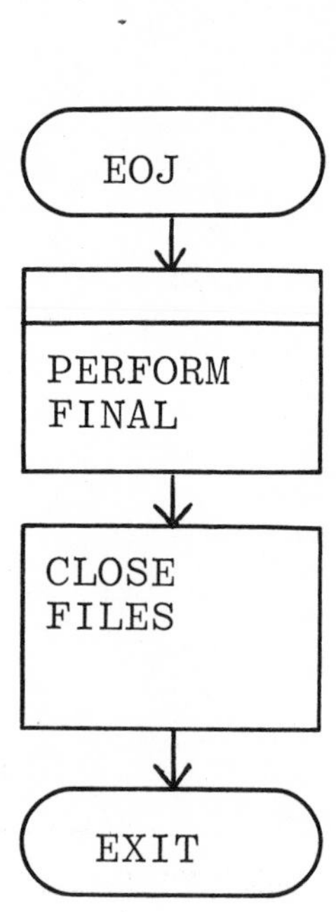

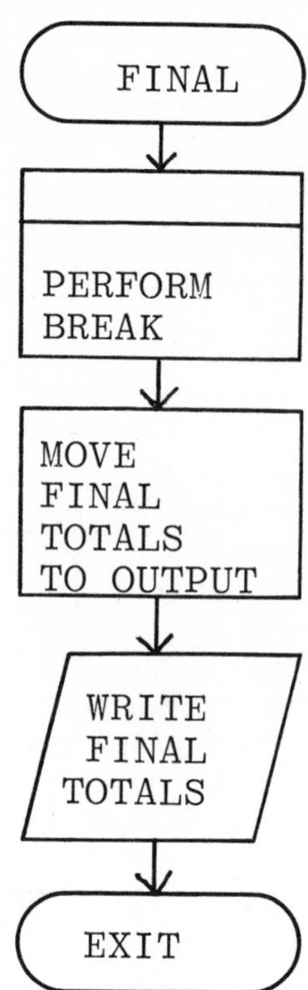

Figure 6-10

The difference between the two approaches is not as important as realizing what it is that needs to be accomplished.

Another type of total which requires resetting to zero that should be mentioned is called page totals. These are subtotals of the various items for which division totals are being produced. Page totals are shown as you reach the bottom of each page in the report. The logic for this is much the same as rolling the division totals into the final totals except that there is one more level of rolling taking place. Let's use the same example as the previous one but also produce page totals as well as division and final totals (see Figure 6-11).

Note that the PAGING routine is performed both on an end of page condition (line count > 50) and as a part of the BREAK routine. It should be relatively obvious that when we reach the end of a page we want to produce the totals for that page before going on to the next page. It may not be as obvious why we want page totals at the control break. If you think about it and follow through on the flowchart, when we change divisions we also go to a new page. If we are going to go to a new page then we need the totals for the present page before producing any division totals or the headings at the top of the next page for the new division.

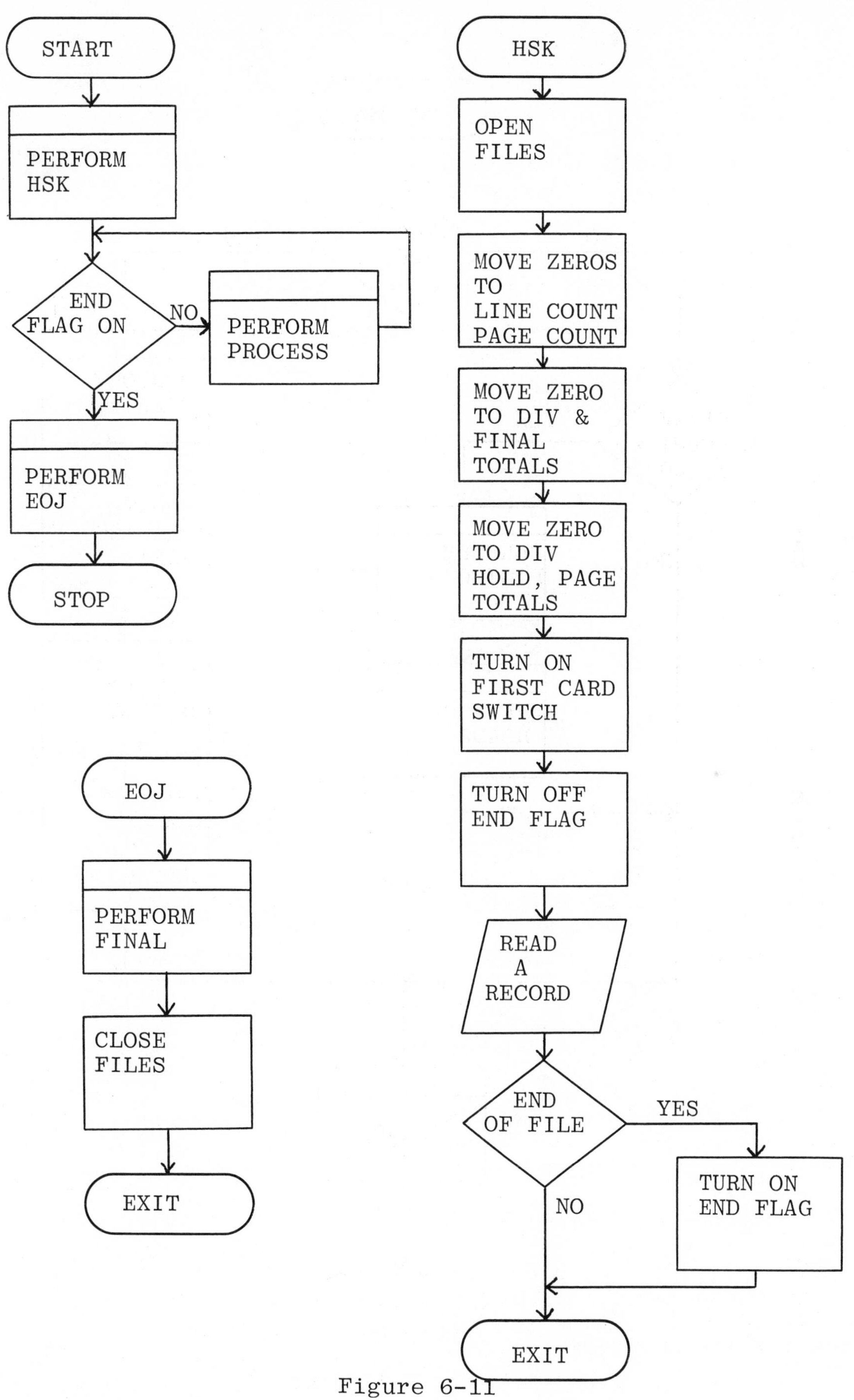
START
PERFORM HSK
END FLAG ON
NO
PERFORM PROCESS
YES
PERFORM EOJ
STOP
HSK
OPEN FILES
MOVE ZEROS TO LINE COUNT PAGE COUNT
MOVE ZERO TO DIV & FINAL TOTALS
MOVE ZERO TO DIV HOLD, PAGE TOTALS
TURN ON FIRST CARD SWITCH
TURN OFF END FLAG
READ A RECORD
END OF FILE
YES
TURN ON END FLAG
NO
EXIT
EOJ
PERFORM FINAL
CLOSE FILES
EXIT

Figure 6-11

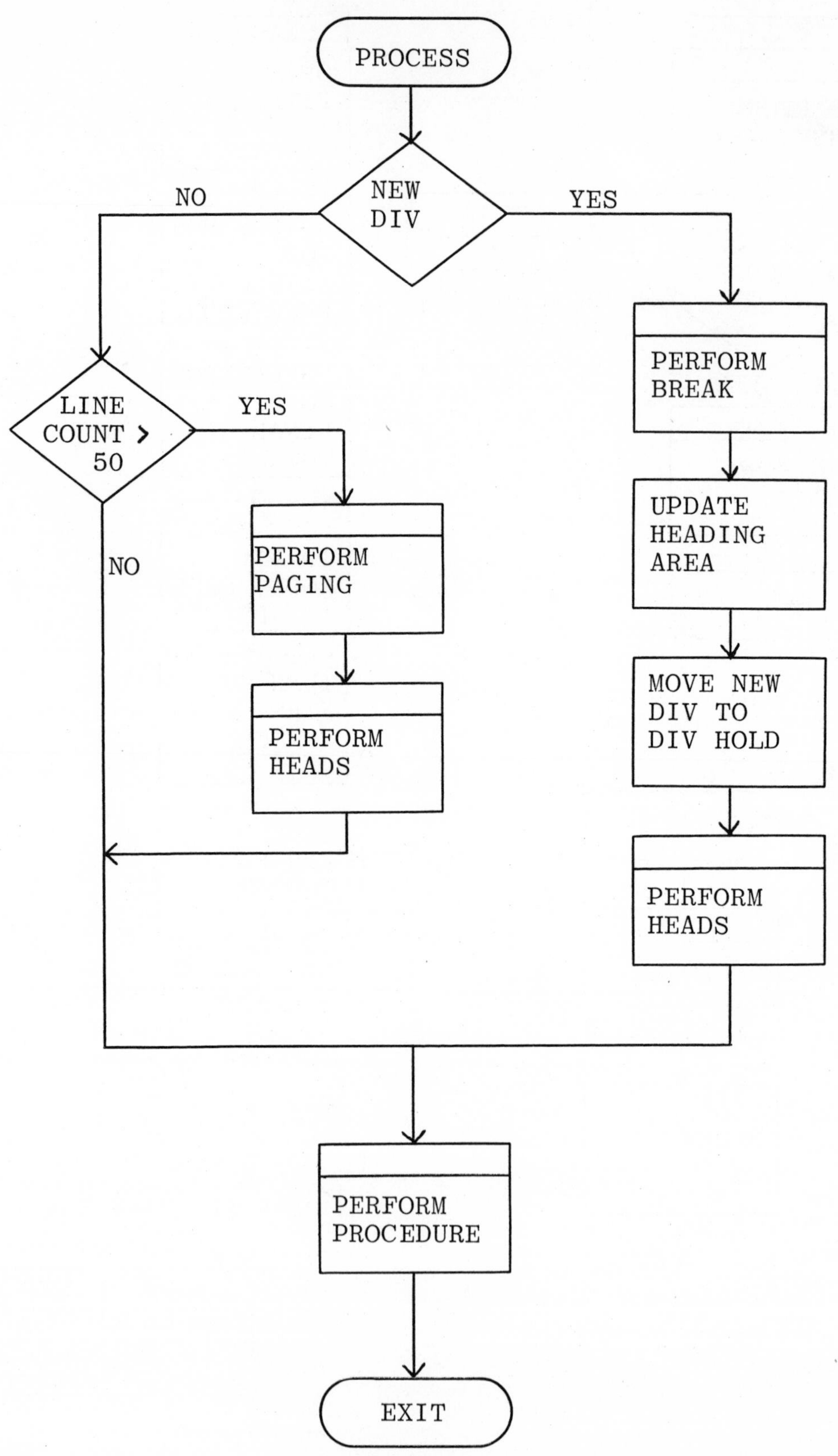

Figure 6-11 (cont.)

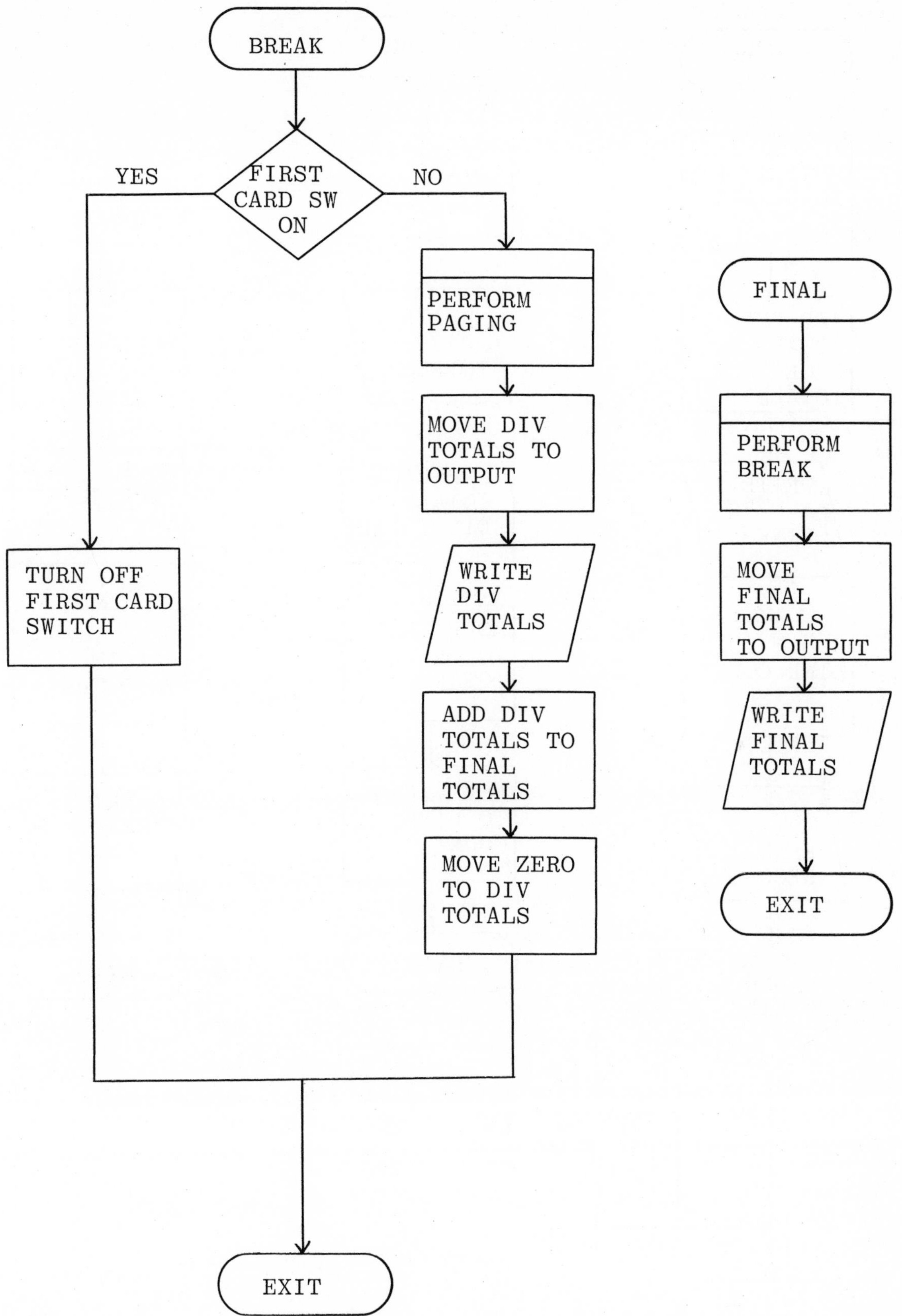

Figure 6-11 (cont.)

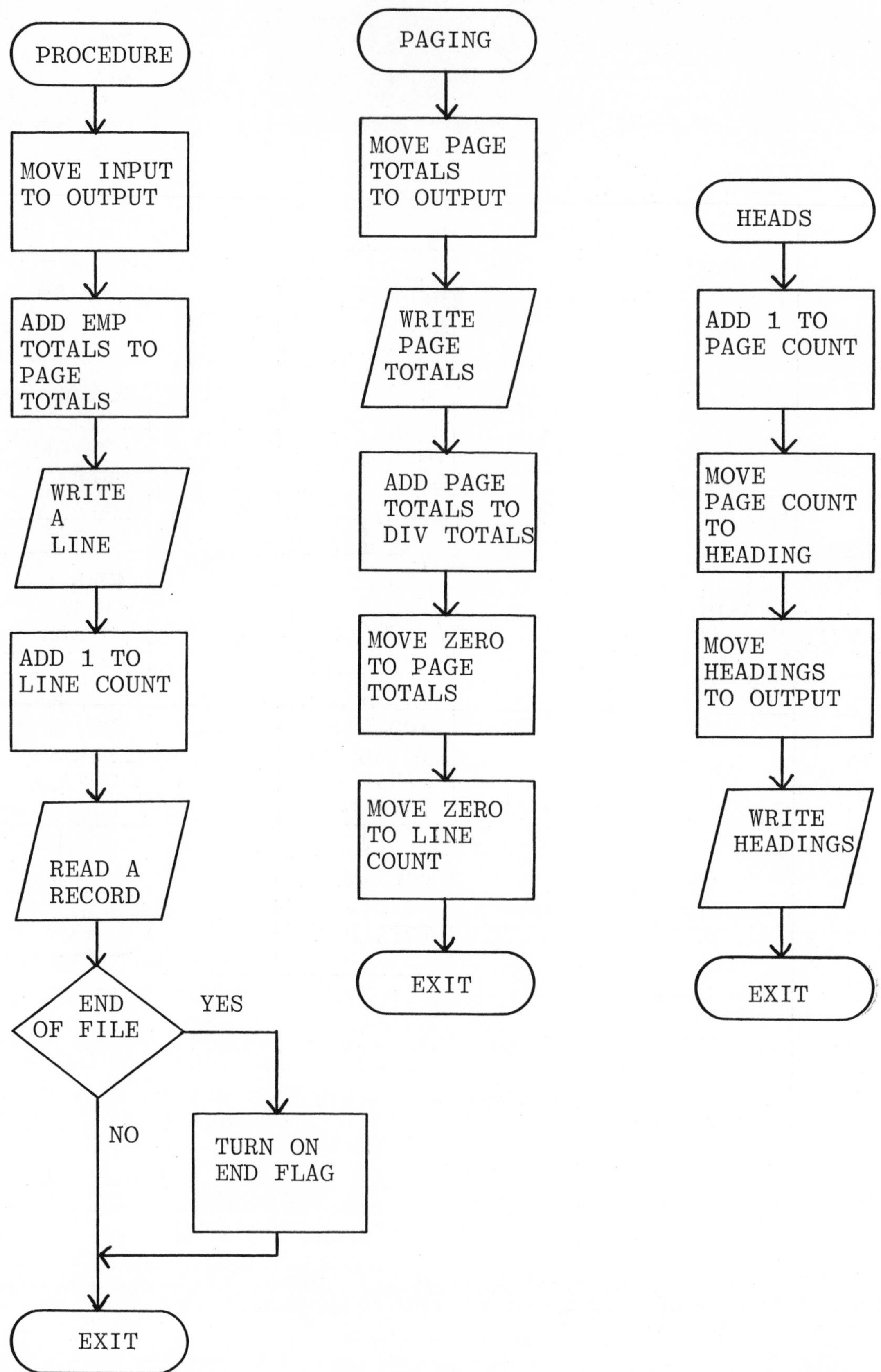

Figure 6-11 (cont.)

It is also important to notice that when the page totals are processed they are first moved and printed and then added (rolled) to the division totals. This prevents any unnecessary addition of the amounts to the division totals for each record that is processed. Saving processing steps and therefore saving time is one of the major reasons behind rolling division totals. Once again, as the page totals are rolled to the division totals, the page totals counter is reset to zero to facilitate the accumulation of the next page totals. These concepts will be further explored in the next section which covers various levels of totals.

TYPES OF MULTIPLE LEVEL TOTALS

The various types of control break totals which have been presented thus far can be grouped into three categories. These are major, intermediate and minor level totals. Grand or final level totals are not included in these three categories. If only one type of control break total is being produced (let's say division totals) then they are referred to as major level totals or major break totals.

If two levels of totals are being produced such as page totals and division totals then the one that happens the most often (page totals in our example) is the minor break total and the one that occurs least frequently (division totals) is the major break total. If you have three levels of totals the same idea is true that the most frequent total is the minor break total, the least frequent total is the major break total and the one in the middle is called the intermediate break total. Four or more levels of totals produce multiple intermediate level totals such as intermediate-1, intermediate-2, etc.

In checking for control breaks with multiple level breaks it is most efficient to check for the highest level breaks (major) first and work down to the lowest level breaks (minor). This is true since a break on any level (except minor) always forces a break to occur for all lower level items.

In our example this means that when a change in division occurs we are going to a new page for the new division and before we do we need to produce both the page totals and division totals for the division just ended. If you glance back at Figure 6-11 you can see that we checked for a change in division before checking for end of page. When a change in division occurs the first item in the BREAK routine is to PERFORM PAGING routine which produces the page totals.

Presuming a problem which has all three levels of totals (major, intermediate and minor) the following items are performed on each level of break.

Minor level break:

1. Move and print minor level totals.

2. Accumulate (roll) minor level totals to intermediate level totals.

3. Zero out minor level totals in order to allow accumulation of the next minor level group.

4. Update minor level control break hold area.

Intermediate level break:

1. Perform minor level break.

2. Move and print intermediate level totals.

3. Accumulate (roll) intermediate level totals to major level totals.

4. Zero out intermediate level totals in order to allow accumulation of the next intermediate level group.

5. Update intermediate level control break hold area.

Major level break:

1. Perform intermediate level break.

2. Move and print major level totals.

3. Accumulate (roll) major level totals to final or grand totals.

4. Zero out major level totals in order to allow accumulation of the next major level group.

5. Update the major level control break hold area.

Let's expand our example so that each division contains several departments. If we want to produce a listing of the employee data so that we have totals by page, by department, by division as well as a final total the details of this logic are shown in Figure 6-12.

Notice that each level of break performs the next lower level break. That is, if a major break (change in division) occurs the major break routine (called MAJOR) performs the intermediate level break routine (called INTER) for an implied change in department. The intermediate level break routine in turn performs the minor level break routine (called MINOR) for an implied change in the page. This is the process by which lower level breaks are forced by higher level breaks.

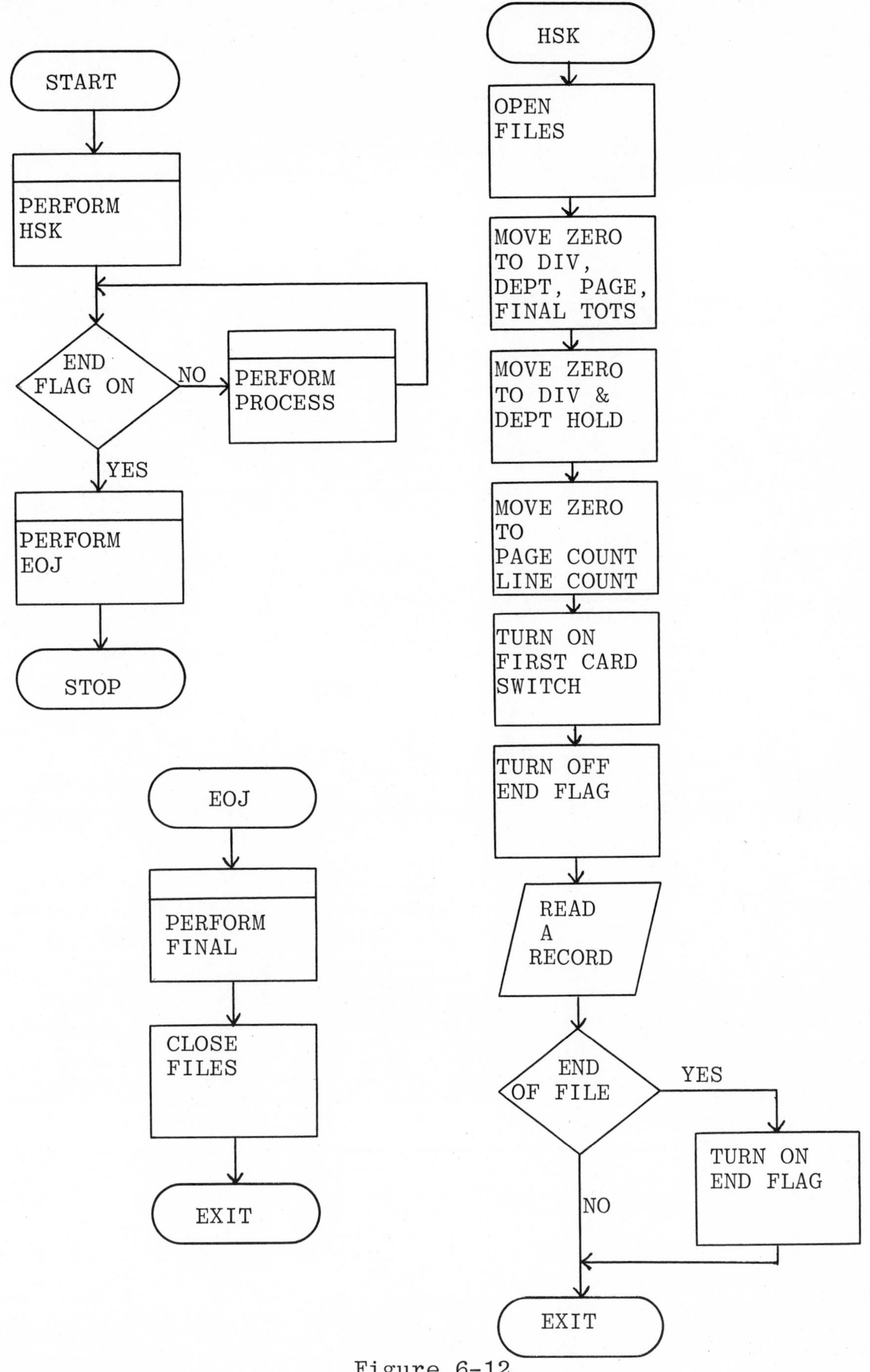
START
PERFORM
HSK
END
FLAG ON
NO
PERFORM
PROCESS
YES
PERFORM
EOJ
STOP
EOJ
PERFORM
FINAL
CLOSE
FILES
EXIT
HSK
OPEN
FILES
MOVE ZERO
TO DIV,
DEPT, PAGE,
FINAL TOTS
MOVE ZERO
TO DIV &
DEPT HOLD
MOVE ZERO
TO
PAGE COUNT
LINE COUNT
TURN ON
FIRST CARD
SWITCH
TURN OFF
END FLAG
READ
A
RECORD
END
OF FILE
YES
TURN ON
END FLAG
NO
EXIT

Figure 6-12

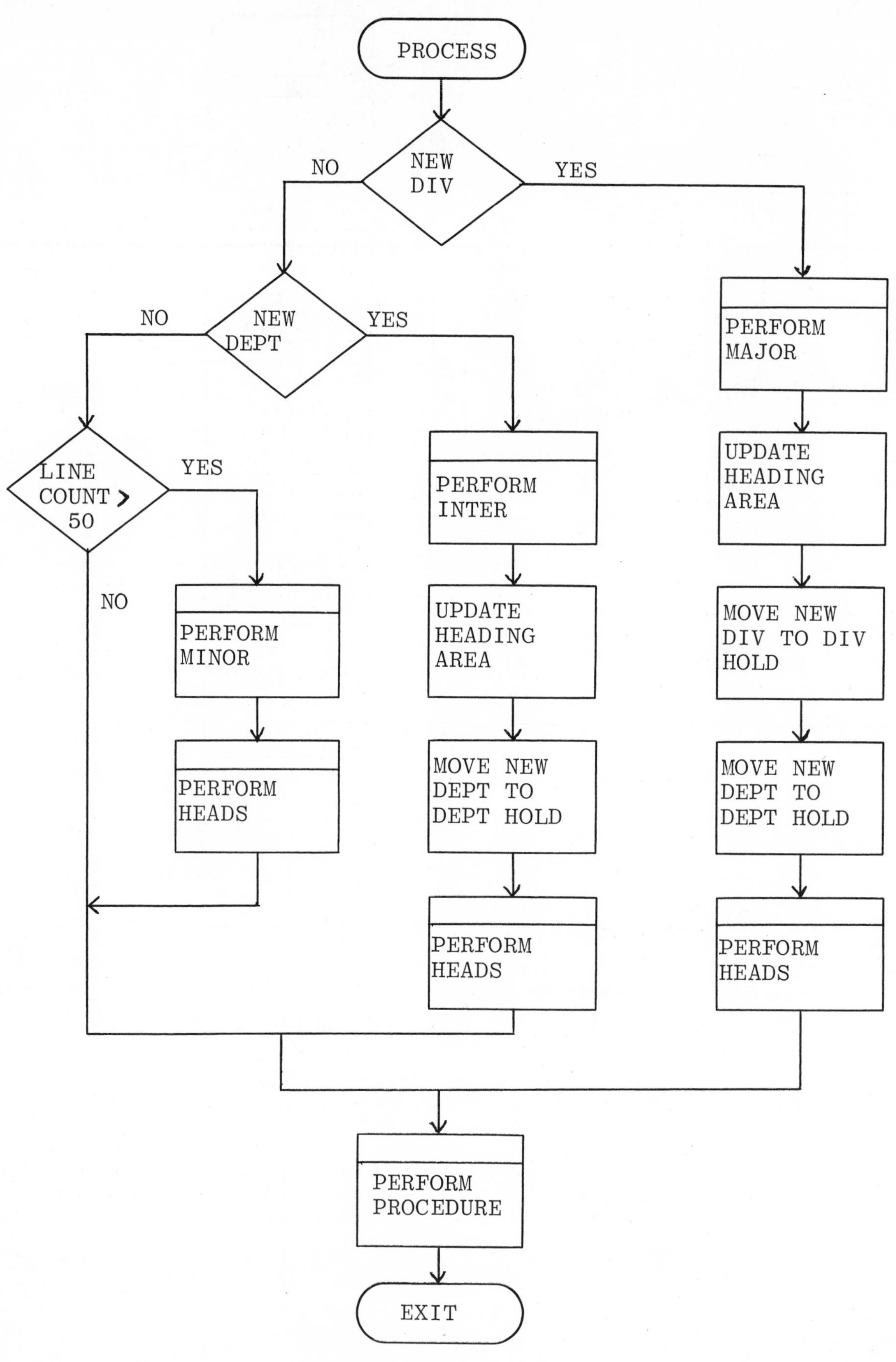

Figure 6-12 (cont.)

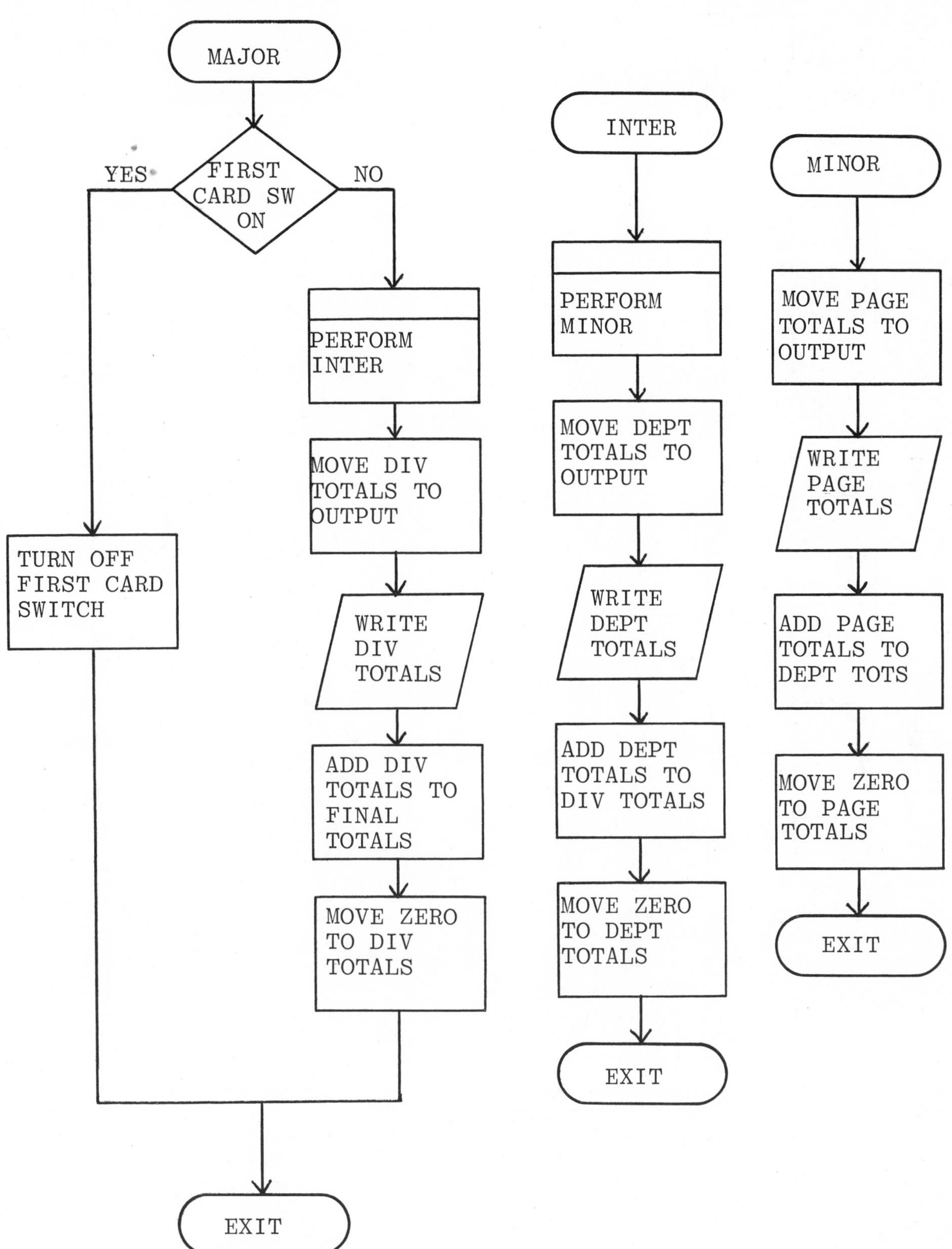

Figure 6-12 (cont.)

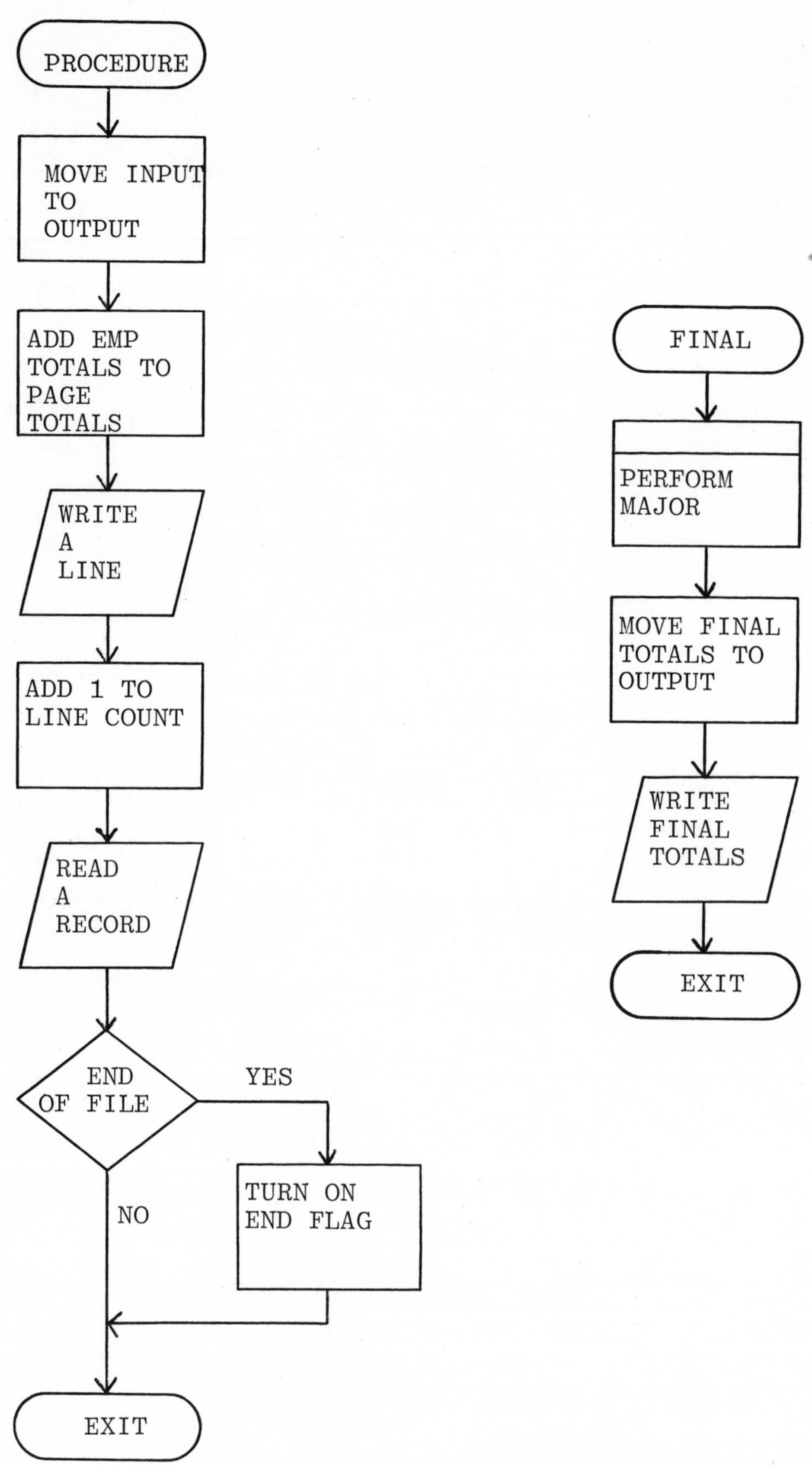

Figure 6-12 (cont.)

At the end of job the FINAL routine is performed. The first step in the final routine is to perform a major break. After all of the minor, intermediate and major level totals have been processed the final totals are moved and printed and processing is terminated.

If multiple intermediate level breaks are present the process is simply expanded to handle more levels of totals. The steps would be the same as already exist for intermediate level breaks.

Chapter 7 will get into how smaller amounts of data can be retrieved or extracted from a file. These extracted items can then be used to produce specialized (extract) reports.

REVIEW QUESTIONS

Matching

Indicate in which routines the following items are usually found. One or more of the lettered items may be used for any item and the lettered items may be used in more than one place.

A. Housekeeping routine

B. Major break routine

C. End of job routine (final routine)

D. Heading routine (including updating processes)

E. Minor break routine

__________ 1. Opening files.

__________ 2. Turning off first card switch.

__________ 3. Incrementing the page number.

__________ 4. Printing major level totals.

__________ 5. Turning on a first card switch.

__________ 6. Updating the minor break hold area.

__________ 7. Ejecting to a new page.

__________ 8. Updating the major break hold area.

__________ 9. Closing files.

__________ 10. Printing minor level totals.

__________ 11. Printing grand totals.

__________ 12. Rolling minor level totals to intermediate level totals.

True/False

T F 1. Record counts are normally set to zero only once at the beginning of the program.

T F 2. First card switches are typically used to prevent control break totals as the first card is processed.

T F 3. A first card switch is usually turned on in the major break routine.

T F 4. Grand totals are usually set to zero in an intermediate level control break routine.

T F 5. Page totals are printed and reset to zero on both control breaks and end of page conditions.

T F 6. The process of rolling totals can be a time saving technique.

T F 7. Final totals are a type of intermediate level total.

T F 8. When only one level of control break total is being produced it is called a major level total.

T F 9. Lower level control breaks always force higher level control breaks.

T F 10. The maximum number of levels of control breaks is three.

T F 11. It is presumed that if a major control break occurs that an intermediate and a minor break also occur.

T F 12. First card switches are normally turned off in the housekeeping routine.

T F 13. If control break totals were not reset to zero when breaks occur the result would be to produce cumulative totals.

Exercises

1. Draw a flowchart to read a card file and write each of the cards on tape. A final record should be written on the tape indicating the number of cards that were read and written (excluding the totals record). If no records were present in the card file (record count = 0) write a message on the printer indicating that no file was present. In addition, write the totals record on tape with a record count of zero.

2. Same as number 1 except also list the cards as they are read. No headings are to be shown on the report but no more than 40 cards should be listed on any one page of the report and the pages should be sequentially numbered. Also the record count should be written both on the tape and the report at the end of job as well as the message for no file being present if the record count = 0.

3. Draw a flowchart to produce a departmentalized listing of the assets in a company. The file is maintained on tape with each record containing the information about one of

the asset types in a given department. The file is in sequence by department. Among the information on each record are the following items:

a. the number of the asset
b. the quantity on hand
c. the cost per unit
d. the description of the asset
e. the department number where the asset is located
f. the name of the department

Total asset costs are to be developed and printed for both the individual departments and the entire company. The answer should incorporate rolling totals.

4. Same as number three with the following additions. A heading should appear at the top of each page showing the name of the department (from the record) and a page total should appear at the end of each page showing the total asset cost for all the items on the page. The last record on the tape (indicated by all *'s in the description field) contains the total number of records on the tape at the time that the tape was created. This should be compared with the total number of records that you read and a message should be printed on a separate page at the end of the report showing both record counts and whether they agree or not.

Discussion Questions

1. Describe typical single level totals that are not reset to zero during processing and indicate why they are not reset.

2. Describe what is meant by rolling totals.

3. Describe why and how higher level breaks force lower level breaks.

4. Describe the activities that take place on:

   a. Minor breaks
   b. Intermediate breaks
   c. Major breaks
   d. End of job

5. Describe the use of a first card switch in relation to control break totals, including when it is turned on and off.

6. Discuss how the process of rolling totals can save processing time in a program.

7. Describe the effect of not setting control break total areas to zero when control breaks occur including which items should be reset to zero on which type of breaks.

CHAPTER 7

Extracts

OBJECTIVES

As a result of studying this chapter the student should be able to perform the following activities:

1. Define an extract program.
2. Formulate the necessary decision steps to meet particular criteria.
3. Arrange the decision steps in an efficient manner.
4. Count selected records as well as total records processed.
5. Handle input and output routines for programming languages with an embedded sort.
6. Create non-print extract files for use in the same or subsequent programs.

INTRODUCTION

An extract program is a program used to select out certain records or fields from a file. These records are used to create a new file. The new file may be a printed listing or a file created on a media suitable for input to another program within the system.

In the first type of extract program a file is created (usually in printed form) containing only those items which meet a particular set of criteria. The user of the data processing output no longer has to scan through a long list of items looking for those of interest. He will have specified in advance the items he wishes to see on the report. The input file to this process may be read sequentially using its normal order or it may be sorted into some order other than its normal one prior to the extract program.

The second type of extract program selects one or more fields from a record, creates a new file of the selected items and then sorts the new file into the desired order if necessary. The size of the new file is smaller than the original. This saves storage space on the media and reading time when the extracted file is used as input to other programs in the system.

PRINTED REPORTS

For the discussion of the first type of extract process, we will start with a printed listing as the output to be created. Assume that we have a file containing records of both male and female employees (see Figure 7-1). The listing we require should contain only the records of the male employees (see Figure 7-2).

Figure 7-3 illustrates the process steps necessary to extract the records of the male employees from the file. Notice that once a record is read and it can be determined that it is not the record of a male employee, a branch is taken to read another record. No further processing takes place for the 'non-male' record.

In Figure 7-3, we considered only two possibilities for the question, SEX = M (yes or no). We have assumed that the contents of our records have been verified prior to this program. Such a verification would assure us that the field representing sex contains either an M or an F for all of the records in the file.

NAME	SOCIAL SECURITY NUMBER	SEX
KENNEDY, KENNETH	123456789	M
GABLE, ANDREW	163234534	M
SIMPSON, JANET	203469729	F
CARUSO, LUCY	239659387	F
GONZALES, JUANITA	316249532	F
EDISON, KEITH	326498765	M
HILL, ANNA	361269016	F
SMITH, ALICE	385312117	F
JOHNSON, EDWARD	396942219	M
ALEXANDER, WILLIAM	419623491	M
EVERETT, GRACE	479809381	F
SWANSON, SHARON	491236125	F
JONES, JAMES	543234534	M
LONG, MARILYN	591632701	F
STANDFORD, ALLEN	619211613	M
METTLESON, GREGORY	632912365	M

Figure 7-1

NAME	SOCIAL SECURITY NUMBER	SEX
KENNEDY, KENNETH	123456789	M
GABLE, ANDREW	163234534	M
EDISON, KEITH	326498765	M
JOHNSON, EDWARD	396942219	M
ALEXANDER, WILLIAM	419623491	M
JONES, JAMES	543234534	M
STANDFORD, ALLEN	619211613	M
METTLESON, GREGORY	632912365	M

Figure 7-2

If some prior verification of the contents of the file had not been made, we run the risk of rejecting records of male employees. A data entry error could result in some character other than an M or an F in the field used for the sex code. Since the character would not be an M, we would bypass the record.

DECISION SEQUENCE

Often a field has more than two possible values which are reasonable. In such a case the order in which we test for the possibilities will make a difference to the actual number of comparisons made by the computer.

In the company we are preparing a payroll for we have five divisions. This means that there are five correct possibilities for the field DIVISION (1 - 5). There is also the possibility of some other incorrect character appearing in

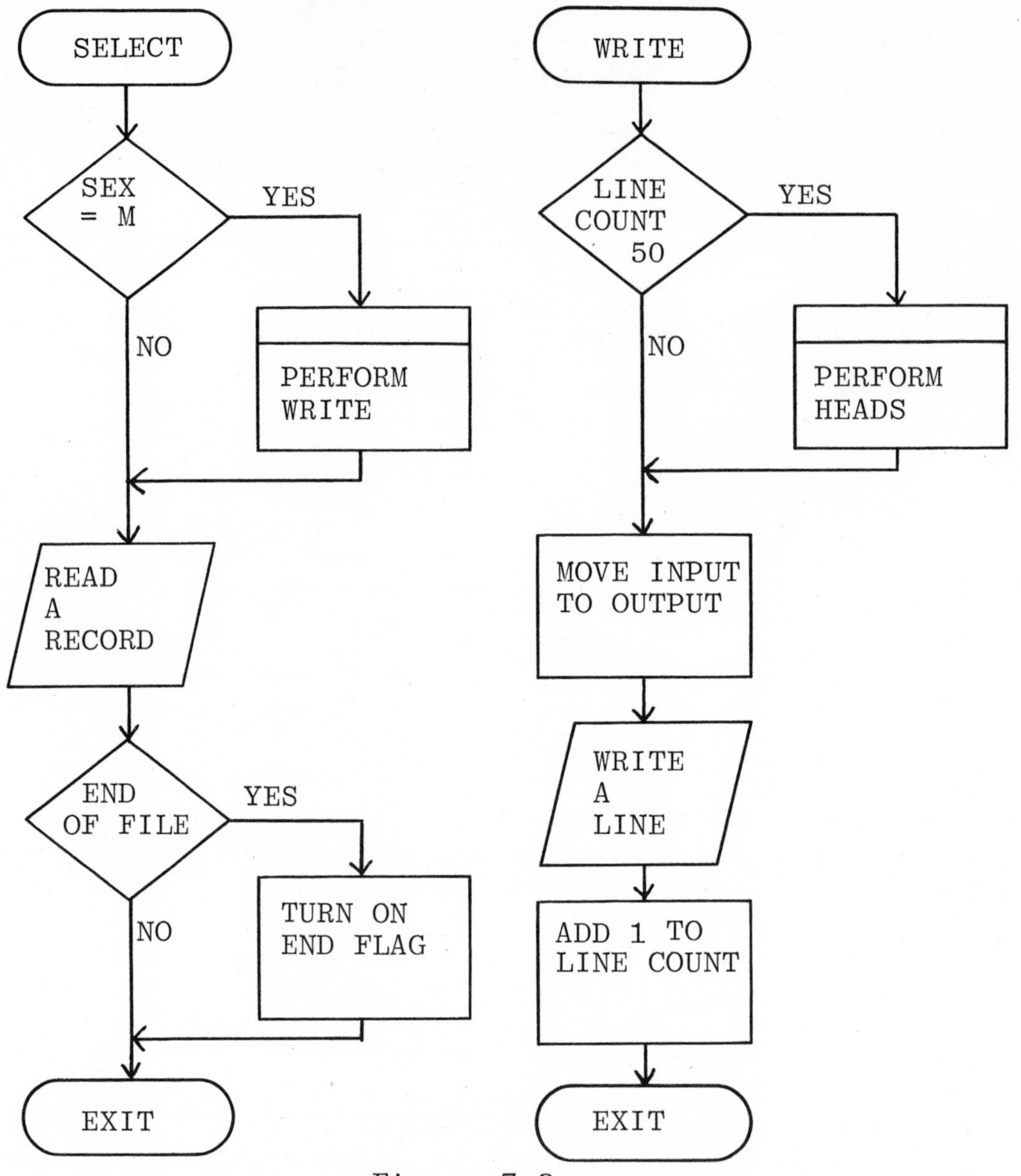

Figure 7-3

this field. If we were required to make a listing in which the data from divisions 1 and 4 only were printed, the extract flowchart would be shown in Figure 7-4.

For each of the criteria that must be met, one or more decision symbols or steps are needed. Although it is possible to make logical (and, or) decisions which combine a number of tests into one decision statement, each test in our examples will be treated separately.

If the possibilities are tested individually, the field must be checked for each additional acceptable possibility after it has been rejected on one possibility. The arrangement of decision symbols which will produce the least number of comparisons is to compare from the most likely possibility

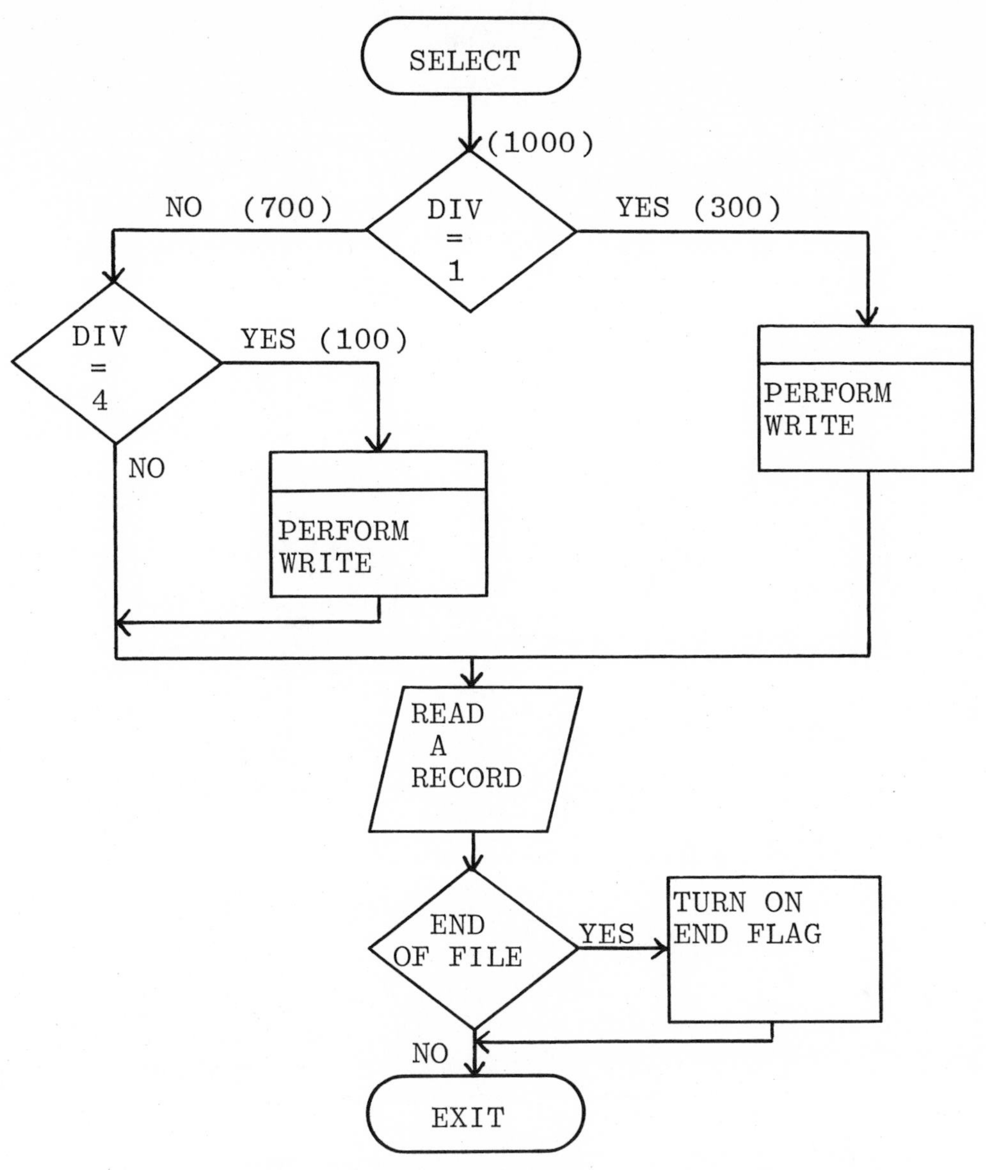

Figure 7-4

to the least likely possibility. For our example, the company has 1000 employees with 300 people in division 1 and 100 people in division 4. The number of comparisons made by using the flowchart in Figure 7-4 is 1000 at the first extract decision symbol (DIV = 1) and 700 at the second decision symbol (DIV = 4). The 700 tested at the second decision represent the records rejected at the first test (DIV = 1). The numbers in parenthesis represent the numerical results of tests on the actual data. The 300 and 100 represent the number of records in divisions 1 and 4 respectively. A total of 400 records will be represented on the report.

If the order of the symbols were reversed, there would be 1000 decisions at the first symbol and 900 decisions at the second symbol. This would result in an increase of 200 decision instructions to be performed thus increasing the time necessary to do the job.

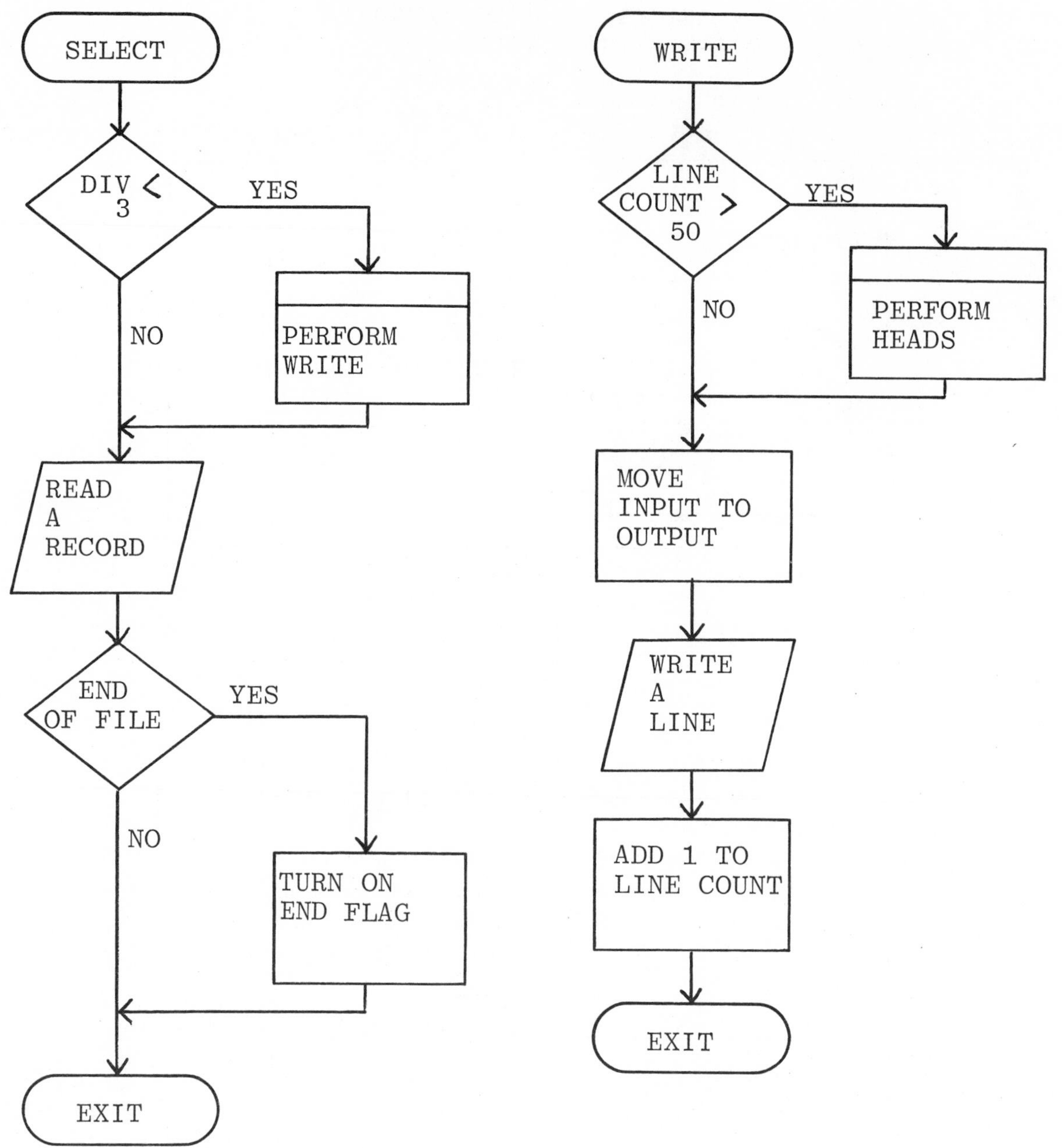

Figure 7-5

It is possible to test for more than two possibilities in a field with a single test if they can be tested using a greater than or less than type of decision. To print all employees in division 1 or division 2, the flowchart shown in Figure 7-5 could be used. This type of test leaves room for error if the division number has been incorrectly entered. On some computer systems the test 'LESS THAN 3' would produce a yes answer for all of the letters of the alphabet and all special characters as well as the 1 and 2 we were interested in. For this reason a more specific test is safer.

When examining more than one field on a card, the opposite priority for testing (least to most) results in the lowest number of tests for the computer.

To illustrate this point, let us produce a list of all males who are in division 1 and who also belong to the credit union. In this case there are 3 separate criteria, all of which must be met before the record is listed. This means tests must be made on three fields before we can be sure we will accept and list the record. To illustrate the idea of testing for the least likely first, assume a test where we expect only 20% of the records to pass. This means 80% of the records will not have to be tested on the other two fields, if they fail the first test. An example of such an extract is shown in Figure 7-6.

The particular order for the decisions was chosen because the members of the credit union represent the smallest percentage of the file, 200 members or 20%. Division 1 contains 300 employees or 30% of the file. Half of the employees are male, making this the decision most likely to produce a yes.

All of the records or 1000 are tested at the first extract decision. Since 800 or 80% are rejected, we have only 200 records to test at the second extract decision symbol. Of these 200 records, 70% or 140 are rejected leaving 60 records to be tested at the third decision. Of the 60 tested at the third decision 30 are accepted and 30 are rejected. A total of 1260 comparisons were made to select the 30 extracted records. Realize that our illustration assumes that the credit union and division 1 are equally divided between male and female members. It also assumes that credit union membership is evenly divided among the divisions of the company.

If we were to reverse the order of the tests it would illustrate the additional comparisons necessary when we do not follow the least to most likely sequence. At the first extract decision symbol we would test 1000 records. One-half of these would be rejected leaving us 500 records to test at the second decision symbol. Since the middle test is still 30% in division 1, we reject 350 of the records and 150 of them go on the the third test. The third test is for the credit union. We will reject 80% or 120 of the records and list 20% or 30 records. In this example we made 1650 comparisons but the final results were the same.

The process of extracting records using the minimum number of tests is more complex when some fields to be tested have only a yes or no alternative and other fields offer multiple possibilities such as the division field. The actual arrangement of the decisions will vary depending upon the probability of a yes or no answer in each case. Figure 7-7 is an example of a listing in which we wish to extract the records of all males in division 1 or division 4 who belong to the credit union.

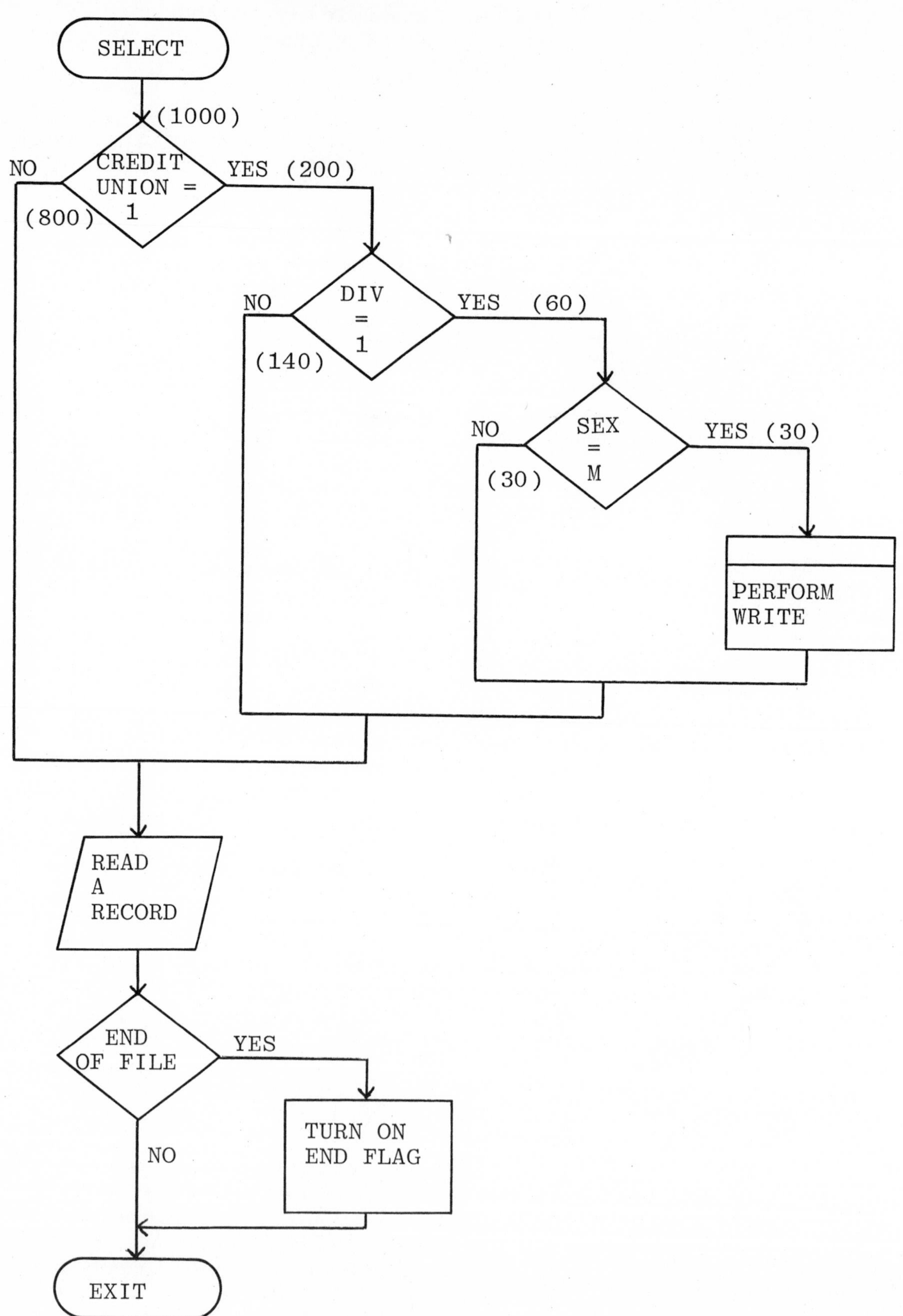
SELECT
(1000)
NO
CREDIT
UNION =
1
YES (200)
(800)
NO
DIV
=
1
YES (60)
(140)
NO
SEX
=
M
YES (30)
(30)
PERFORM
WRITE
READ
A
RECORD
END
OF FILE
YES
TURN ON
END FLAG
NO
EXIT

Figure 7-6

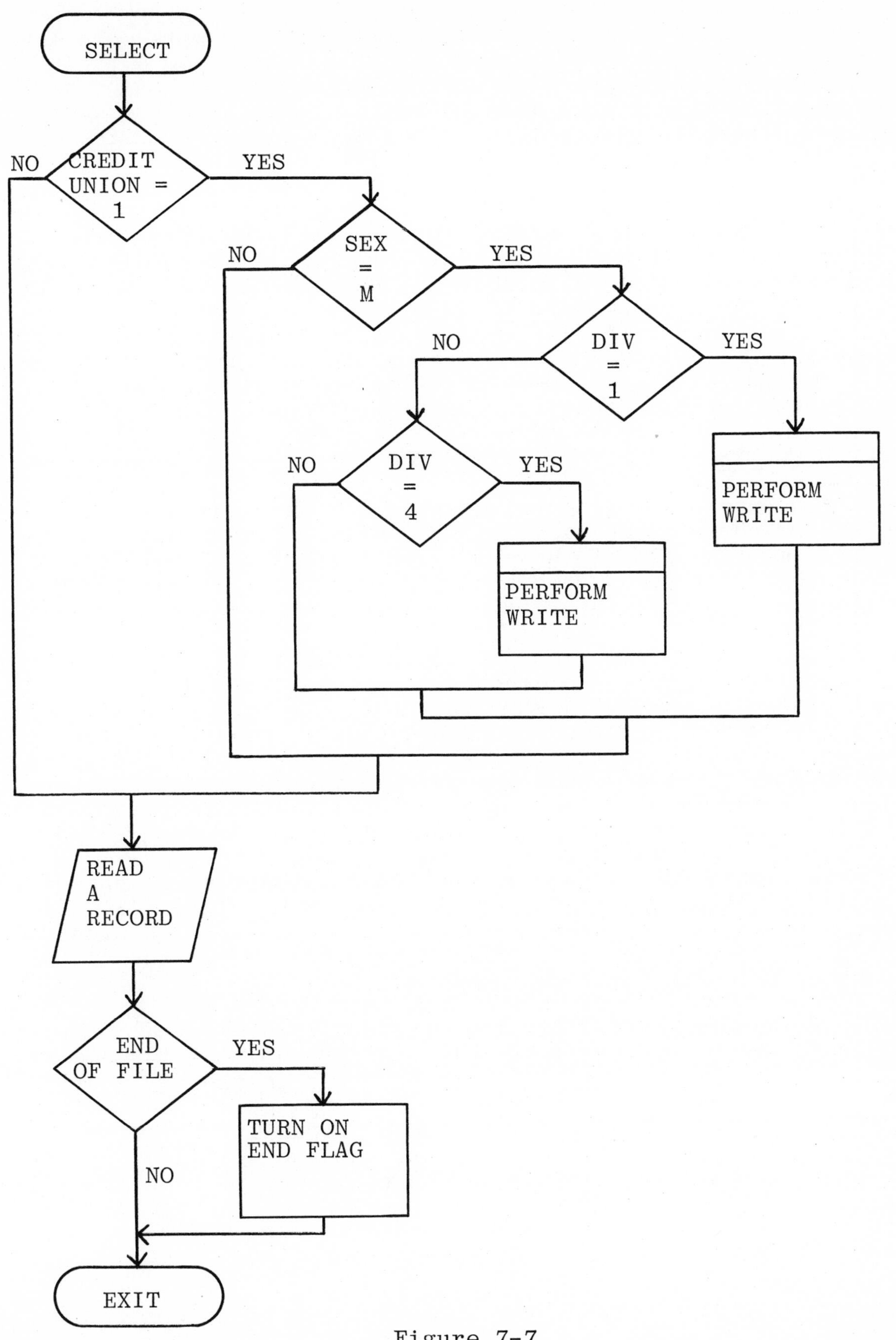
SELECT
CREDIT UNION = 1
NO
YES
SEX = M
NO
YES
DIV = 1
NO
YES
DIV = 4
NO
YES
PERFORM WRITE
PERFORM WRITE
READ A RECORD
END OF FILE
YES
NO
TURN ON END FLAG
EXIT

Figure 7-7

Fields having only two possibilities (male, not male), should be tested first in a least to most likely order. These decisions should be followed by tests on fields with more than one acceptable possibility (division 1 or division 4). The decisions on the fields with more than one acceptable possibility are also tested in a least likely to most likely order. However, the multiple tests on one field (either division 1 or division 4) are done in the most likely to least likely order.

The information necessary to determine least or most likely is not always readily available. Any informed judgment made along this line will, however, usually increase the efficiency of the program when it is put into production. If the information is not readily available, it is not practical to spend large amounts of time figuring out the frequency factors. This is true primarily because of the speed of today's computers and the ever increasing cost of programming time.

RECORD COUNTS

The extraction process as explained thus far has not counted records in any way. It has simply listed out the records meeting all of the selection criteria. Totals of both the number of records processed and the number of records selected can be useful information. Sometimes a count such as the number of records is already known. In the case of the number of records processed it is the number of employees in the company. Even so, producing this total provides an important control figure to insure that the file does actually contain the number of employees assumed to be working for the company. It is less likely that the number of selected records is known in advance. Such a count is often a useful summary figure to the user of the extract report. The flowchart depicting the extract and totaling process is shown in Figure 7-8.

In Figure 7-8 the portion of the flowchart which does the actual selection was indicated only as a subroutine. We now have a basic extract program which totals the records processed and only the routine called SELECT need be changed to suit the requirements of a particular extract.

Notice, in particular, that the addition of each record to the total records count takes place after the test for end of file. Remember, the first record was read in the HSK routine. The end of file test in many programming languages is an integral part of the read statement and no capability exists to insert commands between the read and the end of file test. If such an insertion were possible, then the record count would exceed the actual count by 1. This would be true because the end of file indicator would be counted as a record when, in fact, it is not a part of the data on the file.

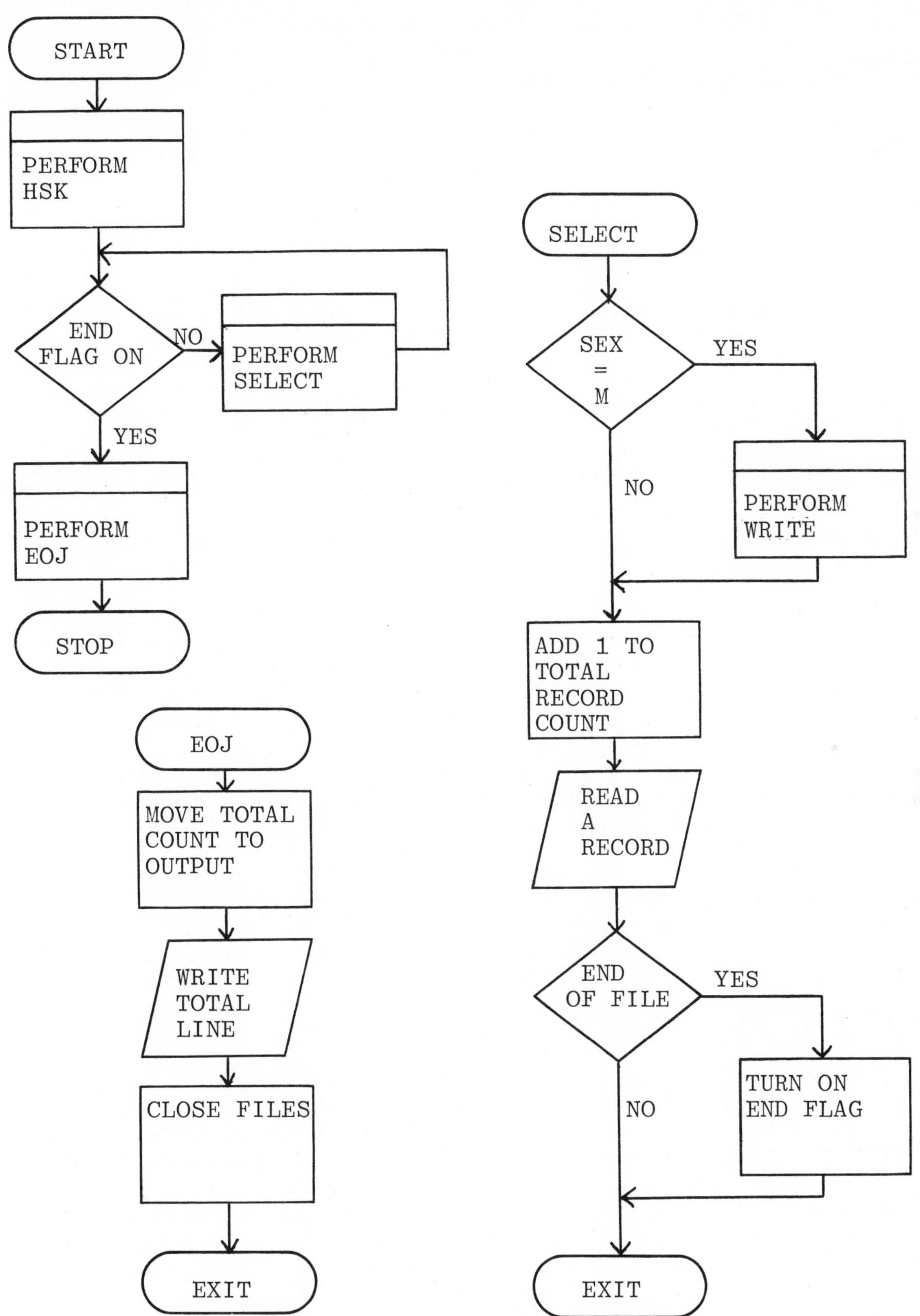
START
PERFORM HSK
END FLAG ON
NO
PERFORM SELECT
YES
PERFORM EOJ
STOP
EOJ
MOVE TOTAL COUNT TO OUTPUT
WRITE TOTAL LINE
CLOSE FILES
EXIT
SELECT
SEX = M
YES
PERFORM WRITE
NO
ADD 1 TO TOTAL RECORD COUNT
READ A RECORD
END OF FILE
YES
TURN ON END FLAG
NO
EXIT

Figure 7-8

In order to count selected records the counting process must come after all selection criteria have been met and prior to reading the next record (see Figure 7-9).

RELEASING RECORDS TO A SORT

In addition to extracting records and listing them in the order they appear in the input file, it is often useful to extract the records required, write them to a separate file and then sort the selected records. After the selected records are sorted they may be used as input to another program or a different section of the same program.

It depends on the programming language used whether this sort is an integral part of the program itself. When the programming language has an embedded sort capability the input records are read, released to a sort routine and then accepted by a third portion of the program in their sorted format. If the programming language has no sort capability, then a program will have to be written to select the records and write them on another file. This file will be sorted with a utility type program and the resulting file will be used as input for another program in the system which will process the sorted output.

Figure 7-10 shows a flowchart of records being selected, released to a sort and then listed. The listing uses the concept of control breaks which has been previously introduced. Since we are taking a control break on division, the sort is necessary to put the records in division number order.

The SORT IN routine reads the records and passes them through a selection routine. The SELECT routine is similar to the ones described thus far in the chapter. If the record meets all of the selection criteria, it is transferred to a sort file. When all of the input records have been read and tested, the sort file is considered complete and the records in it are sorted into a new sequence. After the sort is completed, the records are read through the SORT OUT routine and listed.

EXTRACTING MULTIPLE RECORDS

In the extract program examined thus far the same amount of data was taken from each record and eventually listed. It is also possible to extract differing amounts of data from each record and create a new file. In a payroll system we might require a file which is devoted to voluntary deductions only. This file could later be used to list the deduction amounts in order by the organization for which they were deducted.

Since the number and type of deductions vary from employee to employee, the original record is examined and each deduction is copied to the new file. The flowchart to accomplish this is shown in Figure 7-11.

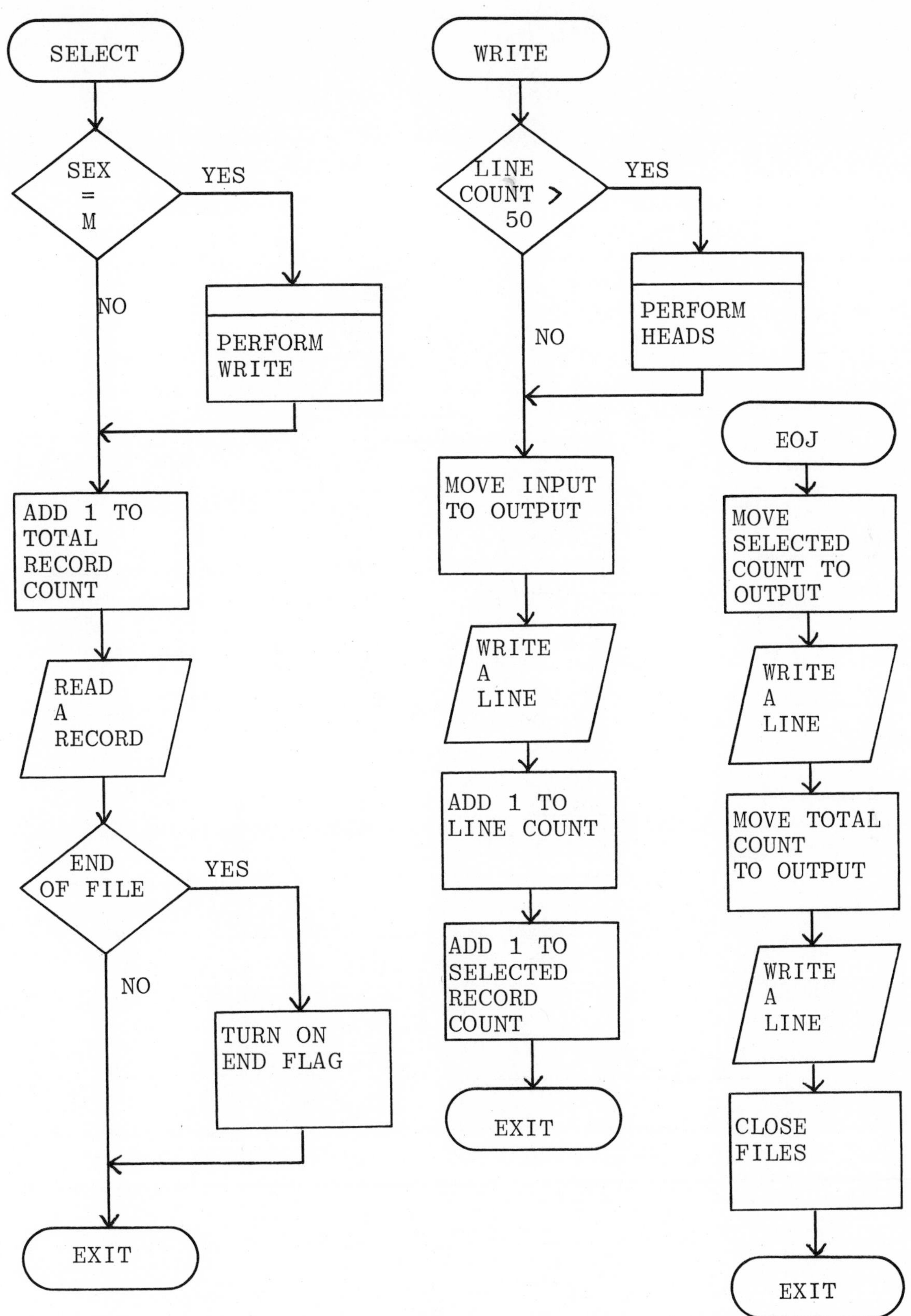
SELECT
SEX = M
YES
NO
PERFORM WRITE
ADD 1 TO TOTAL RECORD COUNT
READ A RECORD
END OF FILE
YES
NO
TURN ON END FLAG
EXIT
WRITE
LINE COUNT > 50
YES
NO
PERFORM HEADS
MOVE INPUT TO OUTPUT
WRITE A LINE
ADD 1 TO LINE COUNT
ADD 1 TO SELECTED RECORD COUNT
EXIT
EOJ
MOVE SELECTED COUNT TO OUTPUT
WRITE A LINE
MOVE TOTAL COUNT TO OUTPUT
WRITE A LINE
CLOSE FILES
EXIT

Figure 7-9

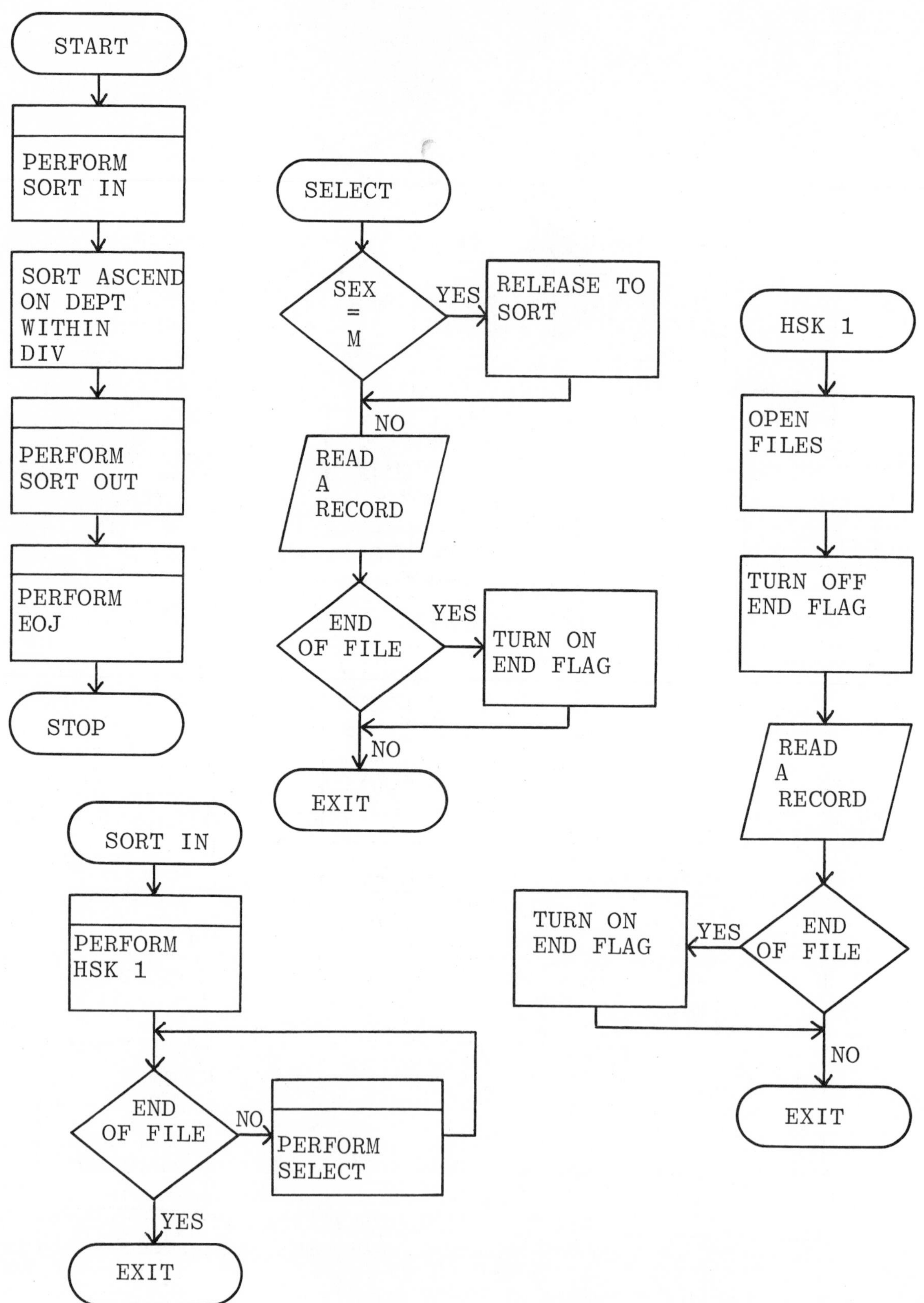
START
PERFORM SORT IN
SORT ASCEND ON DEPT WITHIN DIV
PERFORM SORT OUT
PERFORM EOJ
STOP
SELECT
SEX = M
YES
RELEASE TO SORT
NO
READ A RECORD
END OF FILE
YES
TURN ON END FLAG
NO
EXIT
HSK 1
OPEN FILES
TURN OFF END FLAG
READ A RECORD
END OF FILE
YES
TURN ON END FLAG
NO
EXIT
SORT IN
PERFORM HSK 1
END OF FILE
NO
PERFORM SELECT
YES
EXIT

Figure 7-10

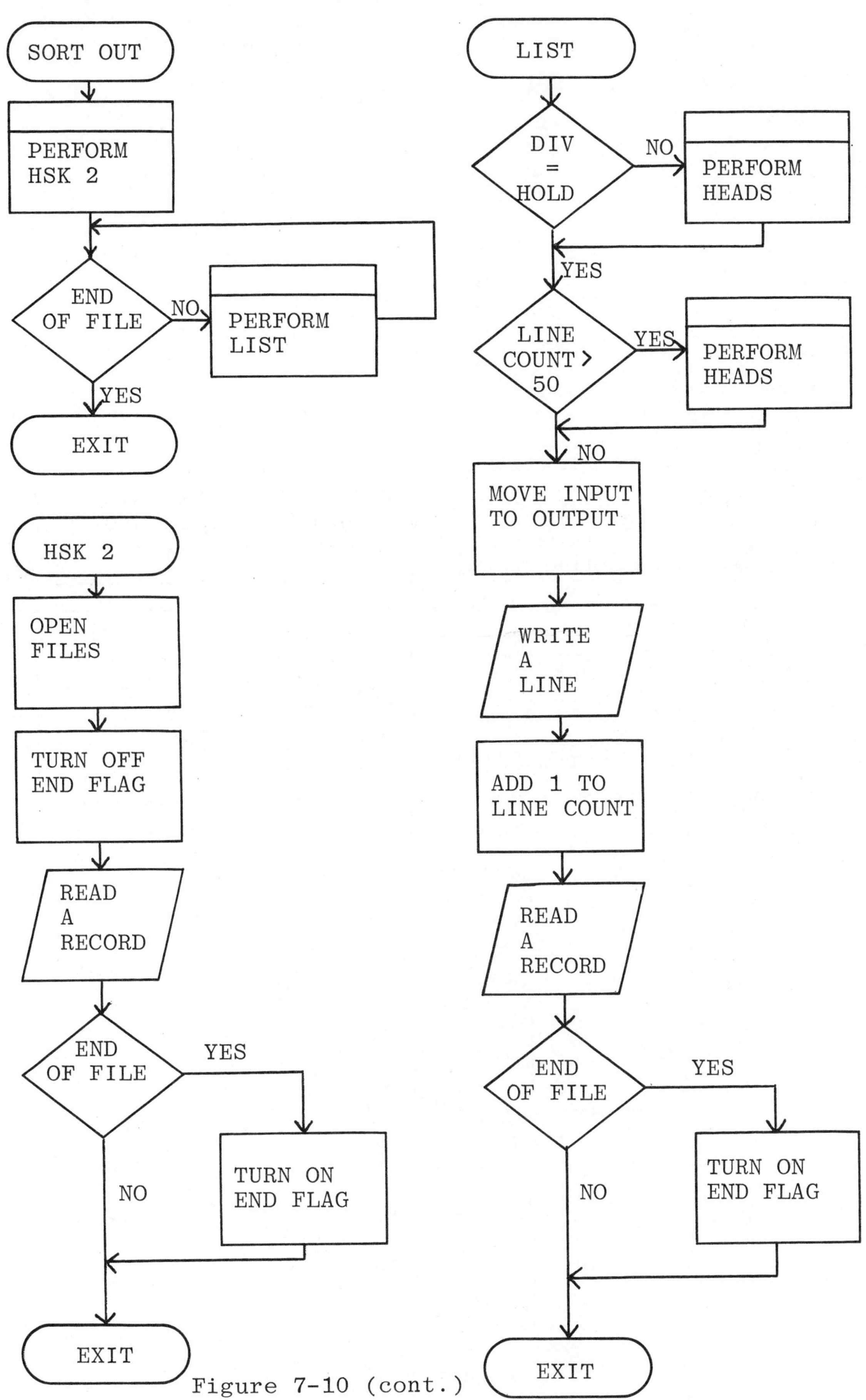

Figure 7-10 (cont.)

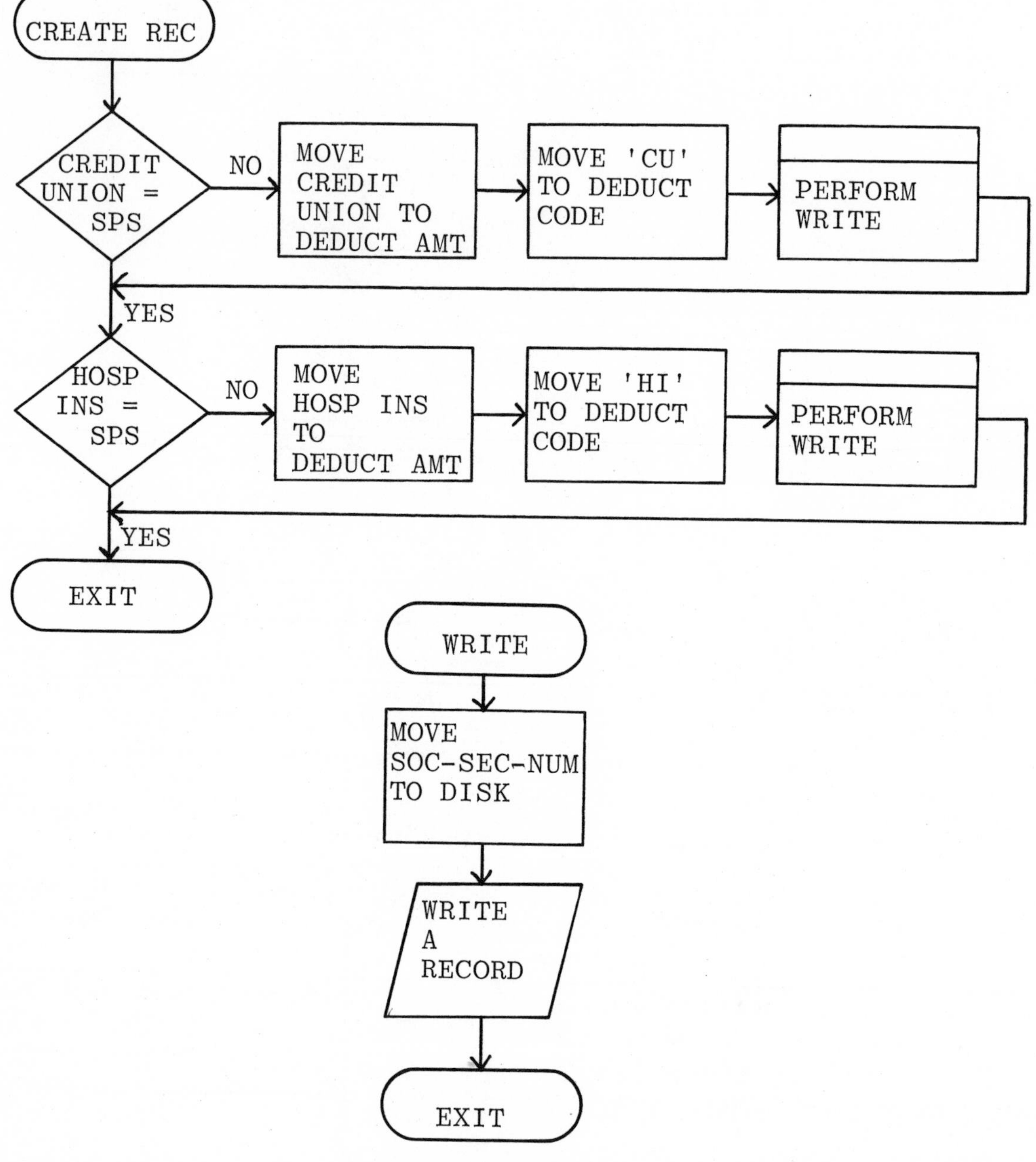
CREATE REC
CREDIT UNION = SPS
NO
MOVE CREDIT UNION TO DEDUCT AMT
MOVE 'CU' TO DEDUCT CODE
PERFORM WRITE
YES
HOSP INS = SPS
NO
MOVE HOSP INS TO DEDUCT AMT
MOVE 'HI' TO DEDUCT CODE
PERFORM WRITE
YES
EXIT
WRITE
MOVE SOC-SEC-NUM TO DISK
WRITE A RECORD
EXIT

Figure 7-11

REVIEW QUESTIONS

Matching

A. Extract programs

B. Criteria

C. Least to most

D. Most to least

E. Embedded sort

F. Total record count

G. Selected record count

H. Utility sort

__________ 1. A language feature of a high-level language.

__________ 2. Used to make efficient comparisons when only one value is acceptable from each field.

__________ 3. The sum of all records processed.

__________ 4. Written to selectively choose records from a file.

__________ 5. The sum of all records which meet the selection criteria.

__________ 6. Standards on which decisions may be based.

__________ 7. Used to make efficient comparisons when multiple possibilities are acceptable from one field.

__________ 8. A software routine, independent of any high-level programming language.

True/False

T F 1. Extract programs are only used to create printed files.

T F 2. One is added to the selected record count after each selection criteria test is passed.

T F 3. A utility sort is a feature of some high-level languages.

T F 4. The order in which selection criteria are tested has an effect on the efficiency of the program.

T F 5. The total record count is accumulated at end of file time.

T F 6. When more than one value in a field is acceptable for extract the most likely value in that field should be tested for first.

T F 7. An embedded sort accepts records from an input procedure within a program.

T F 8. Selected record counts have little value since the user can see the length of the listing.

Exercises

1. Draw a flowchart to select all males over 25 enrolled in a course. The program should print a report with name and address. Provide appropriate headings for first page and overflow.

2. Same as No. 1, but in addition, count selected, rejected, and total records.

3. Draw a flowchart to create two non-print files concurrently. One should contain all males and the other all females. Count selected records for each file as well as total records. Print the results of the counts as a part of a successful end of job message.

4. Draw a flowchart for a personnel search. We are looking for any employees with a business undergraduate degree, an MBA, two or more years teaching experience whose current salary is under $12,000 per year. Design an input record to help you make the search. Keep the design flexible, next week you may be looking for a dentist.

Discussion Questions

1. Identify business situations in which a user would request an extract type report.

2. Is there any advantage to putting all selection criteria testing into a subroutine?

3. Why bother to count the number of total records processed if you have a previous count.

4. Since computers are so fast, does it really make any difference whether you arrange decisions for selection criteria in an order that minimizes the number of tests made?

5. Once a non-print extract file has been created, can it be used within the same program?

6. How can you know what order to make tests of selection criteria in?

CHAPTER 8

Input Edit Programs

OBJECTIVES

After studying this chapter the student should be able to perform the following activities:

1. Describe what an edit program is.

2. Describe the types of undetected errors in data that can cause a program interrupt.

3. Describe the types of undetected errors in data that may cause incorrect output.

4. Flowchart an edit program using the types of errors from number 2 and number 3 above.

5. Flowchart a program which has multiple record types in one file.

6. Flowchart programs in which the files must contain multiple record types in a particular sequence.

7. Flowchart the building of a master file from multiple record types within one file.

INTRODUCTION

Data entry (keypunch, terminals, etc.) is an expensive part of data processing operations. In spite of precautions taken to insure accuracy (verifying, sight checking, etc.) of data entry, many things 'slip through'.

If these items are allowed into a computer program as data, they can cause program interruptions or incorrect output. While it is possible to check for such problems and bypass them during a program run, the best you can hope for if errors are encountered is an incomplete and therefore a potentially incorrect report.

To avoid this situation data is often tested by a program called an edit program. The only purpose of this program is to check the validity of the data and prepare an error report. This error report is used to correct the data prior to its use as input to a program which will manipulate it in some manner.

TYPES OF ERRORS

Before it is possible to write an edit program, the data and the programs it will be used as input for must be analyzed in terms of potential trouble spots. We cannot check for problems without an understanding of what the problems may be.

There are two general problem areas common to most business programming. The first type of problem will cause a program interrupt called a data exception. A program interrupt of this type means that processing stops and an error message is printed out. This message will lead us to the instruction which was being executed when data of an unacceptable form or value was detected.

Some of the possible causes of a data exception are listed below:

1. Non-numeric data in a numeric field.

2. Input fields used to index an array which are zero or exceed the size of the array.

3. Numeric fields stored in a format other than what is described in the program.

4. A zero value when zero may not be permissible. An example is a number that will be used as a divisor. Division by zero is not allowed in most programming languages.

Since we cannot afford to stop and restart continually, it is better to edit the data, prepare an error list to be corrected and then run the production program with correct data.

The second type of data error which can be checked for will cause incorrect output. When looking for these types of errors the particular programs for which the data has been prepared must be considred. One such possibility is the need to check the sequence of the records in the file.

In many programs we are interested in the sequence the records are in. This is particularly true of programs with control breaks. Prior to this type of program a sort program is normally executed if the sequence of the file requires changing. These sorts are relatively foolproof and in general, the data is assumed to be coming into a program in the proper sequence. Trusting card records sorted on a manual sorter to be in the proper sequence is a little more shaky proposition. In either case a part of the edit process could be a test for sequence. A test is made checking each time for a greater than or less than condition in the field determining the sequence. Our choice of greater than or less than depends on whether the file is to be in ascending or descending order.

In a sample payroll system edit the input could be a punched card. The hours could be reported weekly and a card prepared with the following format:

1 - 2	CARD CODE
3 - 11	SOCIAL SECURITY NUMBER
12 - 16	ACCOUNT NUMBER
17 - 20	REGULAR HOURS
21 - 24	OVERTIME HOURS
25 - 30	PAY RATE

The fields called REGULAR HOURS,OVERTIME HOURS AND PAY RATE must all be checked in insure that they contain numeric data to avoid data exceptions. This is necessary because these fields will be used in calculations. To insure correct output, other checks can be made.

1. The SOCIAL SECURITY NUMBER can be 'looked up' in a table of employee social security numbers to confirm that the employee is on our company's payroll.

2. The ACCOUNT NUMBER can be 'looked up' in a table of account numbers to insure that a valid account number is being charged for the salary paid.

3. If any overtime hours are present, the REGULAR HOURS can be tested for a minimum number (such as 40).

4. The PAY RATE can be tested to make sure that it falls within a given range for a particular category of job.

5. The sequence can be checked on SOCIAL SECURITY NUMBER or any other designated control field.

6. A part of the sequence check can include a test for duplicate records.

The flowchart in Figure 8-1 is an example of such an edit program. The data names have been shortened to fit into the symbols. This program creates a listing of the items in error. The list is used to correct the input prior to the running of the programs which calculate the payroll. It is desirable to have sufficient time lapse between the running of the edit program and the actual payroll to allow orderly correction of any data found to be incorrect.

In Figure 8-1 each of the edit decisions is tested until the data fails to pass an edit test. At this time an error message appropriate to the test being made is moved to output and written. The entire record is also moved to output so that its contents may be inspected. Notice that if more than one error were in a record only the first one would be detected using this flowchart.

If we wish to print any multiple errors that appear on the record, then we must continue the testing of the record after any one error has been discovered. The flowchart in Figure 8-2 shows the logic for this type of checking.

MULTIPLE RECORD TYPES

A complicating factor in edits as well as other types of programming is when there is more than one type of record in a file. An example is a master record followed by one or more transactions. These record types share the same input area when they are read into storage. The record types must have an identifying characteristic which can be tested after the read so we can tell the record types apart. Since there are one or more transactions, we cannot anticipate in advance which record type will be read.

Assume a card file as input and an 80 character area reserved for storing input for that file inside the computer. The computer would reserve a particular series of core locations for the storage of the input card. We will use core locations 4000 to 4079 for our example. Therefore, when <u>any</u> card type is read from our file it will reside in core locations 4000 - 4079. Since we have master cards followed by one or more transaction cards, the type of card read can only be

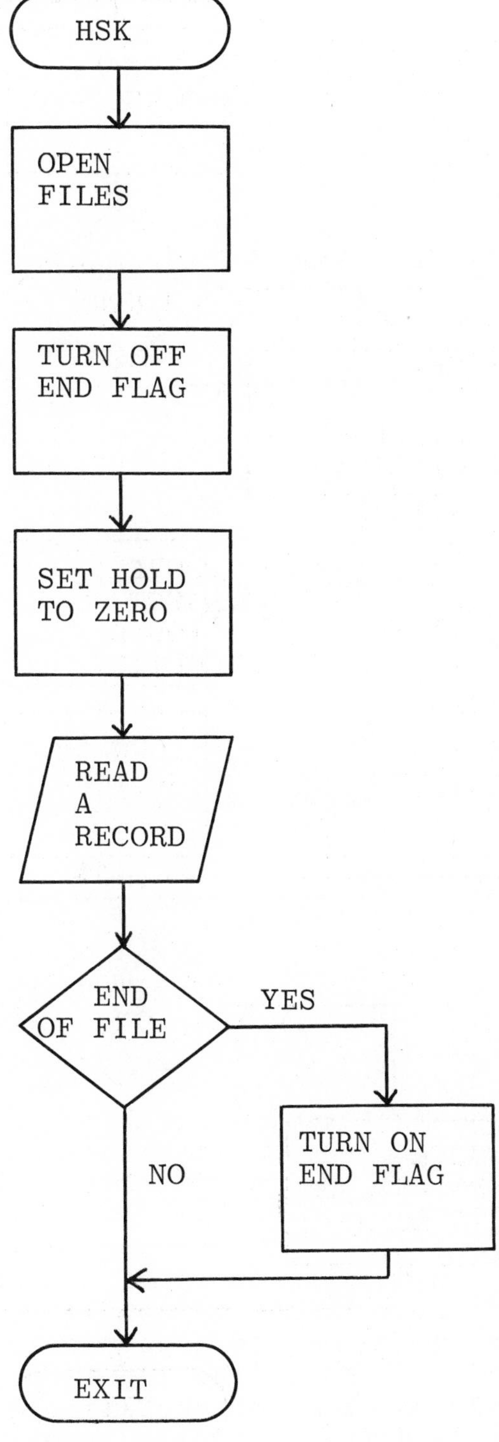
HSK
OPEN FILES
TURN OFF END FLAG
SET HOLD TO ZERO
READ A RECORD
END OF FILE
YES
NO
TURN ON END FLAG
EXIT

Figure 8-1

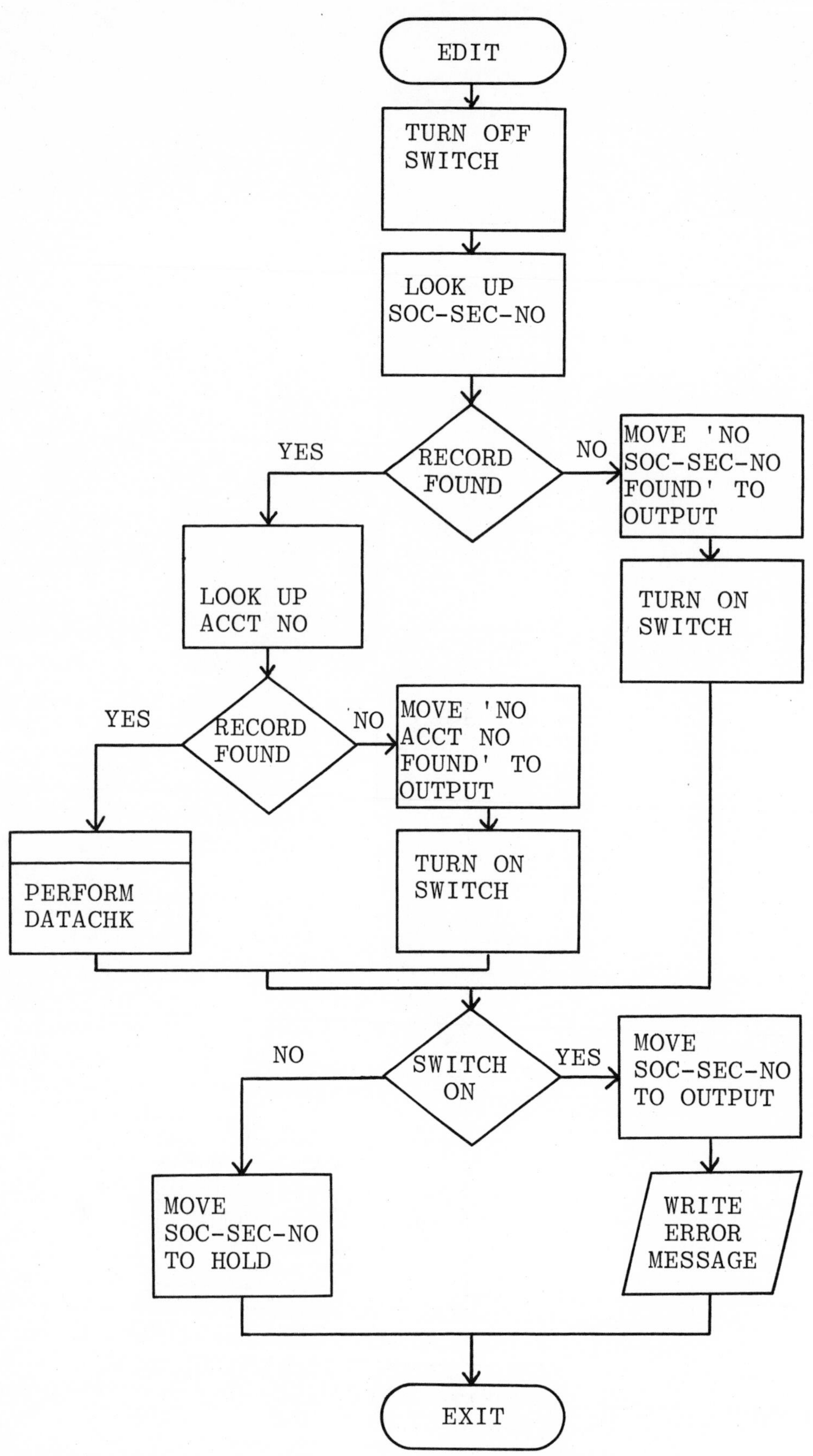

Figure 8-1 (cont.)

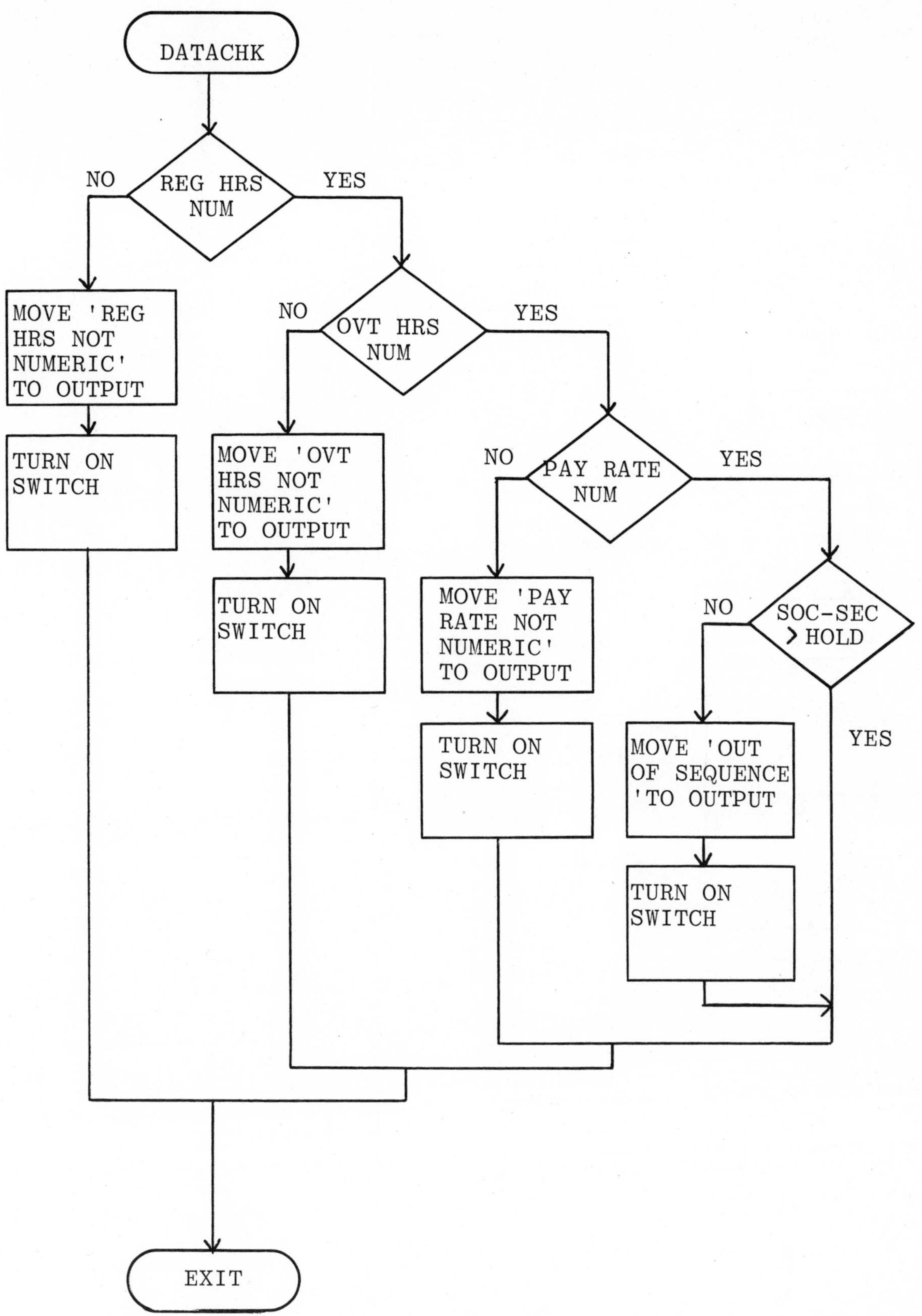

Figure 8-1 (cont.)

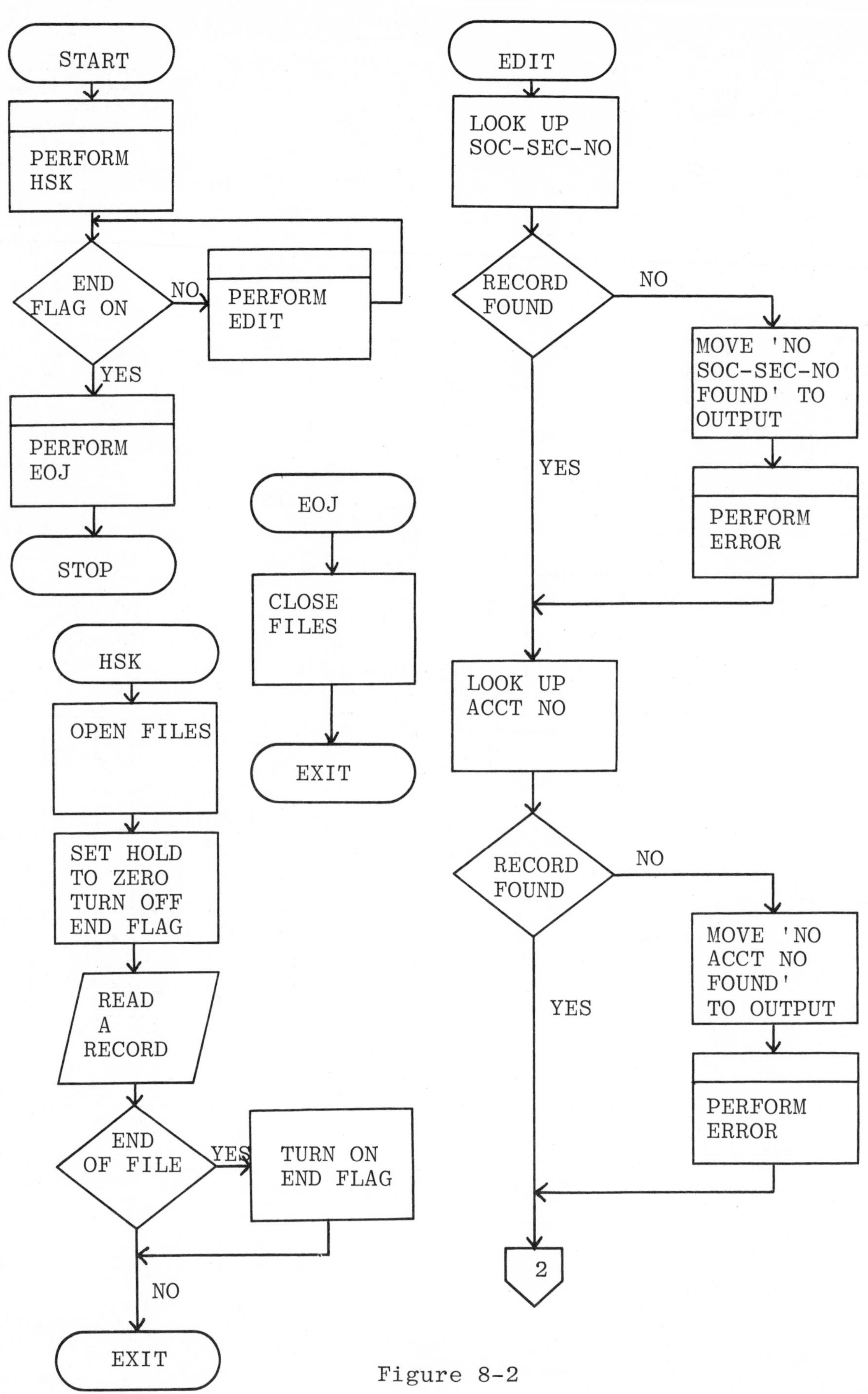
START
PERFORM HSK
END FLAG ON
NO
PERFORM EDIT
YES
PERFORM EOJ
STOP
EOJ
CLOSE FILES
EXIT
HSK
OPEN FILES
SET HOLD TO ZERO TURN OFF END FLAG
READ A RECORD
END OF FILE
YES
TURN ON END FLAG
NO
EXIT
EDIT
LOOK UP SOC-SEC-NO
RECORD FOUND
NO
MOVE 'NO SOC-SEC-NO FOUND' TO OUTPUT
YES
PERFORM ERROR
LOOK UP ACCT NO
RECORD FOUND
NO
MOVE 'NO ACCT NO FOUND' TO OUTPUT
YES
PERFORM ERROR
2

Figure 8-2

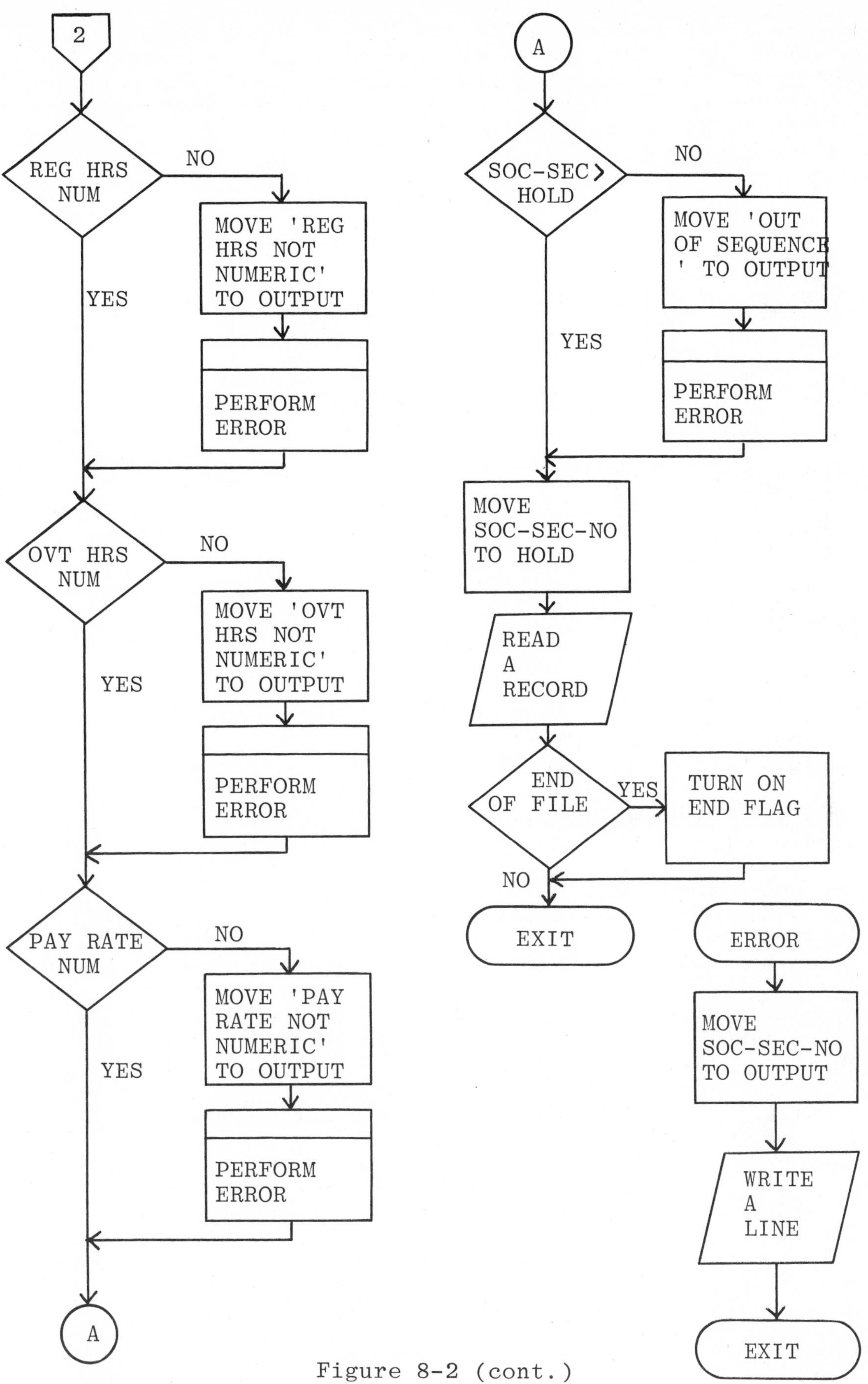

Figure 8-2 (cont.)

determined after it is in the input area where a test can be performed on it. Consequently, the test for the card type should come after the READ and test for END OF FILE portion of the flowchart. To attempt to edit a field prior to determining the card type will result in either a data exception or incorrect test results.

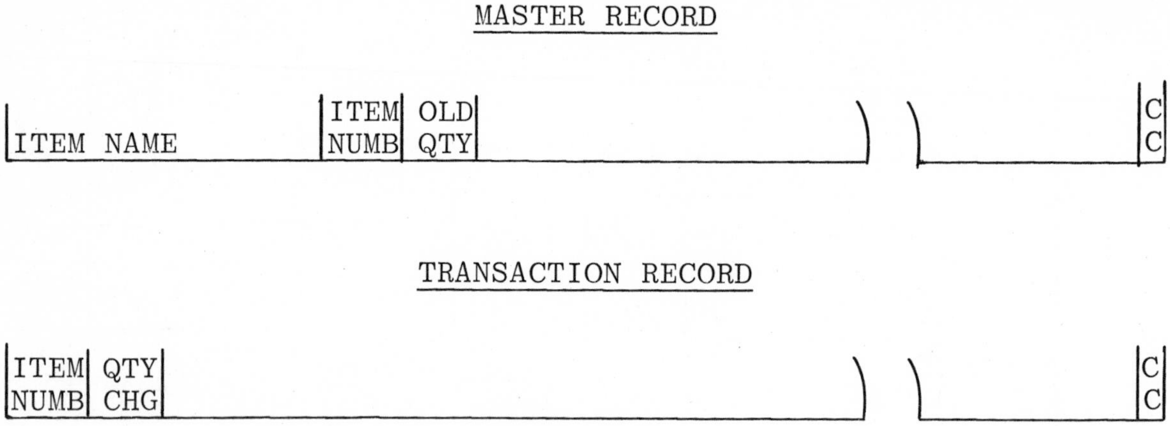

MASTER RECORD

ITEM NAME	ITEM NUMB	OLD QTY	...	CC

TRANSACTION RECORD

ITEM NUMB	QTY CHG	...	CC

Figure 8-3

When a master record is read into the computer, its contents are stored as follows:

4000 - 4016	ITEM NAME
4017 - 4020	ITEM NUMBER M
4021 - 4024	OLD QUANTITY
4025 - 4078	UNUSED
4079 - 4079	CONTROL CODE (0 indicates a master card)

When a transaction record is read into the computer, its contents are stored as follows:

4000 - 4003	ITEM NUMBER T
4004 - 4007	QUANTITY CHANGE
4008 - 4078	UNUSED
4079 - 4079	CONTROL CODE (1 indicates a transaction card)

All locations of storage labeled unused will contain blanks. The blanks or spaces will be transferred from the card when it is read.

If any tests are made on fields prior to determining the type of record in the input area (see Figure 8-4) the following might result. The test QUANTITY CHANGE NUMERIC would check the contents of core locations 4004 - 4007 for numeric data. If there is a transaction record in the input area at the time, the test results will be valid. If it is a master card the master record will be rejected as a transaction with a non-numeric field. This is because core locations 4004 - 4007 are a part of the ITEM NAME field on the master record.

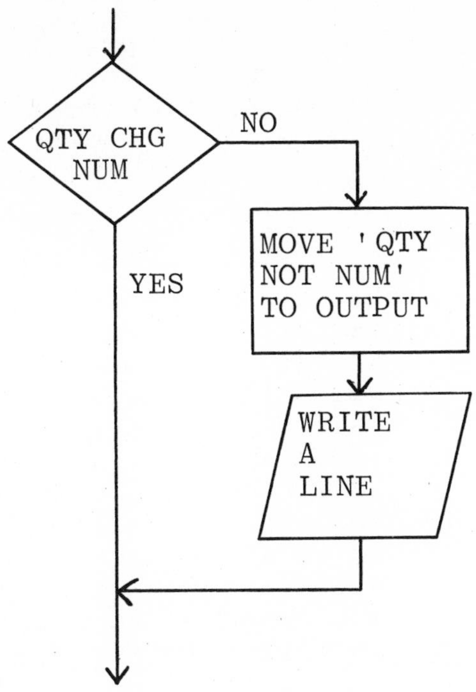

Figure 8-4

Another potential problem would be to have read a master record and upon reading a transaction, ADD QUANTITY CHANGE TO OLD QUANTITY. Since we just read a transaction the QUANTITY CHANGE field will be correct, but OLD QUANTITY will be taken from core locations 4021 - 4024 which currently contain blanks. Let's put actual data in our record formats (see Figure 8-5) and follow through the explanation above. We have just read a transaction record and knowing that we have read a master record previously, we issue the instruction ADD QUANTITY CHANGE TO OLD QUANTITY. QUANTITY CHANGE (4004 - 4007) contains 0003, an acceptable value for a numeric field. OLD QUANTITY (4021 - 4024) contains blanks, not an acceptable value for a numeric field. If two fields from different record types within the same file must be used together, it will be necessary to transfer the first one read to a hold area.

MASTER RECORD

|RECLINER |8686|0012| \ \ |0|

TRANSACTION RECORD

|8686|0003| \ \ |1|

Figure 8-5

The flowchart in Figure 8-6 shows the proper method for checking records which share a common area in storage. The two edit routines would ordinarily contain more than a single test.

MULTIPLE RECORD TYPES

When editing a file in which there are multiple record types which must appear in a certain sequence it is necessary to keep track of all records read for each control field. Since, in the long run, we need only know of the existence of a valid record or records of each type and their sequence we can handle it as we would a control break situation (see Figure 8-7). After the record type has been identified it is put through the appropriate edit routine. A switch may be turned on if the record is in the proper sequence and successfully complete the edit. When we discover a change in the control field indicating a new group of records a test is made on the status of the switches representing the various types of records. If the appropriate combination is on no action is taken. If any switches remain off an error message is written. Having completed the check and having written a message, if necessary, the switches are set off to begin the testing of a new group.

The building of a master file from multiple record types is a similar situation. In this case though, the actual data from each record would be held in storage in an area separate from the input area until all record types were accounted for then the master record would be written.

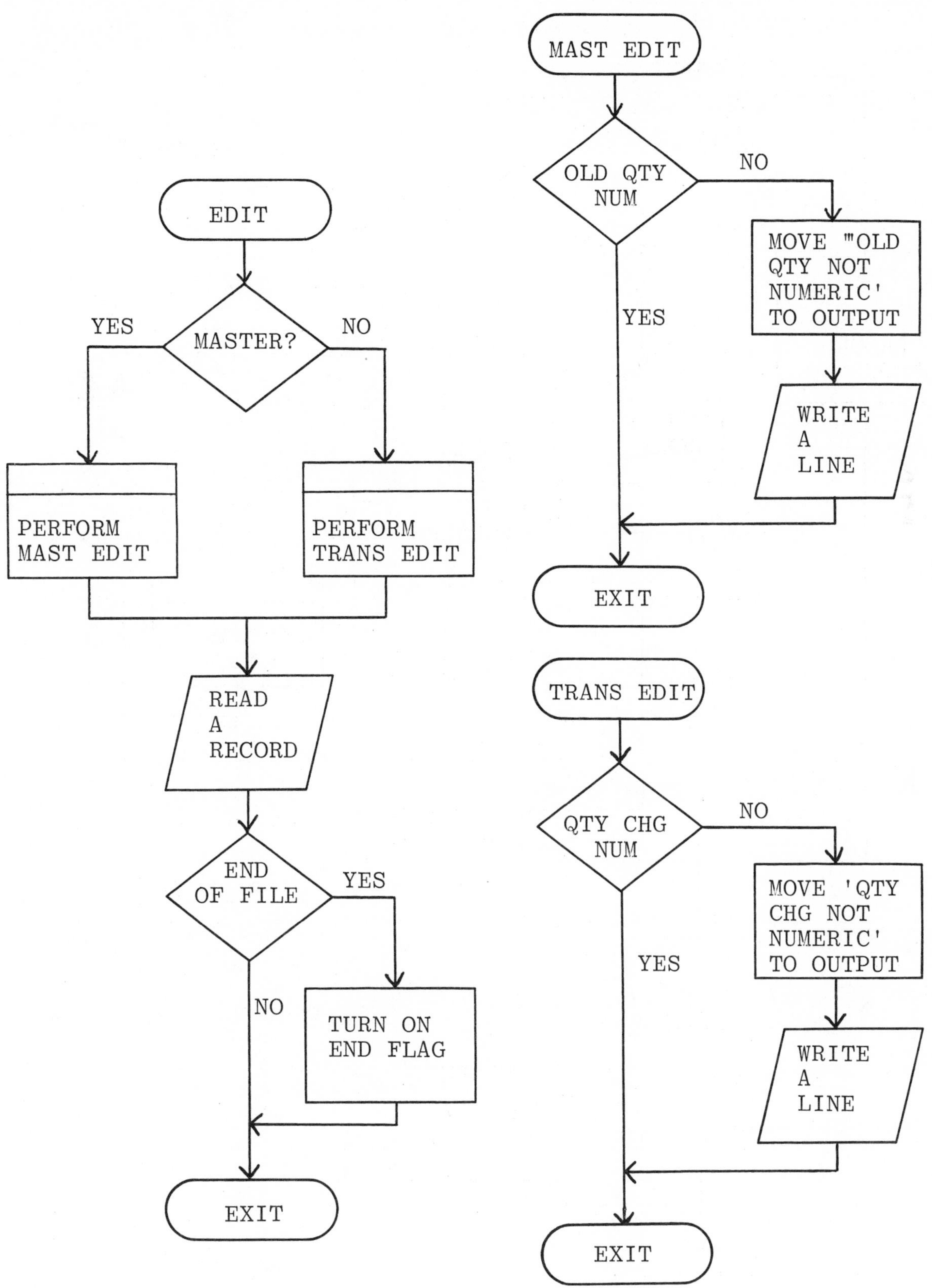
EDIT
MASTER?
YES
NO
PERFORM MAST EDIT
PERFORM TRANS EDIT
READ A RECORD
END OF FILE
YES
NO
TURN ON END FLAG
EXIT
MAST EDIT
OLD QTY NUM
NO
YES
MOVE "OLD QTY NOT NUMERIC' TO OUTPUT
WRITE A LINE
EXIT
TRANS EDIT
QTY CHG NUM
NO
YES
MOVE 'QTY CHG NOT NUMERIC' TO OUTPUT
WRITE A LINE
EXIT

Figure 8-6

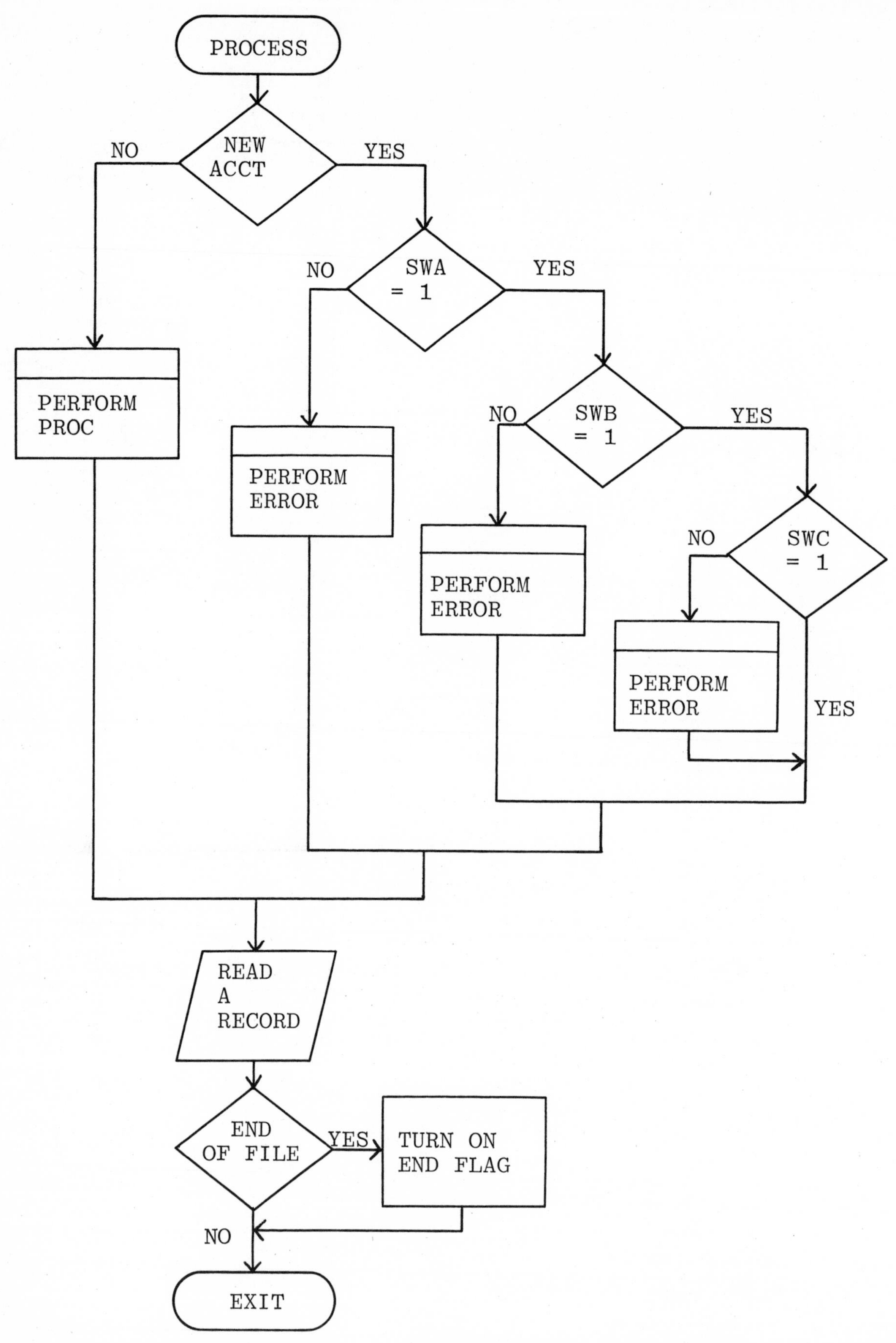

PROCESS
NEW ACCT
NO
YES
SWA = 1
NO
YES
PERFORM PROC
PERFORM ERROR
SWB = 1
NO
YES
PERFORM ERROR
SWC = 1
NO
PERFORM ERROR
YES
READ A RECORD
END OF FILE
YES
TURN ON END FLAG
NO
EXIT

Figure 8-7

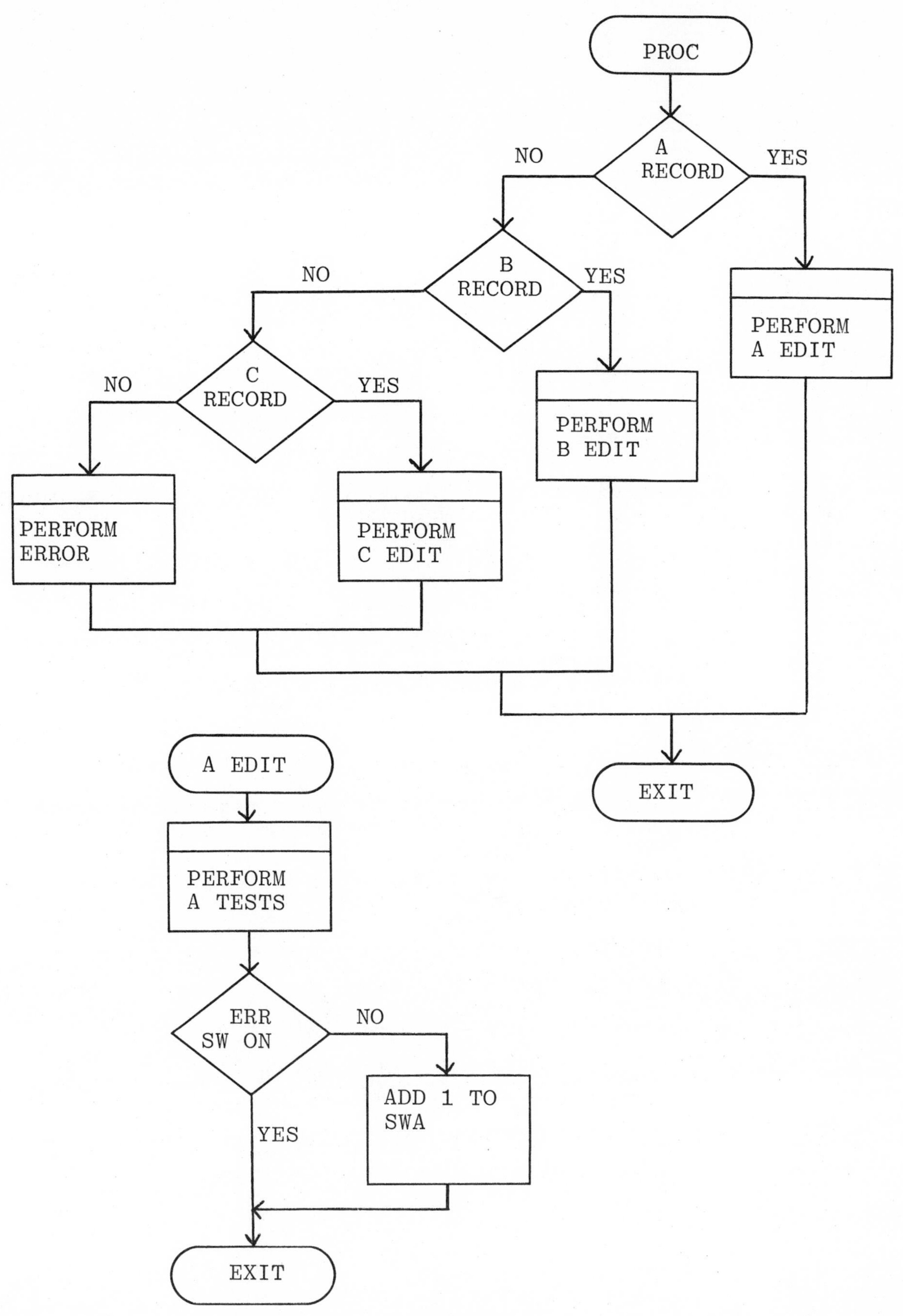

Figure 8-7 (cont.)

REVIEW QUESTIONS

Matching

A. Edit program

B. Program interrupt

C. Multiple input files

D. Error list

E. Record code

F. Multiple record types

__________ 1. Two or more record formats in a single file.

__________ 2. The premature termination of a program, sometimes caused by data in the wrong format.

__________ 3. More than one file used to provide data for a program.

__________ 4. A program which checks the input in various ways in order to avoid problems at a later point.

__________ 5. Data in a field which is used to identify the record type.

__________ 6. A report which indicates those items needing correction prior to the use of the data in subsequent programs.

True/False

T F 1. Data entry is one of the least expensive parts of a data processing operation.

T F 2. Update programs should be run immediately after edit programs.

T F 3. Division by zero is not permissible in most programming languages.

T F 4. Data exceptions are one form of program interrupt.

T F 5 The purpose of an edit program is to check the validity of the data and prepare an error list.

T F 6. When multiple record types are in a file, each type is automatically stored in a separate core location.

Exercises

1. Draw a flowchart to edit the following input in order to avoid incorrect output or program interrupts.

   CUSTOMER NUMBER
   ORDER NUMBER
   STYLE
   COLOR (a two digit number, color name is in a table)
   SIZE
   QUANTITY ORDERED

2. Draw a flowchart to edit a file which has two record types, a master and a transaction. Indicate the routines needed by performing subroutines but do not expand the subroutines.

3. Draw a flowchart which edits data about to be used for preparing an invoice. Identify the fields you would expect to be present that require editing.

Discussion Questions

1. What type of tests would you expect to find in a payroll transaction edit?

2. What types of tests would you expect to find in an order entry edit?

3. What types of tests would you expect to find in an accounts receivable edit of cash receipts?

4. Name other business data processing applications where edits can be usefully applied.

5. What types of problems might arise from not editing input data?

CHAPTER 9

Two Input Files

OBJECTIVES

As a result of studying this chapter the student should be able to perform the following activities:

1. Describe and flowchart the necessary activities in the housekeeping routine of a file matching program.

2. Describe what the high/equal/low paths mean when comparing master and transaction records.

3. Describe and flowchart the necessary processing needed for the high/equal/low paths when comparing master and transaction records.

4. Describe and flowchart the use of end master and and end transaction switches.

5. Describe and flowchart the use of an END FLAG switch.

6. Flowchart the read master and read transaction subroutines for a file matching program.

7. Describe error handling in terms of why it is needed and what should be done in file matching programs.

INTRODUCTION

Up to now, input has been in the form of a single sequentially organized file. It is very common to have multiple sequential input files (usually two) coming into a program. In order for this to be accomplished each of the files must be in sequence on the same item such as part number, division number, etc. There are several types of applications where this type of processing is typically found. One possible program in a payroll system (see Figure 9-1) might be to read the employee file for the current period and check to see if the employees who are to be paid actually work for the company.

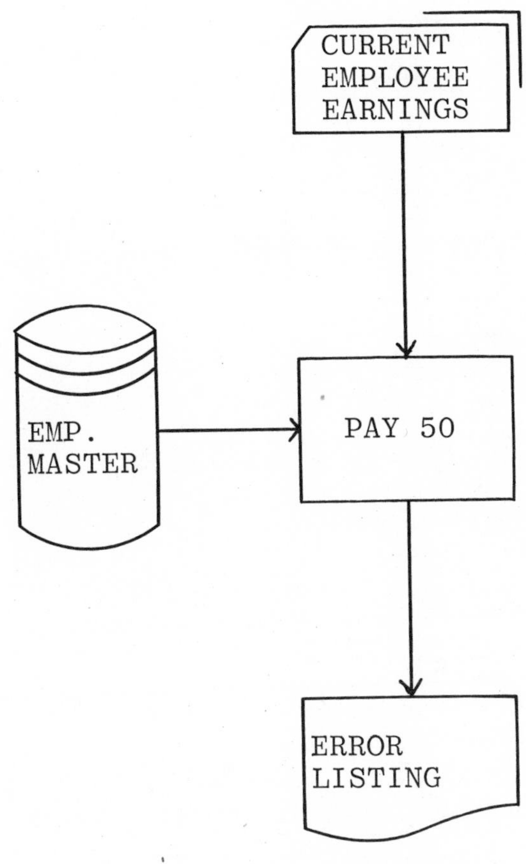

Figure 9-1

This is done by cross-referencing the current payroll file for earnings during a given period with a master file of employee numbers. If there are current earnings for which there is no matching master employee number, it raises some doubts as to who is being paid and why. If there are master items for which there are no current earnings it needs to be shown someplace that certain employees are not being paid this period. If the master employee number agrees with the current earnings employee number, things are presumed to be okay at this point.

In order for unmatched situations to be uncovered, both files (employee master number file and employee current earnings file) need to be read and processed at the same time. It should also be noted that there may be multiple current earnings records for each employee whose record should be on the file. However, our example will presume only one current earnings record for each employee.

FIRST RECORD PROCESSING

The typical method of starting this process is to read the first record from both the master (employee number master) and the transaction (current earnings) files. This is shown in Figure 9-2.

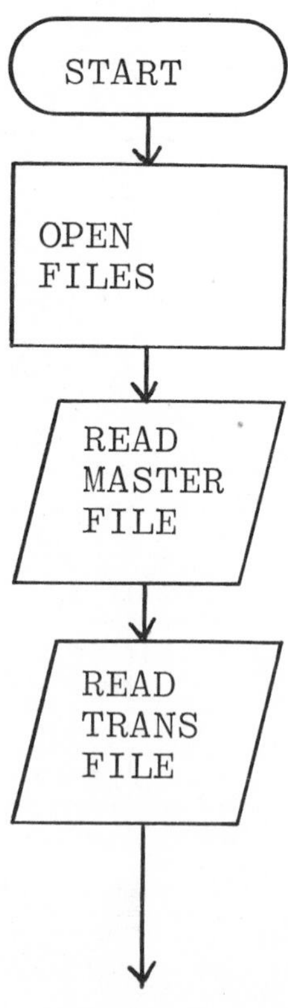

Figure 9-2

If an end of file condition is reached on trying to read the first record of either file an error condition exists which should force special processing and the termination of the run. The flowcharting for this is seen in Figure 9-3. The NO MAST and NO TRANS subroutines will be expanded later on in the chapter.

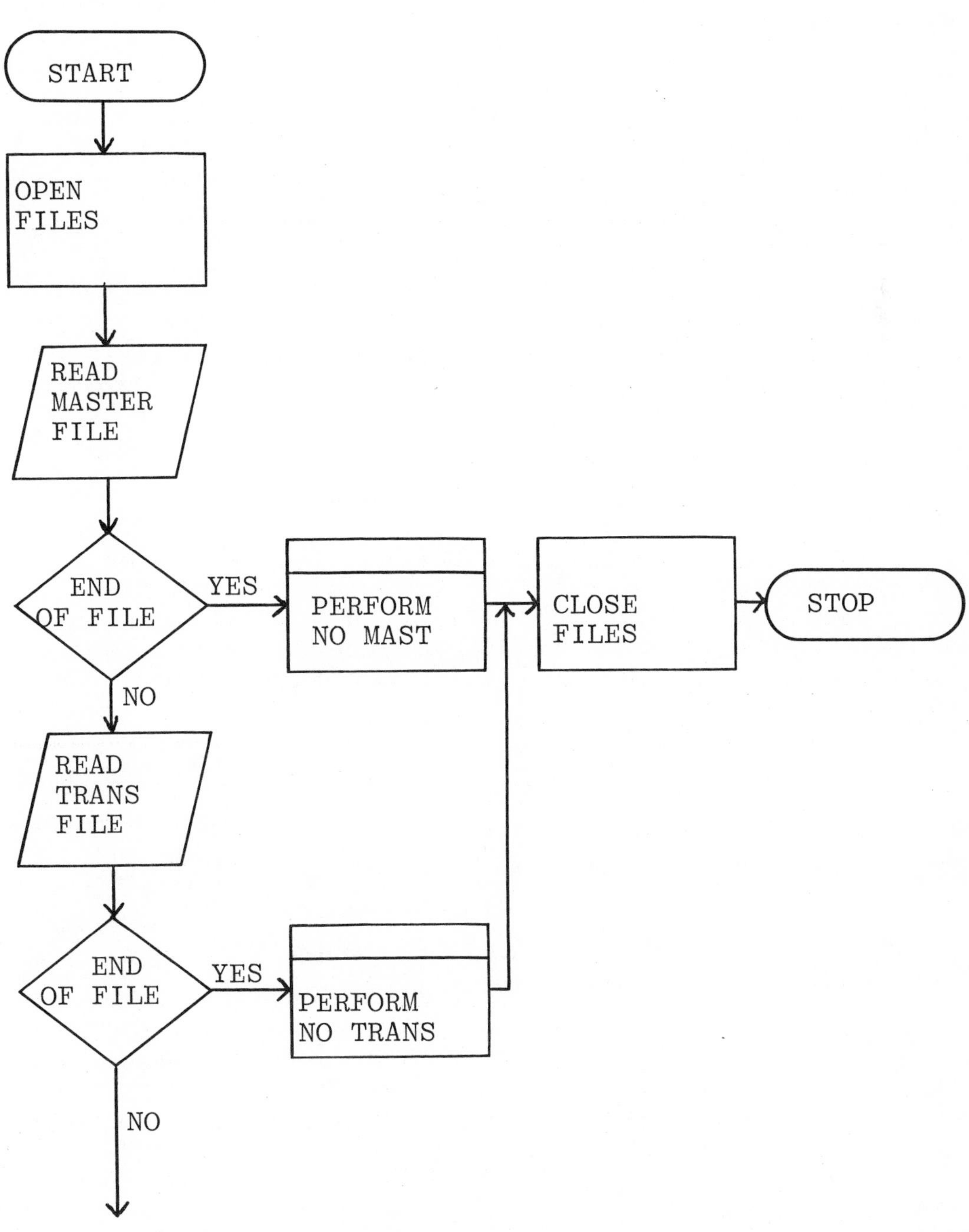

Figure 9-3

MATCHING THE FILES

Once the first record from each of the two files has been read into storage (there is a separate input area for each file) the next step is to see if they match. In our case this means to see if the current earnings employee number has a match on the employee master file. Whenever two items such as a field on a master record and a field on a transaction record are being compared, there are only three possible outcomes. Either the master item is higher in value or the transaction item is higher in value or the two values are equal. This type of comparison is shown in Figure 9-4.

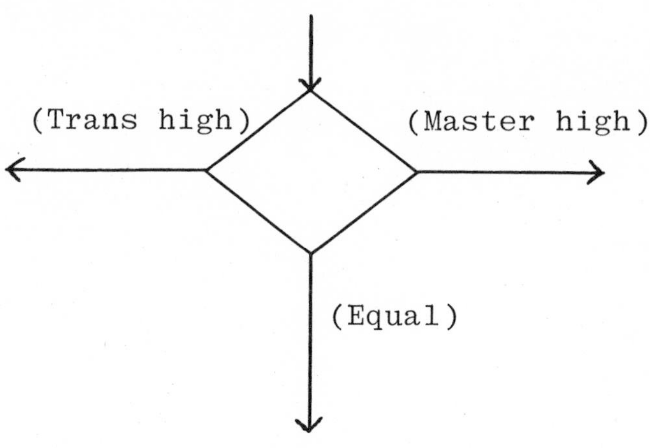

Figure 9-4

In order to be able to show how this works we need some sample items. The first few employees on both files (at least their numbers) are shown in Figure 9-5. Although in reality the employee number would probably be the social security number we will use single digit numbers to make the explanation easier to follow.

Master File	Trans File
1	1
2	3
3	4
5	5

Figure 9-5

Upon entering the master/trans comparison we have read the first record from both files. When we do the comparison we find that the employee numbers are equal (1 = 1). Thus the first employee on the current earnings file does in fact work for the company. Since all we are interested in knowing about are the mismatched or unequal situations, no further processing of these items is currently needed. The next step then is to read the next record from both files and go back to the comparison. This is shown in Figure 9-6.

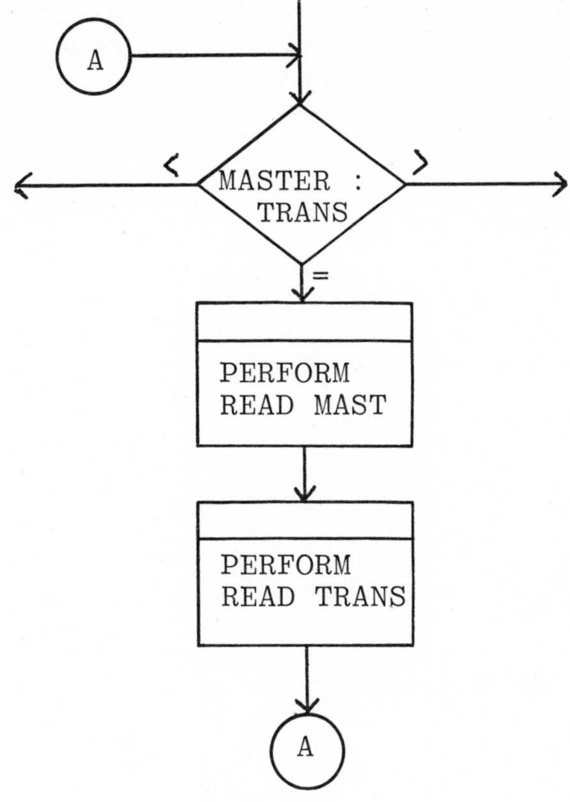

Figure 9-6

Because of the logic required in reading the next records, they are shown at this point as two separate performed routines for reading the master and transaction files. Presuming that the files have been read, we now have master employee number 2 and transaction employee number 3 in storage when we go back to the comparing step.

When we do the comparison we find that the transaction item is high (3 > 2). In our case this means that there are no current earnings for employee number 2. This should be noted someplace so that proper records can be maintained. For our purposes we will print a message on the printer indicating that there are no current earnings for employee number 2 this period. This action is shown in Figure 9-7.

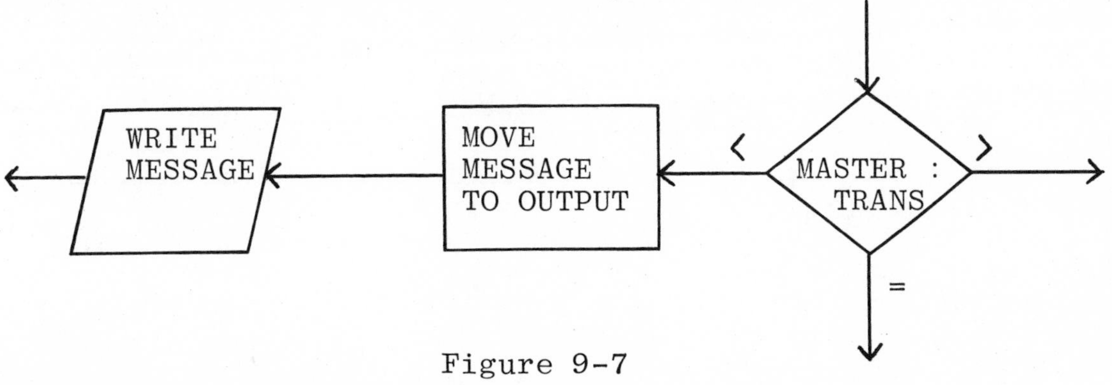

Figure 9-7

After writing the message we are done processing the master record and need to once again read the master file before returning to the comparison. We do not want to read the transaction file yet since we have not verified that employee number 3 exists. This addition to the logic is shown in Figure 9-8.

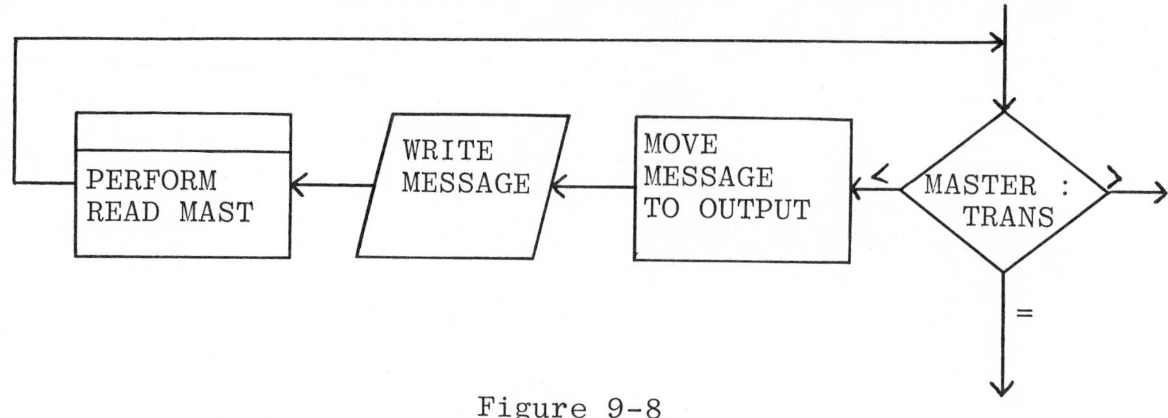

Figure 9-8

After reading the next master record (employee number 3) and going back to the comparison we find another equal situation (3 = 3). This results in both files being read and returning to the comparison. At this point we now have Master number 5 and transaction number 4 in storage. When the comparison is made the result is that the master item is high (5 > 4). What this means is that there was no 4 on the master file or in other words, somebody is being paid who does not work for the company or that the master file is being poorly maintained. This situation definitely needs to be noted for investigation. We will print an error message on the printer and continue on with the processing.

It is important to note that we do continue processing and do not stop the program. Since we are now finished with the transaction record we also need to read the next transaction record before returning to the comparison. This process is shown in Figure 9-9.

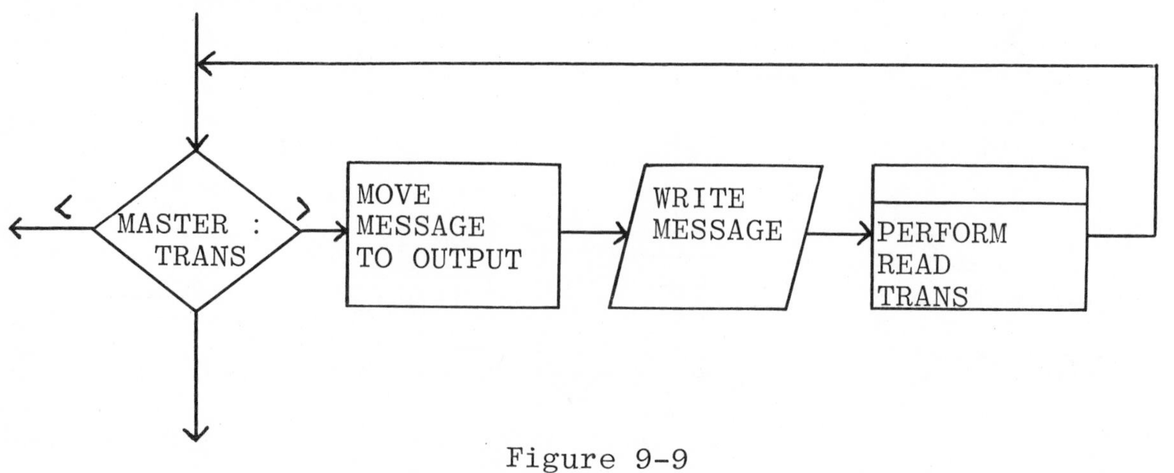

Figure 9-9

If you put all of this together the entire matching process (less the reading routines) is as shown in Figure 9-10.

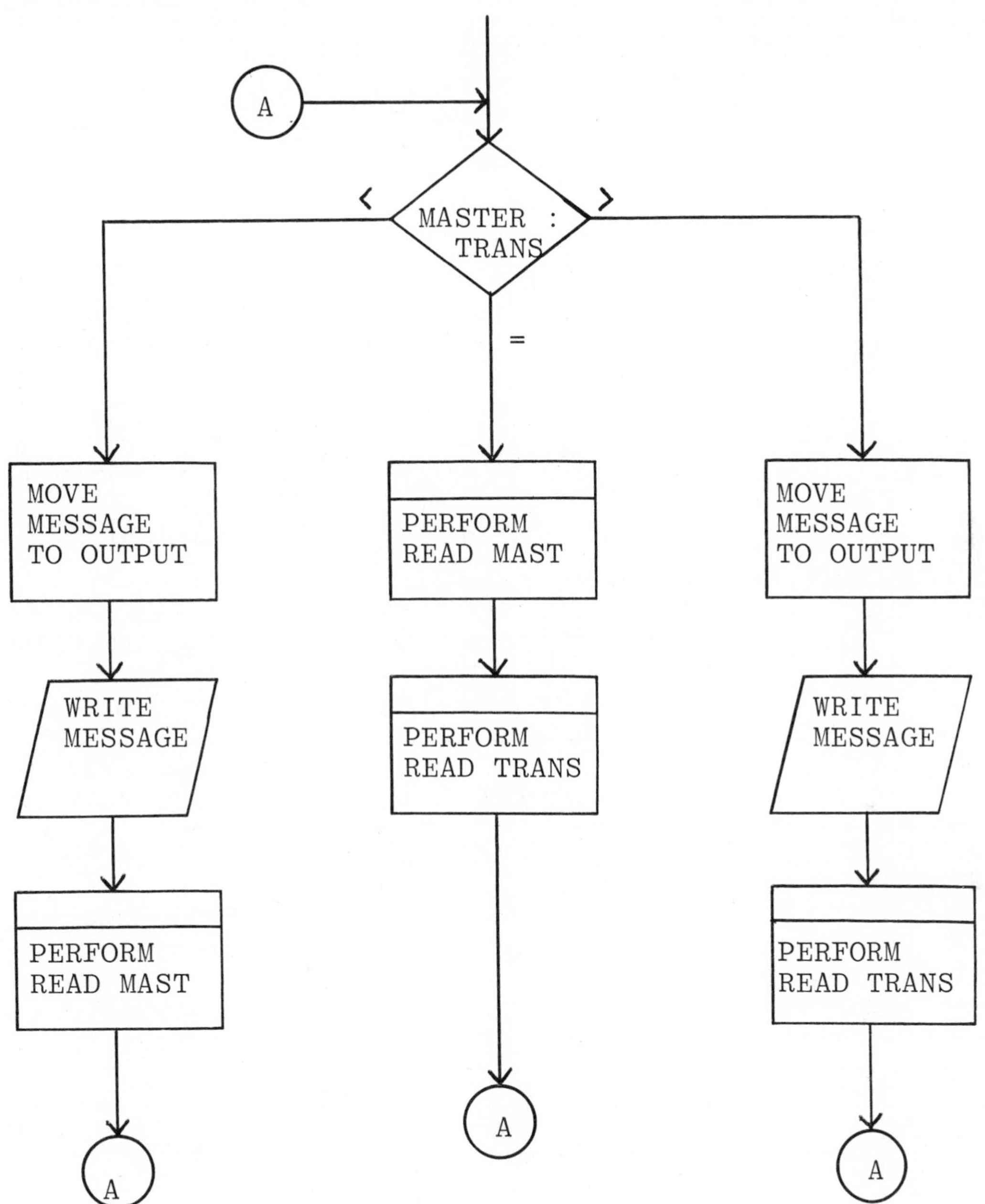

Figure 9-10

Before going on the reading process for master and transaction files, let's put what we have so far together in the standard format we have been using as shown in Figure 9-11.

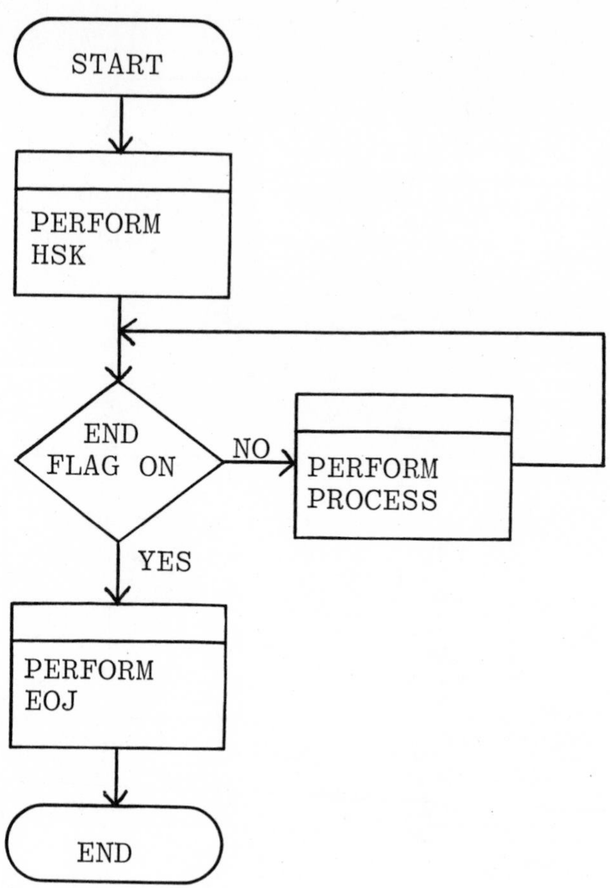

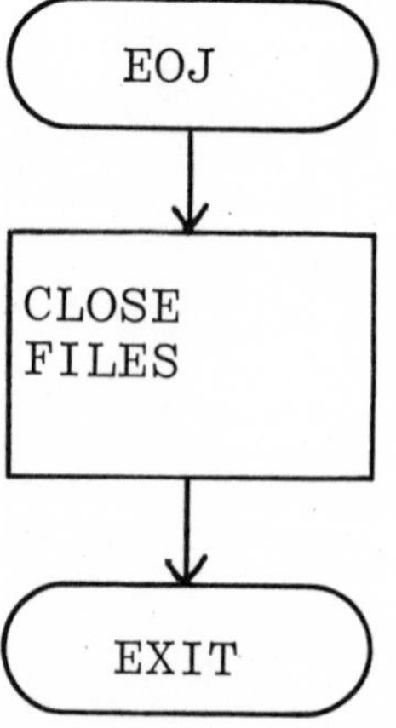

Figure 9-11

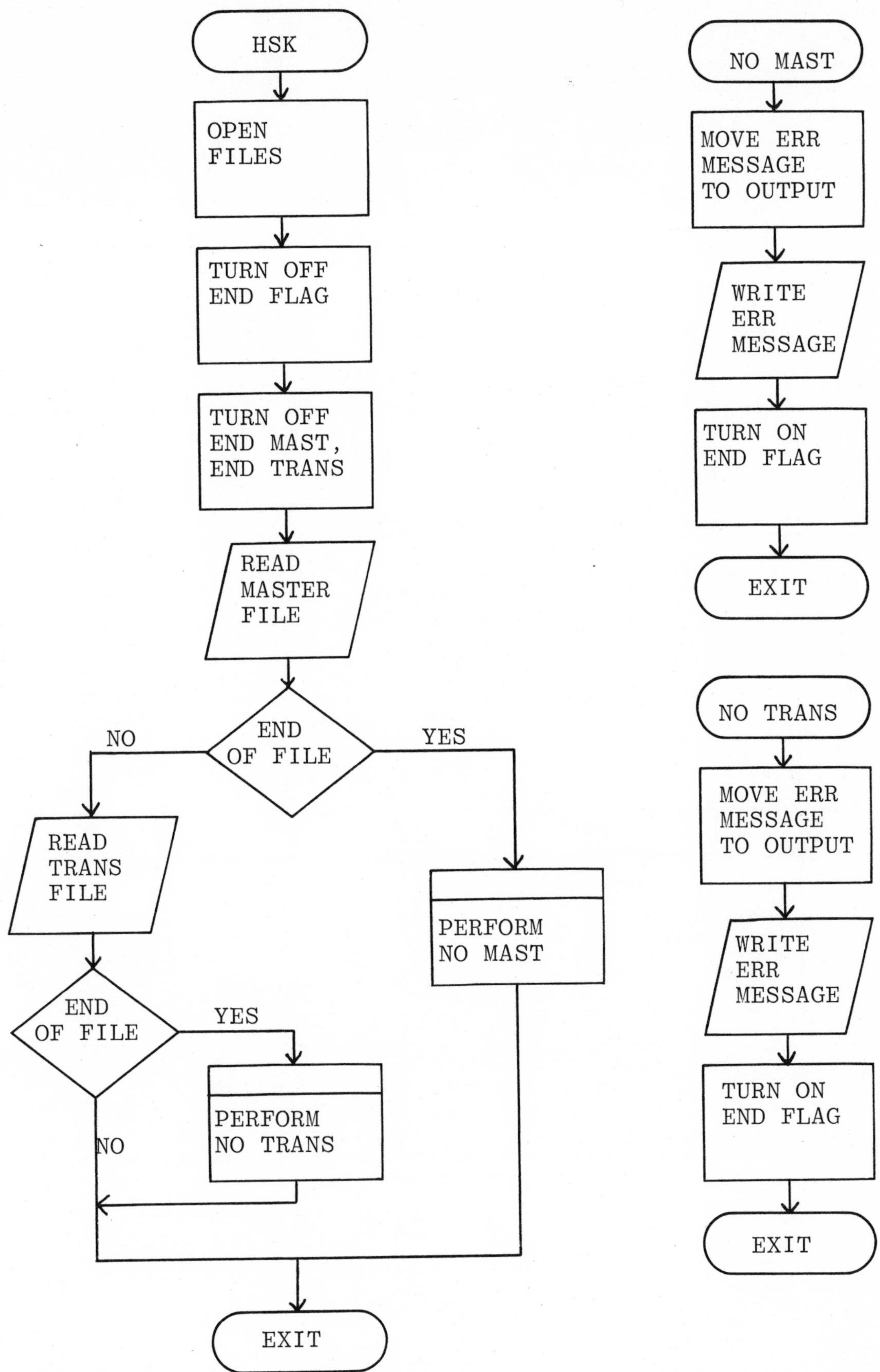

Figure 9-11 (cont.)

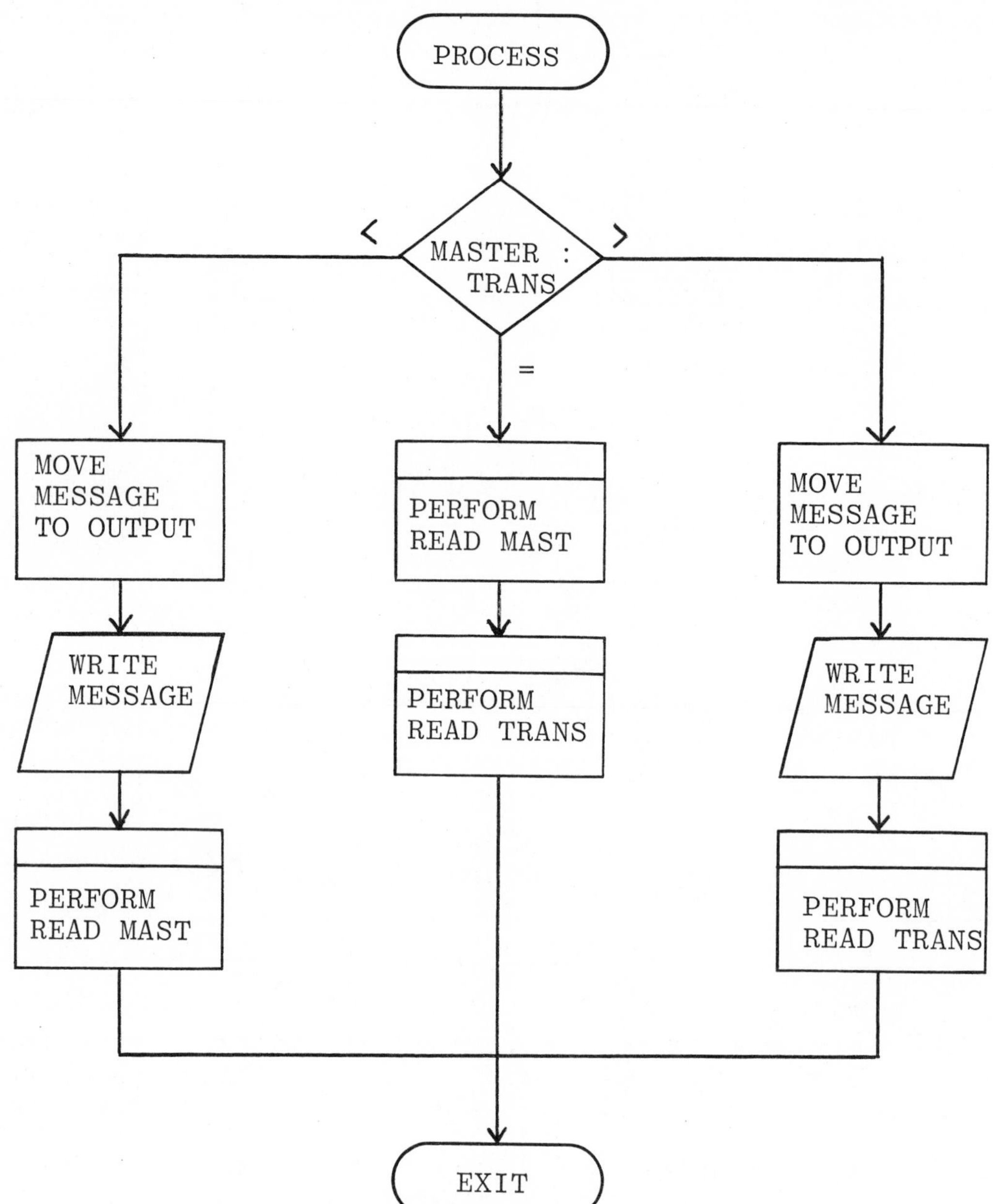

Figure 9-11 (cont.)

Let's walk through this version of the flowchart using the same data as before (see Figure 9-5). The first step is to perform the HSK routine. In HSK we open the files, turn off END FLAG, END MAST, END TRANS and read the first master record (employee number 1). The use of END MAST, END TRANS and END FLAG will be pointed out later following explanations of the routines. Had the master file contained no records we would have performed the NO MAST routine and dropped through to the exit in HSK. The NO MAST routine would have printed an error message indicating the absence of any master data and turned on the END FLAG switch.

After reading the first master record we then read the first transaction record (employee number 1). Had the transaction file contained no records we would have performed the NO TRANS routine and dropped through to the exit in HSK. The NO TRANS routine would have printed an error message indicating no activity against the master file and turned on the END FLAG switch.

Once we leave the HSK routine through the exit we will either have read the first master record and the first transaction record (both number 1 in our case) or printed an error message and turned on END FLAG. The next step is to see if the END FLAG switch has been turned on. If it is on then one or the other file had no records so we perform EOJ and terminate the program.

Since we have read a record from both master and transaction files when we test the END FLAG switch it is off. Thus we fall through and perform the PROCESS routine. The first step in the PROCESS routine is to compare the master and transaction value. Both values are equal to 1 so we follow the equal path. In our case there is no further processing needed as we are only interested in unmatched situations. We then read the next master record (employee number 2) and the next transaction record (employee number 3) and exit the PROCESS routine.

Upon leaving the PROCESS routine we return to checking the END FLAG switch. Since a record was successfully read from both files, this switch should still be off. The only time END FLAG will be turned on at this point is when both files have reached the end. The switch will be turned on in the reading process. Finding the END FLAG switch off we once again fall through to the PROCESS routine.

When entering the PROCESS routine this time we find that the master is less then the transaction ($2 < 3$). As with the previous example this indicates an employee with no earnings this period. This is indicated by writing an appropriate message on the printer. After writing the message we are done processing the master record and need to read the next master. In performing READ MAST we read employee number 3. Next, we exit the PROCESS routine and return to check the END FLAG.

The END FLAG switch is still off since we have not yet reached the end of both files. Therefore, we again enter the PROCESS routine and compare master and transaction employee numbers. At this point we find an equal condition (3 = 3). As in the previous equal situation we read the next master (employee number 5) and transaction (employee number 4) records on each file. Following the reading of these records we exit the process routine and return to comparing the END FLAG switch.

Still finding the END FLAG switch off we fall through into the PROCESS routine. In comparing master and transaction values the master is found to be high (5 > 4). In this case we have an employee with earnings who is not on the master file. This error needs to be noted. In our case we move and write an error message and proceed on to read the next transaction record. After reading the next transaction record (employee number 5) we exit the PROCESS routine and return to checking the END FLAG switch.

The END FLAG switch is still off so we again fall through into the PROCESS routine. On this pass through the PROCESS routine the master and transaction values are equal (5 = 5). As before we read another master and transaction record. However, as can be seen from the data, we are at the end of both files.

END OF FILE LOGIC

This brings up the point of end of file logic. That is how do we handle the reading process when one or both of the files has ended? Figure 9-12 shows the logic for reading the master file.

Let's take a look at how this fits in the PROCESS routine. There are two places in the PROCESS routine where the READ MAST routine is performed. One place where it is performed is on the master less than transaction path. This path of the PROCESS routine represents those employees who have no earnings this period. Any time this path is encountered the master record was printed along with a message indicating the no salary status. While performing READ MAST the first step is to check whether the master file has already ended. If it has already ended then we obviously cannot read the next record. Since we will be returning to check the status of END FLAG, if the END MAST switch is on and the end of the transaction file has already been reached, we need to turn on the END FLAG switch (Figure 9-13). The same thing is true if the END MAST switch was off when entering READ MAST but an attempt to read the master file found the end of file. See Figure 9-14.

If the END MAST switch is off and we do not find an end of file condition when reading the master file, we fall through to the exit of the READ MAST routine (Figure 9-15). The one remaining path through READ MAST is for END MAST being off when entering the routine, finding an end of file when

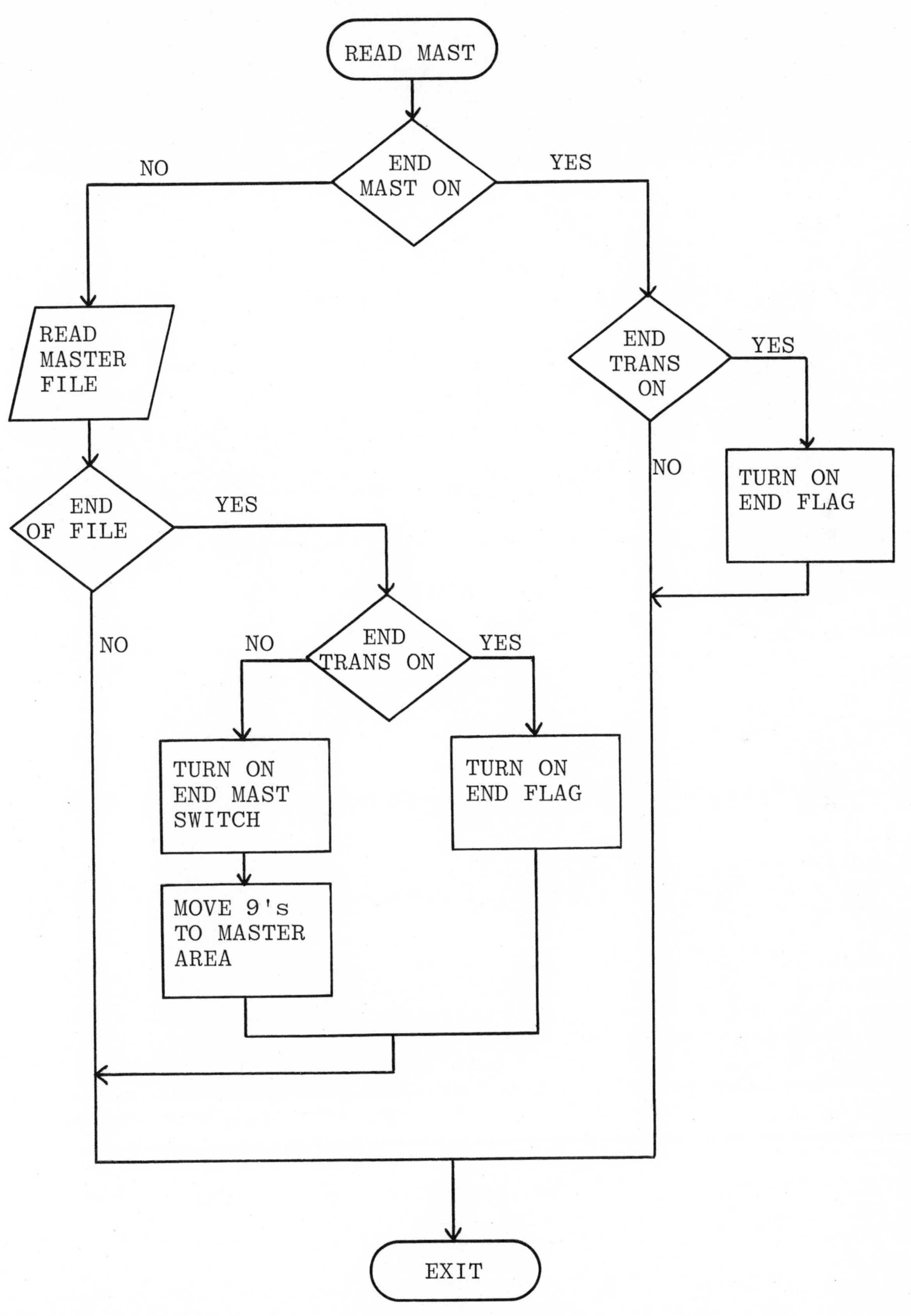
READ MAST
END MAST ON
NO
YES
READ MASTER FILE
END TRANS ON
YES
NO
TURN ON END FLAG
END OF FILE
YES
NO
END TRANS ON
NO
YES
TURN ON END MAST SWITCH
TURN ON END FLAG
MOVE 9's TO MASTER AREA
EXIT

Figure 9-12

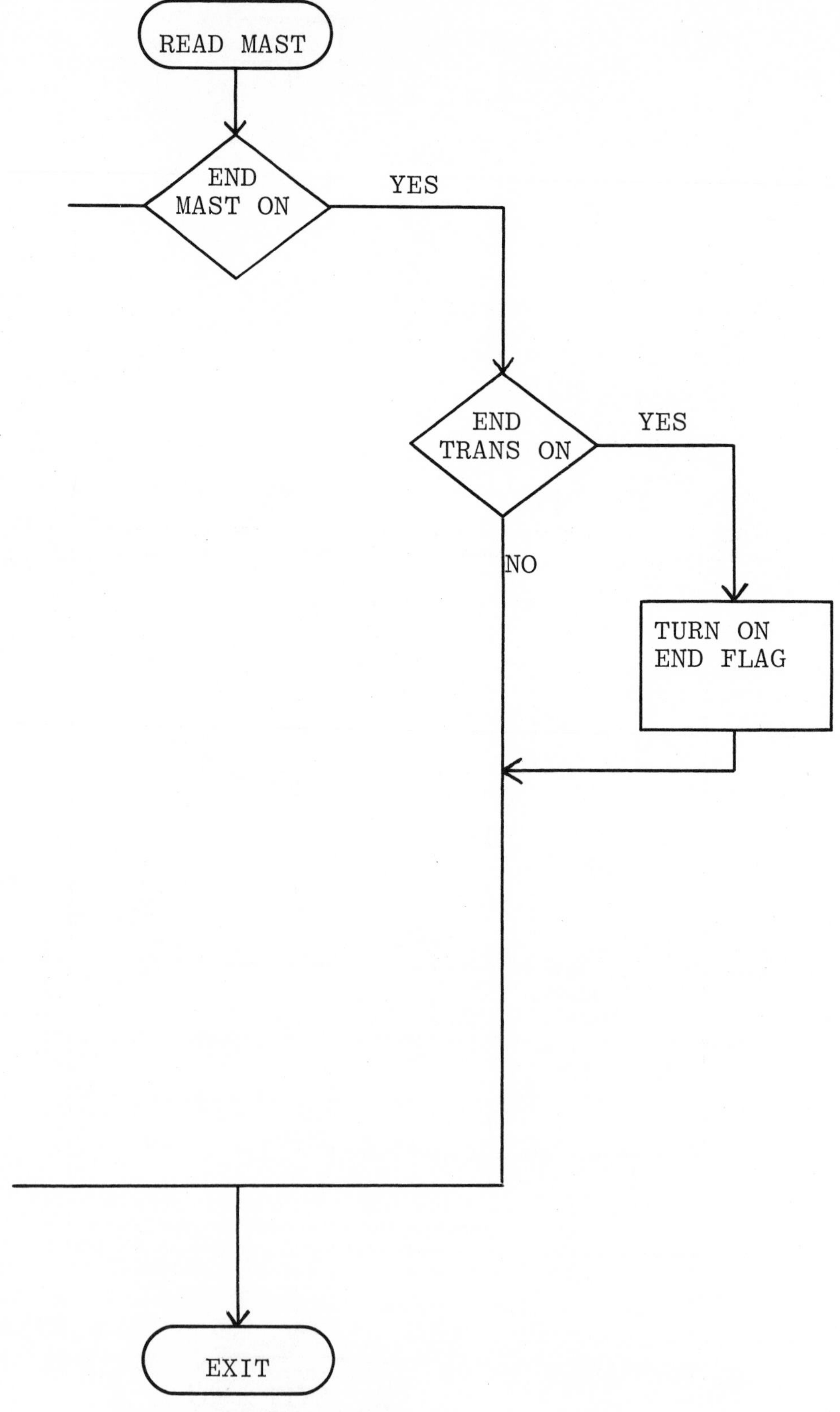
READ MAST
END
MAST ON
YES
END
TRANS ON
YES
NO
TURN ON
END FLAG
EXIT

Figure 9-13

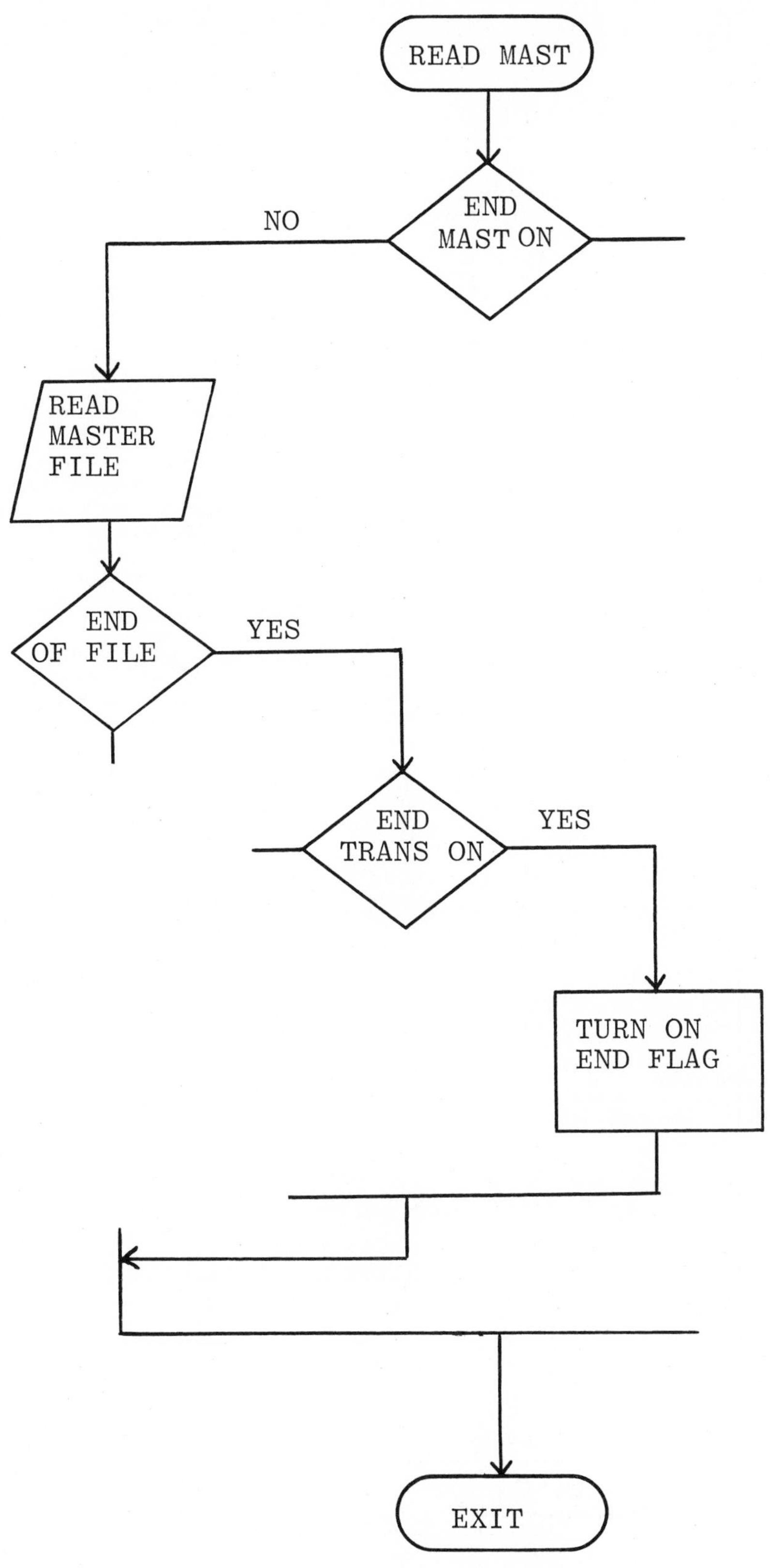
READ MAST
END
MAST ON
NO
READ
MASTER
FILE
END
OF FILE
YES
END
TRANS ON
YES
TURN ON
END FLAG
EXIT

Figure 9-14

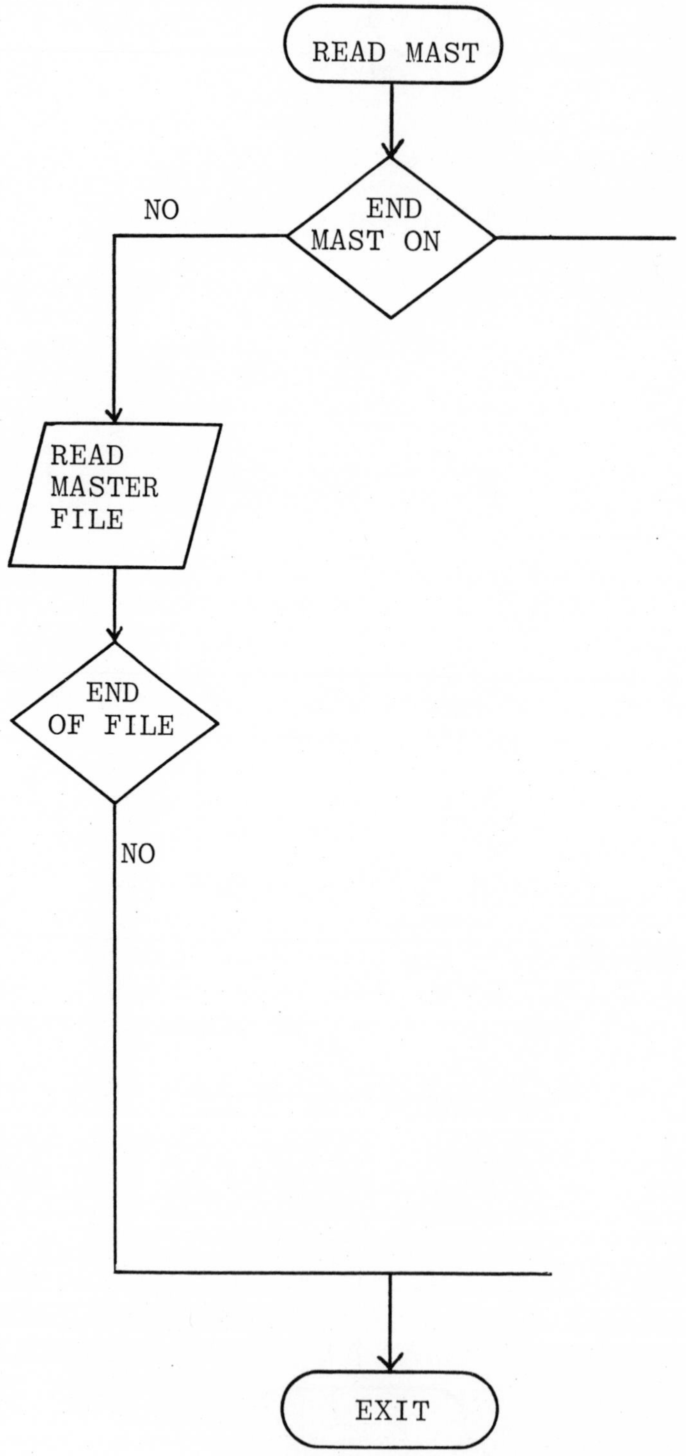

Figure 9-15

reading the master file, and the transaction file not yet having ended. In this case all remaining transaction items represent people being paid who are not on the master or in other words MASTER > TRANS conditions. To force this situation we move 9's (or a value higher than the largest employee number possible) to the master area. In this way any other transaction items will compare low and cause the appropriate error message to be printed. The END MAST switch is turned on at the same time.

The other place where the READ MAST routine is performed within PROCESS is on the MAST = TRANS path. The explanation given above also fits this execution of READ MAST. The logic for reading the transaction file is similar. This can be seen in Figure 9-16. Notice that the END MAST and END TRANS switches were turned off initially in the HSK routine.

Now let's return to the point where we had just processed master and transaction number 5 and were about to read the master and transaction files. The first step is to perform READ MAST. In READ MAST we find the END MAST switch off so we attempt to read the next record. In doing so we find the end of file. Thus we check to see if the transaction file has already ended. It has not, so we move 9's to the master area, turn on the END MAST switch and exit the READ MAST routine.

The next step is to perform the READ TRANS routine. In doing so the END TRANS switch is off so we attempt to read the transaction file. This produces an end of file condition on the transaction file so we check to find out if the master file has ended. Since the master file has also ended, we turn on the END FLAG switch and exit the READ TRANS routine.

This time when we return to check the END FLAG it is on. Therefore, we perform the EOJ routine and terminate processing.

TRANSACTION FILE ENDING FIRST

Realistically the odds are very good that both files will not end at the same time. One possibility is that the transaction file will end before the master file.

Presuming that the HSK routine has been executed and that both files do exist, the END FLAG switch is off the first time that it is tested, thus we perform the PROCESS routine. The data presented earlier is shown below except that we have added one more master record (employee number 6) to insure that the transaction file ends first.

Master File	Trans File
1	1
2	3
3	4
5	5
6	

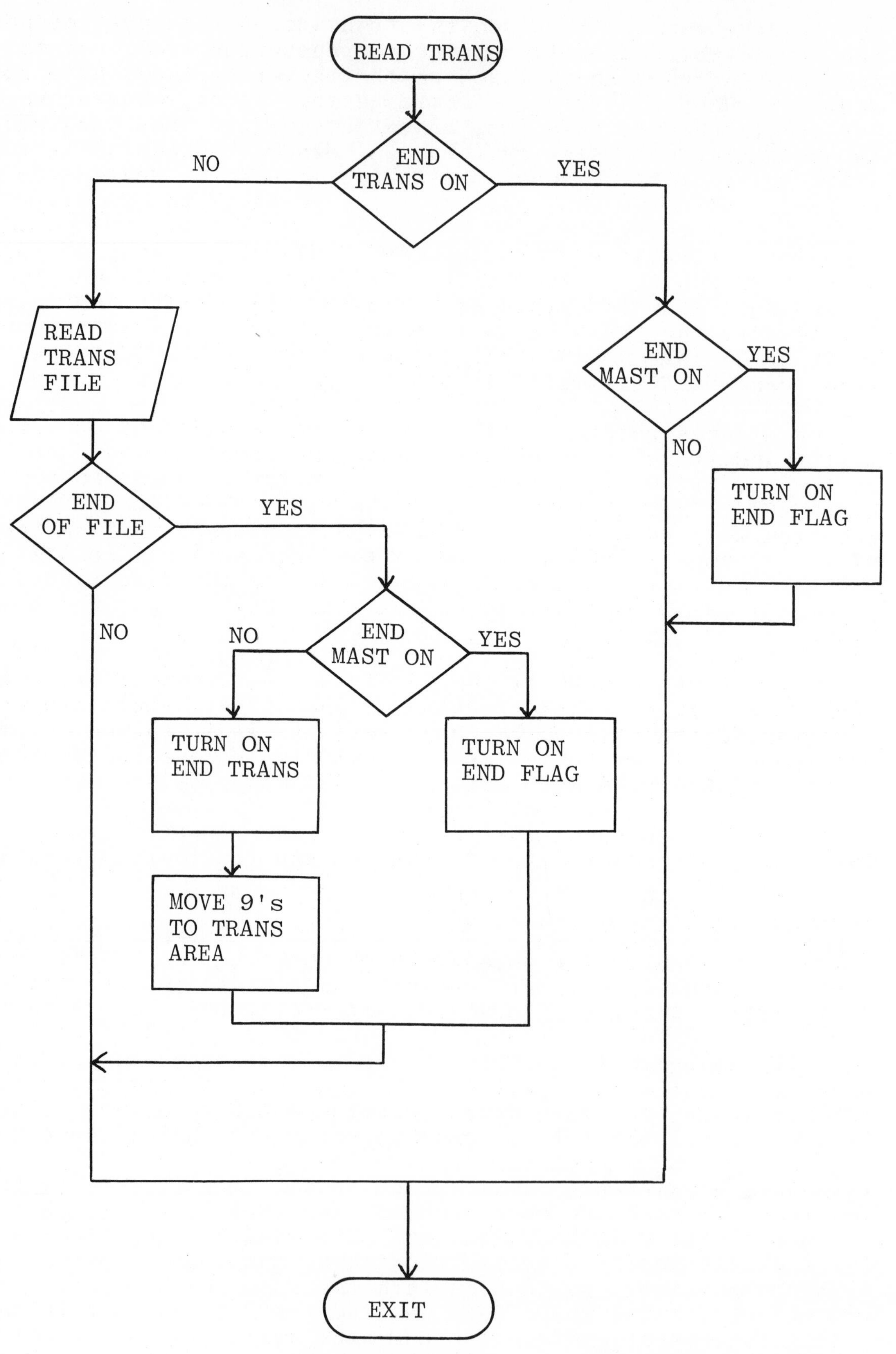
READ TRANS
END
TRANS ON
NO
YES
READ
TRANS
FILE
END
MAST ON
YES
NO
TURN ON
END FLAG
END
OF FILE
YES
NO
END
MAST ON
NO
YES
TURN ON
END TRANS
TURN ON
END FLAG
MOVE 9's
TO TRANS
AREA
EXIT

Figure 9-16

Since the housekeeping (HSK) routine is already finished, the first record from both files (employee number 1 in both cases) is already in storage. When the master and transaction items are compared they are found equal (1 = 1). Therefore, our next step is to perform the READ MAST routine. READ MAST reads the next record (employee number 2), finds no end of file and exits the routine. The next step is to perform READ TRANS.

In performing the READ TRANS routine we read the next transaction record (employee number 3) and finding no end of file, exit the routine. Having read both a master and a transaction record we now exit the PROCESS routine. The next step in the mainline logic is to test whether the END FLAG switch is on or off. It is off so we return to the PROCESS routine. Upon entering the PROCESS routine we now have master record number 2 and transaction record number 3.

When the two records are compared the master is found to be low (2 < 3) so we print a message showing no earnings this period of employee number 2 and then perform the READ MAST routine. In performing the READ MAST routine we read the next master record (employee number 3) and finding no end of file, exit the routine. We once again exit the PROCESS routine and return to test the END FLAG switch. Since it is still off we return to performing the PROCESS routine.

This time when we do the comparison the results are equal (3 = 3) so the READ MAST routine is performed. In reading the next master record (employee number 5) there is no end of file condition so we exit the READ MAST routine. Next, we perform the READ TRANS routine. This causes employee number 4 to be read in from the transaction file. Since no end of file exists, we exit the READ TRANS routine after reading the record. At this point we once again exit the PROCESS routine and return to check the END FLAG switch.

END FLAG is still off so we reenter the PROCESS routine and compare the master and transaction records. This time the master is high (5 > 4) so we print a message indicating that we have current earnings for a non-existent employee and then perform the READ TRANS routine. In performing the READ TRANS routine, employee number 5's record is read into storage and finding no end of file we exit the routine. We also exit the PROCESS routine and return to check the END FLAG switch. Finding it still off we once again enter the PROCESS routine.

When comparing the master and transaction items this time we find that they are equal (5 = 5) and thus fall through to performing the READ MAST routine. The READ MAST routine reads the employee number 6 record finding no end of file so we exit the routine. We then perform the READ TRANS routine. This time in performing READ TRANS we find that an end of file condition is present. Since the END MAST switch is not on we turn on the END TRANS switch, move 9's to the transaction area and exit the READ TRANS routine.

We also exit the PROCESS routine and return to checking the END FLAG switch. END FLAG is still off so we again enter the PROCESS routine. This time when comparing the master and transaction values, we find the master to be low (6 < 9's). A message indicating no current salary for employee number 6 is printed and the READ MAST routine is performed.

On this performance of READ MAST an end of file condition is found on the master file. Since the END TRANS switch is also on we turn on the END FLAG switch (both files have now ended) and exit both the READ MAST and PROCESS routines. When we return to check END FLAG this time we find it on. As a result we perform EOJ and terminate processing.

MASTER FILE ENDING FIRST

Now let's switch the data around just a little to cause the master file to end first.

Master File	Trans File	
1	1	
2	3	
3	4	
5	5	←Items being processed
	6	

Presume that we are at the point where the employee number 5 records from both files have been read (as indicated above). We compare the master with the transaction within the PROCESS routine and they are found to be equal. We fall through on the equal path to performing the READ MAST routine. In trying to read a master record we find an end of file condition on the master file. Since the END TRANS switch is not on, we turn on the END MAST switch, move 9's to the master area and exit READ MAST. After reading the next transaction record (employee number 6) we exit PROCESS and check END FLAG. END FLAG is still off so we fall through into the PROCESS routine.

When comparing the master and transaction values the master is found to be high (9's > 6). Accordingly a message is printed to indicate that employee number 6 is being paid but is not on the master file and READ TRANS is performed. When performing READ TRANS an end of file condition is found on the transaction file. Since the END MAST switch is also on the END FLAG switch is turned on and we exit the READ TRANS and PROCESS routines. Returning to the check for END FLAG it is now on so we perform EOJ and terminate processing.

ERROR PROCESSING

Errors that are found in matching two input files may be handled in many ways. How they are handled depends on the severity of the error and individual company practices. In our examples the initial file reading in the HSK routine was the only place where an error caused the program to be terminated. This was based on one or the other files not being present which obviously would prevent any reasonable processing from being done.

The rest of the errors, which were basically unmatched master or transaction records, caused an error message to be printed and processing continued. While these may seem drastic enough errors to stop processing (especially earnings for employees who do not exist on the master file) this program's function was to find these types of errors. As such we want to know what all of the errors are so that they can be checked, corrected and made ready for future processing. In general most errors in this type of a program are not enough to cause termination of the program.

The process of matching multiple sequential input files will be further explained in Chapter 10 which covers the updating process for sequential files.

REVIEW QUESTIONS

Matching

A. Causes processing to be terminated

B. Handled in the housekeeping routine

C. Master > transaction

D. Master < transaction

E. END MAST switch

F. END FLAG switch

G. READ TRANS

H. READ MAST

__________ 1. Indicates that there is a master record with no matching transaction record.

__________ 2. Reading the first record from both master and transaction files.

__________ 3. Set on when both files have ended.

__________ 4. No master or no transaction file present.

__________ 5. Indicates that there is a transaction record with no matching master record.

__________ 6. Done on both the equal and master greater than transaction paths of the PROCESS routine.

__________ 7. Set on in the READ MAST routine.

__________ 8. Done on both the equal and master less than transaction paths of the PROCESS routine.

True/False

T F 1. It is very uncommon to find two sequential files being used as input to the same program.

T F 2. It is valid to have multiple transactions for a single master in a file matching program.

T F 3. The first master and transaction records are usually read in the READ MAST routine.

T F 4. An error condition is usually indicated when the master and transaction records are equal.

T F 5. Master records for which there are no transactions during the period are usually a master greater than transaction situation.

T F 6. The END FLAG switch is typically turned off in the housekeeping routine.

T F 7. Any time the master file ends before the transaction file in file matching programs the remaining transactions are in error.

T F 8. The END MAST and END TRANS switches, if used, must be turned off in the HSK routine.

T F 9. End of Job (EOJ) processing is done only when the END FLAG switch is off.

T F 10. The END FLAG switch is turned on after only the master file has ended.

T F 11. All error conditions usually cause the job to be terminated.

T F 12. Files are opened and closed in the housekeeping (HSK) routine.

Exercises

1. Flowchart the routines for reading the master and transaction files in a two input file program.

2. Flowchart the housekeeping routine.

3. Flowchart the entire program for reading two sequential input files with the following requirements. Each record on the transaction file is to be checked to see if there is a corresponding record on the master file. Unmatched masters should cause the message 'NO TRANSACTION FOR MASTER NUMBER X' to be printed. Matching master and transaction records should cause the message "MASTER AND TRANS NUMBERS X FOUND EQUAL' to be printed. Unmatched transactions should cause the message 'NO MASTER FOR TRANSACTION NUMBER X' to be printed.

Discussion Questions

1. Describe the use of the END MAST and END TRANS switches including why they are used, how they are initialized and how they are modified.

2. Describe how the first records from the master and transaction files are read and how end of file conditions are handled in the housekeeping routine.

CHAPTER 10

The Update Program

OBJECTIVES

As a result of studying this chapter the student should be able to perform the following activities:

1. Describe the function of a file update program.
2. Identify and describe the types of transaction records in an update program.
3. Flowchart the logic for additions to a master file.
4. Flowchart the logic for deletions from as master file.
5. Flowchart the logic for changes to a master file.
6. Describe why a sequential file update needs to produce a new file for the updated version of the file.
7. Flowchart a file updating procedure for single card image masters.
8. Describe some of the necessary additional steps when masters might take 2, 3 or 4 cards to create or change them.

INTRODUCTION

One of the more common types of programs that requires two sequential input files to be matched is an update program. An update program is used to bring the data in a file (usually a master file) up to date so that it reflects the current situation. The transaction records which provide the updating data may be one of three types. They can be additions to the master file, deletions from the master file and changes to items already in the master file.

Additions - Add records are records that are to be added to the master file. Adds are only valid if no similar record already exists on the master file. Additions are found on the master greater than transaction branch when comparing the records from the two files.

Deletions - Deletions are records that are to be removed from the master file. Deletions are only valid if there is a record on the master file similar to the one that is to be deleted. Deletions are found on the equal path of the master/transaction comparison.

Changes - Change records are those that will modify the contents of the records already on the master file. Like deletions, change records are only valid if there is a record on the master file similar to the change record. Changes also happen on the equal branch of the master/transaction comparison. Changes may occur to any part of the master record except the field on which the file has been sequenced (called the control field).

In order to know which type of transaction record is being processed at any given time it is necessary to have some sort of code such as A (addition), C (change), or D (deletion) in the transaction record. This is in addition to any data that is in the record. As these records are processed, a record or report should be produced showing any activity (updating) that takes place. The first few steps in the update program are the same as the file matching program. These steps are shown in Figure 10-1.

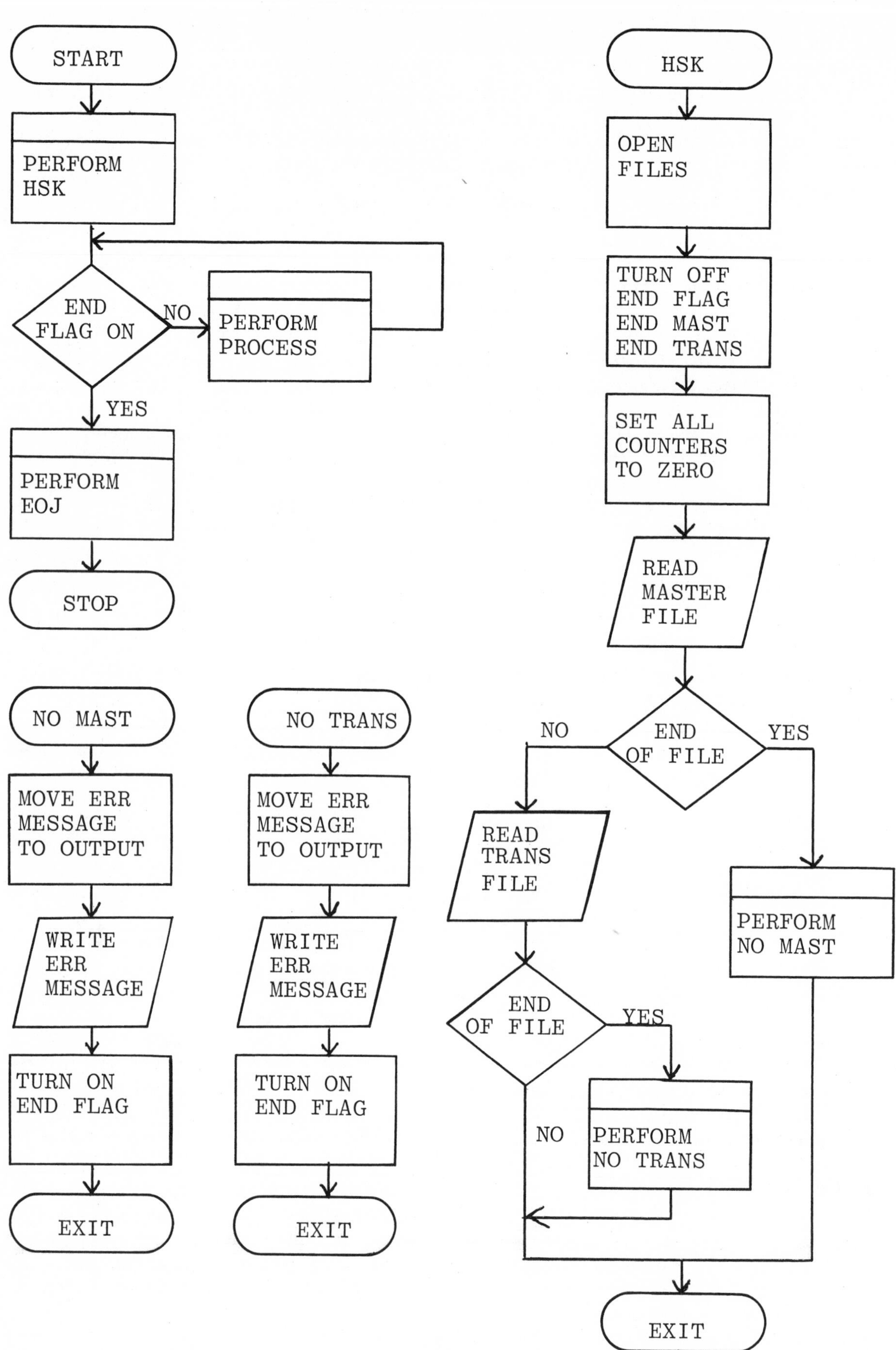

START
PERFORM HSK
END FLAG ON
NO
PERFORM PROCESS
YES
PERFORM EOJ
STOP
HSK
OPEN FILES
TURN OFF END FLAG END MAST END TRANS
SET ALL COUNTERS TO ZERO
READ MASTER FILE
END OF FILE
NO
YES
READ TRANS FILE
PERFORM NO MAST
END OF FILE
YES
NO
PERFORM NO TRANS
EXIT
NO MAST
MOVE ERR MESSAGE TO OUTPUT
WRITE ERR MESSAGE
TURN ON END FLAG
EXIT
NO TRANS
MOVE ERR MESSAGE TO OUTPUT
WRITE ERR MESSAGE
TURN ON END FLAG
EXIT

Figure 10-1

MASTER GREATER THAN TRANSACTION

The PROCESS routine is a little more complicated than the one in Chapter 9. The same basics that were true in file matching are still true, but more steps are now needed. One path of this process is shown in Figure 10-2.

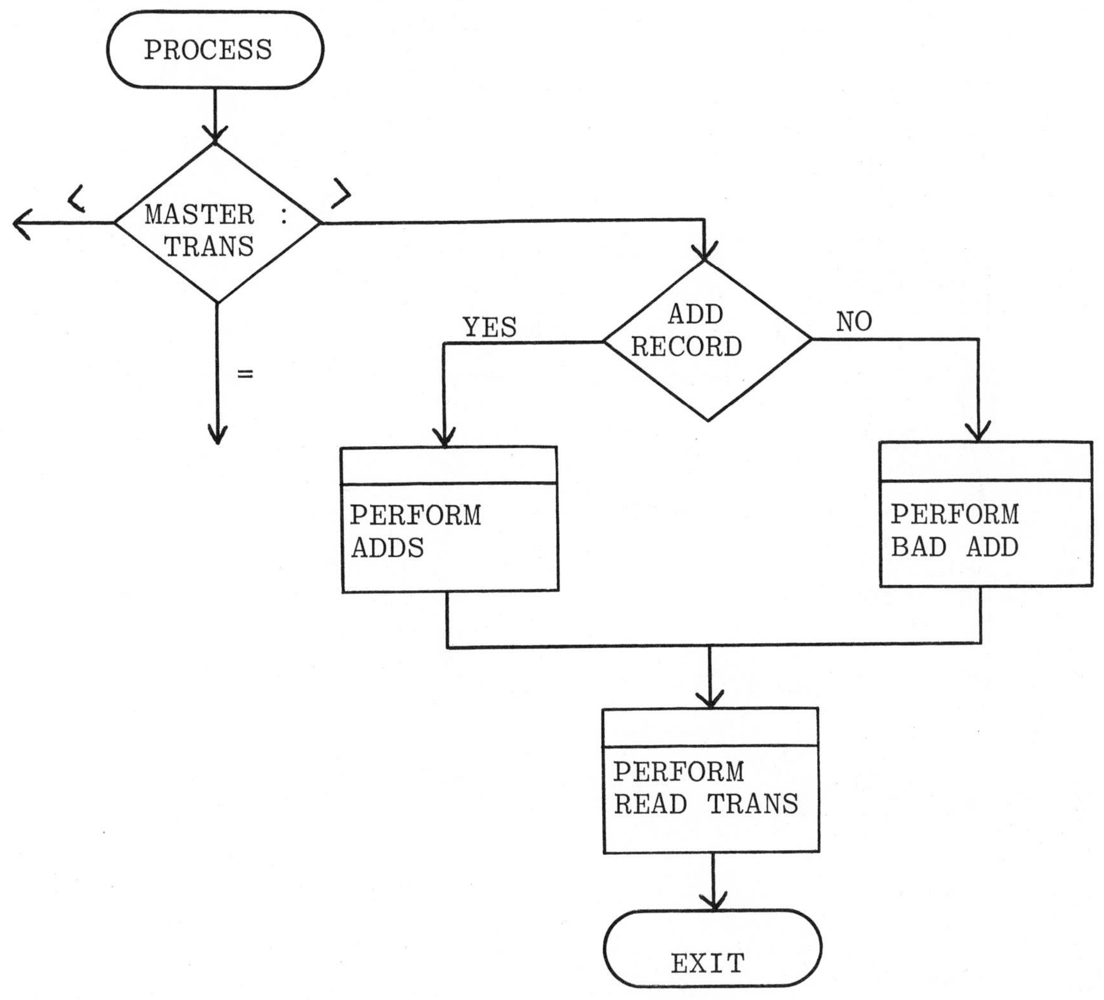

Figure 10-2

Any time the master is greater than the transaction the record should be an addition to the file. It is, however, necessary to check to see if the transaction record had a valid add code. If it does not have an add code, it is in error and we perform the BAD ADD routine to handle the error. If it does have an add code we perform the ADDS routine to add the record to the file. In either case, after processing the add or the error transaction record, we need to read the next transaction record and return to the mainline program. The logic for the BAD ADD and ADDS routines is shown in Figure 10-3 and 10-4 respectively.

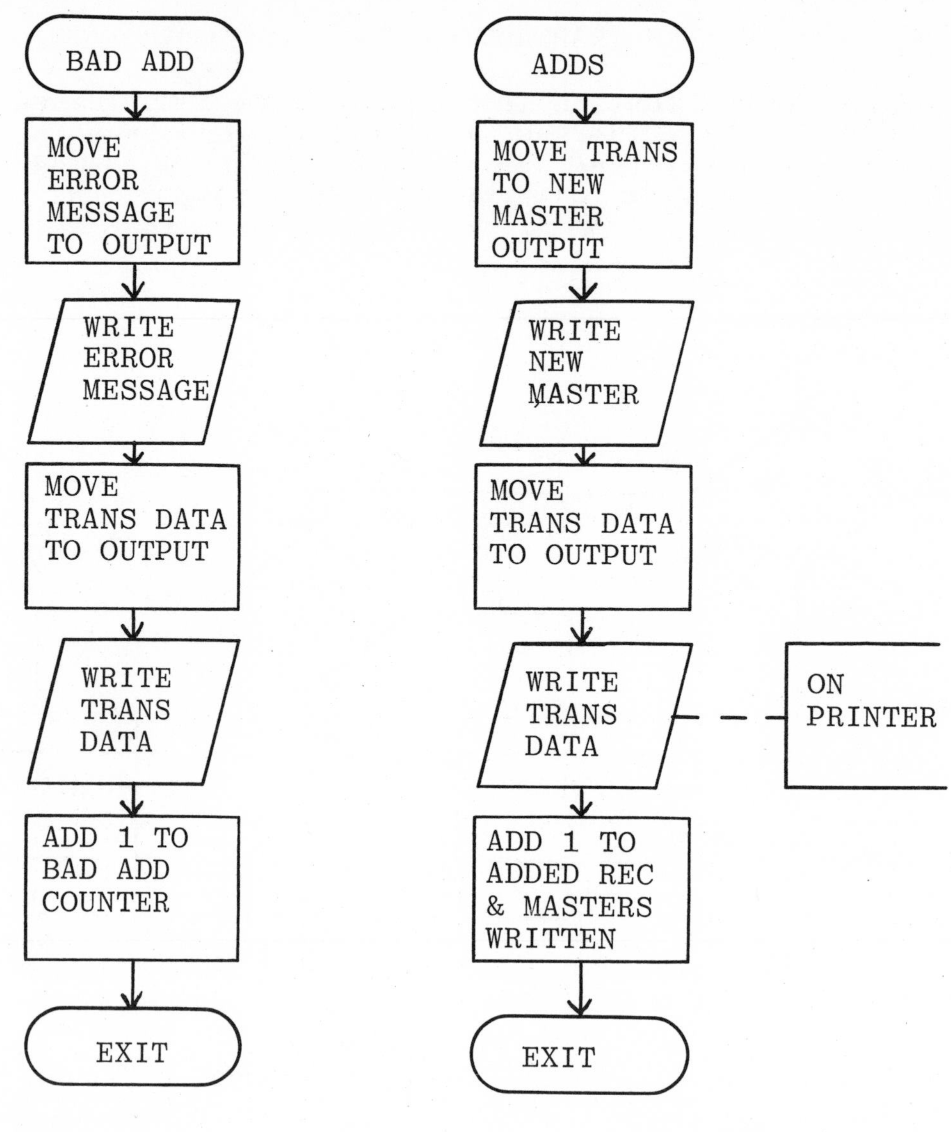

Figure 10-3

Figure 10-4

All we are doing for invalid add records in our example is printing a message to indicate what occurred, printing the bad transaction and incrementing a BAD ADD counter. The counter is needed so that after all the records have been processed from both files we will know how many invalid addition records were present in the transaction file.

The ADDS routine first moves all the data from the transaction record to the output area for the new master file and then writes the new master record. You may be asking yourself what new master record and why? A simple analogy should serve to explain the situation. If you have a casette tape of music that you wish to add songs to and you wish to add them in the middle of the tape, you have much the same problem. That is, you cannot do it on the existing tape. You must create a new tape by copying those songs from the original tape that you still want and inserting the new songs that you want on the tape at the places you want them to appear.

Much the same process is true in updating a standard sequential file. Since there is no room between existing records to add new records, then a new file needs to be created with the new records added at the desired points. This insertion process is what was done in the ADDS routine.

In addition to adding the record to the new master, we also printed a message indicating that this addition to the file was done. This serves as a visual indication of the processing taking place. A records added (ADDED REC) counter was incremented so that at the end of the processing we will know how many new records have been added to the master file. We also increment a MASTERS WRITTEN counter.

MASTER LESS THAN TRANSACTION

One of the other paths possible after comparing the master and transaction records is the master being less than the transaction. This situation means that the master record from the old master file is to be copied in its present form on the new master file. This is shown in Figure 10-5 along with the COPY routine that actually moves the record from the old to the new file.

Notice once again that in addition to moving the data from the old master to the new master and writing the new master that we also incremented the MASTERS WRITTEN counter. This counter is for the same control purposes as the previous examples of additions and errors.

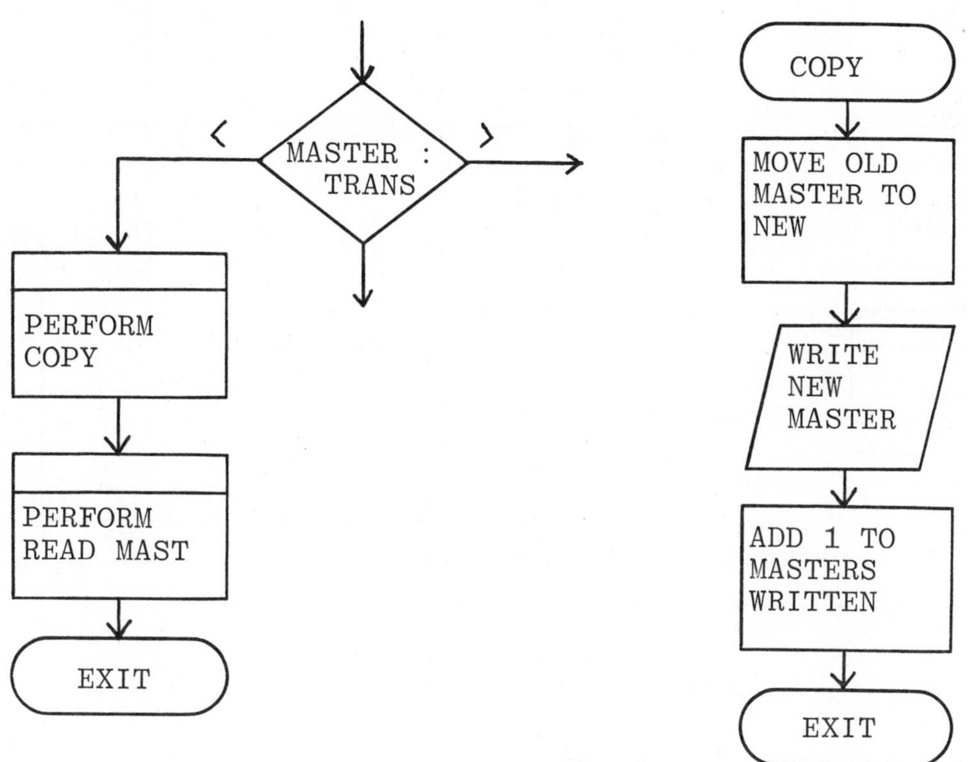

Figure 10-5

MASTER EQUAL TO TRANSACTION (GENERAL)

The one remaining path left on the master/transaction comparison is that of the master and transaction records being equal. If the equal path is followed, then the transaction records must be either deletions or changes in order to be valid. The logic for this is shown in Figure 10-6.

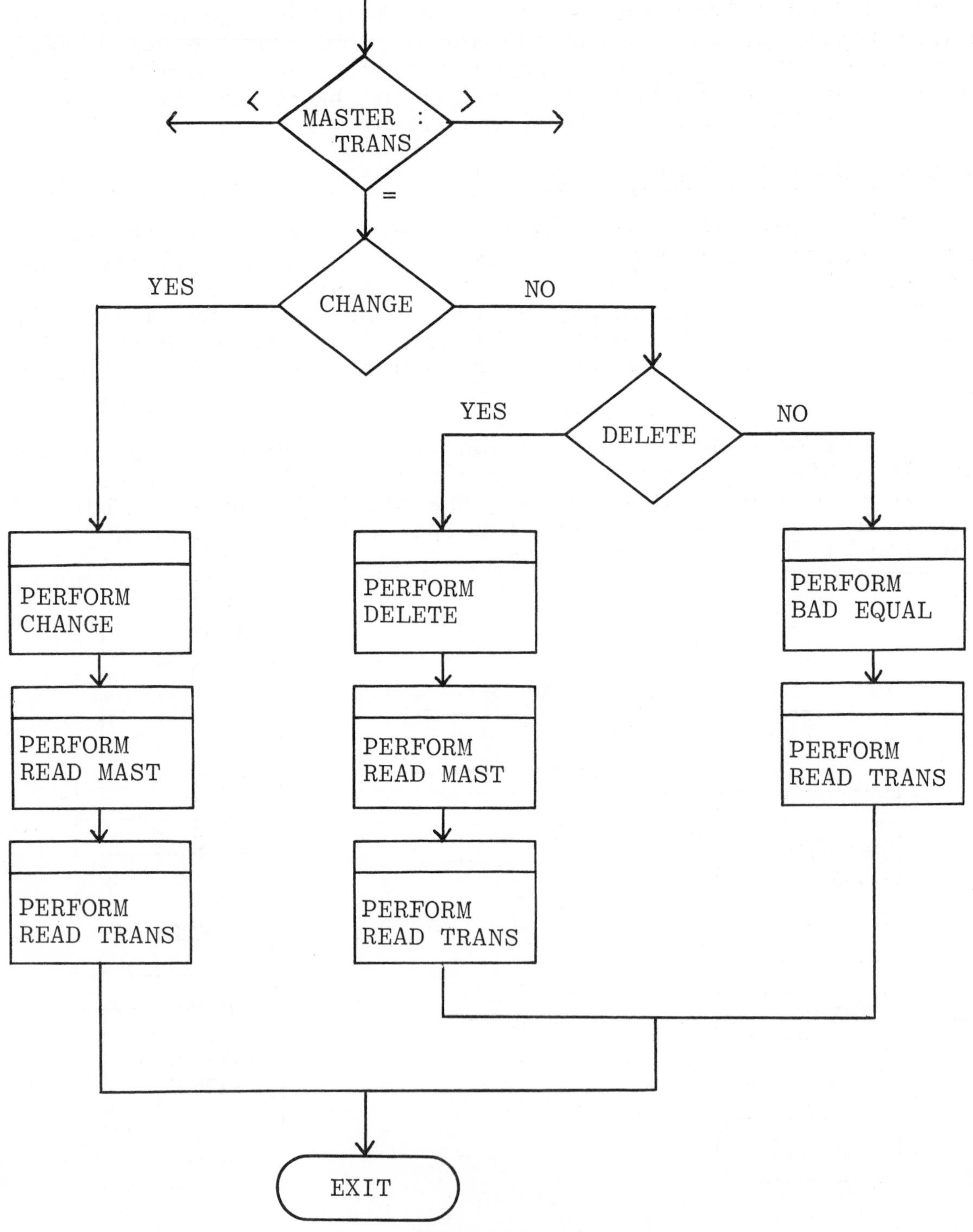

Figure 10-6

Once we have determined that the master and transaction records are equal we need to know if the transaction item represents a change or a delete. If it is a change, we perform the CHANGE routine to modify the existing master record's contents and perform the READ MAST and READ TRANS routines to get the next master and transaction records. After reading the next record from both files we exit the routine.

If the transaction is not a change, we check to see if it is a delete. If it is not a delete it is in error and we perform the BAD EQUAL error routine to indicate the error and the READ TRANS routine to get the next transaction record. If on the other hand it is a delete, we perform the DELETE routine to drop the record from the master file and then perform both the READ MAST and READ TRANS routines to continue processing. After reading both files we exit the routine.

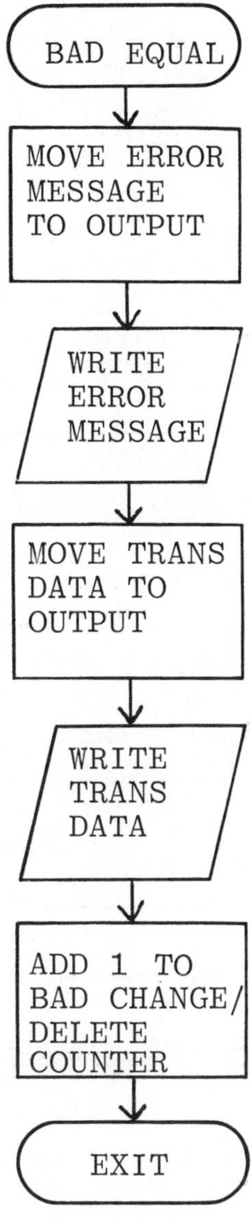

Figure 10-7

MASTER EQUAL TO TRANSACTION (BAD EQUAL)

The BAD EQUAL routine shown in Figure 10-7 builds and prints an error message indicating that you have something other than a change or a delete for an existing master record and prints the transaction record that is in error. Also, a counter is incremented so that at the end of the program we will know how many of this type of error occurred.

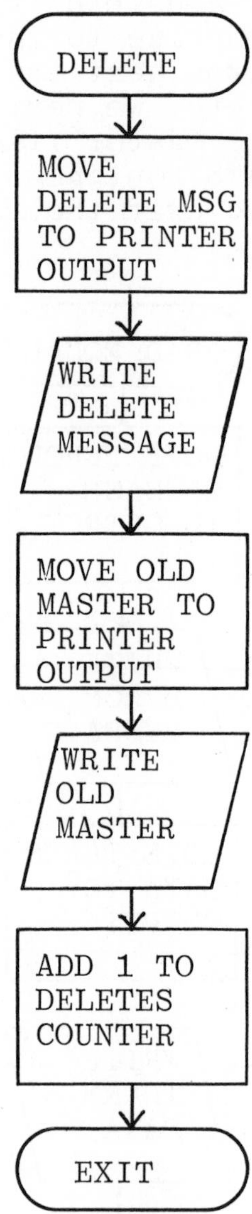

Figure 10-8

MASTER EQUAL TO TRANSACTION (DELETE)

The DELETE routine shown in Figure 10-8 builds and prints a message indicating that a master record has been deleted and prints the deleted master record. Once again a counter is incremented so that at the end of the program we will know how many master records have been deleted.

MASTER EQUAL TO TRANSACTION (CHANGE)

Change records require a little explanation prior to showing their logic. Change records contain all the same fields as the master record. If any fields in the change record are blank, then no change is being made to those particular fields. If any of the fields in the change record are not blank, then the contents of the non-blank fields in the change record will replace the contents of the same fields in the master record.

Let's presume that the fields in our master and transaction record are NAME, date of birth (BIRTH), SEX, PAY RATE, and marital status code (MCODE). In addition the transaction record contains the EMPLOYEE NUMBER and CHANGE CODE and the master record contains the EMPLOYEE NUMBER. The logic for a change record would be as shown in Figure 10-9.

The first step in the CHANGE routine is to print a record showing the original contents of the master record before any changes are made. Also, a counter is incremented so that we will know how many change records have been processed at the end of the program.

Next comes a series of decisions which check each field on the change record to see if it is blank. If it is blank, nothing is done except to go on to the next decision. If it is not blank then its contents are moved to the corresponding field in the old master record. It is important that the old master fields are the ones that are modified. It is also important to note that all of the fields in the transaction record are individually checked regardless of whether any of the fields are blank or have changes in them.

Once all of the fields have been checked and changes have been made, the modified contents of the entire old master record are once again printed out to reflect its current status. After printing the modified contents we move the modified master record to the new master and write the new master. We also increment the MASTERS WRITTEN counter. Following this we exit the CHANGE routine.

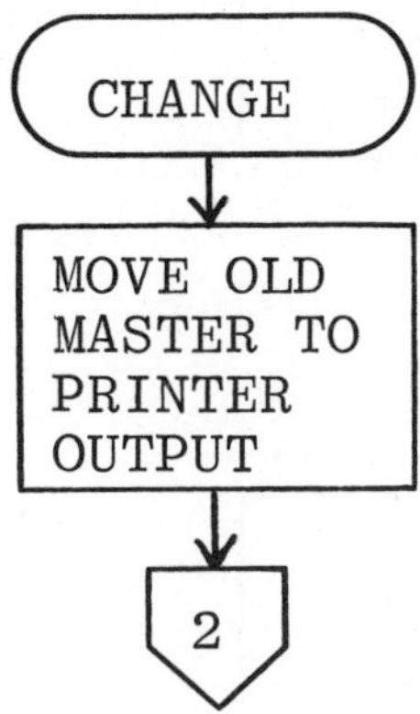

Figure 10-9

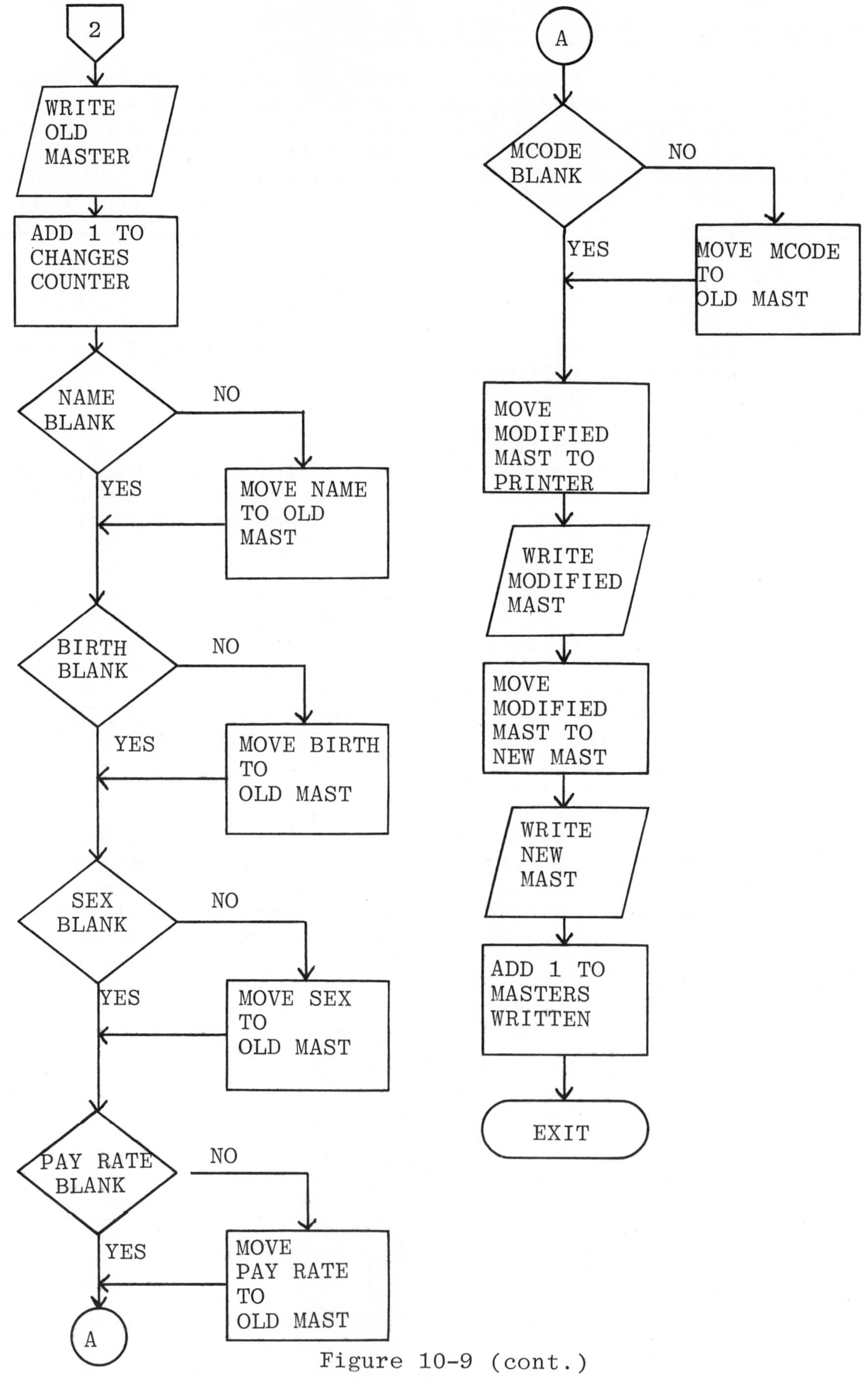

Figure 10-9 (cont.)

READ MASTER

Now for the READ MAST routine. Its logic is shown in Figure 10-10. Notice that the READ MAST routine in Figure 10-10 is the same as the READ MAST routine presented in Chapter 9. When attempting to read the master file, if no end of file is found, we exit the routine after incrementing the MASTERS READ counter. If an end of file is found and the transaction file is not yet finished, we move 9's to the master employee number area, turn on the END MAST switch and exit READ MAST.

If an end of file is found and the transaction file is also ended, we turn on END FLAG and exit READ MAST. If both the END MAST and END TRANS switches are on when entering READ MAST we turn on the END FLAG switch and exit the READ MAST routine. Subsequently, we will also exit the PROCESS routine, perform the EOJ routine and stop.

If the transaction file is not already finished (END TRANS off) but the master file is finished (END MAST on), we exit READ MAST without any other processing. Any further transactions that are adds will be added to the new master (via ADDS) and any further transactions that are not adds will be handled as errors (via BAD ADDS). When the end of the transaction file is finally reached the END FLAG swich will be turned on in READ TRANS and we will terminate the program.

READ TRANS

The logic for reading the transaction file is shown in Figure 10-11. The logic in READ TRANS is the same as it was in Chapter 9. If END TRANS is on when entering READ TRANS one of two paths are followed. First, if the master file is also ended (END MAST is on), we turn on END FLAG and exit READ TRANS. Second, if the master file is not yet finished (END MAST is off), we do nothing but exit READ TRANS.

If, one the other hand, END TRANS is not on when we enter the READ TRANS routine we will attempt to read another transaction record. If another transaction is successfully read (i.e. no end of file is found) we exit the READ TRANS routine. If an end of file is found when attempting to read a transaction record there are two possible paths left open. First, if the master file is also finished (END MAST is on), we turn on END FLAG and exit READ TRANS. Second, if the master file is not yet finished (END MAST is off), we move 9's to the transaction employee number area, turn on END TRANS and exit the READ TRANS routine.

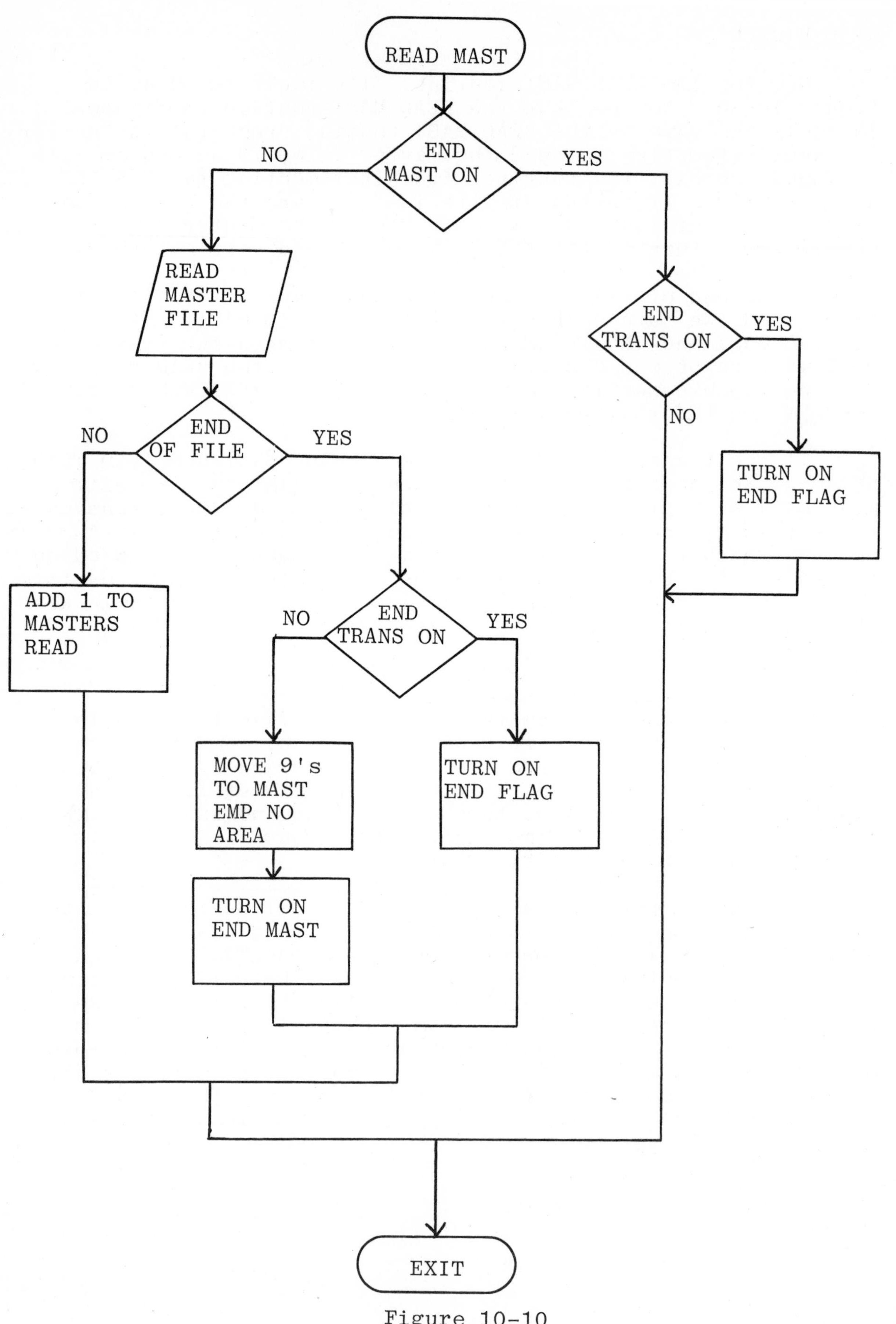
READ MAST
END MAST ON
NO
YES
READ MASTER FILE
END TRANS ON
YES
NO
END OF FILE
NO
YES
TURN ON END FLAG
ADD 1 TO MASTERS READ
END TRANS ON
NO
YES
MOVE 9's TO MAST EMP NO AREA
TURN ON END FLAG
TURN ON END MAST
EXIT

Figure 10-10

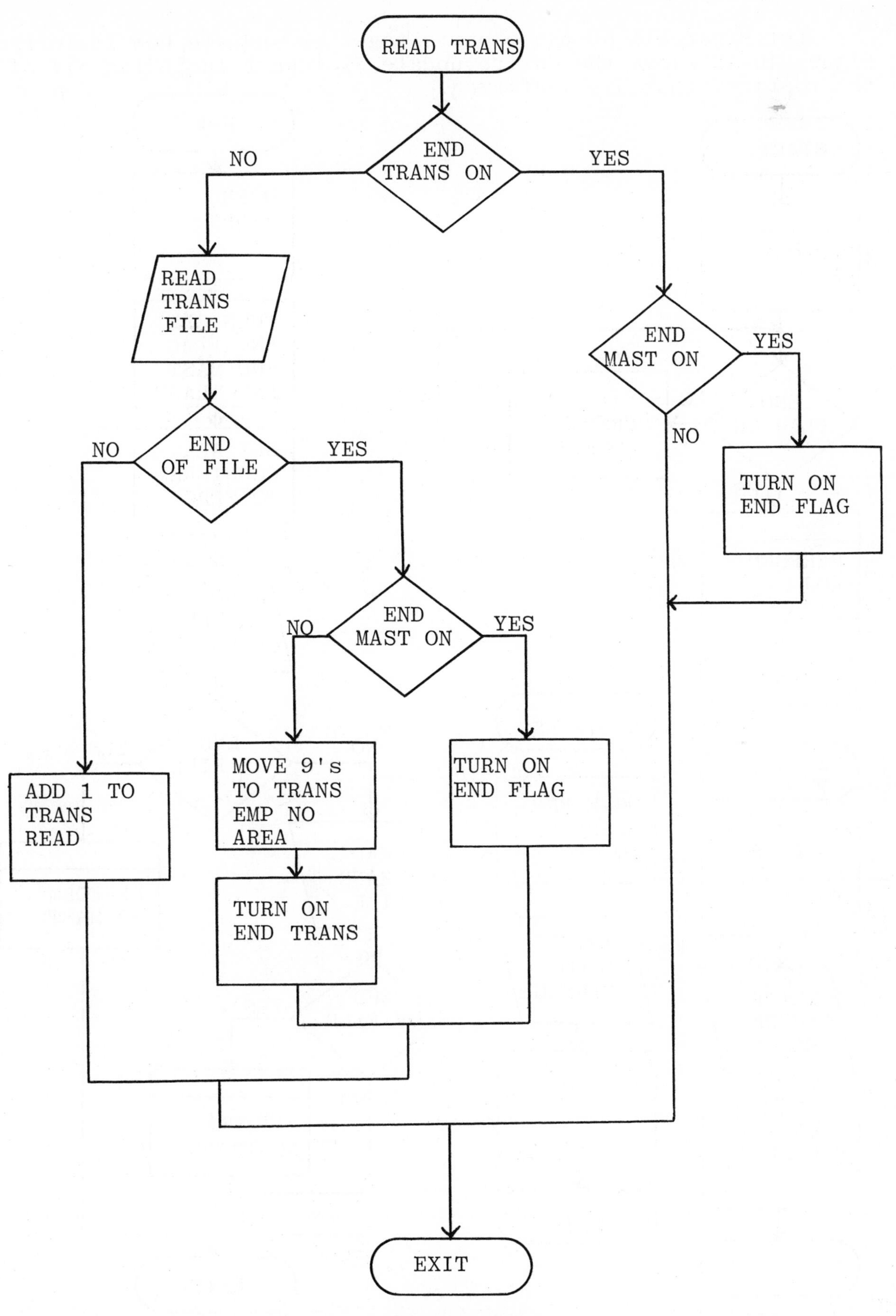
READ TRANS
END TRANS ON
NO
YES
READ TRANS FILE
END MAST ON
YES
NO
END OF FILE
NO
YES
TURN ON END FLAG
END MAST ON
NO
YES
ADD 1 TO TRANS READ
MOVE 9's TO TRANS EMP NO AREA
TURN ON END FLAG
TURN ON END TRANS
EXIT

Figure 10-11

Let's put all of these parts together and see how it works. Figure 10-12 shows the entire update flowchart including all of the routines that are performed.

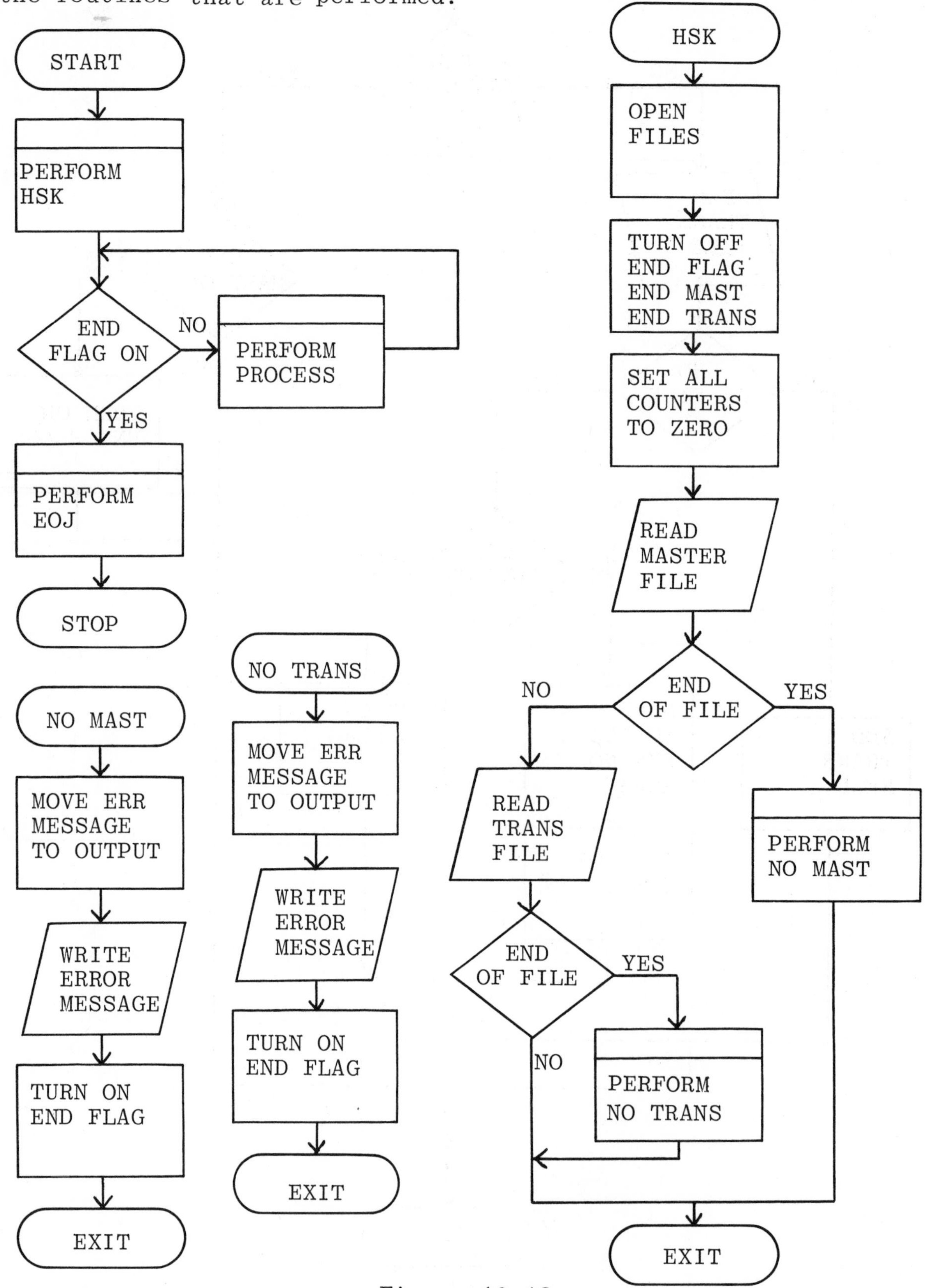

Figure 10-12

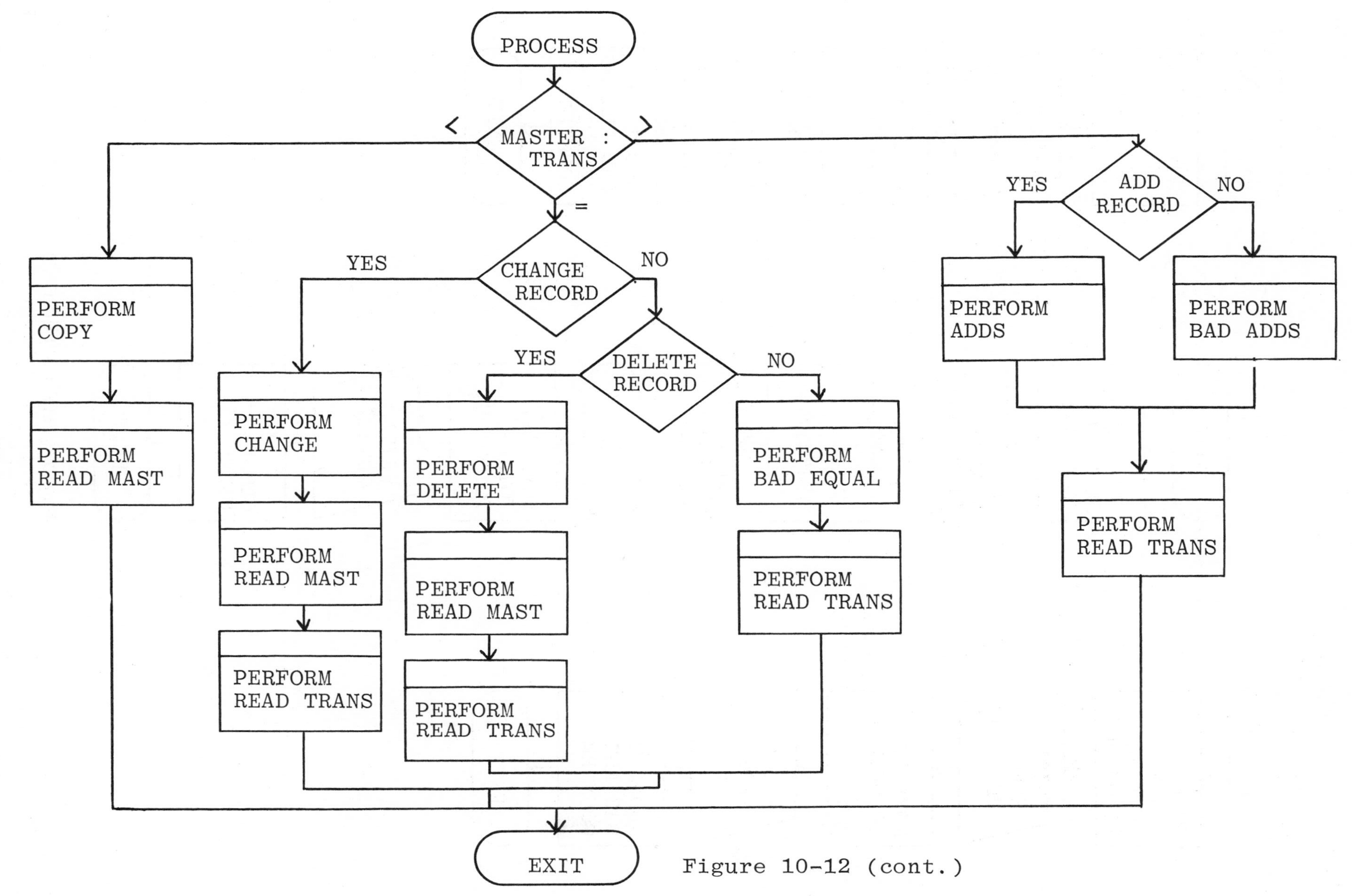

Figure 10-12 (cont.)

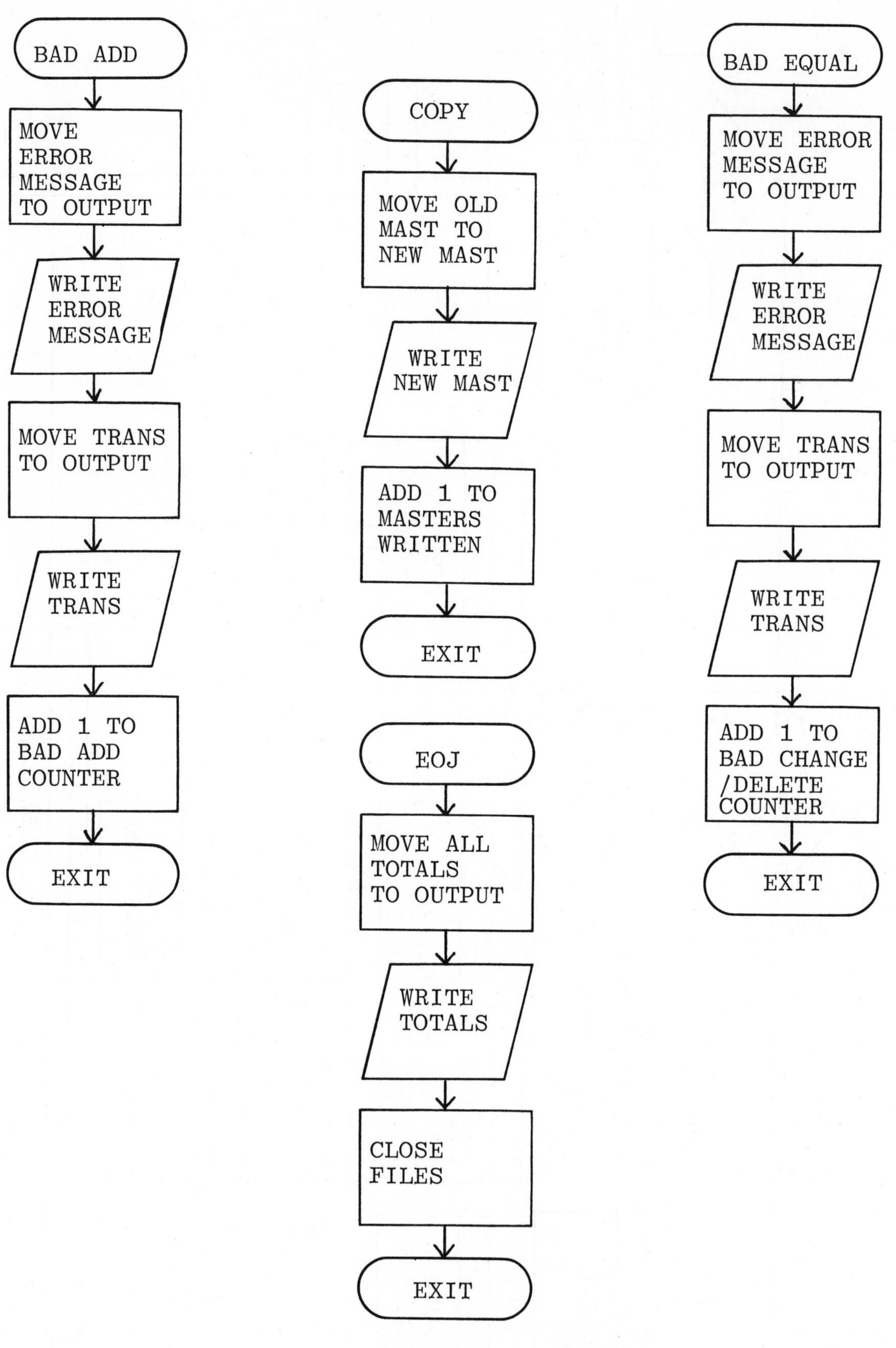

Figure 10-12 (cont.)

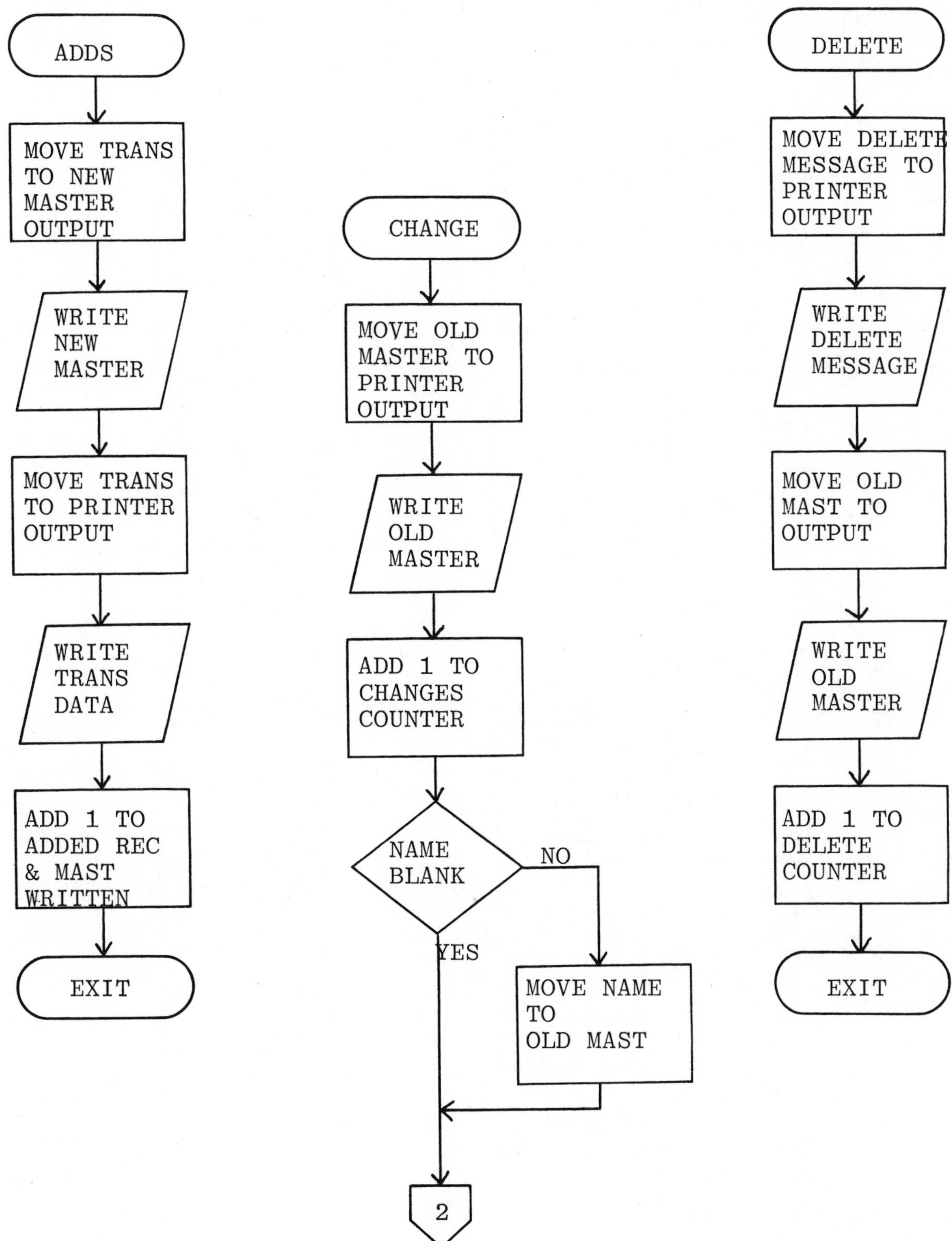

Figure 10-12 (cont.)

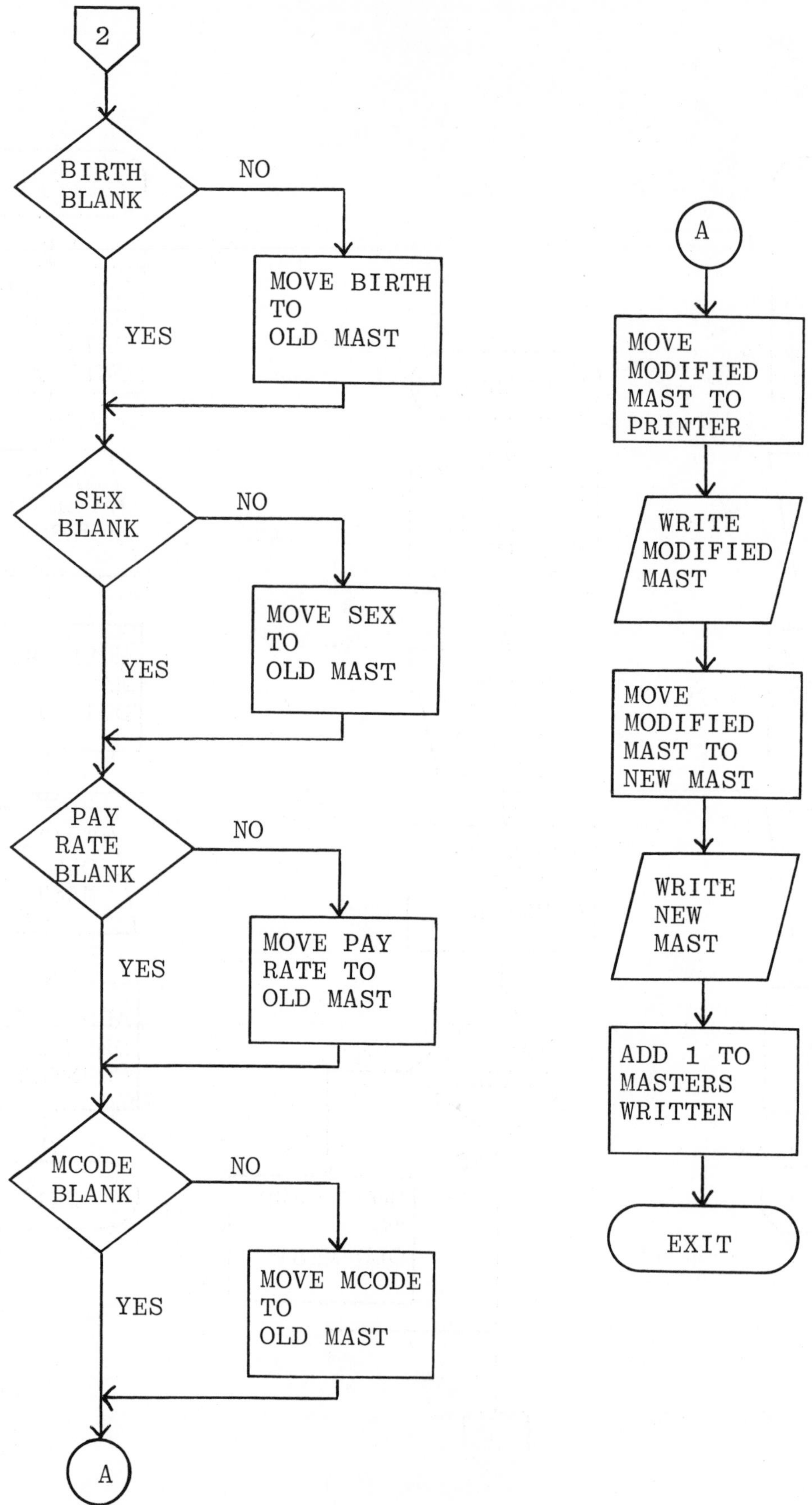

Figure 10-12 (cont.)

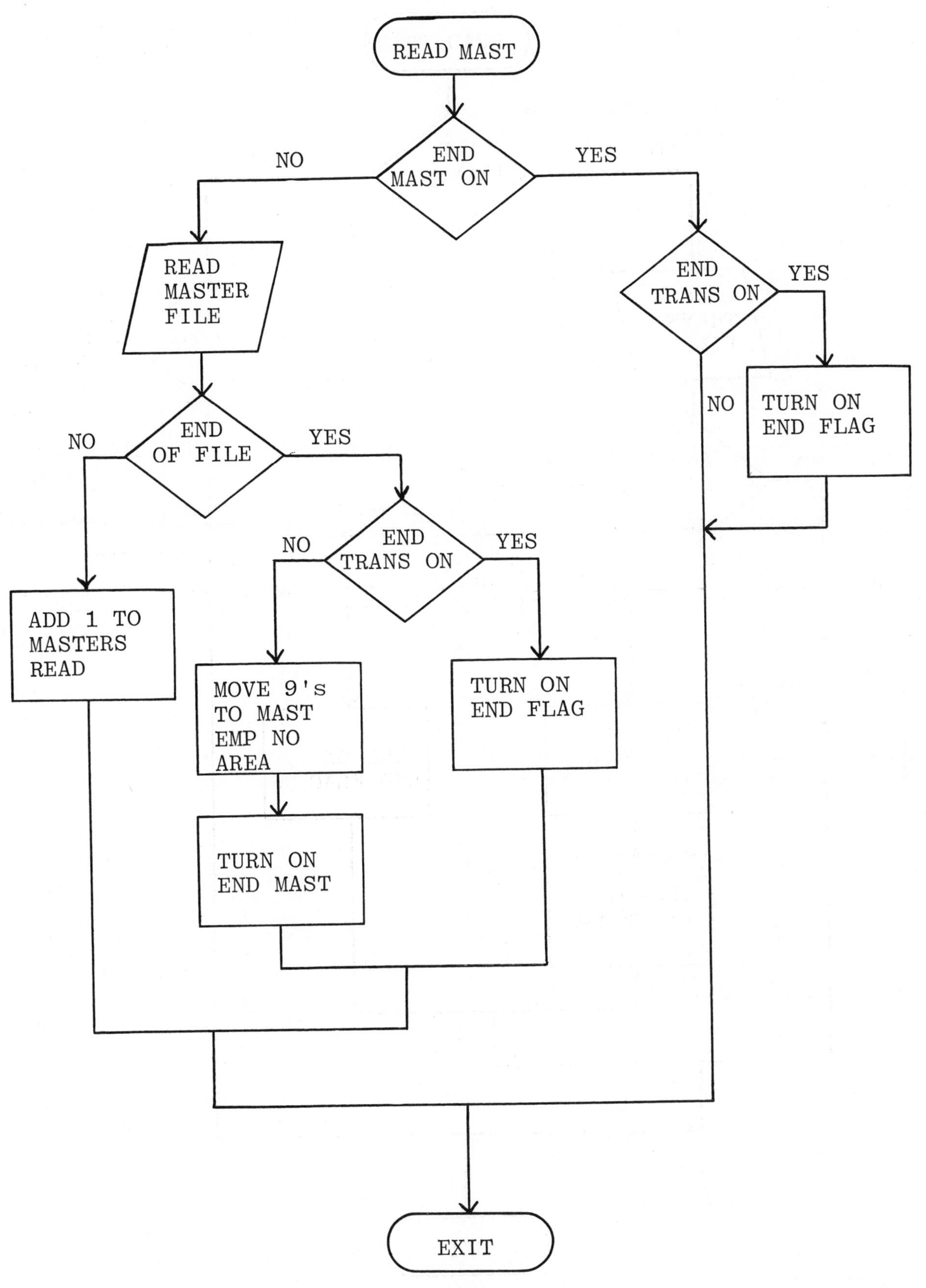

Figure 10-12 (cont.)

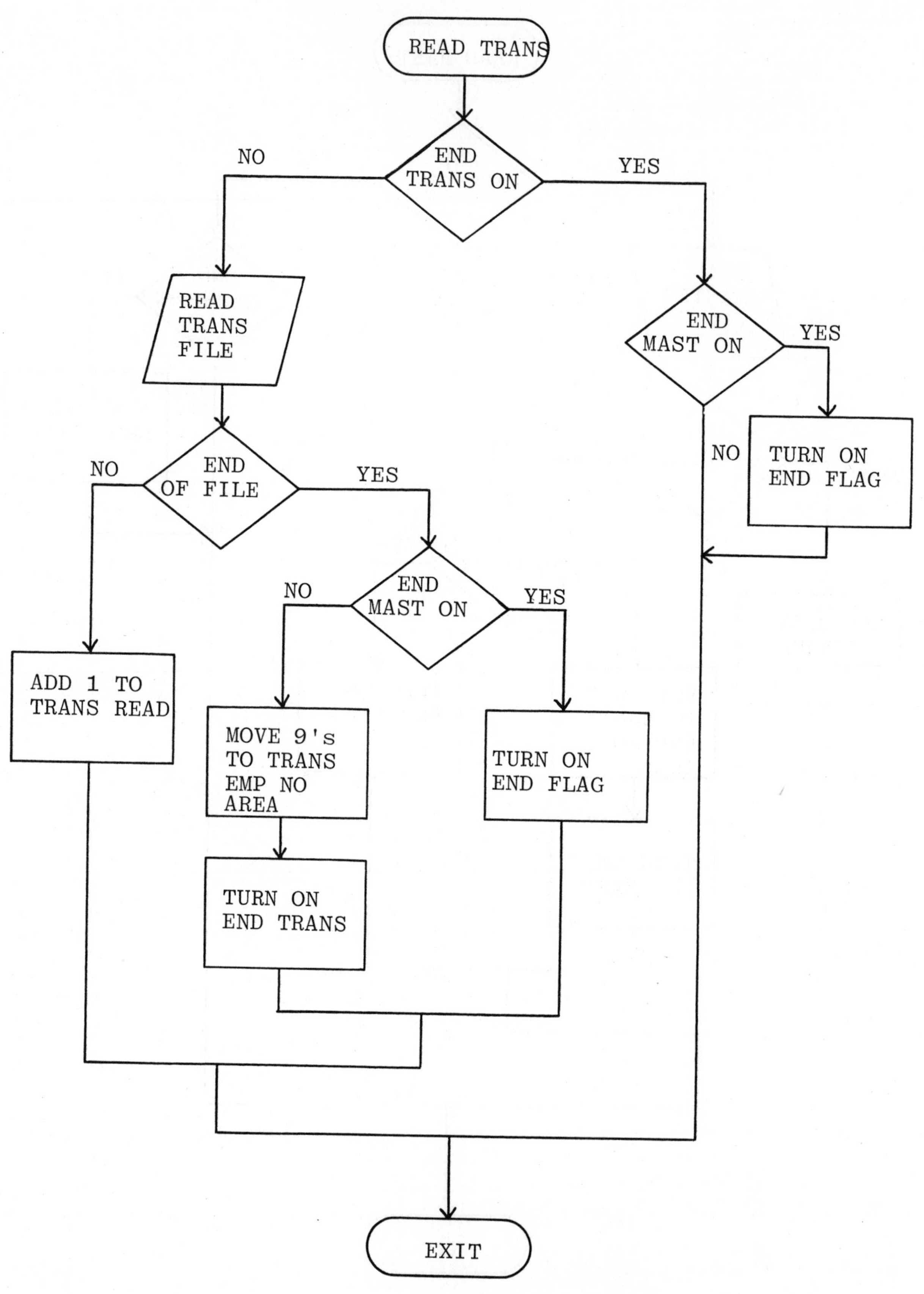

Figure 10-12 (cont.)

TEST DATA

We need a sample set of data to see how this will actually work. The formats for the master and transaction records are shown in Figure 10-13. The size of the records as been kept small only for simplicity. In reality, many more fields would probably be present in the records.

MASTER RECORD FORMAT

DESCRIPTION	POSITION IN RECORD	
EMPLOYEE NUMBER	1 - 9	
EMPLOYEE NAME	10 - 30	
BIRTH DATE	31 - 36	
SEX CODE	37 - 37	
PAY RATE	38 - 44	(7.2)
MARITAL STATUS CODE	45 - 45	
UNUSED	46 - 80	

TRANSACTION RECORD FORMAT

DESCRIPTION	POSITION IN RECORD	
EMPLOYEE NUMBER	1 - 9	
EMPLOYEE NAME	10 - 30	
BIRTH DATE	31 - 36	
SEX CODE	37 - 37	
PAY RATE	38 - 44	(7.2)
MARITAL STATUS CODE	45 - 45	
UNUSED	46 - 79	
TRANSACTION CODE	80 - 80	

Figure 10-13

The sample data to be used is shown in Figure 10-14. The high order (leftmost) zeros of the employee numbers have been deleted for simplicity.

OLD MASTER DATA

EMP. NO.	EMP. NAME	BIRTH DATE	SEX	PAY RATE	MAR	UNUSED
1	TIMOTHY ABBOTT	101240	M	0200000	S	
2	ROGER BENDER	033044	M	0180000	M	
4	DONALD CANTERBURY	092435	M	0090000	D	
6	BEN DONALDSON	122560	M	9500000	M	

Figure 10-14

TRANSACTION DATA

EMP. NO.	EMP. NAME	BIRTH DATE	SEX	PAY RATE	MAR	UNUSED	CODE
1							D
2	ROGER FENDER						C
3	SALLY BUTTONS	072540	F	0079000	S		C
4	DENISE DARNELL	091430	F	0098000	M		A
5	ROWLAND ROBERTS						C

Figure 10-14 (cont.)

Before going through the actual handling of these records it should be noted that in addition to both the master and transaction files being in employee number sequence the transaction file is also in transaction sequence within each employee. What this means is that all the transactions for a given employee are also in sequence in such a manner that add records come first followed by any change records followed by any delete records.

Changes and deletes for an added record will show on the report as being in error. This is reasonable because you would not try to change or delete records that you were preparing to add to the file. You would either modify the add record itself instead of changing it or you would not add it at all instead of deleting it.

In performing the housekeeping routine the first record from both the master (employee number 1) and transaction (employee number 1) files is read into storage. Since the END FLAG switch is off we fall through to performing the PROCESS routine.

When the master and transaction items are compared they are found equal (1 = 1). The next step is to check whether the transaction item is a change record (C in column 80). Since it is not a change we take the no path and check to see if it is a delete record (D in column 80). It is a delete record so we follow the yes path where we perform the DELETE routine. This routine prints a copy of the record being deleted and a message indicating that it has been deleted. It also increments the DELETES counter. After performing DELETE, the next step is to perform the READ MAST routine.

In reading the master file we do not find an end of file so all that happens is we read the next master record (employee number 2) and exit the routine. The next step is to perform READ TRANS. In reading the transaction file, no end of file is found so we read the next transaction record (employee number 2) and exit the routine. At this point we also exit the PROCESS routine.

This brings us back to the point in the mainline program where we check to see if the END FLAG switch is on. It is not on so we again perform the PROCESS routine. In comparing the master and transaction items, they are found to be equal (2 = 2). Taking the equal path we check to see if the transaction is a change record. It is a change record (it has a C in column 80) so the next step is to perform the CHANGE routine.

The CHANGE routine first prints a copy of the original master record and increments a counter for the number of change records processed. Then each of the fields in the change record are individually checked to see if they are blank. The only non-blank field is the NAME field (ROGER FENDER) which is moved to the old master name field and replaces what was there (ROGER BENDER). The modified version of the master record is then written on the printer. The last things done by CHANGE are to move the modified contents of the master record to the new master, write the new master and increment the MASTERS WRITTEN counter.

After leaving the CHANGE routine, we perform READ MAST which reads the next master record (employee number 4) into storage. Since no end of file condition was encountered in reading the master file, we increment the MASTERS READ counter and exit the READ MAST routine.

Next we perform the READ TRANS routine which reads the record for employee number 3 into storage. With no end of file condition occurring on the transaction file we increment the TRANS READ counter and exit the READ TRANS routine. We also exit the PROCESS routine and return to checking the END FLAG switch which is still off.

While performing PROCESS this time we compare the master and transaction items and find the master greater than the transaction (4 > 3). This being the case we then check to see if the transaction is an add record. It is an add record, so we perform the ADD routine. The ADD routine moves the data (each of the individual fields) to the new master area and writes the new master record. The new master now has two records. The ADD routine also prints a message indicating that this record has been added and increments counters for the total records added and master records written.

The next step is to perform the READ TRANS routine. In performing READ TRANS we read the next transaction record (employee number 4) into storage and finding no end of file exit the READ TRANS routine. This in turn causes us to exit the PROCESS routine and return to check the END FLAG switch. Since END FLAG is still not turned on, we perform the PROCESS routine.

When comparing master and transaction items they are found equal (4 = 4). The next step is to check to see if we have a change record. It is not a change record so we check to see if it is a delete record. Since it is neither a change nor a delete, it is an error. At this point we perform the BAD EQUAL routine which prints a message showing the error, prints the error transaction and increments a counter for the total number of this type of error. Following this we will perform the READ TRANS routine. READ TRANS brings the next transaction record (employee number 5) into storage. At this point we exit the PROCESS routine and check the END FLAG switch

Still finding END FLAG off we compare master and transaction items and find the master less than the transaction (4 < 5). This in turn will cause the old master to be moved and written on the new master. The NEW MASTER counter will be incremented and the next master (employee number 6) will be read into storage.

The next pass through the PROCESS routine finds the master high (6 > 5). When checking for an add record we find it is in error since there is not an A in column 80 and we perform the BAD ADD routine. BAD ADD prints a message indicating the error, prints the error transaction and increments a counter for this type of error. After finishing BAD ADD we perform the READ TRANS routine.

This time when performing READ TRANS we find an end of file condition. This causes us to turn on the END TRANS switch and move 9's to the transaction area. Following this we exit the READ TRANS and PROCESS routines and return to check END FLAG. END FLAG is still off since both files have not yet ended. Therefore, we again fall through to the PROCESS routine.

This pass through PROCESS finds the master less than the transaction (6 < 9's). Remember that 9's were moved to the transaction area when an end of file was found on the transaction file. Since the master is low we perform the COPY routine to move the old record to the new master and increment the MASTERS WRITTEN counter. Following COPY, we perform the READ MAST routine. This time when we execute READ MAST an end of file occurs on the master file. Since END TRANS is also on at this point, we turn on END FLAG and exit the READ MAST routine.

Finding END FLAG now turned on, we perform the EOJ routine and terminate processing. EOJ moves and prints each of the individual totals (transactions read, masters read, masters written, adds, changes, deletes, bad adds and bad equals) along with a message identifying each total. The files are also closed in the EOJ routine.

The new master file contents are shown in Figure 10-15 and the update report is shown in Figure 10-16.

NEW MASTER

EMP. NO.	EMP. NAME	BIRTH DATE	SEX	PAY RATE	MAR	UNUSED
2	ROGER FENDER	033044	M	0180000	M	
3	SALLY BUTTONS	072540	F	0079000	S	
4	DONALD CANTERBURY	092435	M	0090000	D	
6	BEN DONALDSON	122560	M	9500000	M	

Figure 10-15

STATUS MESSAGE	EMP. NO.	EMPLOYEE NAME	BIRTH DATE	SEX	PAY RATE	MAR
THE FOLLOWING RECORD HAS BEEN DELETED						
	1	TIMOTHY ABBOT	101240	M	0200000	S
OLD	2	ROGER BENDER	033044	M	0180000	M
NEW	2	ROGER FENDER	033044	M	0180000	M
ADD	3	SALLY BUTTONS	072540	F	0079000	S
THE FOLLOWING RECORD SHOULD BE A CHANGE OR A DELETE						
	4	DENISE DARNELL	091430	F	0980000	M
THE FOLLOWING RECORD SHOULD BE AN ADD						
	5	ROWLAND ROBERTS				

MASTERS READ	4
TRANSACTIONS READ	5
MASTERS WRITTEN	4
BAD ADDS	1
ADDED RECS	1
BAD CHANGE OR DELETE	1
DELETED RECS	1
CHANGED RECS	1
NEW MASTER	4

Figure 10-16

In looking at the report shown in Figure 10-16 a couple of points need to be made. First, notice the status message on the left side of the report. This column is used to indicate the status of each record on the report which does not have an error message. Second, the totals show how many of each type of activity took place. These totals are for control purposes to indicate the processing that took place during the updating operation. One of these totals, however, was not created during the updating. The NEW MASTER total is generated as the totals are printed out and is computed as follows:

NEW MASTER = MASTERS READ + ADDS - DELETES

4 = 4 + 1 - 1

The process of updating a standard sequential file is one of the most complicated file handling situations. This is true because of the logic needed in end of file situations. It is however, one of the most common types of programs.

MULTIPLE CARD TRANSACTIONS

There is the situation where it takes multiple cards to effect a change or an addition to a file. Often some of the cards must be present and others may be optional. The only difficult part of this type of updating is that you have to save each of the required cards separately in storage. If the required items are all present, you build and write the record in the conventional manner. If they are not all present a message is printed indicating which ones are missing and the add does not take place. This also necessitates the use of an additional code in the transaction card indicating which card it is in the sequence. This in turn means that in making changes to existing records you must first determine which number card is being processed.

REVIEW QUESTIONS

Matching

A. Adds

B. Deletes

C. Master > Transaction

D. END FLAG switch

E. Changes

F. EOJ routine

G. Master < Transaction

H. 9's

__________ 1. Condition indicating that the record should be an add record.

__________ 2. Transaction records used to modify the data in the file.

__________ 3. Moved to the master or transaction areas on an end of file condition.

__________ 4. Produces the final totals of the various record types encountered during processing.

__________ 5. Transaction records to be included in the new master file which were not in the old master file.

__________ 6. Turned on only after both files have ended.

__________ 7. Condition that forces the old master to be moved and written as is on the new master file.

__________ 8. Transaction records which cause old master records not to be included on the new master file.

True/False

T F 1. The DELETE routine should be the result of a master = transaction comparison in the PROCESS routine.

T F 2. Adds are permitted on a master = transaction comparison in the PROCESS routine.

T F 3. The purpose of a file updating program is to cause the file to reflect the current situation.

T F 4. The only portion of a master file record that should not be changed is the contents of the field on which the file is sequenced.

T F 5. The new master file can be created right over the old master file in order to save a second tape or other media.

T F 6. The only place that records are written on the new master is in the COPY routine.

T F 7. When the master compares lower than the transaction the COPY routine will be performed.

T F 8. Deletes cause a null record to be created on the master indicating that a record has been deleted.

T F 9. Blank fields in a change record cause the master file fields to be changed to blanks.

T F 10. The READ MAST routine checks transaction records to see if they are additions to the file.

T F 11. Files are typically closed in the PROCESS routine.

T F 12. END FLAG is sometimes turned on when only one file has ended.

Exercises

1. Flowchart the PROCESS routine for a master file update program (less subroutines).

2. Flowchart the READ MAST routine for a master file update program.

3. Flowchart the READ TRANS routine for a master file update program.

4. Flowchart the entire update program for a master file update program including all subroutines. The master file has the following fields:

   EMPLOYEE NAME
   EMPLOYEE NUMBER
   DATE OF BIRTH
   SEX
   RATE OF PAY
   POSITION
   ADDRESS
   CITY
   STATE

Discussion Questions

1. Discuss the use of control totals including when they are initialized, incremented and printed. Of what use are they?

2. Describe the various types of transaction records in a master file update program and what they signify.

3. Describe why it is necessary to create a separate new master file when doing a sequential file update.

4. Discuss additional items which need to be considered when multiple transaction records are needed to add or change a master file record.

5. Describe the function of a sequential file update program and what might be done if file updating in this manner were not possible.

CHAPTER 11

Miscellaneous Routines

OBJECTIVES

As a result of studying this chapter the student should be able to perform the following activities:

1. Flowchart a date record routine.
2. Flowchart a parameter record routine.
3. Describe the methods for loading a table.
4. Flowchart a table lookup for both a high level language and an assembler language.
5. Flowchart a routine for forms alignment.

Chapter 11 is devoted to the miscellaneous routines which are not in themselves a type of program but rather additional techniques used in the program types we have described thus far.

DATE RECORD

Often a single record is read at the beginning of a program run to provide information concerning that execution of the program only. A common example is a date record. While the current date is available on most computers, not all reports carry the current date. Sales and inventory reports in particular, often should carry a month ending date, even though they may not actually be run until early the following month.

In order to furnish the appropriate date a single record is prepared and often read into storage (a one-record file). It is then moved to output and usually used as a part of the heading. It is also possible to make use of the date in calculations such as computing the age of asset in a depreciation report.

The flowcharting of a special date record is simple. It generally is represented by a read statement in the housekeeping routine (see Figure 11-1). Any further processing of the date record would depend on the needs of the particular program.

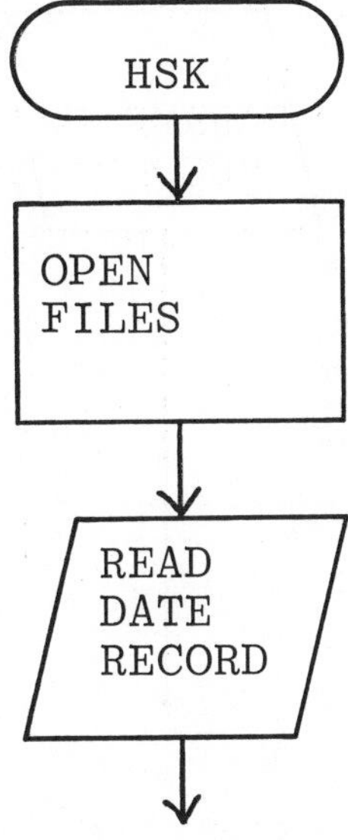

Figure 11-1

PARAMETERS

One of the definitions of parameter is a fixed limit or guideline. In this sense, parameter records are used to define some processing limit within a program.

First, what is a parameter record in a physical sense? It is an input record generally read at the beginning of the program. The reading of the record would occur as a part of housekeeping in a manner similar to a date record. It usually is a one-time need. Once the information from the parameter card has been saved, repeated tests or uses of the information may be made.

We have three choices for the input of a parameter record or records. It may have a file of its own or it may be the first record of a file used for other purposes. As long as the parameter record has a file of its own, its contents will remain in the input/output area for its own file and be available to us throughout the program. If the parameter record is the first record of a file used for other purposes in the program, we must move its contents from the input/output area to

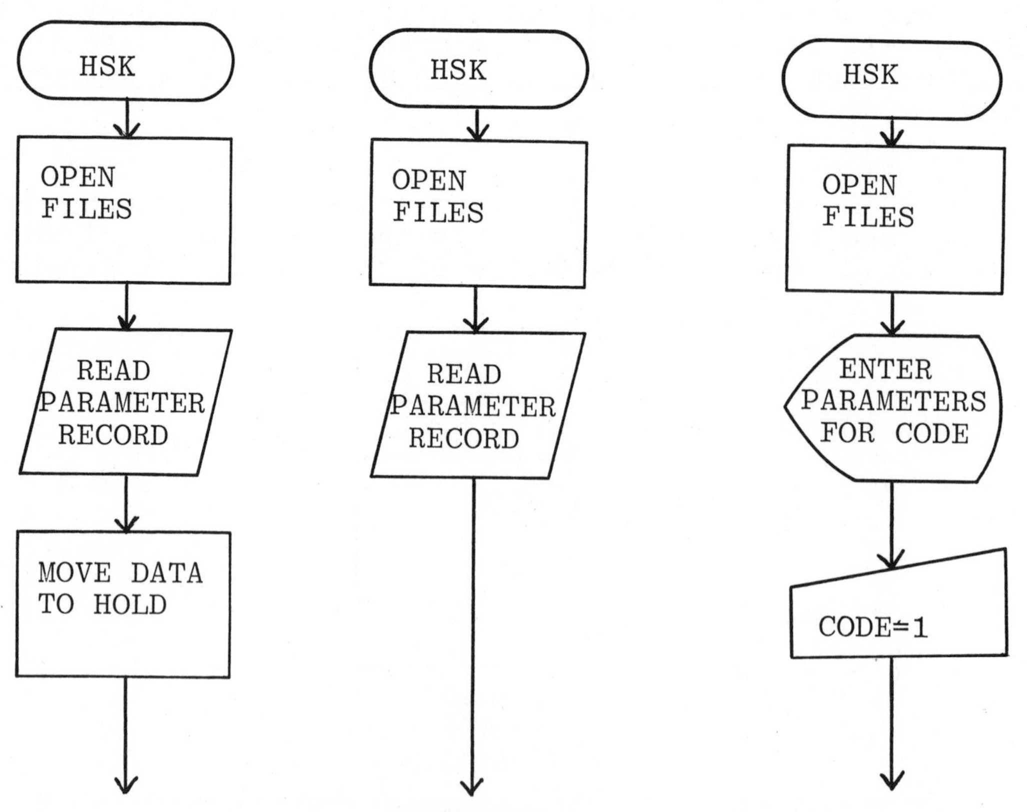

(1st record of a file) (separate file) (entered via console)

Figure 11-2 (a) Figure 11-2 (b) Figure 11-2 (c)

another area to save them. Otherwise when additional records are read from that file our parameter data will be overlayed and destroyed.

Another possibility is to have the computer operator enter the parameters for processing through the console typewriter at the beginning of the program execution.

The flowcharts for these three possibilities are shown in a general way in Figure 11-2 (a), (b) and (c). These represent only a portion of a housekeeping routine.

The uses of parameter records are varied. They are generally included as a part of the logic to make a program more flexible.

Sometimes a company may operate under more than one trade name. All of the order, inventory and billing information may be kept in a single file with only a code to designate the trade name under which it is to be invoiced. Some information is necessary then at the beginning of the program to indicate which records are to be billed in a particular program run and under what name. The selected code could be entered as a parameter record and any records with a different code would be bypassed.

Rather than selected individual records from a file as in the case above, sometimes a block of records are desired. On a small system in particular some programs may take hours to run and no such uninterrupted stretch of time is available. It is possible to start the program at a specific point in the file (specifying the contents of a key field as the starting point) and stop at a predetermined point. This allows you to run the program in segments, making it easier to schedule.

For example, a file might contain part numbers ranging from 00000 through 99999. Not all of the part numbers will necessarily be present. By entering 00000 and 33333 as the beginning and ending limits we could process approximately one-third of the file. When we want to continue the job, 33333 would be the beginning limit and the ending limit would be whatever we wish to make it. Notice in the logic shown in Figure 11-3 that the first record to be processed would be 33334. The numbers you would choose when setting the limits will depend on your choice of greater than or less than tests in the logic.

Equal is not a suitable test for this kind of a problem because not all part numbers within the range are required to be present. A test for equal might never be successful.

This particular type of parameter record is often used with processing methods other than sequential and will be explored further in Chapter 12.

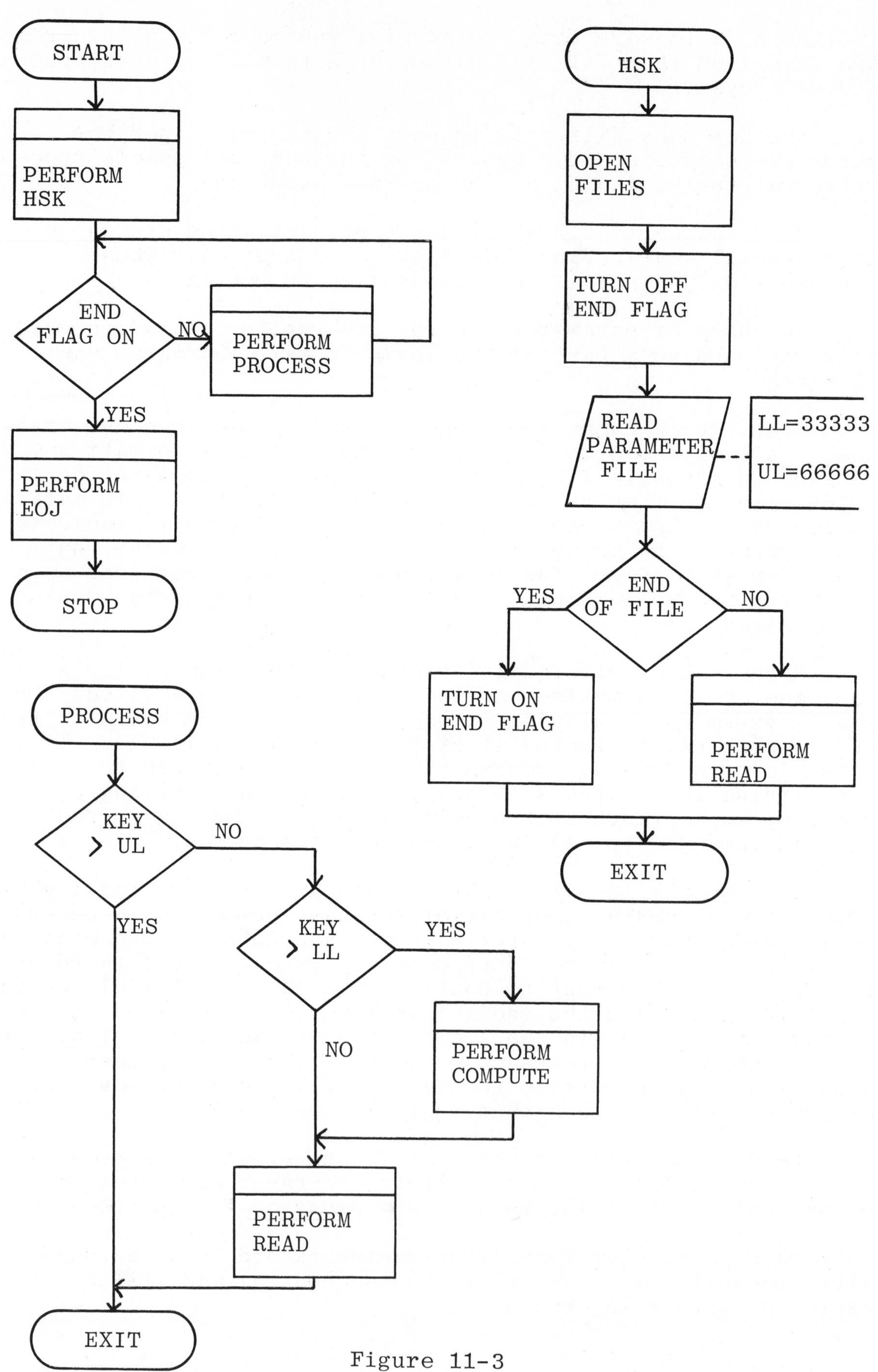
START
PERFORM HSK
END FLAG ON
NO
PERFORM PROCESS
YES
PERFORM EOJ
STOP
HSK
OPEN FILES
TURN OFF END FLAG
READ PARAMETER FILE
LL=33333
UL=66666
END OF FILE
YES
NO
TURN ON END FLAG
PERFORM READ
EXIT
PROCESS
KEY > UL
NO
YES
KEY > LL
YES
NO
PERFORM COMPUTE
PERFORM READ
EXIT

Figure 11-3

Another parameter record usage example can be found in a payroll system. A section of a systems flowchart where this might exist is shown in Figure 11-4.

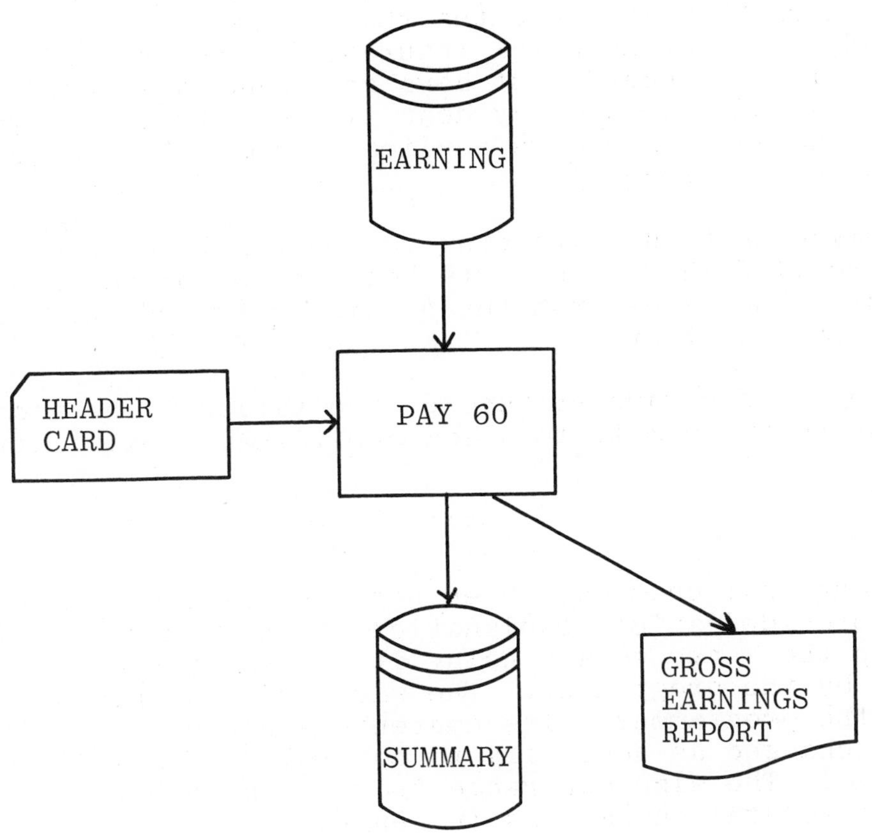

Figure 11-4

In this system the header record is being used as a parameter record. It is a file containing a single card. The card layout is as follows:

COLUMNS	FIELD
1 - 2	CARD CODE
3 - 8	PAY PERIOD ENDING
9 - 14	CHECK DATE
15 - 20	TIME CARD DATE
21 - 21	CREDIT UNION
22 - 22	HOSPITAL INSURANCE

This record is read near the beginning of the payroll run and will determine the date printed on the check, the period ending date for the check stub and the date for any time card labels produced. It will also determine which of the voluntary deductions will be taken for this pay period. For example, the payroll might be run twice a month but hospital insurance is deducted only once a month. The contents of column 22 (X if yes) in this record would be the determining factor in making payroll deductions for hospital insurance. An X in column 22 only indicates that it is the appropriate pay period to deduct hospital insurance. The individual employee's master record must have an amount allocated for hospital insurance before any deduction for that employee will be made. The same procedure applies to the other voluntary deduction on this record.

Assuming that the parameter record was read in housekeeping, Figure 11-5 shows the tests being made for voluntary deductions. The dates from the parameter record only require moving to an output area.

The uses of parameter records are varied. The underlying reason for using them is to allow additional flexibility in programs.

SWITCHES

Although switches have been used in previous chapters we have not provided a full explanation of their nature. A switch, in the sense we are using it, is an area of storage set aside by the programmer. The size and contents of the area is up to the programmer. Its contents are given an initial value and changed as necessary to control the logic flow of the program. The size can range from a single bit (BI nary digi T) to several characters in length.

A switch is initialized by naming it, specifying its contents and in some languages specifying its size. What name it is given depends only on the rules of the particular programming language for forming variable names and the concept of using meaningful names. An example in COBOL would be:

```
77  END-FLAG          PICTURE 9    VALUE ZERO.
```

END-FLAG is the name of the switch. It is only one character in size, should contain a numeric value and is initialized at zero. What the initial value of zero means to the program is up to the programmer. Expressions such as on or off are often used. Which value represents on and which value represents off is not important. It is the fact that the value is changed from one value to another that is important.

A switch does not have to be numeric nor is it restricted to only two possible values. The contents of a switch are usually changed with a move statement.

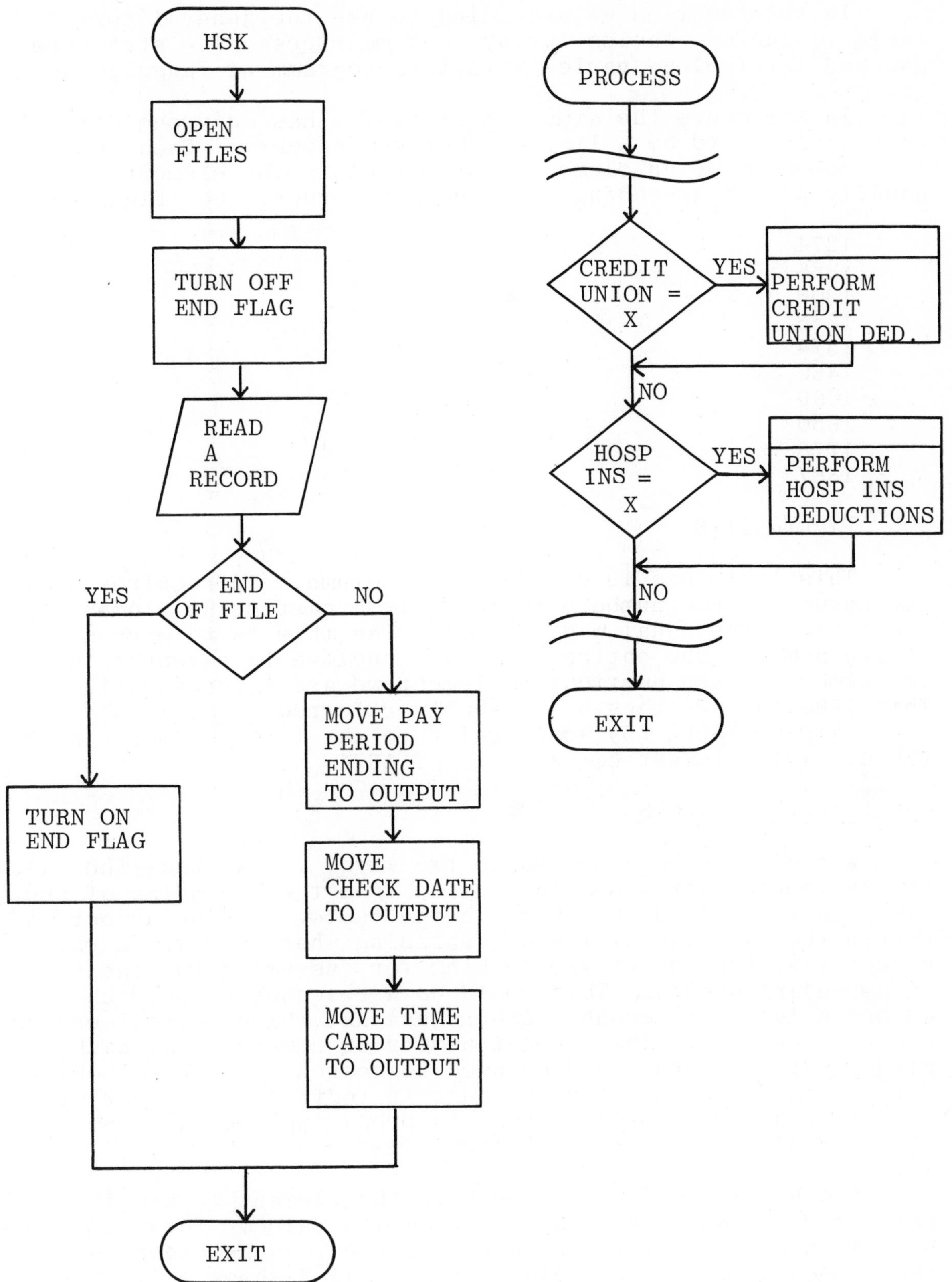
HSK
OPEN FILES
TURN OFF END FLAG
READ A RECORD
END OF FILE
YES
NO
TURN ON END FLAG
MOVE PAY PERIOD ENDING TO OUTPUT
MOVE CHECK DATE TO OUTPUT
MOVE TIME CARD DATE TO OUTPUT
EXIT
PROCESS
CREDIT UNION = X
YES
PERFORM CREDIT UNION DED.
NO
HOSP INS = X
YES
PERFORM HOSP INS DEDUCTIONS
NO
EXIT

Figure 11-5

TABLES

In this section we are going to use the general term table to include tables, arrays and matrices. The structure, use and terminology varies with the programming language used.

In structure the simplest of tables has only one dimension. An example would be a list of employee numbers. Each number is considered to be an element in the table. The elements are usually put in ascending or descending order. See Figure 11-6.

1274
1285
1306
1356
1374
1486
1590
1650
1776
1887

Figure 11-6

This table has 10 rows and one column. It requires only one number (a row number) to identify a particular element in the table. The usual way of specifying this is to give a single name to the entire table and enclose in parenthesis the number of the particular element we are interested in. This item in parenthesis is usually referred to as a subscript. For example, TABLE (5) would refer to the fifth element in the table. This element has a value of 1374.

TABLE ACCESS METHODS

A table can be accessed in two ways. If we know the value we are looking for a search is made from the beginning of the table until we find the value in the table. If the number is not in the table we will stop searching when we reach a value higher than the one we are looking for (assuming the table is in ascending order). This would be a reasonable approach if we had a table of account numbers against which payroll expenses could be charged. The account number or numbers from each person's pay record would be used to search the table looking for a match. If no match is found it indicates an error of some kind has been made, either in preparing the pay record or maintaining the table. See Figure 11-7.

Another method is when we know the element we are interested in but do not necessarily know its value. This is the case when particular values are assigned to an element in a table because of its position. Figure 11-8 shows a list of product prices. The prices are arranged in the table so that the first price (10.00) represents product 1. The second price (12.00) represents product 2 and so on.

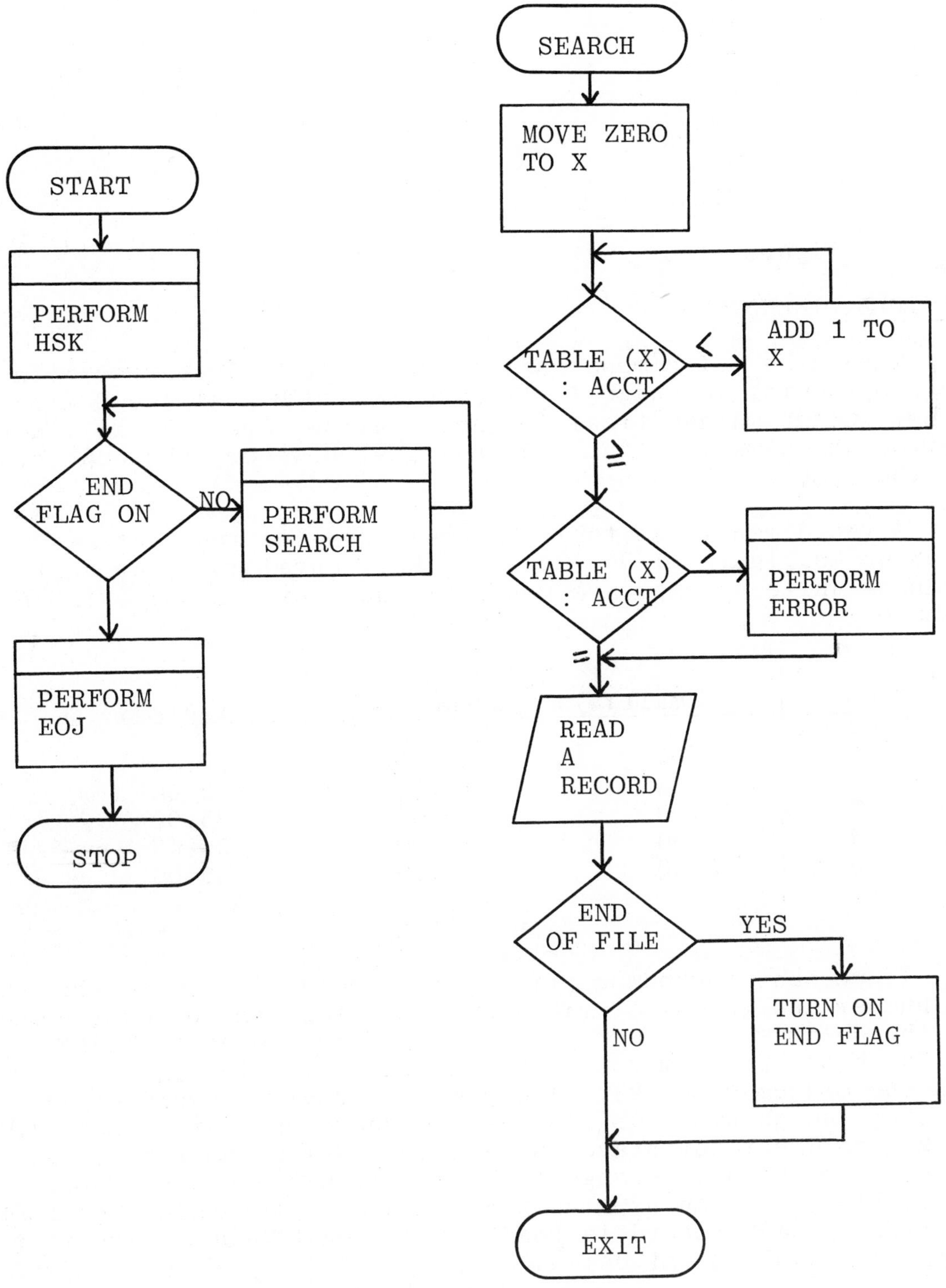
START
PERFORM HSK
END FLAG ON
NO
PERFORM SEARCH
PERFORM EOJ
STOP
SEARCH
MOVE ZERO TO X
TABLE (X) : ACCT
<
ADD 1 TO X
≥
TABLE (X) : ACCT
>
PERFORM ERROR
=
READ A RECORD
END OF FILE
YES
TURN ON END FLAG
NO
EXIT

Figure 11-7

In this example we are not looking for a specific value. We are looking for the price which corresponds to a product number. For example, whatever value is in the table at TABLE (4) represents the price of product number 4.

10.00
12.00
14.00
17.00
19.00
22.00
25.00
28.00
31.00
35.00

Figure 11-8

MULTIPLE DIMENSIONS

The number of dimensions allowed in a table varies with the programming language it is used in. COBOL allows 3 dimensions. Other mathematical languages allow more. We will not provide an example beyond 3 dimensions; however, the concepts are the same.

A two-dimensional table has rows and columns. An example is shown in Figure 11-9. Rows are horizontal and represent products while columns are vertical and represent size in this example.

Size / Product	1 (small)	2 (medium)	3 (large)
1	5.00	10.00	15.00
2	10.00	15.00	20.00
3	15.00	20.00	25.00
4	20.00	25.00	30.00
5	25.00	30.00	35.00

Figure 11-9

If we want to know a price for a product, we need the product number and the size. The rows represent the product number and the columns represent the sizes. A reference to TABLE (3, 2) in the program would give us the price for product number 3 in the medium size (2). The row is normally specified first and then the column. As long as the subscripts are constants (3, 2), no great advantage is gained by using the table. If on the other hand we change them to variables such as TABLE (PROD, SIZE); we can use input data to give the values of PROD and SIZE as each record is read. A typical COBOL instruction using this table might be:

```
MULTIPLY TABLE (PROD, SIZE) BY UNITS-SOLD GIVING AMOUNT.
```

This instruction would appear in a process box on the flowchart and would be the only instruction required to make the price available. Values for PROD, SIZE and UNITS-SOLD would, of course, have to be available to us.

To visualize 3 dimensions we can increase the number of manufacturers from 1 to 4. Now we need 3 subscripts to identify an element in the table. One each is needed for the manufacturer, the product and the size. Combined into one table would be 4 tables similar to the one in Figure 11-9. The data would be placed in storage starting with manufacturer number 1 (see Figure 11-10). The part of an instruction used to identify one element in the table could be written as follows:

TABLE (MANUFACTURER, PROD, SIZE)

	Size	1 (small)	2 (medium)	3 (large)
	Product			
	1	5.00	10.00	15.00
	2	10.00	15.00	20.00
1	3	15.00	20.00	25.00
	4	20.00	25.00	30.00
	5	25.00	30.00	35.00
	1	5.25	10.25	15.25
	2	10.25	15.25	20.25
2	3	15.25	20.25	25.25
	4	20.25	25.25	30.25
	5	25.25	30.25	35.25
	1	5.50	10.50	15.50
	2	10.50	15.50	20.50
3	3	15.50	20.50	25.50
	4	20.50	25.50	30.50
	5	25.50	30.50	35.50
	1	5.75	10.75	15.75
	2	10.75	15.75	20.75
4	3	15.75	20.75	25.75
	4	20.75	25.75	30.75
	5	25.75	30.75	35.75

Figure 11-10

LOADING TABLES

Tables can be loaded into storage by three methods. The first (often called a compile time table) is a method which describes the exact contents of the table in the program itself. An example of a part of this procedure for the COBOL language is shown in Figure 11-11.

```
01  ARRAY1.

    02 FILLER       PICTURE 9(12)  VALUE 050010001500.
    02 FILLER       PICTURE 9(12)  VALUE 100015002000.
    02 FILLER       PICTURE 9(12)  VALUE 150020002500.
    02 FILLER       PICTURE 9(12)  VALUE 200025003000.
    02 FILLER       PICUTRE 9(12)  VALUE 250030003500.

01  ARRAY2 REDEFINES ARRAY1.

    02 PRODUCT      OCCURS 5 TIMES.
       03 PRICE     OCCURS 3 TIMES  PICTURE 9(4).
```

Figure 11-11

The important part of this illustration is the assigning of the actual numeric values needed for the table as a part of the program. The OCCURS clause in the second portion is used to subdivide the table so we can specify one element in the table. In the COBOL language PRICE (3, 2) would identify the third product and a medium size.

Entering the table data as a part of the program causes the information to be stored at the time the program is compiled. If the table information is of a rather permanent nature this approach is suitable. Realize that any change to the table information will mean that the table data in the program must be changed and the program recompiled.

For the second way of loading a table we could reserve the storage we need for the table but not assign the values. In this way the information in the table could be read in from an input file. We would normally read the table information in as input when it is of a less permanent nature and needs to be changed often. This is called an execution time table.

A third way is when storage is reserved without values and then the values are created by calculations within the program. Often information is created during processing that lends itself to storage in a table. Imagine a company with 10 division and 4 departments within each division. We are interested in keeping totals of some amount for each of the departments and printing it out as a summarization at the end of the program. We can establish 40 separate counters or we can use a 10 by 4 table (see Figure 11-12) subscripted as follows:

```
TABLE (DIVISION, DEPARTMENT)
```

DIVISION \ DEPARTMENT			
0984323	1290928	0943940	2909828
0789378	0345781	0123578	0347812
8903730	0378291	0782973	0723482
0348927	0278921	1287495	1874902
0347864	0347893	0237784	0984732
0982674	0487632	0578391	0283746
0785326	0853847	0895322	0543783
0758472	0674653	2947653	0487365
0648763	2764585	1847653	1847653
0874676	0873652	3774685	2746875

Figure 11-12

TABLE SEARCH LOGIC

In high level languages a relatively automatic table search is possible. We specify the position we are interested in through controlling the subscripts (either by input or an incrementing process) and the computer does the rest. In a lower level language such as an assembler, the table search is not automatic. The programmer must write the logic for the search. While this book is not intended to teach assembler language techniques, a demonstration of such a routine may aid your understanding of how a computer can locate a given element in a table.

We will assume that the table data has already been placed in core. See Figure 11-13 for the data only.

PROD \ SIZE	1 2 3
1	050010001500
2	100015002000
3	150020002500
4	200025003000
5	250030003500

Figure 11-13

The address in core at which the table begins may be referred to by a data name in assembler language. We will call it BTABLE.

In order to locate any price we need to know the product number and size. A record can be read which contains this information. See Figure 11-14.

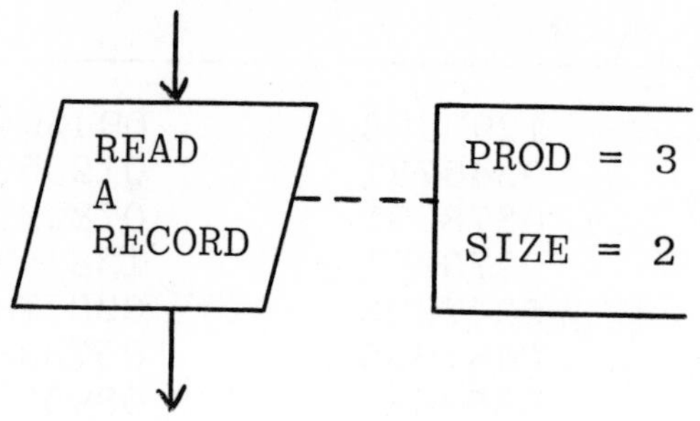

Figure 11-14

Other information we need is the total width of a row in the table (the number of characters in a row representing all possible prices for one product). This character width will be 12 in our example. We also need the width of each item in a row (4 in our example representing 1 price). As a programmer we would know this information since we were responsible for allocating the storage space for the table. Figure 11-15 shows the rest of the steps for locating the desired element in the table. Follow the arithmetic of this flowchart through using PROD = 3, SIZE = 2 and the address of BTABLE = 4000.

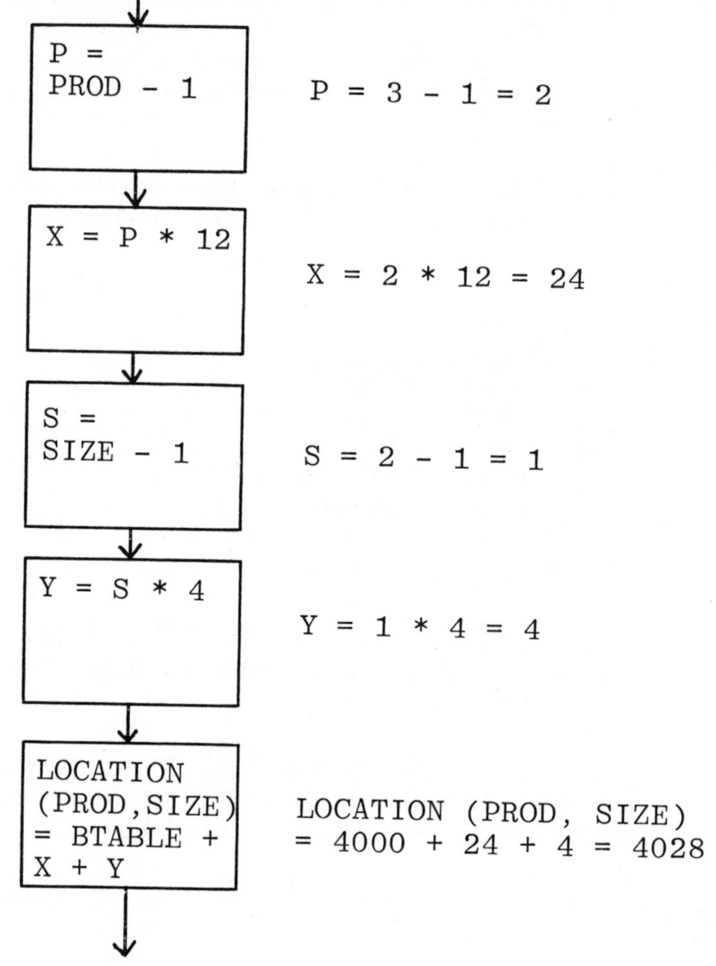

Figure 11-15

If the beginning of the table is at 4000, count 28 characters into the table and you will find 2000 which represents a 20.00 price for product number 3, size number 2. The location of the decimal point is handled separately in this type of programming language. Try a few sets of numbers on your own.

FORMS ALIGNMENT

Much of the printed output from programs must be placed on special forms. Some examples are purchase orders, invoices, W2's, checks, report cards and other notifications which are generated often. An example of such a form is shown in Figure 11-16.

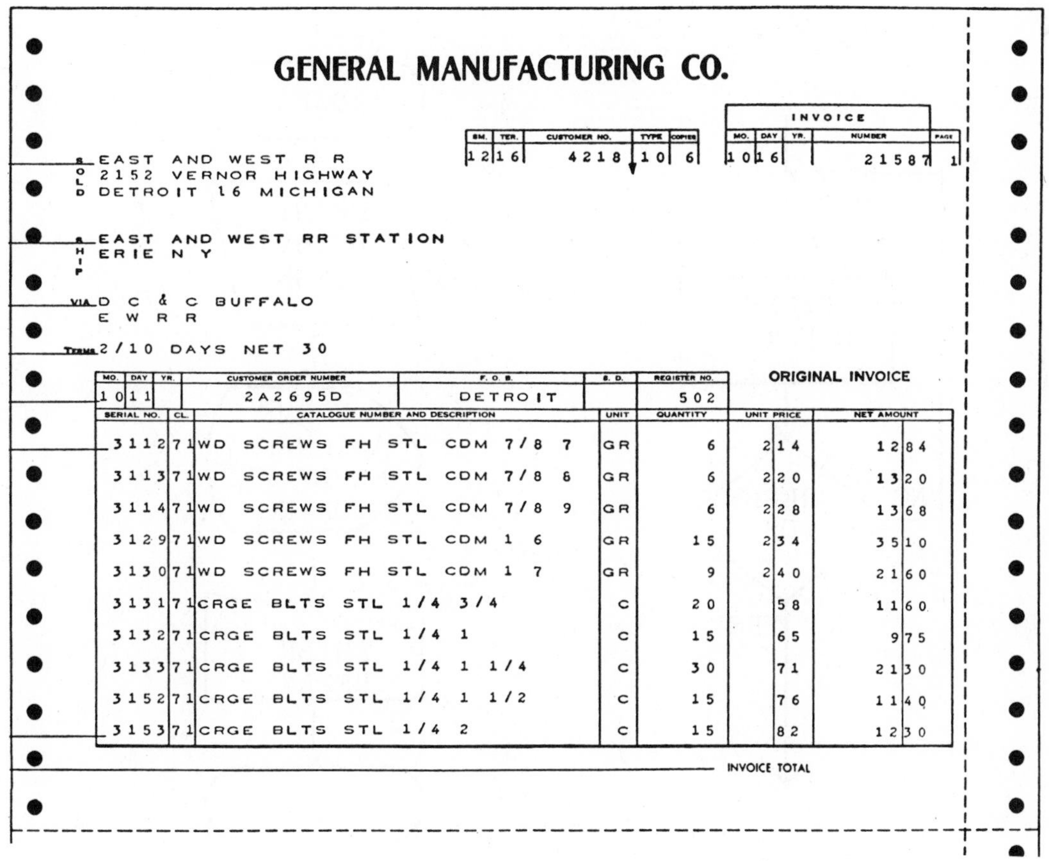

GENERAL MANUFACTURING CO.

SM.	TER.	CUSTOMER NO.	TYPE	COPIES
12	16	4218	10	6

INVOICE

MO.	DAY	YR.	NUMBER	PAGE
10	16		21587	1

SOLD: EAST AND WEST R R
2152 VERNOR HIGHWAY
DETROIT 16 MICHIGAN

SHIP: EAST AND WEST RR STATION
ERIE N Y

VIA: D C & C BUFFALO
E W R R

TERMS: 2/10 DAYS NET 30

ORIGINAL INVOICE

MO.	DAY	YR.	CUSTOMER ORDER NUMBER	F. O. B.	S. D.	REGISTER NO.
10	11		2A2695D	DETROIT		502

SERIAL NO.	CL.	CATALOGUE NUMBER AND DESCRIPTION	UNIT	QUANTITY	UNIT PRICE	NET AMOUNT
3112	71	WD SCREWS FH STL CDM 7/8 7	GR	6	2 14	12 84
3113	71	WD SCREWS FH STL CDM 7/8 6	GR	6	2 20	13 20
3114	71	WD SCREWS FH STL CDM 7/8 9	GR	6	2 28	13 68
3129	71	WD SCREWS FH STL CDM 1 6	GR	15	2 34	35 10
3130	71	WD SCREWS FH STL CDM 1 7	GR	9	2 40	21 60
3131	71	CRGE BLTS STL 1/4 3/4	C	20	58	11 60
3132	71	CRGE BLTS STL 1/4 1	C	15	65	9 75
3133	71	CRGE BLTS STL 1/4 1 1/4	C	30	71	21 30
3152	71	CRGE BLTS STL 1/4 1 1/2	C	15	76	11 40
3153	71	CRGE BLTS STL 1/4 2	C	15	82	12 30

INVOICE TOTAL

Figure 11-16

There are a number of lined areas on the form where accurate placement of the printing is necessary. This means that the form must be adjusted both vertically and horizontally when loaded into the printer. A portion of the run sheet is usually devoted to instructions to the computer operator concerning forms alignment. The operator uses these instructions to align the form as accurately as he can.

A routine can be incorporated into a program producing such printed material to double check the physical alignment of the form. It would be a part of housekeeping or performed in housekeeping. The routine prints dummy information for the first few lines of the form (usually a single character like X's). The printer then stops and an inquiry goes to the operator through the console to approve or disapprove the alignment. This gives the operator a change to adjust the form if necessary and proceed with the program or he may send it through the test loop again to make sure his adjustment was correct. See Figure 11-17.

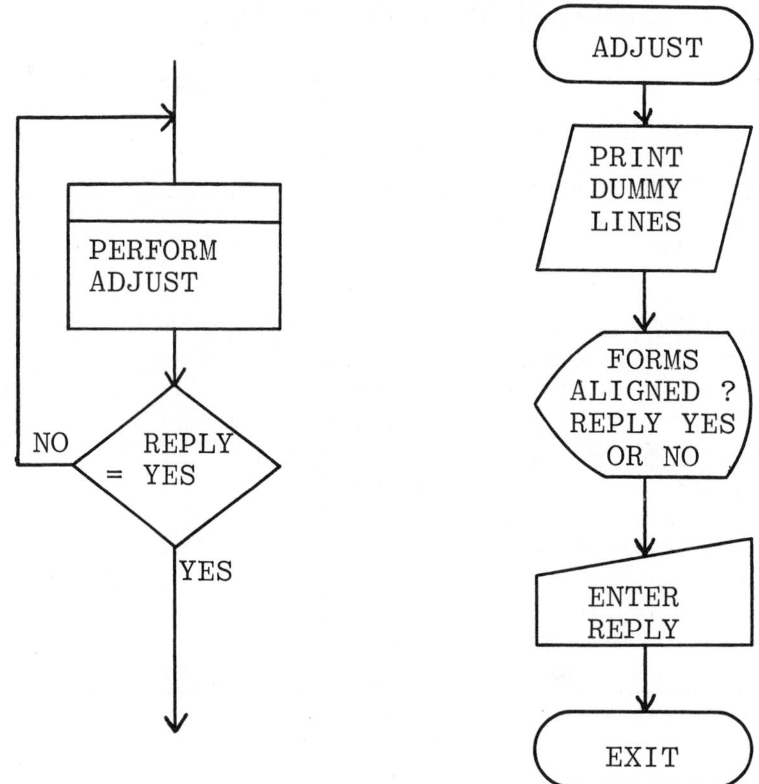

Figure 11-17

This procedure can be important since some programs update master files during their execution (such as adding current pay to year-to-date totals). If, halfway through the payroll run, it is discovered that the forms are ruined the program must be rerun.

REVIEW QUESTIONS

Matching

A. Parameter

B. Date record

C. Switch

D. Subscript

E. Compile time table

F. Execution time table

__________ 1. An area of core whose contents are changed to control the logic flow of the program.

__________ 2. A limit or guideline.

__________ 3. A table loaded from a data file.

__________ 4. Used when something other than the current date is required.

__________ 5. Used to identify one element in a table.

__________ 6. A table whose values are written as a part the program.

True/False

T F 1. The current date is suitable for the heading of all programs.

T F 2. Parameter records always have a file of their own.

T F 3. Parameter records may be used to select a portion of the file to be processed.

T F 4. A switch should be a numeric field.

T F 5. A one-dimensional table would be subscripted as TABLE (5, 2).

T F 6. Tables in which we are looking for a particular value should be loaded in ascending or descending order.

T F 7. A three-dimensional table would have three subscripts.

T F 8. Forms alignment is normally a part of the EOJ routine.

Exercises

1. Flowchart a program (using a parameter record) which bills only those customers whose last name begins with the letters J - R.

2. Construct and label a table for pricing a piece of furniture which comes in 2 sizes and 4 grades of upholstery fabric. Use your own prices but use a five digit number.

3. Locate the (2, 3) position of the table in exercise 2. Use an assembler language type routine and perform the actual calculations. Assume that the table is loaded in storage beginning at location 2000.

4. Given the taxable wages as input, flowchart a routine to search a tax table for the appropriate row and calculate the tax.

SINGLE person - SEMIMONTHLY PAYROLL

If the amount of wages is		The amount of income tax to be withheld shall be:	
Not over $71 0			
Over --	But not over		of excess over-----
$ 71	--$165 . . .	16%	$ 71
$165	--$310 . . .	$ 15.04 plus 18%	$165
$310	--$394 . . .	$ 41.14 plus 22%	$310
$394	--$477 . . .	$ 59.62 plus 24%	$394
$477	--$644 . . .	$ 79.54 plus 28%	$477
$644	--$769 . . .	$126.30 plus 32%	$644
$769	. . .	$166.30 plus 36%	$769

5. Flowchart a routine to move out and print a table which has 5 rows and 5 columns. All items from a single row are to be printed on the same line.

Discussion Questions

1. Give possible uses for parameter records.

2. Name some tables that should be loaded at compile time, at execution time.

3. What are some advantages of using tables in program.

CHAPTER 12

Nonsequential Files

OBJECTIVES

As a result of studying this chapter the student should be able to perform the following activities:

1. Describe the difference between a sequential and a nonsequential file.
2. Describe appropriate media for nonsequential files.
3. Describe the types of applications suitable for nonsequential files.
4. Describe types of nonsequential files.
5. Flowchart the creation of an ISAM file.
6. Flowchart the updating of an ISAM file.

INTRODUCTION

Although the use of nonsequential files is common, we have left the flowcharting techniques for them until the end of program flowcharting. The reason for this is the ease with which we can flowchart some of the more difficult sequential file routines (matching, updating, etc.) when using a nonsequential file. In this chapter we will describe the difference between the types of files, the appropriate media for each and the types of applications suitable for each. While there are many types of nonsequential access methods, we have elected to describe the Indexed Sequential Access Method (ISAM) in greatest detail.

SEQUENTIAL VS. NONSEQUENTIAL

A sequential file is one whose records must be accessed starting at the beginning of the file and passing over (or reading) every record. This means we must read every record whether we are interested in it or not.

A file with nonsequential access allows us to read any one record just as easily as any other record in the file. We are able to go directly to that record without having to read all prior records in order to get the one we want. This makes a record in the middle of the file available to us without having to read the first half of the file.

FILE MEDIA

Two types of media that are suitable only for sequential files are punched cards and magnetic tape. When punched cards are loaded into a card reader, they must be read one at a time from the beginning to the end of the deck. We are free to sort them into a particular sequence before loading them. After that we must access one card at a time until we have completed the reading of the deck.

Magnetic tape functions in a similar manner. Once the records are on the tape in a sequence of our choosing, reading is generally started at the beginning of the tape and continued record by record until we have either reached the end of the file or passed all of the records we are interested in.

Nonsequential files are most often found on magnetic disk. There are other less often used media such as magnetic drum and magnetic card strips. A series of magnetic disk surfaces are assembled together in what is commonly referred to as a disk pack. The assembly includes read-write heads which move over the disk surfaces either reading or writing data. The ability of these read-write heads to move across the disk surface to a predetermined location gives us nonsequential or direct access. Figure 12-1 is an illustration of a disk pack.

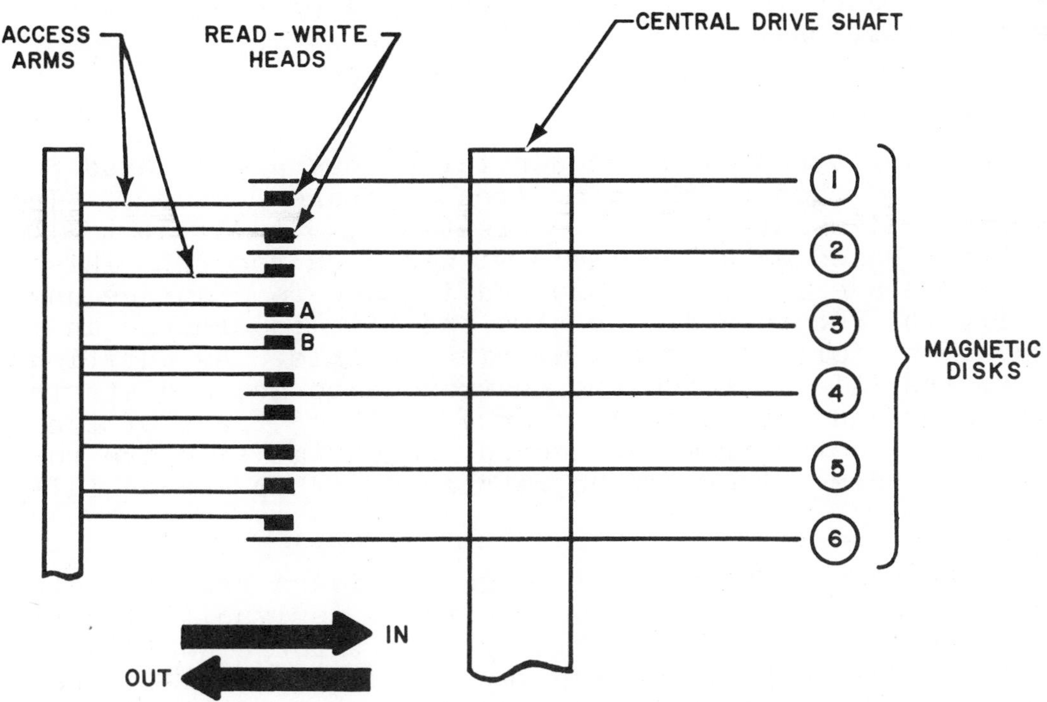

Figure 12-1

TYPES OF APPLICATIONS

There are a number of factors which affect the decision to use sequential or nonsequential files. One of these factors is the speed with which we can complete a given job. A second factor is convenience.

A part of the decision on which method to use is based on the number of records from the file that need to be read. In comparing speeds for the two methods, sequential processing is the fastest method per record read. If we must read a high percentage of the records in the file, then sequentail processing may be our choice. If, on the other hand, we need only a small percentage of the records from a file; nonsequential processing may be our choice.

We have to balance the slower reading speed on a nonsequential file against the number of records we actually need to read from a file. Assume that it takes 3 times as long to access the average nonsequential record as the average sequential record in a file. This would mean that if we needed at least one-third of the records in a file, sequential processing would be just as fast.

Another factor is convenience. Many on-line real-time systems are built around the concept of direct access. A student coming to register for classes wants to know if a seat is available in the class. A person buying an airline ticket wants to know if there is space available for him. Neither of these people want to wait until every class or every flight with a lower number has been checked out. This need for a real-time reply makes the use of nonsequential processing a necessity is such situations.

TYPES OF ACCESS

Two major types of nonsequential access are Indexed Sequential Access Method (ISAM) and direct or random access. Indexed sequential files are loaded or created originally in a sequential order based on a key field within each record. This key field is unique to each record and is used to sequence and identify the record. At the time the file is created an index is developed for each record within the file. As additions are made to the file, records are rearranged to accommodate the new records and the index is changed to keep track of the new location. Records from an indexed sequential file are retrieved using the index. They may be retrieved either sequentially or randomly.

In the case of direct file organization a relationship is developed using the key of the record to assign its location within the file. This is normally done through applying a formula to the contents of the key field and using the results to assign a location to the record within the file. When you retrieve the record the same formula is applied.

CREATING AN ISAM FILE

The flowchart to create an ISAM file is shown in Figure 12-2. This flowchart assumes an initial read in housekeeping. In the CREATE routine the key of each record is moved to an area where it is recognized by the computer to be the key used for indexing. Next, the record is written. The computer handles the creation of the index for the record.

When we write a record we must test for INVALID KEY. We will take the yes path if for any reason the computer cannot use the key of the record just written. If it is invalid an error message is moved to output and written. Then we turn on END FLAG. It is necessary to turn on END FLAG because the loading of the file cannot continue if an invalid key is discovered. As long as we do not find an invalid key we continue to read records and write them on the file.

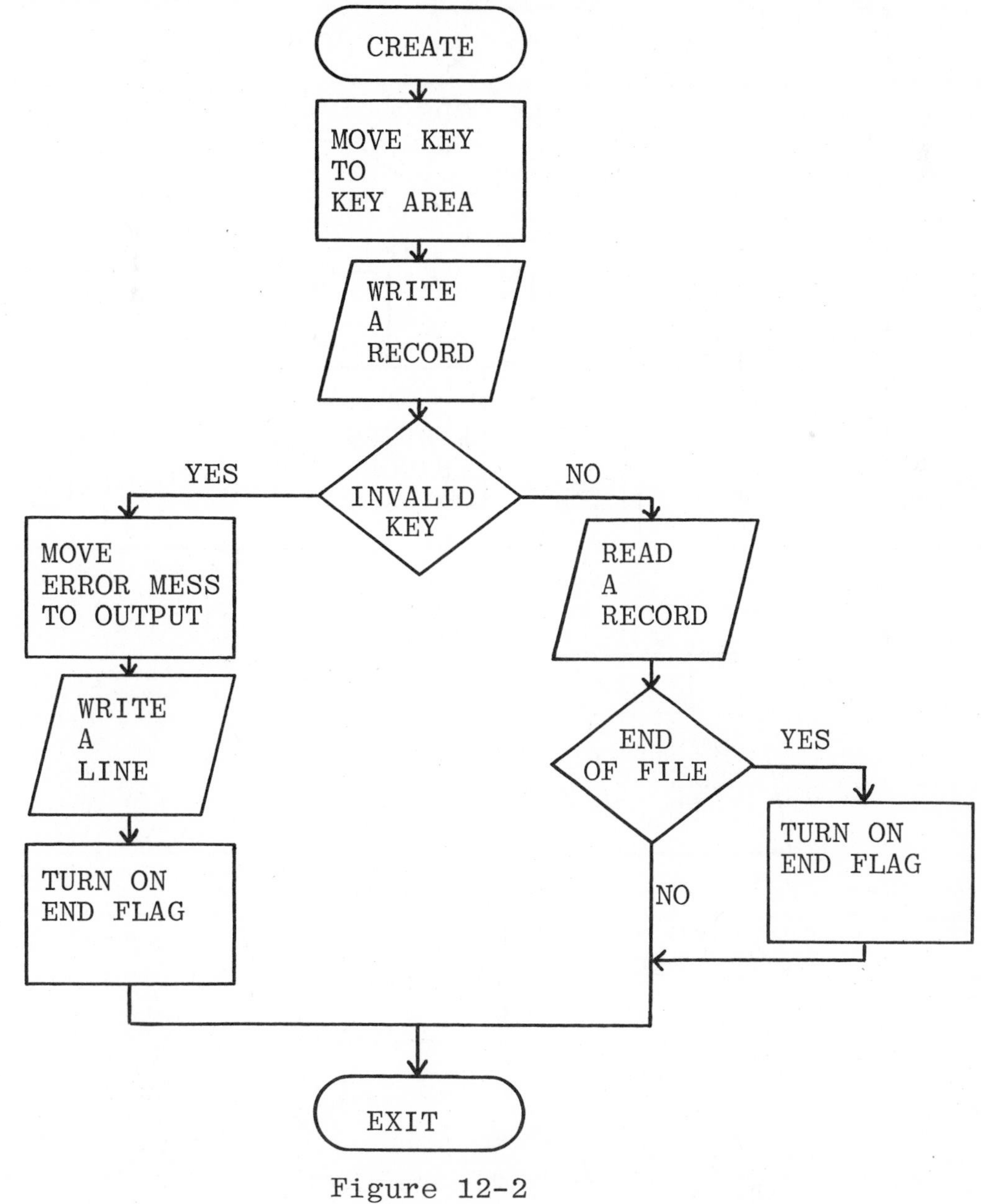

Figure 12-2

UPDATING AN ISAM FILE

To update an ISAM master file we need a transaction file which contains all of the additions, deletions and changes. After reading the initial transaction record in housekeeping we enter the UPDATE routine and test the transaction code. If it is not an addition, deletion or change we perform an error routine. If the answer is yes to any of these codes we perform the appropriate routine. After our return from the routine we read another transaction record. If END FLAG is not on we perform UPDATE again (See Figure 12-3).

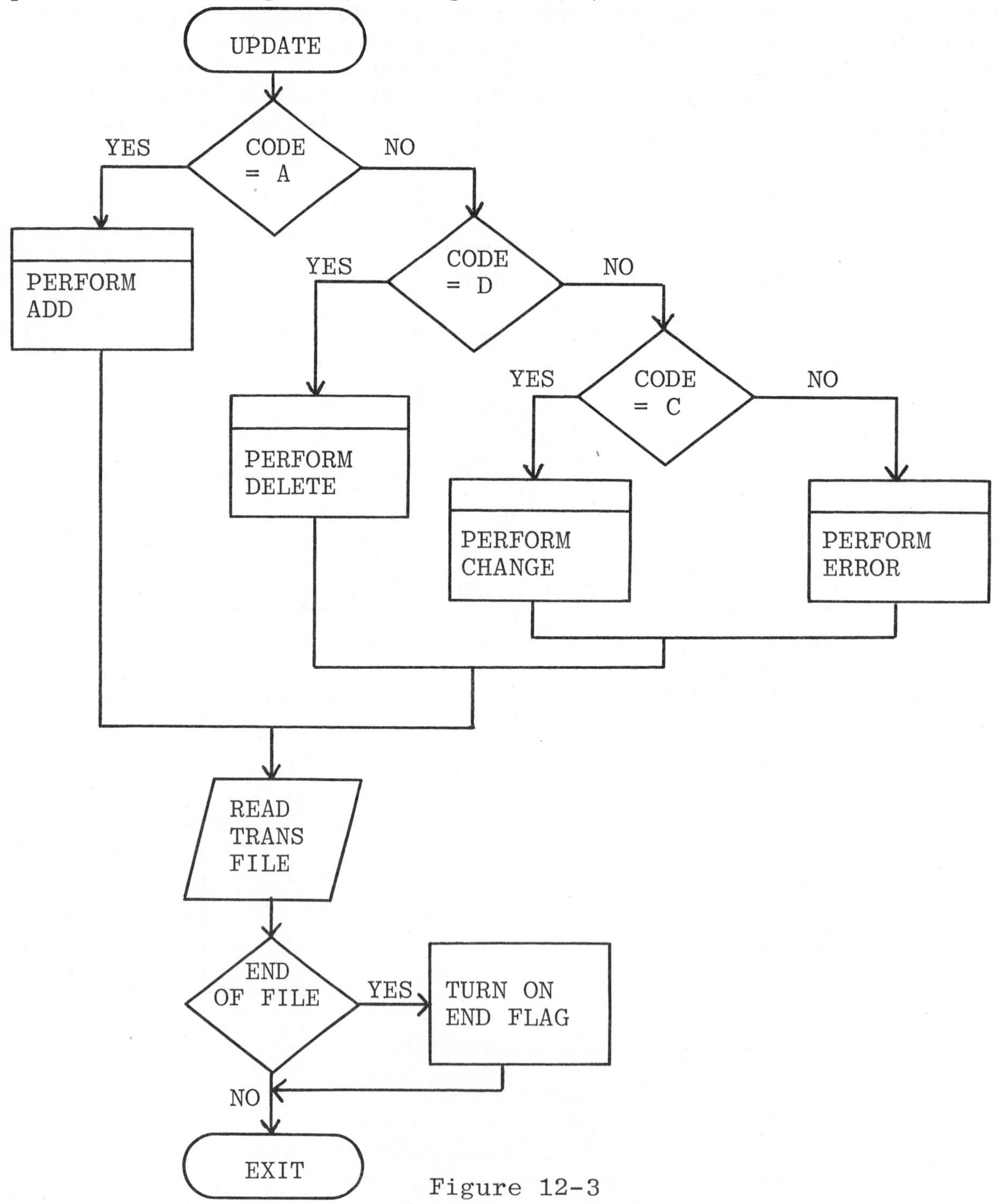

Figure 12-3

The ADD routine requires us to move the key to the control field used by the computer to establish an index. We then move the data and write the added record. Each time we write we must test for INVALID KEY. If the answer is yes, we move and write a message indicating a bad add. Next, we exit the routine.

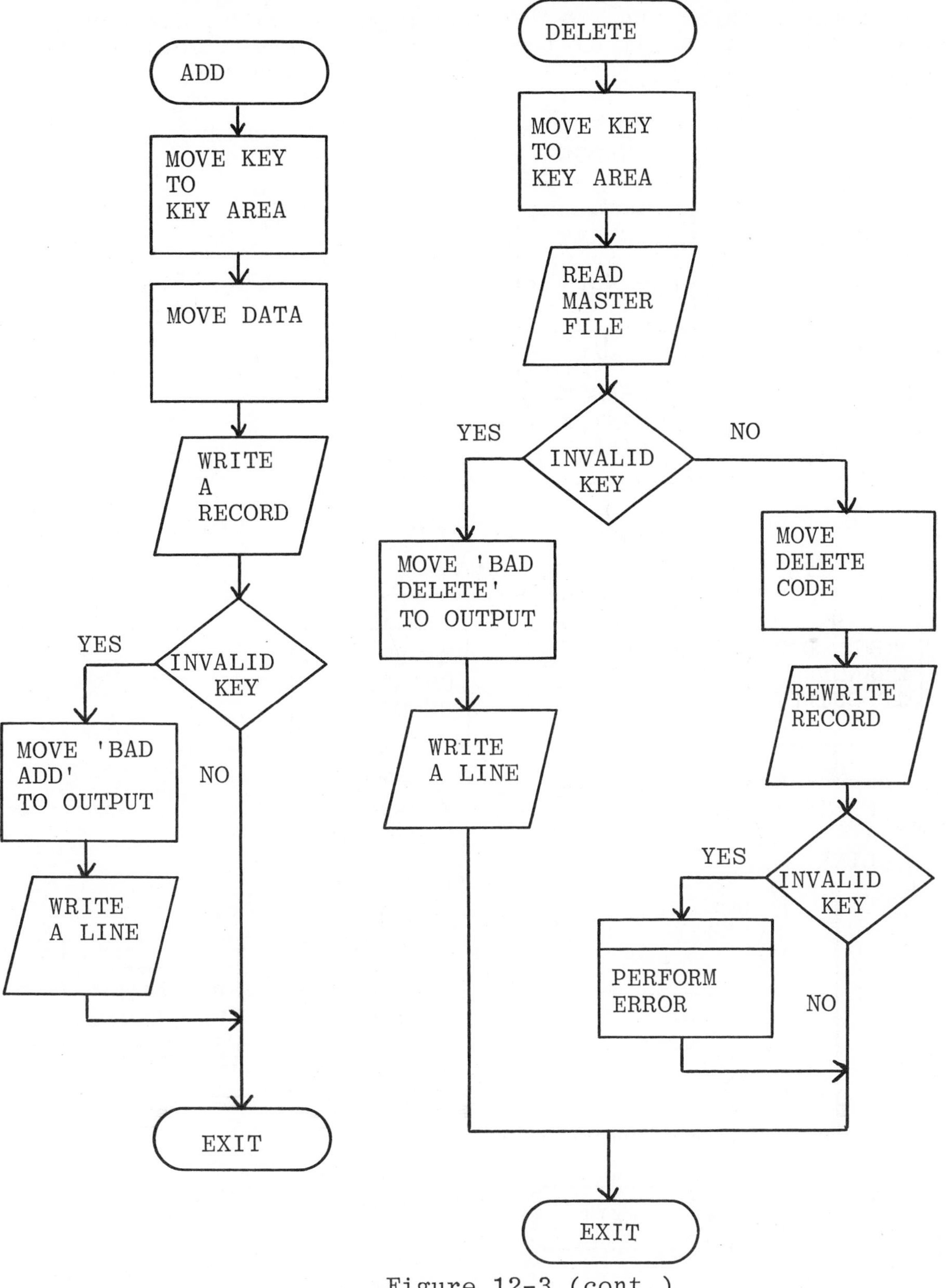

Figure 12-3 (cont.)

The DELETE and CHANGE routines are similar. In both cases we must establish the key and read the master file. After an attempt at reading if we have an INVALID KEY, we were not able to find the record we wanted to change or delete. In this case an appropriate message is written. If our read was successful we either move in a delete code and rewrite the record or we move in the changes and rewrite the record. If we have an INVALID KEY as a result of the rewrite, we have a serious processing problem and perform a suitable error routine.

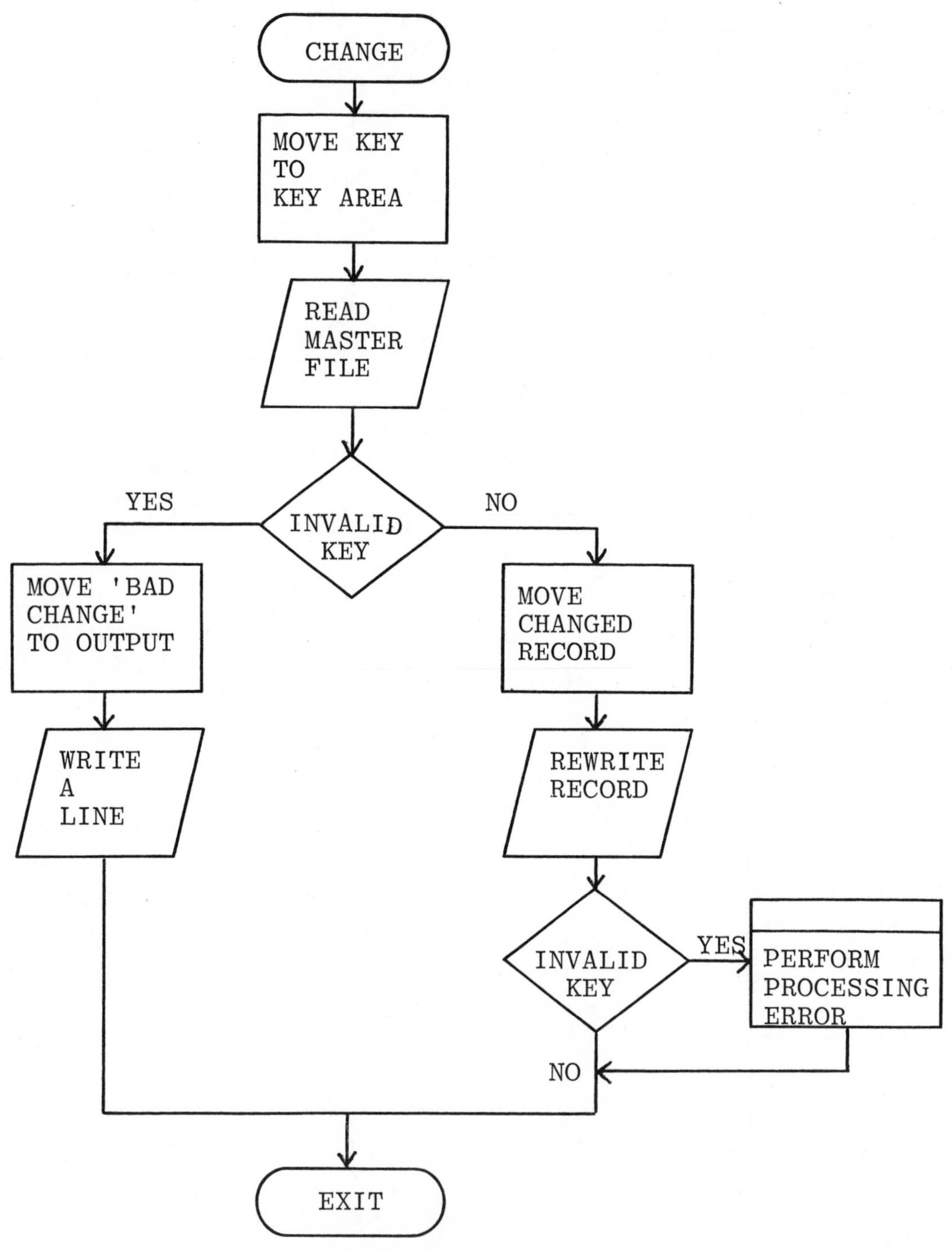

Figure 12-3 (cont.)

REVIEW QUESTIONS

Matching

A. Magnetic disk

B. Magnetic tape

C. Key field

D. Index

E. ISAM

F. Sequential

__________ 1. A field in a record (unique to that record) used to access the record.

__________ 2. An access method whose records are available in a sequential or nonsequential manner.

__________ 3. A media suitable only for sequential processing.

__________ 4. Used to locate records on an ISAM file.

__________ 5. The most common media for nonsequential processing.

__________ 6. The fastest access method.

True/False

T F 1. The flowcharting for nonsequential files is more difficult than that for sequential processing.

T F 2. Sequential processing is only practical when 90 to 100 per cent of the records in a file are needed.

T F 3. Sequential processing is the fastest method per record processed.

T F 4. Magnetic tape may be used only for sequential files.

T F 5. An ISAM file is created by performing a randomizing routine on the key field.

T F 6. On-line real-time systems rely mainly on sequential files.

T F 7. An ISAM file is created or loaded with the records in sequence by a key field.

T F 8. When an ISAM file is updated, all transactions are read but only the master records needed are read.

Exercises

1. Flowchart a routine to check on the availability of an inventory item in a sales office.

2. Flowchart a routine to print transcripts for students who have requested them during the previous 24 hours.

3. Flowchart a routine to update a payroll master file.

4. Flowchart a routine to print a student's schedule. You will need more than one master file to do this. Identify the files you will need and the general type of data they will contain.

5. Flowchart a routine to answer customer inquiries about their account balances.

Discussion Questions

1. What on-line real-time systems are you familiar with that must rely on a nonsequential access method?

2. Is there something in your job that could be made more efficient if it were handled with an on-line real-time system?

3. Who should be responsible for the maintenance of master files within an organization?

CHAPTER 13

Systems Flowcharting

OBJECTIVES

As a result of studying this chapter the student should be able to perform the following activities:

1. Recognize the systems flowcharting symbols and be able to use them in a systems flowchart.
2. Describe what file maintenance is in terms of the updating process.
3. Describe a GFS file retention system.
4. Describe the systems flowcharting process and show where programs such as updates, edits, extracts, listings and sorts fit into an overall systems flowchart.
5. Draw systems flowcharts for a file updating process all the way from source documents to an updated file.

INTRODUCTION

As mentioned earlier, systems flowcharting is used to show the flow of data through a system. The logic of any given program within a system is not shown in a systems flowchart. Similar to program flowcharts, systems flowcharts have their own set of symbols.

SYSTEMS FLOWCHARTING SYMBOLS

Punched Card Symbol

This symbol represents an input/output function in which cards are used as the medium. This symbol represents all types of cards (mark sense, stub, etc.). It also includes both card decks and card files. There are two variations on this symbol which may be used to specifically represent card decks and card files. They are shown below.

Punched Card Deck

This symbol represents a deck of cards. The cards are not necessarily related to each other. Additional cards may be depicted, each card representing a single card or group of cards (see Figure 13-1). The cards can be labeled to represent each component of the deck.

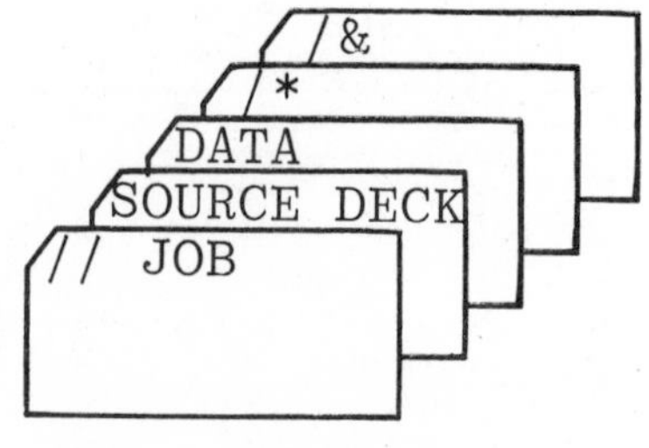

Figure 13-1

File of Cards

This symbol is used to depict a group of related punched cards. Since a file is a group of related records, this symbol is used to represent related punched card records comprising a file.

Online Storage Symbol

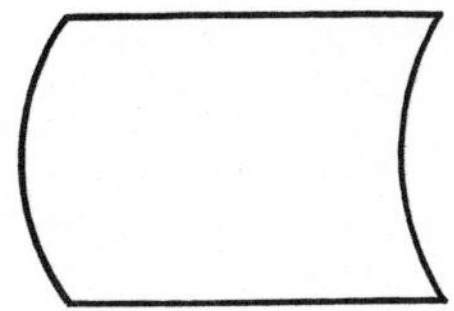

This is a general symbol for an input/output function using any type of online storage. It can represent magnetic tape, disk or drum storage.

Magnetic Tape Symbol

This symbol is used when you wish to show that the input or output is on magnetic tape.

Punched Tape Symbol

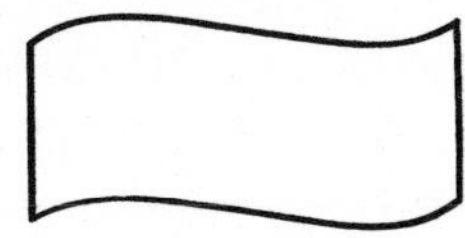

This symbol is used when you are using punched tape as an input or output medium.

Magnetic Drum Symbol

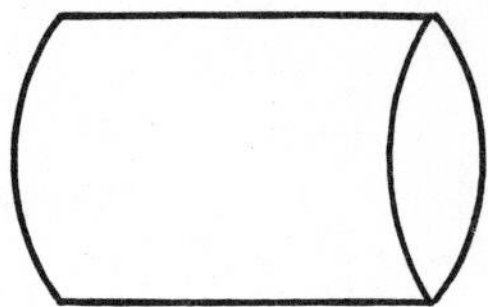

This symbol indicates that the input or output medium being used is a magnetic drum.

Magnetic Disk Symbol

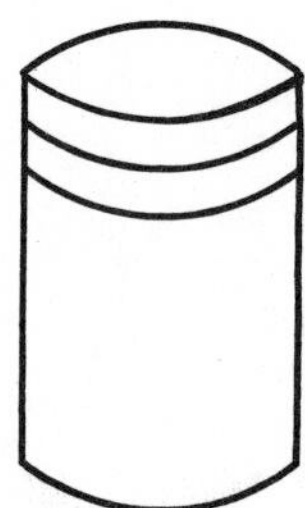

This symbol is used when you wish to show that the input or output medium is magnetic disk. If we are using more than one file which resides on a single disk, the names of the files are sometimes placed between the bands of the symbol (Figure 13-2).

Figure 13-2

Core Symbol

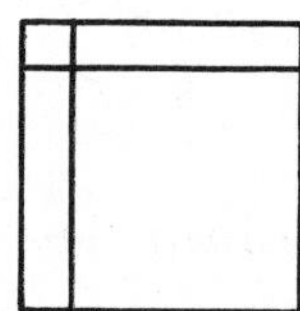

This symbol represents an input/output function in which the medium is magnetic core.

Document Symbol

This symbol represents either an input or an output function where the medium is a document. It is generally used to represent a source document or an output listing.

Manual Input Symbol

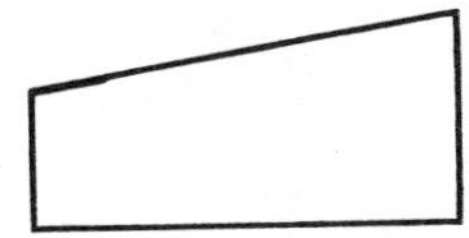

This symbol represents an input function in which the data is entered manually at the time of processing. An example would be input through a console typewriter.

Display Symbol

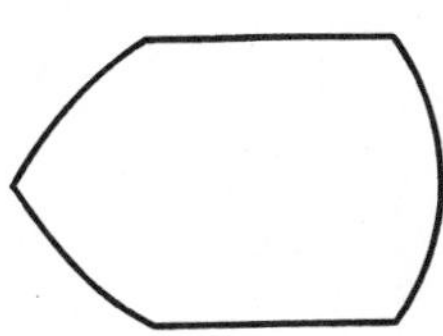

This symbol represents an input or output function in which the information is displayed for human use at the time of processing. Examples would be video devices, console printers and plotters.

Communication Link Symbol

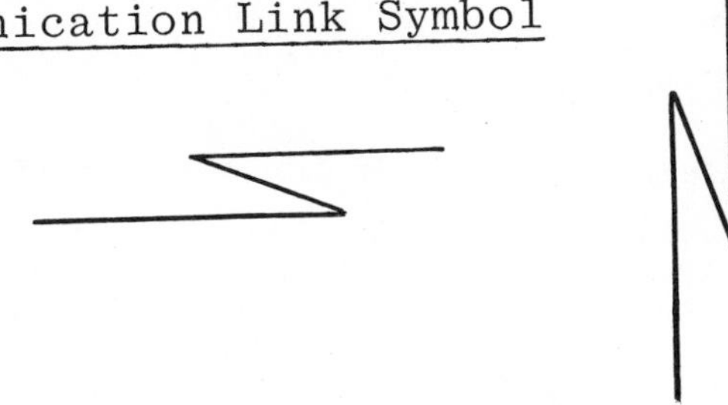

This symbol represents a situation where information is being transmitted by a telecommunication link. This could include telephone, telegraph, microwave, etc. types of data transmission.

Offline Storage Symbol

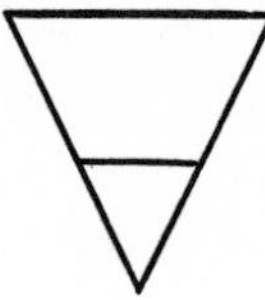

This symbol represents the function of storing information offline, regardless of the medium on which the information is recorded. Offline storage is storage not currently accessible by the computer. This could range from reports filed in a folder to cards on a shelf.

Preparation Symbol

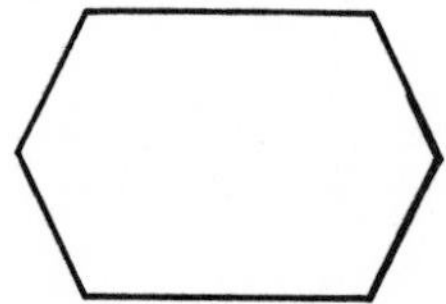

This symbol represents modifications of an instruction or group of instructions which change the program itself.

Manual Operation Symbol

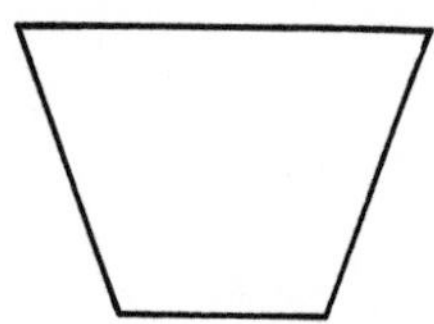

This symbol represents an offline operation performed at the speed of a human being using no mechanical aid. This could include many things such as physically sorting or altering parameter cards or making out a report for a program that just ended abnormally.

Auxiliary Operation Symbol

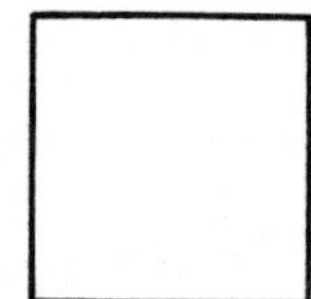

This symbol represents an offline operation performed on equipment not under the control of the central processing unit. A typical example would be putting cards or optically read input on a tape from a stand alone device.

Merge Symbol

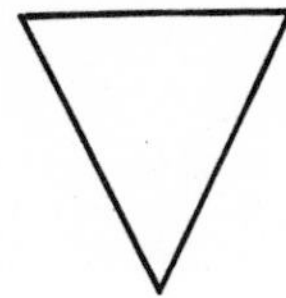

This symbol represents the combining of two or more sets of items into one set. It can be used to show the combining of a master and a transaction file.

Extract Symbol

This symbol represents the removal of one or more specific sets of items from a single larger set of items. The extract is based on a set of criteria which could be similar to those we used in Chapter 7.

Sort Symbol

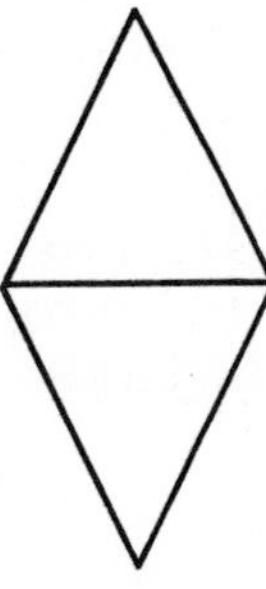

This symbol represents the arranging of a set of items into a particular sequence. This operation is used to order a file on some field in preparation for using it in a program.

Collate Symbol

This symbol represents merging with extracting. It is the formation of two or more sets of items from two or more other sets.

Process Symbol

Although this symbol was presented in Chapter 2 as a part of program flowcharting, it is also used in systems flowcharting. In the case of systems flowcharting it represents an entire program, rather than a single instruction or group of instructions.

In addition to these symbols the flowlines presented in program flowcharting symbols (Chapter 2) are still used in the same manner with systems flowcharts.

THE UPDATING PROCESS

Systems in general (i.e. payroll, accounts receivable, inventory, etc.) have a master file which contains the data relative to the particular system. Periodically this master file needs to be updated so that it reflects the current situation. This process of updating the master file is a part of the overall topic of systems maintenance and is shown in Figure 13-3.

Figure 13-3 is the updating process for a standard sequential file. Non sequential file updating contains many of the same steps and was covered in Chapter 12. Let's take a look at the symbols in Figure 13-3 one at a time.

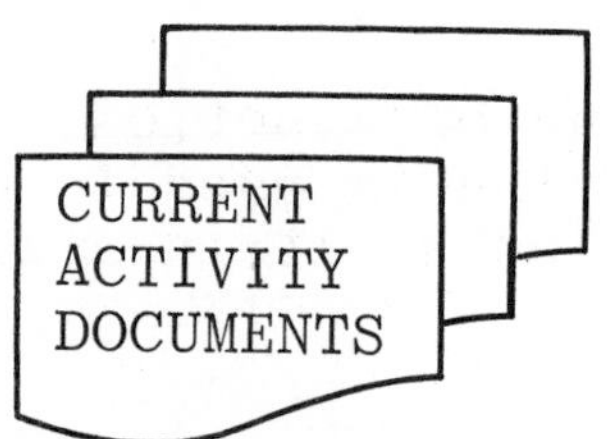

Current activity documents are changes that need to be made to the master file. These changes occurred since the last time the master file was updated and need to be recorded so that the master file reflects the current situation.

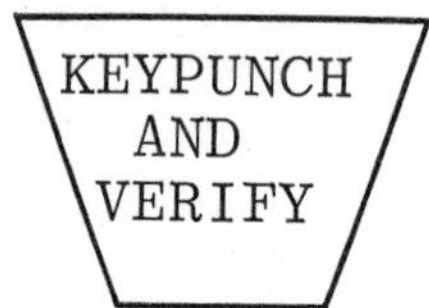

This step shows the conversion of the change items into a form that can be machine processed.

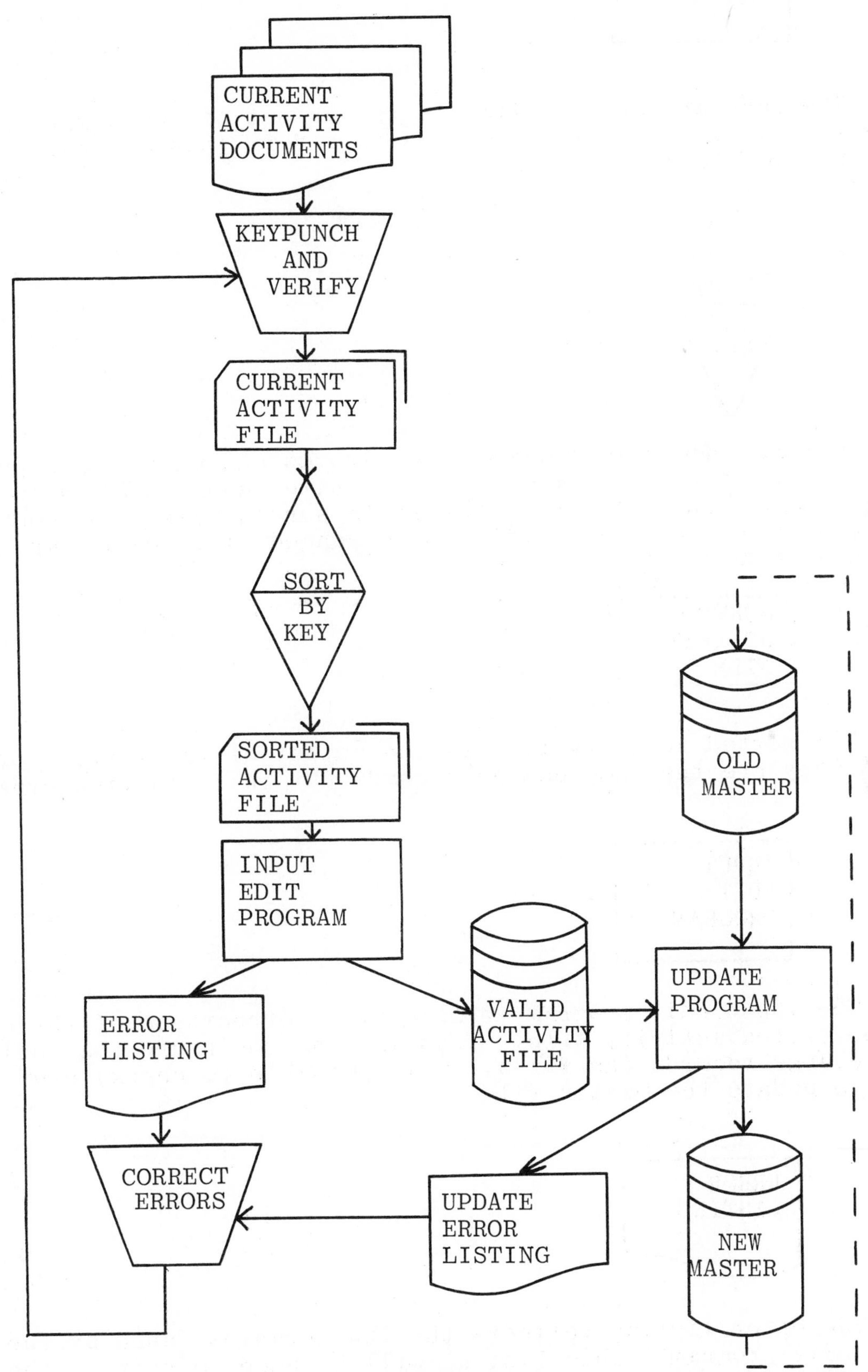
CURRENT
ACTIVITY
DOCUMENTS
KEYPUNCH
AND
VERIFY
CURRENT
ACTIVITY
FILE
SORT
BY
KEY
SORTED
ACTIVITY
FILE
INPUT
EDIT
PROGRAM
OLD
MASTER
ERROR
LISTING
VALID
ACTIVITY
FILE
UPDATE
PROGRAM
CORRECT
ERRORS
UPDATE
ERROR
LISTING
NEW
MASTER

Figure 13-3

CURRENT
ACTIVITY
FILE

The current activity file is the output of the keypunching process. It is the change records in a form (punched cards) suitable for future processing.

In order for the changes to be processed against a sequential master file, they must be in the same sequence as the master file. The KEY field that it is sorted by is the control field on which the master file is sequenced (i.e. part number, employee number, etc.).

SORTED
ACTIVITY
FILE

The sorted activity file is the output of the sorting process. They are the same change records but in a modified order.

INPUT
EDIT
PROGRAM

The input edit program verifies the correctness of the data in the sorted activity file. This is done to insure that only good change records (as far as it is possible to check) are used to update the master file.

ERROR
LISTING

The error listing reflects the inaccuracies found by the input edit program. This listing will be used to correct the invalid change items for future processing.

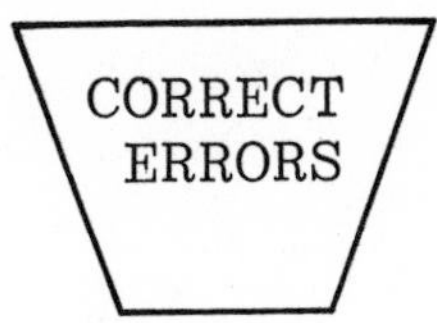

Errors in the change records shown on the error listing are corrected manually. These corrections are then turned back to the keypunch department. The corrected items will be rekeypunched and submitted the next time the update program is to be run.

The valid activity file is made up of those change items not found to be in error in the input edit program. These valid items are the ones that will be used to update the master file.

UPDATE
PROGRAM

The update program will combine the change records (adds, deletes and changes) with the old version of the master file and produce the updated (new) version of the master file. It is possible that other errors, not detectable by the input edit program, may be found in updating the master file. These errors are printed out on an update error listing.

UPDATE
ERROR
LISTING

The update error listing is used for manual correction of the errors encountered in updating the master file.

The old master file is the one which is updated to produce the new master. It is the most recent of the master files. Typically there are three copies (at least) of a master file that are retained at any time. These are the three most current versions of the master file. This type of file retention is referred to as GFS (Grandfather, Father, Son). The most current is called the son. The next most current is the father. The third most current is the grandfather. Every time an updating process is done a new son is created. The oldest version of the file (the grandfather) is destroyed when the new son has been successfully created. This cycling of the files is indicated by the dotted line on Figure 13-3.

The new master is the output of the updating process. It is the new son in the GFS file retention system and reflects the current status of the master file.

The updating process is done at various time intervals depending upon the particular system. Some files need to be updated every day while others may only need to be updated every other day or once a week.

Now let's apply this generalized updating process to a specific system. The system is a personnel system and the master file is an employee master file. This is shown in Figure 13-4.

USING THE MASTER FILE

The employee master file is used in a variety of programs. These range from simple employee listings to such things as deduction listings, insurance reports, and reports to governmental agencies. In many cases the employee master file is also accessible to various company personnel so they can get quick answers relative to the employee information that is in the file. This quick response information is usually retrieved over some sort of terminal. This process is shown in Figure 13-5.

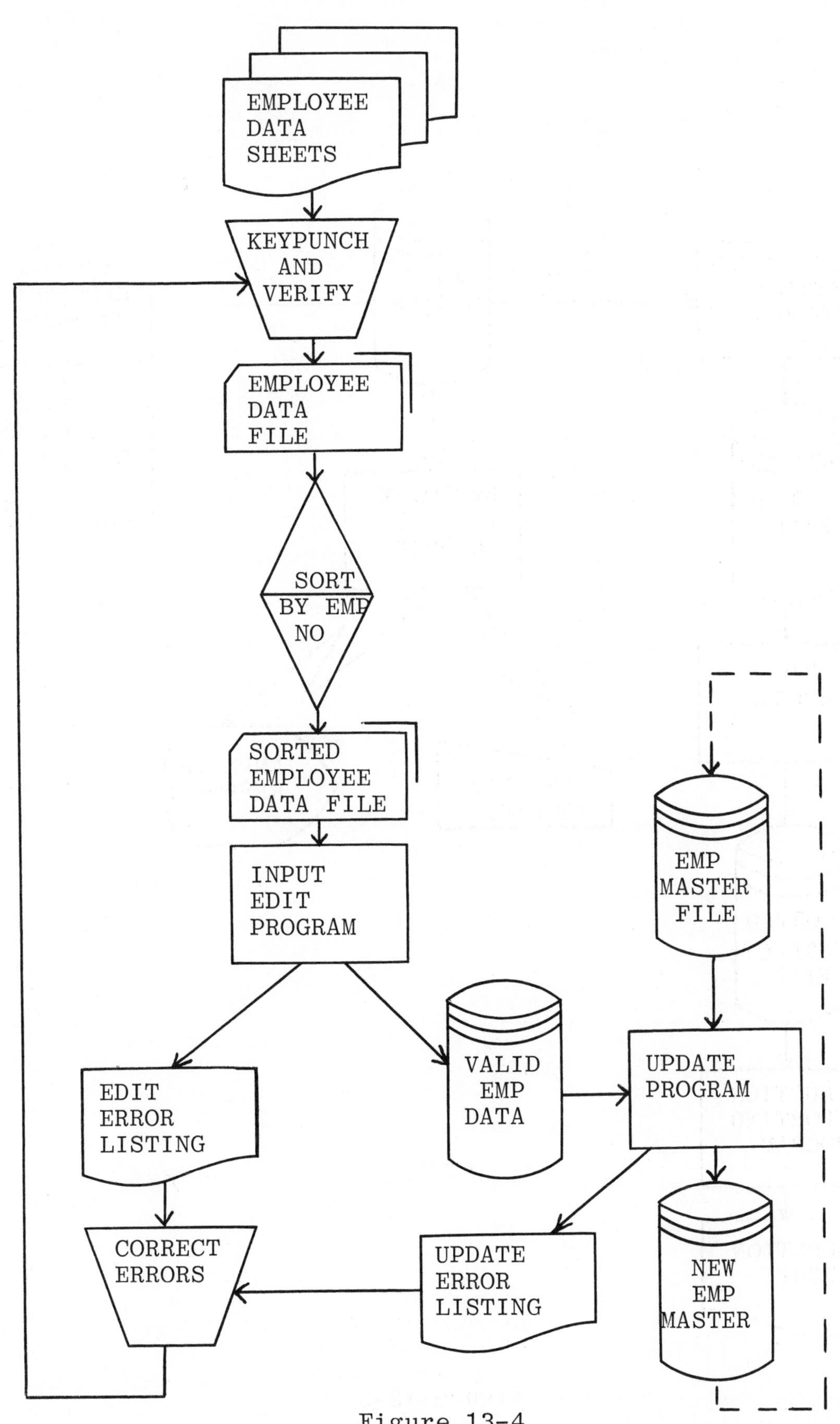
EMPLOYEE
DATA
SHEETS
KEYPUNCH
AND
VERIFY
EMPLOYEE
DATA
FILE
SORT
BY EMP
NO
SORTED
EMPLOYEE
DATA FILE
INPUT
EDIT
PROGRAM
EMP
MASTER
FILE
EDIT
ERROR
LISTING
VALID
EMP
DATA
UPDATE
PROGRAM
CORRECT
ERRORS
UPDATE
ERROR
LISTING
NEW
EMP
MASTER

Figure 13-4

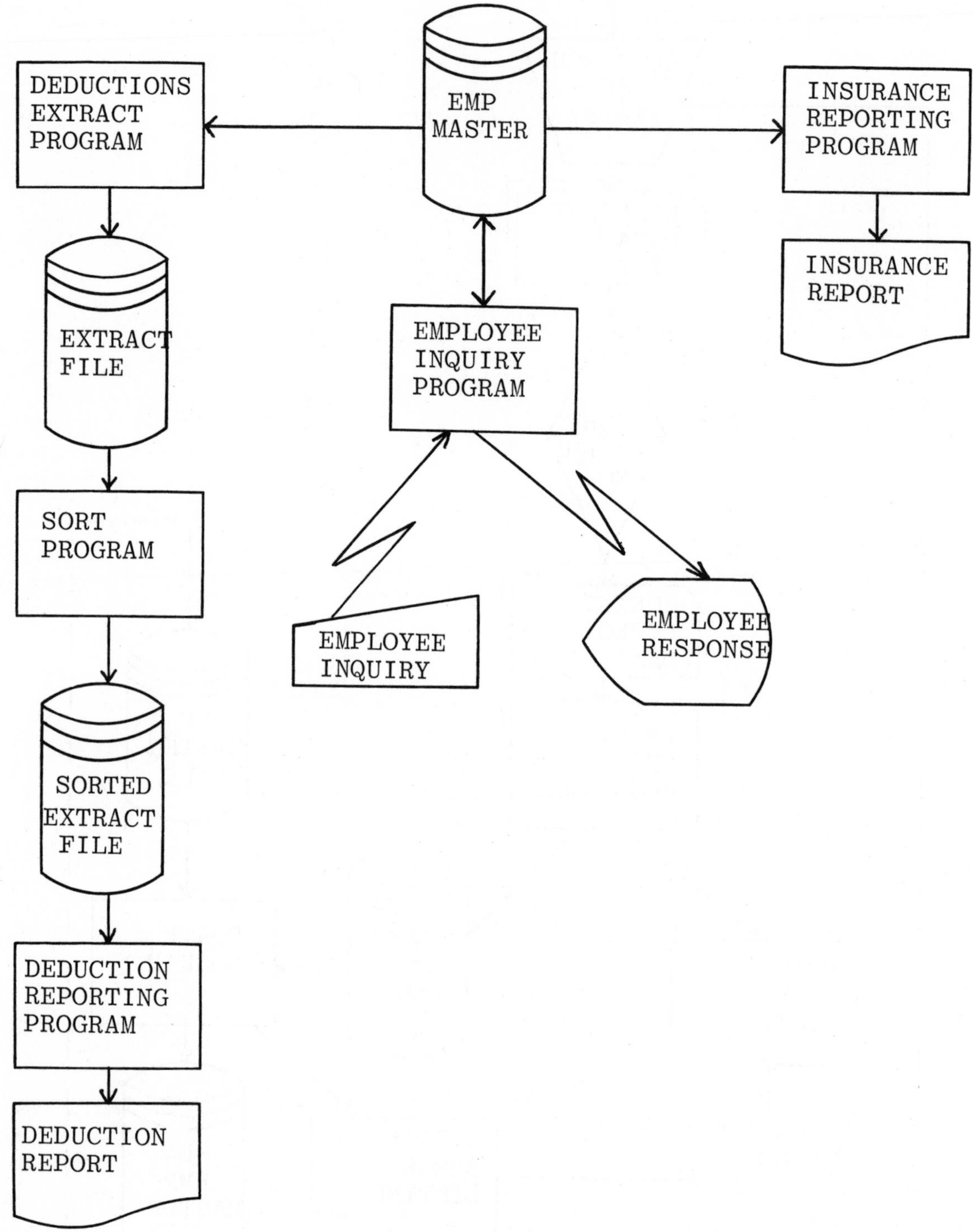
DEDUCTIONS
EXTRACT
PROGRAM
EMP
MASTER
INSURANCE
REPORTING
PROGRAM
INSURANCE
REPORT
EXTRACT
FILE
EMPLOYEE
INQUIRY
PROGRAM
SORT
PROGRAM
EMPLOYEE
INQUIRY
EMPLOYEE
RESPONSE
SORTED
EXTRACT
FILE
DEDUCTION
REPORTING
PROGRAM
DEDUCTION
REPORT

Figure 13-5

REVIEW QUESTIONS

Matching

________ 1. Sort symbol

________ 2. Card file symbol

________ 3. Communication link symbol

________ 4. Magnetic disk symbol

________ 5. Merge symbol

________ 6. Document symbol

________ 7. Punched card deck symbol

________ 8. Manual input symbol

________ 9. Collate symbol

________ 10. Punched tape symbol

________ 11. Display symbol

________ 12. Manual operation symbol

________ 13. Punched card symbol

________ 14. Auxiliary operation symbol

________ 15. Extract symbol

________ 16. Online storage symbol

________ 17. Magnetic drum symbol

________ 18. Offline storage symbol

________ 19. Magnetic tape symbol

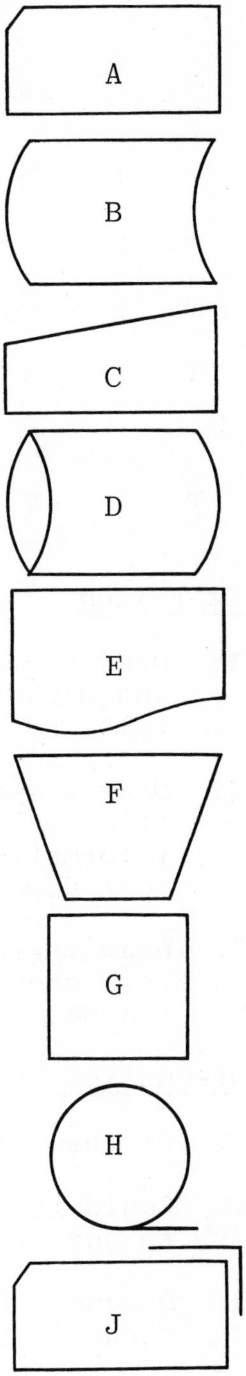

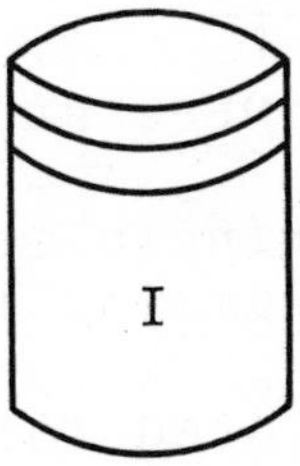

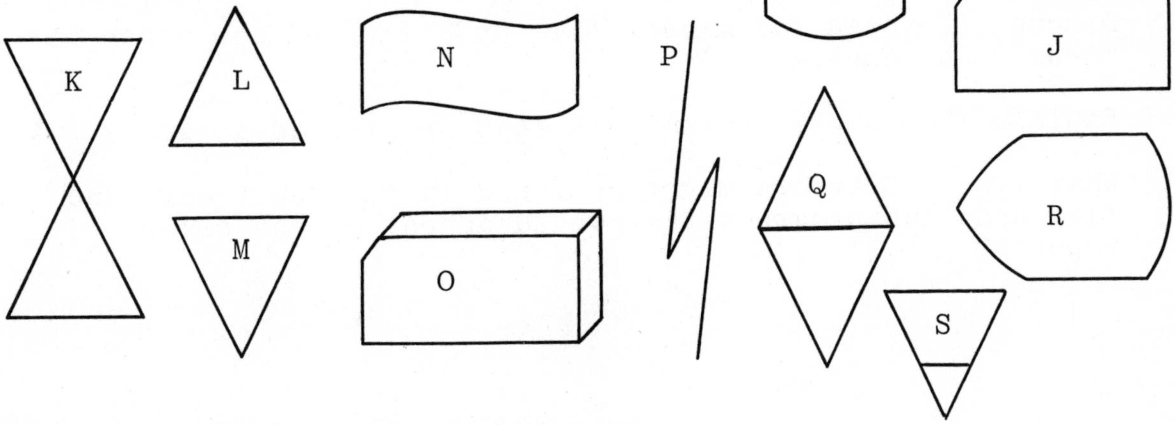

A

B

C

D

E

F

G

H

I

J

K

L

N

P

M

O

Q

R

S

True/False

T F 1. Systems flowcharts depict the logic of the programs in a system.

T F 2. The punched card symbol can be used to represent mark sense cards.

T F 3. Multiple files may be shown on the disk symbol.

T F 4. Offline storage could be used for any media.

T F 5. Flowlines are not needed in systems flowcharting.

T F 6. Sequential file updating requires that the transaction items be in the same sequence as the master file.

T F 7. One of the outputs of a file update program in a GFS system is a new grandfather.

Exercises

1. Draw a systems flowchart of a program that has a card file and magnetic tape file as inputs and outputs of a disk file and a printed report.

2. Draw a systems flowchart for the following list of activities. Keypunch and verify the data from personnel information sheets. The cards produced are then to be sorted on employee number.

3. Draw a generalized flowchart for updating a master file. This should include the handling of both master and transaction files.

Discussion Questions

1. Discuss the uses and value of systems flowcharting.

2. Could the principles of systems flowcharting be applied to non-programming tasks?

3. Discuss the need for master file updating and how often it needs to be done.

4. Explain what a GFS system is. What are its advantages?

5. What types of errors might be found in the input edit and file updating programs that would appear on the error reports?

CHAPTER 14

Decision Tables

OBJECTIVES

As a result of studying this chapter the student should be able to perform the following activities.

1. Name the parts of a decision table.
2. Describe the advantages of a decision table over a flowchart.
3. Describe the disadvantages of decision tables.
4. Differentiate between limited entry, extended entry and mixed entry tables.
5. Construct a decision table for a situation with which the student is familiar.

INTRODUCTION

Decision tables are planning tools used in ways similar to flowcharting. Decision tables provide a concise format for examining a situation with many decision steps. While their compact nature makes them an excellent planning and documentation tool it also limits them. This is because each individual table usually deals with only the logic decisions present in a situation and does not show the overall flow of logic that a flowchart shows.

LIMITED ENTRY TABLES

In order to build a decision table we first need a problem to solve. Given a college setting, an ongoing problem seems to be registration. In particular, people are disappointed at general registration by the lack of openings in classes they wish to take. The circumstances we will describe cover the registration process as it is currently handled at a typical college. It reflects the timing of the registration process. We will use what is know as a limited entry table for our first example. A limited entry table is a table in which each condition has only two possibilities, Yes or No (True or False).

First, let's examine the construction of a decision table. Decision tables are divided into four parts (see Figure 14-1). The two on the left are referred to as stubs and the two on the right are referred to an entries.

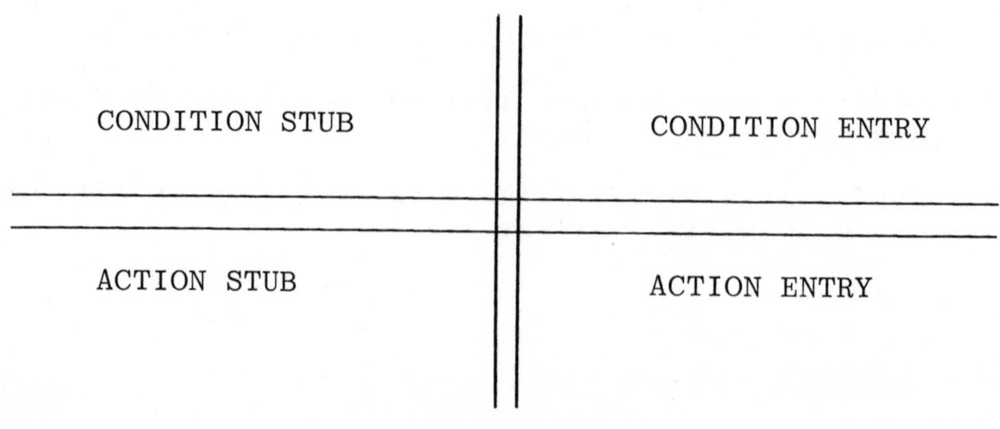

Figure 14-1

The condition stub lists all of the important, usual conditions. It would be nice to say all of the possible conditions, but that would be like asking you to describe the universe in ten words or less and give three examples. Each condition that we can identify is listed on a separate line. For our conditions we have chosen those in Figure 14-2. The fourth condition may seem out of place, but if you watch where the X's fall you will find that it is an overriding factor in the registration process.

TIMING OF REGISTRATION	
APPLICATION COMPLETE	
FULL-TIME STUDENT	
RETURNING STUDENT	
PROCRASTINATOR	

Figure 14-2

TIMING OF REGISTRATION	
APPLICATION COMPLETE	
FULL-TIME STUDENT	
RETURNING STUDENT	
PROCRASTINATOR	
PRE-REGISTRATION	
TELEPHONE RESISTRATION	
ORIENTATION & SPECIAL REGISTRATION	
GENERAL REGISTRATION	

Figure 14-3

The lower or Action Stub lists all the usual actions that may be taken as a result of the Condition Stub. The actions in our example reflect the time of registration for each of the possible combinations of conditions (see Figure 14-3).

Once you have formulated the conditions and the actions possible based on those conditions, it is time to start systematically examining the results of the possible combinations of conditions. This is done in our limited entry table by starting in the first column of our condition entry with all Y's (yes).

In many tables one specified condition may make other listed conditions not feasible. In this case the square is left blank or a hyphen is inserted. In our example as long as an application has been completed we are able to fill our all of the other squares (see Figure 14-4). Notice in particular the systematic way the Y's and N's are grouped. This is not always possible but proceeding in this manner will assure that you have not overlooked any of the possibilities.

TIMING OF REGISTRATION

APPLICATION COMPLETE	Y	Y	Y	Y	Y	Y	Y	Y	N
FULL-TIME STUDENT	Y	Y	Y	Y	N	N	N	N	
RETURNING STUDENT	Y	Y	N	N	Y	Y	N	N	
PROCRASTINATOR	Y	N	Y	N	Y	N	Y	N	
PRE-REGISTRATION									TABLE 2
TELEPHONE REGISTRATION									
ORIENTATION & SPECIAL REGISTRATION									
GENERAL REGISTRATION									

Figure 14-4

The remainder of the decision table is shown in Figure 14-5. As our table is constructed it can only deal effectively with people who have made application. Therefore, when an N is encountered on this line, we refer to another table which will handle the circumstances of making an application. The ability to leave this table and move to another table if necessary makes it an open end table. If we were not able to, it would be considered a closed table.

TIMING OF REGISTRATION

APPLICATION COMPLETE	Y	Y	Y	Y	Y	Y	Y	Y	N
FULL-TIME STUDENT	Y	Y	Y	Y	N	N	N	N	
RETURNING STUDENT	Y	Y	N	N	Y	Y	N	N	
PROCRASTINATOR	Y	N	Y	N	Y	N	Y	N	
PRE-REGISTRATION		X				X			TABLE 2
TELEPHONE REGISTRATION								X	
ORIENTATION & SPECIAL REGISTRATION				X					
GENERAL RESISTRATION	X		X		X		X		

Figure 14-5

EXTENDED ENTRY TABLES

Thus far we have shown only limited entries. An extended entry table would allow such entries in the condition entry area as $\leq$, $\geq$, $<$, or $>$ with each of these related to a quantity. Limited and extended entries are not allowed on the same horizontal line of a table but they are allowed in the same table on separate line in the condition entry portion of the table. If both types of entries appear in one table it is called a mixed entry table. For an example of an extended entry table see Figure 14-6. It represents the grading scale in a course.

GRADING SCALE

POINTS EARNED	≥ 378	≥ 336	≥ 294	≥ 252	< 252
A	X				
B		X			
C			X		
D				X	
F					X

Figure 14-6

REVIEW QUESTIONS

Matching

A. Condition Stub

B. Action Stub

C. Condition Entry

D. Action Entry

E. Limited Entry

F. Extended Entry

__________ 1. The area where we specify a specific status for each condition.

__________ 2. A list of the conditions we have to consider.

__________ 3. A table in which only yes or no, true or false is allowed in the condition entries.

__________ 4. A list of actions that may be taken.

__________ 5. A table in which > or < may be used.

__________ 6. The area where an action is identified for each combination of conditions.

True/False

T F 1. Each decision table is divided into four parts.

T F 2. The left side of the decision table contains all of the conditions and the right side contains all of the actions.

T F 3. Limited entry tables use yes or no condition entries, while extended entry tables use true and false.

T F 4. If a condition makes other conditions infeasible, a blank or a hyphen may be used to indicate this.

T F 5. An open table allows us to refer to another table for additional areas of decision.

T F 6. Yes, no, > , and < are all permissible on a single horizontal line of a decision table.

Exercises

1. Draw a decision table to determine if you should attend a movie. Consider homework, money and the appeal of the movie.

2. Draw a decision table to aid in granting credit in a retail establishment. Set your own conditions.

3. Draw a decision table to aid in buying a house. Set your own conditions.

4. Draw a decision table to aid in selecting a career.

Discussion Questions

1. What are the advantages of decision tables versus flowcharting.

2. What are the disadvantages of decision tables versus flowcharting.

3. Discuss uses for decision tables outside the area of computer programming.

Index